Wind over Water

Foundations in Asia Pacific Studies

Editors:

Malcolm Cooper, Vice President, International Cooperation and Research at Ritsumeikan Asia Pacific University.

Jerry Eades, Dean of Asia Pacific Studies at Ritsumeikan Asia Pacific University.

The Asia Pacific Region is establishing itself as the new center of the world economy in the 21st Century, reflected by a growing political and cultural influence. This series documents its rise and examines its structure through accessible accounts from leading social science experts and perspectives from inside and outside the region. Invaluable to students and researchers alike, this series will form a basis for our knowledge of the region and the changes taking place within it.

VOLUME 1
China in Oceania: Reshaping the Pacific?
Edited by Terence Wesley-Smith and Edgar A. Porter

VOLUME 2
Wind over Water: Migration in an East Asian Context
Edited by David W. Haines, Keiko Yamanaka, and Shinji Yamashita

Wind over Water

Migration in an East Asian Context

EDITED BY

David W. Haines, Keiko Yamanaka,
and
Shinji Yamashita

berghahn
NEW YORK · OXFORD
www.berghahnbooks.com

First published in 2012 by

Berghahn Books

www.berghahnbooks.com

Library of Congress Cataloging-in-Publication Data

Wind over water : migration in an east Asian context / edited by David W.
Haines, Keiko Yamanaka, Shinji Yamashita.
     p. cm. -- (Foundations in Asia Pacific Studies ; v. 2)
     Includes bibliographical references and index.
     ISBN 978-0-85745-740-0 (hardback : alk. paper) -- ISBN 978-1-78533-039-1
(paperback : alk. paper) -- ISBN 978-0-85745-741-7 (ebook)
     1. Ethnology--East Asia. 2. East Asia--Emigration and immigration. 3. East Asia-
-Ethnic relations. 4. East Asia--Social life and customs. I. Haines, David W. II. Yamanaka, Keiko. III. Yamashita, Shinji.
     GN635.E5W56 2012
     305.80095--dc23

2012012507

British Library Cataloguing in Publication Data

A catalogue record for this book is available from the British Library

ISBN 978-0-85745-740-0 (hardback)
ISBN 978-1-78533-039-1 (paperback)
ISBN 978-0-85745-741-7 (ebook)

利涉大川

Contents

✦ Tables

Figures

Preface

This volume has a very simple premise: that contemporary migration in East Asia presents a valuable opportunity to rethink a mass of migration research and theory that has tended to be dominated by North American and European data, and by North American and European scholars. To that end, we have been involved with a series of panels, workshops, and conferences – a kind of traveling discussion – that has extended from 2006 in Vancouver, Canada (a general panel on Asian migration at the annual meeting of the Society for Applied Anthropology), through Hong Kong later that year (a panel on international marriage at the meeting of the Society for East Asian Anthropology), and then three separate segments in Japan in 2007: a two-day conference at the National Museum of Ethnology in Osaka; an academic panel at the annual meeting of the Japan Society of Cultural Anthropology in Nagoya; and a one-day workshop on migration and human security at the University of Tokyo. 2008, in turn, provided two segments in the United States (a two-day workshop at U.C. Berkeley's Institute of East Asian Studies and an invited session at the annual meeting of the American Anthropological Association in San Francisco). It was then back to Japan – Beppu this time – for three migration panels at a conference at Ritsumeikan Asia Pacific University in December 2008 and, finally, to Kunming, China for four academic panels at the International Congress of the Anthropological and Ethnological Sciences in July 2009.

The fruits of these interactions, especially the Berkeley and Beppu meetings that form the basis of this book, can be seen in the chapters that follow. However, it is worth making three general points by way of a preface. First, this effort represents a coalescence of our own three individual interests, and in a fuller way than perhaps we originally imagined. Shinji's interests in exploring the nature of Asian anthropologies, and what they can contribute to a more globally interactive anthropology, find in the issue of migration a rather good test case. Keiko's long interest in labor issues and civic activism on behalf of migrants finds here a broader comparative framework for migration and perhaps a broader role for civil society's involvement in migration and diversity issues. This project has enabled David to make a productive link between his North American work on refugees and immigrants and the more Asia-related parts of his experience: as a child and then foreign student in Japan; as a translator/interpreter in, and then academic observer of, Vietnam; and as a 2004 Fulbright senior lecturer at Seoul National University in South Korea in 2004, an experience that was the original spur to this comparative effort on East Asian migration.

Second, this book is hardly the first on East Asian migration, but we do believe it provides a broader framework for considering different kinds of migration in different East Asian countries, and thus may be especially valuable in showing the variations in how migrants, the societies from which they come, and the societies to which they go, develop in interaction with each other. Furthermore, we hope that this volume will illustrate the value of taking a regional approach to migration, located somewhere between the specific stories of particular migrants in particular places and the frequent emphasis on the causes and consequences of migration as a global phenomenon. The study of migration at the mid-range regional level has significant advantages in assessing cultural similarities and dissimilarities and what are often very long-term interactions among migrants, their "old" and "new" societies, and the people – like those represented in this book – who aim to understand migration and the lives of migrants.

Third, we do have some regrets. Both Keiko and David, for example, would have wished for more attention to be paid to forced migration both because of the poor situation of most forced migrants in East Asia and because the response to forced migration is so crucial to a country's self-identity and affiliation with world human rights conventions. In addition, David would have wished for further progress on a more fully cross-linguistic and cross-cognitive examination of the personal and cultural meanings of migration. Certainly all three of us recognize that in aiming for a broad scope we have left many kinds of migrants and many migrant origins and destinations either under-represented or not represented at all. A book of this kind can be but a beginning.

David W. Haines
Keiko Yamanaka
Shinji Yamashita

Acknowledgments

We would like to express appreciation to the many people who have been involved in this multi-year project, only some of whose work appears in this volume. In terms of organizations, we are greatly indebted to Japan's National Museum of Ethnology (Minpaku) for providing the setting and resources for the two-day conference on migration in Japan in 2007, subsequently published as *Transnational Migration in East Asia*. Makito Minami deserves special thanks for his management of that conference. We are especially indebted to the Wenner-Gren Foundation, which provided funding for the two-day workshop in 2008 that provided our most intensive period of discussion and the basic structure and thinking behind this book. For that workshop we would also like to thank the Institute of East Asian Studies at the University of California, Berkeley, which provided facilities for that workshop – and to Caverlee Cary for her unfailing courtesy and helpfulness. We are also indebted to the Research Center on Asia Pacific Studies at Ritsumeikan Asia Pacific University for travel support that enabled several of us to participate in the series of three panels there in December 2008, which were especially helpful in expanding the Korean and Vietnamese representation in this book.

Finally, we are indebted to many of our professional associations for stretching their usual rules to permit more international composition of panels, perhaps especially the Japan Society of Cultural Anthropology for its willingness to let us have a panel in English at its 2007 meeting. Other debts incurred include those to the Human Security Program at the University of Tokyo, and the Global Studies Program at George Mason University.

INTRODUCTION

David W. HAINES, Shinji YAMASHITA, and J.S. EADES

This book focuses on the dynamics, trends, and meanings of East Asian migration, paying particular attention to the ways in which East Asian migration is important in its own right but also to how it can complement the broader literature on migration research and theory. The East Asian material is especially helpful, for example, in indicating the interaction between internal and international migration (thus helping to reunite two long-separated areas of human movement), the degree to which out and in-migration often offset each other (thus counterbalancing the common emphasis on immigration alone), and the extent to which migration is of unclear duration (thus challenging conventional categorizations of temporary versus permanent migration).

The East Asian material also permits an initial reconnaissance of what a general theory of migration might entail, especially the need to recognize the fluid nature of human movements that vary in intention and actuality, the variable and often unplanned length of migration, how instances of migration channel subsequent decisions about migration, and how the processes of migration must be separated conceptually from the histories of those who migrate. To move, it appears, is human – and to move again perhaps even more so. Such a broad view of migration, based on the East Asian experience (Haines 2008, Yamashita 2008b), may help to provide a better orientation to the much less geographically fixed social order of the twenty-first century and help to bring about a better understanding of the many human options and constraints in an increasingly globalized – yet also atomized – world.[1]

In this introductory chapter we provide some general comments on the major trends in contemporary East Asian migration and then introduce the organization of the book and the kinds of issues it raises for what we will hope will be an enhanced – and more internationally collaborative – understanding of human migration.

Rising Affluence, Changing Lifestyles

As has often been noted, the increasing affluence in most East Asia countries has led to new demographic patterns, kinds of work, and lifestyle choices. This has been documented with increasing interest by social scientists, who have focused on consumption, mobility, and the kinds of industries that accompany them. The new middle classes are more highly educated than previous generations, and also more highly urbanized. Their families are smaller. The effects of the one-child policy in China are well known, but Hong Kong, Korea, Japan, and Taiwan have also become statistically one-child societies, without the need for such draconian policies. Part of the reason for the decline in family size is economic: more and more women with higher levels of education are part of the labor force, and have less time for childcare. Part of the reason is demographic: as child mortality sinks towards zero, there is less need to reproduce in order to produce heirs as security in old age. As families shrink, many of the functions of the family have been taken over by the state, or the market in the wealthier countries, often utilizing migrants from outside – a process described by Douglass (2009) as "global householding." Another factor is the expense of education. Paradoxically, increasing affluence means that children may remain dependent on their parents for a longer rather than a shorter period. The period of education financed by parents now often extends beyond compulsory education to high school and even university and beyond. The phenomenon of "parasite singles" (Tran 2006), adult children continuing to live with their parents and enjoying the benefits of free or very inexpensive housing, cooking, and laundry services, is well known in Japan, and could be spreading to the rest of the region. At the other end of the lifespan, older people are living longer and, for an increasing number, this is spent in relatively affluent retirement. Generous pensions mean that people can travel and experience other lifestyle options, resulting in new flows of international migration in search of recreation, medical services, health care, and a more desirable lifestyle for less money.

One of the most obvious results of the new affluence is the emergence of the tourist industry. In the Asia Pacific area, many regions and smaller countries are increasingly basing their strategies of economic development on the tourism industry, selling images of paradise whether in Bali, Thailand, Southern China, the Philippines, Australia, or the Pacific Islands (Yamashita, Din, and Eades 1997, Picard and Wood 1997, Yamashita 2003). Their clienteles come increasingly from the richer countries of East Asia – from Japan, Taiwan, Korea, Hong Kong, and Singapore.

Like tourism, education has also become increasingly globalized and international. Once more, this has been largely driven by the middle classes, either by the parents looking for the best education for their children's job prospects and mobility, or by the students themselves looking for education and training which they cannot find at home. This may start at a young age. There is a long tradition of "parachute" children from Taiwan – and now from Korea – who are sent to the United States for their education, where they may spend much of the time living on their own or with relatives, and thus become used to fending for themselves. Education has also become an important element in governmental manpower recruitment and training programs, and this too is having an enormous impact on patterns of international migration and the responses of states to it. The highly developed countries have long made up for a skills shortage in areas such as mathematics, science, and technology through recruiting from overseas, and the education system has been an important part of this. Students who arrive to study at the undergraduate or postgraduate level often stay on and become integrated into the local skilled labor market (Mani 2005). Singapore takes this one stage further, by recruiting students at the high school level as well as the university level, and offering them scholarships in return for a period spent working in Singapore after they graduate (Ko 2004).

The decline in fertility coupled with rising life expectancy also contributes to new forms of movement in the region. Medical tourism, for example, is on the rise and the search for medical care, often coupled with the desire for a more affluent retirement lifestyle, may result in permanent settlement.[2] In East Asia, the largest market is probably Japan, and Thailand and Malaysia have both begun to offer deals for retiring Japanese looking to improve their lifestyles within the limits of their pensions (Miyazaki 2008, Ono 2008). Some have acquired second homes in the sun, while others have moved there permanently. Another driver in this respect is the diminishing availability of family support in old age. Families are now much smaller and more scattered than they were, especially in low-fertility societies such as Japan, so even though the government's policies throw much of the burden of care on the family, the family is often simply not there. This results in two flows of migrants: the flow of care workers from countries like the Philippines to take over the responsibility of care from family members in countries like Hong Kong and Singapore (Toyota 2008); and the flow of the elderly looking for the sun, recreation, and eventually cheaper care services in Southeast Asia and elsewhere. These issues are illustrated in particular detail in this volume's chapters by Mika Toyota (Chapter 16), and Shinji Yamashita (Chapter 11).

All of these flows have been facilitated by the falling cost of transport thanks to a new generation of cost-efficient wide-bodied airplanes and competition in the airline industry. The costs of international travel are in many cases the same as, or cheaper than, domestic travel, with the result that people prefer to spend the same money on traveling abroad, where they get better, cheaper, and, above all, different service. Migration used to be a one-way process, but it is now just part of the establishment of a transnational network of friends and relatives. The costs of communication have also fallen, with cheap internet connections and email services together with the falling costs of phone calls and mobile phones.

The Economic Impact

Many of these shifts represent a development of what has become known in the literature as the "new international division of labor" or NIDL thesis. In his study of migration, Robin Cohen (2006: chapter 7) summarizes this as follows. In the second half of the twentieth century, industrial capital increasingly moved from the metropolitan countries to the periphery to establish factories. However, unlike earlier attempts of industrialization, these were intended to produce goods for export, rather than for import substitution, and they formed the backbone of the economic success of the Asian Tigers, the newly industrializing countries (NICs) that followed Japan's lead in staging economic "miracles." The reason for the shift was the search for cheaper, skilled labor, due to the increased costs of reproducing labor power in the older advanced industrialized countries which, in turn, was due to the construction of the welfare state and the organization of the workers. As a result, the older industrialized countries shifted from importing migrant workers to exporting production. Meanwhile, the urban labor forces of the NICs were swelled by the movement of rural labor to the cities, while governments set up beneficial fiscal regimes to help foreign companies wishing to come in and invest. Goods exported typically included electronics and clothes, with a high value to weight ratio, so that the cost of transport was less than the savings through cheaper labor. The result was rapid economic development in East Asia coupled with stagnation and rising unemployment in the older industrial countries such as Germany, the United Kingdom, and the United States.

Cohen admits that the NIDL thesis provides a powerful explanation for many of the observed changes in the world economy in the postwar period, though he does criticize it both on conceptual and historical grounds, in that "NIDL theorists have ignored or misconceived the historical evolution and successive phases of the international division of labour" (Cohen 2006: 157–158). He also argues that the current "transnational phase" in the division of labor "should be conceived as embracing a number of different forms of labor utilization not adequately depicted in NIDL theory. These all have implications for the patterning of migration flows" (Cohen 2006: 162). This is the phase of the international division of labor brought about by a number of factors in the postwar period: the collapse of colonialism, the rise of transnational capital, the boom in the oil industry, and the relocation of production to peripheral regions such as East Asia. The resulting shifts in migration patterns include the flow of both unskilled and skilled labor to the oil economies, the growth of demand for new services in the "global cities" which are the centers of the finance industry (Sassen 1992) or competing in the international mega-events and tourism market (Ren 2009), the promotion of labor exports as a development strategy by countries like the Philippines, and the rise of China as an international exporter of cheap labor (cf. Cohen 2006: 1). In other words, the NIDL has provided a platform on which complex movements of people within the newly developing countries are played out, alongside new forms of labor migration to the older industrialized countries, and particularly to the global centers of finance with their insatiable need for cheap labor to provide accommodation, catering, entertainment, and sexual services.

The growth of the middle classes and the rise of lifestyle migration within, between, and from the newly affluent countries of East Asia have made these patterns even more complex. If the NICs became wealthy through taking over the production of consumer goods from the West, their transition to being countries with large middle classes has meant the growth of large consumer and recreational service industries, which themselves can be marketed to the international elite. The current crop of advertisements on international television, portraying the major countries of the region as tropical paradises offering both young and middle-aged jet setters a cornucopia of delights, is one symptom of this. Another genre of advertisement is that of the "shop till you drop" type, branding such places as Hong Kong, Singapore, and Malaysia as glorified supermarkets offering unlimited access to global designer goods. And, of course, transport between them is offered by the airlines with their competing first and business class services, complete with glasses of champagne, stewardesses presenting orchids, and ever more lavish pull-out sleeping arrangements. The increased affluence in East Asia thus indicates that the region may be a particularly valuable site for reconsidering these issues of NIDL theory.

The Contradictions of Transnationalism

At a more mundane level, these movements of people are leading to increasingly transnational social and family structures as well. From the increasing interaction of migrants and locals, there are more transnational partnerships and marriages and more children potentially claiming citizenship in multiple countries. Core institutions that have been taken for granted are now being challenged, forcing states to re-examine these institutions and, if necessary, bring them in line with new realities.

Perhaps the most obvious institution being challenged is citizenship itself. Laws on citizenship vary widely from country to country. Most basically, there is the distinction between the Latin terms *jus soli* and *jus sanguinis*, whether one acquires the right (*jus*) of citizenship by being born of the soil of a country (*soli*) or being of descent from existing citizens through relationships of blood (*sanguinis*). States in which immigration has been common have generally adopted the idea of *jus soli*, given that few citizens are blood relatives of the original inhabitants. Older nations have tended to emphasize *jus sanguinis*: the great majority of residents are the children of previous residents. Originally, many countries adopted a patrilineal rule that the line of descent had to be that of the father, and that children were not entitled to the citizenship of their mothers, but increasingly this has changed, with both the father and the mother recognized as potential sources of citizenship. This then raises the possibility of bi- or multi-national children (e.g. where children of two parents of different nationalities are born in a third country with *jus soli*). Some countries have long allowed the possibility of dual citizenship, the Commonwealth countries with large populations of British origin being good examples. Britain now also has very flexible citizenship arrangements with the Republic of Ireland. In other cases, such as those involving Japanese parentage, children in theory have to decide which nationality to take upon reaching adulthood, though it is probable that at least some continue to exercise both.

It is likely that in the future many countries will relax their citizenship laws and recognize dual citizenship. India has recently been moving in this direction, realizing that the worldwide diaspora of families of Indian descent represents a huge resource in terms of talent and capital, one on which the ancestral homeland could usefully draw. China would also stand to gain in the same way as India, given the vast numbers and economic prominence of the overseas Chinese. In 1990, Japan changed its immigration law to allow the settlement of South Americans of Japanese descent, who now form distinctive Portuguese- and Spanish-speaking minorities in Japan (Tsuda 2003, Sasaki 2008). Increasing numbers of Korean residents are taking citizenship in Japan, as are the highly-skilled Chinese discussed by Liu-Farrer (2010). But whether children will want to exercise certain citizenships will also depend on the economic standing of the countries concerned. In the global migration market, some passports – those of the developed countries – are clearly worth more than others.

Another crucial issue that states have to consider with increasing transnationalism is the welfare system. Are the migrants entitled to the same welfare and pension payments that citizens enjoy? It can be argued that long-term migrants do, in that they have paid taxes and pension contributions and contributed to the national economy over the years, even if they have not taken citizenship. At the other end of the labor market, however, countries generally try to avoid the costs of labor reproduction while reaping the benefits of cheap labor. One extreme example is that of Singapore, where migrant female care givers from the Philippines and Myanmar are forbidden to form partnerships with locals and subjected to regular pregnancy tests – if tested positive, they are deported (Eades 2004). In contrast, Singapore is very generous in providing student scholarships in return for the students' long-term commitment to working in Singapore (Ko 2004). Japan provides another extreme example in not allowing the influx of unskilled labor at all, though it is an open secret that some industries such as construction and the sex trade depend massively on unregistered foreign labor.

A third crucial issue involves nationality and ethnicity. In the general Asia Pacific region, the variation in both is extensive (Eades 2001), ranging from (a) large fairly homogeneous nation states, in which minorities tend to be either assimilated, ignored or given marginal recognition (as in China, Japan, Korea, and perhaps Thailand and Myanmar) to (b) postcolonial states with artificially imposed boundaries dating from the colonial period, in which a variety of ethnic and language groups do their best to coexist (as in Indonesia, Malaysia, the Philippines and, despite its large Chinese majority, Singapore), to (c) settler states populated mainly by immigrants and their descendants, with the aboriginal peoples forming a small and often marginalized minority (as in Australia, New Zealand, Canada, the United States, and perhaps also Taiwan). The East Asian countries described in this book (China, Japan, Korea, and Vietnam) fall into the first of these categories. For all of them, increasing levels of transnationalism are likely in the long run to undermine notions of national homogeneity and identity.

In China, these issues of nationality and ethnicity are dealt with within a framework of officially designated minorities, which were established following the Stalinist model from the Soviet Union in the 1950s. This has so far been resistant to change, though there are clearly minorities which are in fact very diverse, and others that are not recognized at all. More recently, the incorporation of Hong Kong and Macau as special administrative regions has created a new kind of quasi-ethnic enclave with cultural and political arrangements quite different from those of the rest of the country. In Japan the situation is somewhat different. It does not have the kind of minority situation found in China. However, it does have Ainu and Okinawans, and it also has a large resident population of Koreans who are still officially foreign (Ryang 1997, Fukuoka 2000), as well as the *burakumin*, a caste-like group with status problems left over from the stratification system of the Edo period (i.e. up to 1868). More recently, the influx of Latin Americans of Japanese descent has created new and relatively visible minorities who tend to be disadvantaged in the labor market because of their poor command of Japanese. The paradox is that having previously seen themselves as Japanese in Latin America, they are now both seen and define themselves as Latin Americans in Japan (Tsuda 2003, Sasaki 2008).

Global Cities, Global Countryside

The places where all these factors collide are usually the cities. With globalization, East Asian cities function as ever more extensive and complicated intersections of national and international forces and connections. As the core element of the current phase of globalization, David Harvey's notion of "time-space compression" may be particularly helpful. According to him, "time-space compression" is generated by "flexible accumulation," a post-Fordist mode of production (Harvey 1990: 147). Importantly, the "compression" of the world generates the transnational mobility of information, products, money, and people all over the world. For East Asia overall, Douglas Massey and his colleagues (1998) noted that, by the

1980s, international migration had spread into Asia, not just to Japan but also to newly industrialized countries and regions such as Korea, Taiwan, Hong Kong, Singapore, Malaysia, and Thailand. By 2000, it was estimated that approximately fifteen million transnational migrants had spread out from East Asia, while Southeast Asian countries such as Singapore, Malaysia, and Thailand had received over four million guest-workers. Even in Japan, where migration control is rather tight, registered foreign residents numbered 2.22 million people (1.74 percent of the total population) in 2008 (although dropping slightly thereafter). This number may seem low compared with migrant-receiving countries such as the United States, Canada, Australia, and many E.U. countries, yet for Japan this number represents nearly a three-fold increase compared with the number of 783,000 in 1980.

This globalization is particularly apparent in the formation of the "global city" (Sassen 1992). In East Asia, cities such as Tokyo, Seoul, Beijing, Shanghai, Hong Kong, and Singapore are good examples. They serve as symbols of global capitalism and as central nodes of what Arjun Appadurai (1997: 33–36) has called "global cultural flows." But they are all very different. For instance, Keiko Yamanaka reports on the distinctive situation in Hamamatsu (Shizuoka Prefecture) in central Japan. She focuses on the emergence of groups of citizens concerned about the legal rights of recently arrived immigrant workers and their children. These immigrants – notably Japanese-Brazilians, undocumented Asians, and industrial trainees (*kenshûsei*) – work as unskilled laborers without full legal protection. As a result, they frequently suffer discrimination and exploitation. In this situation, local citizens have organized groups that work on behalf of the immigrants in labor disputes, and on issues of health, welfare, and equal human rights.

Singapore, as described by Brenda Yeoh and Theodora Lam (Chapter 4), offers a different scenario, a small island nation state with about four million people, but with one of the highest levels of GDP per capita in Asia. The creation of a cosmopolitan and creative city is a key plank of the government's vision for Singapore in the twenty-first century. The plan entails a wide range of strategies to "cosmopolitanize" both people and places in the city. The two possible arenas of tension and slippage seem to be Singapore's founding philosophy of multiracialism based on the Chinese-Malay-Indian-Others model – and here Singapore is indeed more Southeast Asian than East Asian – and the everyday reality of (un)cosmopolitanism in the contact zone of locals and migrants.

The emphasis on such international global cities, however, may elide the more pervasive extent of the sheer number of very large cities in East Asia. Zhang Jijiao (Chapter 3) focuses on the broader Chinese situation through survey work on multiple ethnic groups in multiple Chinese cities, aiming to provide a sketch of this range of urban experience that is changing rapidly because of international and national forces. In China, domestic migration from rural areas to big cities is much more important than transnational migration in the current stage of urban development, yet it is still directly connected to global forces and processes. This kind of ethnic migration to Chinese cities, after all, is interwoven with vibrant communities of those from other countries, such as the Korean enclave discussed by Kwang-Kyoon Yeo (Chapter 5). Here East Asia, and China in particular, provide a valuable site for considering how migrant social networks function comparatively between internal migrants in general, internal ethnic migrants, and international ones, considering, for example, the lives and trajectories of international Korean migrant communities and Korean minority migrant communities.

Yet the forces of increasing globalization are also seen in rural areas. Such areas are affected by global migration in various ways. In Japan, for instance, there has been the phenomenon of the "import" of Asian brides since the late 1980s. Today, the marriage age of Japanese women is one of the highest in the world. Young Japanese women nowadays often seem to find few positive reasons to get married, and they are thus reluctant to do so. In some villages where depopulation continues, the exodus of women to the cities has led to a dearth of younger women, and so brides are "imported" from places such as the Philippines, Sri Lanka, Korea, and China (Yamashita 2008a: 109). The American anthropologist Lieba Faier (2009) has discussed how Filipinas as *oyomesan* (the Japanese word for brides) play an important role in the rural community in Central Kiso, Nagano. Without them the Japanese rural community cannot maintain its family (*ie*) system. One finds similar cases of "bride import" in Taiwan and Korea as well (Yamanaka 2007). Furthermore, in rural Japan, under the legal status of *kenshûsei* (trainees), Chinese grow vegetables in highland Nagano, Filipinos work at orange farms in Ehime, and Indonesians fish for bonitos in Miyazaki. The Japanese rural economy itself is therefore increasingly based on these guest-workers.

The overall issue of guest-workers in Japan also deserves attention in relation to the coming of a "super-aged" society with a low birthrate. Japanese society is likely to face more labor force problems as Japan's population continues the decline that began in 2005. It is estimated that the percentage of the population over sixty-five years will increase to 33.7 percent by 2035, and 40.5 percent by 2055, compared to 23.1 percent in 2010. Given this background, Hidenori Sakanaka, the former director of the Tokyo Immigration Office, and Akihiro Asakawa, a migration policy specialist, have proposed a "10 million foreign migrants plan" for Japan by 2050 (Sakanaka and Asakawa 2007).[3] For Japan, as for several other East Asian societies, migration thus lies at the intersection of policy concerns about economics and about demography.

Structure of the Book

Any attempt to encompass these many strands of East Asian migration must address the fundamental problem of how to pursue a topic as broad as migration across the breadth of East Asia.[4] For this book, we have opted for very broad

inclusion. For example, we have included both internal and international migration, very short-term tourist visits and permanent settlement, and have returned
Vietnam and Singapore to the East Asian fold as vital comparisons to China for
both international and, in the case of Vietnam, internal migration as well. We
have thus attempted to illustrate as far as possible the full range of migration,
rather than focusing on a single kind, whether labor or business, tourism or marriage, short or long term, useful though more focused approaches can be.

In organizational terms, the book is in three sections. The first section addresses the general regional, state, and city contexts in which migration occurs.
Nicolas Lainez opens the discussion with an historical discussion of trafficking in
colonial Vietnam. His discussion establishes at the outset how sharply inscribed
and durable many of the migration channels in East Asia are. Xiang Biao continues with an examination of how the process of migration intersects with the
complex structuring of national and local government in China. Migration, his
chapter suggests, reflects not only passage across terrain and across borders, but
also up and down through complex governmental and commercial hierarchies.
Zhang Jijiao's chapter introduces the topic of internal migration and how – especially in the case of China's very extensive migration of minorities – internal migration has much of the flavor of "transnational" migration since it too requires
crossing legal, economic, and cultural borders. Brenda Yeoh and Theodora Lam
then show a very different kind of "Chinese" city set in a Southeast Asian regional
context of cultural diversity. Finally, Kwang-Kyoon Yeo and Keiko Yamanaka
provide discussions of two very different urban areas and both the formal and
informal ways in which migrants are included in, and excluded from, the societies to which they move. These chapters are a reminder of how diverse East Asian
cities can be, and thus how diverse the experiences of migrants within them are.

The second section focuses on family, gender, lifestyle and culture. The first
three chapters illuminate the range of issues that result from the intersection of
migration and family. Hy Luong starts with a discussion of Vietnam and the
way in which migrants – through family ties – are wound into moral networks
that transcend the divisions of place. Caroline Grillot then takes us to the border between Vietnam and China, showing the complex practical and symbolic
interactions between Vietnamese women looking for Chinese husbands and Chinese men looking for Vietnamese wives. Hung Thai and Masako Kudo then add
two complementary studies of women who marry very different kinds of foreign
men: Vietnamese women marrying overseas Vietnamese and Japanese women
marrying immigrant Pakistanis. Shinji Yamashita and Okpyo Moon complete
the section by bringing tourism into the discussion, thus balancing the implicit
durability of families with the seemingly more evanescent experience of tourists.
Their two chapters bracket the possibilities, from short-term historical tourism
of Koreans in China, to very long-term, "long-stay" movements of Japanese to
Southeast Asia. Tourism, their chapters suggest, has many forms, can sequence

into longer-term migration, and is itself also the result of prior visits of various kinds.

The third section of the book focuses on the intersection of ethnicity and nationality with work. Haeng-ja Sachiko Chung begins with ethnic Korean hostesses and club owners in the Japanese city of Osaka; Gordon Mathews discusses African entrepreneurs in Hong Kong (and how they navigate life in a city which often supports their work but not them); and Brenda Yeoh and Katie Willis discuss the lives of ethnic-Chinese Singaporean women when they move to China (almost inevitably as non-working spouses even though they have well developed careers in Singapore). These cases represent a range of people in a range of occupations with a range of different effects: sometimes expanding economic roles and activities, sometimes constraining them, and sometimes simply changing them. The final chapter of the book, by Mika Toyota, turns to the specific issue of care work and the way in which the skills of women are evaluated differently in sending and receiving countries, but in both cases with similar ambivalence. Thus despite the need for skilled health care, government policies often restrict the free movement, and extended stay, of exactly those people who can provide that care.

Some Cross-Cutting Themes

The concluding chapter of this book will return to the broader implications of these chapters, both individually and collectively. But it may also be useful to indicate from the outset some of the particular themes that emerge in this book and that often cross-cut its formal organization.

The first, and perhaps most obvious, theme that emerges is the degree to which people and objects are in motion in different kinds of ways with varying implications for future additional movement. The migrants themselves are quite varied, from low-skill labor to highly talented professionals, from female entertainers to international brides, from short-term tourists to long-stay retirees. One particularly interesting set of migrants are people who, like the authors of this book, migrate in order to look at migration. They are one of many kinds of short- and mid-term migrants who return as changed people to changed societies, often creating further migrant flows – of their students for example. Whatever the nature of the migrants, it remains hard to predict the exact duration of their stay somewhere else, and the nature and duration of their return to their original country.

A second theme involves the multiple and complex meanings of "skill." Migration researchers often generalize about low-skilled labor versus high-skilled "talent," but the actual nature of skill is often far more complex than those simple categories would suggest. Whether as club hostesses or health care providers, for example, many female migrants have very high levels of social and personal skills – functioning as both managers and psychologists – for which they receive relatively low rewards. Receiving societies often respond to this complexity with policies that are inherently ambivalent, seeking to bring in the labor but also making it difficult to stay, as with the Japanese response to the need for care workers.

A third theme is families. While some chapters are explicitly about families, many more have families as part of their story. The life histories of migrant families, and of families which are mixed migrant/non-migrant, are often very complex, with interweaving strands of general social change (for example, that women generally now have greater access to more jobs) and the developmental cycle of the household (for example, that women may move in or out of the labor force depending on the presence and age of children). Migration adds another unpredictable strand. The presence of in-migrants to help with domestic chores, for example, may give women more latitude to pursue their careers outside the home. But out-migration of those professionals may then reduce their activities outside the home. The discussion by Yeoh and Willis of Singaporean women, for example, suggests how when the women move with their husbands to China, they often end up much more restricted to the home as household managers and parents, and may continue that pattern on their return to Singapore. The implication is that attempts to understand contemporary migration must include consideration of how the future lives of families will develop in response to both internal dynamics and external changes.

A fourth theme involves the blurring of conventional categories. In much of the migration literature, very conventional notions of migration still endure. For example, people are discussed as moving from "here" to "there" (or "there" to "here") and doing so with some finality. The result is sometimes a dichotomy between temporary and permanent migrations. Much of the material in this book, however, suggests the opposite: that short- and long-term moves are intermixed in many migration histories; and that any seeming permanency of migration may evaporate as migrants return to their origins. There is sometimes an analogous assumption that migration constitutes a move from the familiar to the unfamiliar. Yet this too is often misleading. Japanese, for example, often move in retirement to places they already know from their pre-retirement careers or to places that offer much that is somehow familiar, whether in terms of people, culture, and even scenery (such as irrigated rice fields).

A fifth theme involves the complexities of migration processes. For example, in his chapter Xiang Biao traces Chinese migrants who move "downstream" toward destination countries but also "upstairs" in terms of bureaucratic structures in China. Migration, after all, is not just about people moving from place to place and often across national borders. It is also about the local, national, regional, and global domains and institutions that shape the flows of migration and the experiences of migrants. Understanding this multidimensional nature of migration may benefit from ways of looking at migration and society that come out of the East Asian tradition. Zhang Jijiao suggests one such option in his reference to the distinctly Chinese way in which Fei Xiaotong conceptualized human networks. Hy Luong's discussion of moral networks among migrants in Vietnam also invokes a quite distinctly East Asian sense of how individual decisions are also simultaneously set within social, moral, and familial frameworks. The broader suggestion is simply that in dealing with the complexities of East Asian migration we may all benefit from considering the complexities of East Asian thought about human mobility, as well as the complexities of East Asian migration itself. Our title itself is drawn from that tradition,[5] specifically the frequent exhortation of the Yi Jing (I-Ching) that the best course may be to seek one's destiny across the waters – whether they be vast oceans or simple rivers.

Notes

1. There is now much research on various aspects of migration to, from, and within East Asia and much of it is available in English. The edited volumes by Akaha and Vassilieva (2005), and Douglass and Roberts (2003) are perhaps especially crucial, supplemented now by a volume from a conference held at Japan's National Museum of Ethnology (Yamashita, Minami, Haines, and Eades 2008; Haines, Minami, and Yamashita 2007) and a volume on diversity in Japan (Graburn, Ertl, and Tierney 2008). The extensive work on returning Nikkei from South America also deserves note (Linger 2001, Roth 2002, Takenaka 1997, Tsuda 2003). Particularly useful discussions of immigration and minorities policy in Korea and Japan include Bartram (2000), Kashiwazaki and Akaha (2006), Kim (2006), Komai (2001), S. Lee (2003), Lim (2003, 2004, 2009), Park (2004), Seol and Skrentny (2004), Tsuda and Cornelius (2004), Takao (2003). Discussions of labor activism on behalf of migrants in Korea can be found in Chung and Seok (2000), Kim (2003), H.-K. Lee (1997, 2003), Lim (2003), Park (2004), and Seol and Han (2004).

2. The rules of the game are vastly different for the wealthier social classes on the move, compared with the migrant poor. The world is rapidly becoming differentiated into the citizens of rich countries, who are tolerated almost anywhere as long as they bring their credit cards with them and don't stay too long, and those from the poorer countries who are treated with great suspicion. In general, tourists come from the wealthier countries. However, even tourists may come to stay permanently, and not just those ready for retirement. As Yamashita has noted, many Japanese tourists to Bali over the years, particularly women, have ended up becoming enamored both with the place and with Balinese partners, and have settled there, forming transnational and multicultural families (Yamashita 2003; Yamashita, Chapter 11 in this volume). This is part of a growing trend in the Asia Pacific region. The shortage of women of marriageable age in many areas, particularly isolated rural areas with high levels of out-migration, means that either a lot of bachelors stay unmarried, or that wives have to come in from even poorer regions. In China, the flow of wives is generally from West to East, while in Japan, there has been systematic importation of wives from other Asian countries for many years (Douglass 2009). Meanwhile, among the more cosmopolitan populations and the more international wards of the larger cities, the

numbers of international migrants and the local arrangements catering for them will continue to increase (Nagy 2009).

3. There is, in addition, the broader issue of what state reactions are, and should be, to these new types of migration. Many of the lifestyle migrants, for example, are wealthy or have useful skills. The question therefore becomes, how can the destination countries maximize the benefits of these new kinds of migration while minimizing the problems?

In the case of tourists, the benefits are obvious. They spend money locally and create jobs. There are potential problem areas. Many commentators see tourism as destroying the local culture, though others have suggested that cultures are always changing anyway, and that tourism creates new forms of culture that are often beneficial (Yamashita 2003). In providing income, tourism also provides resources for maintaining local cultural forms – forms of culture that lack market value are often very difficult to perpetuate. Casinos can also be a way of generating revenue, although without regulation they often create opportunities for corruption or attract the unwelcome attentions of organized crime (Lintner 2002). Sex tourism is another problem area, though historically sex has always been linked strongly with tourism, and the problem will probably persist as long as do the huge differences in wealth within developing countries that give rise to the problem. One other problem is that tourism facilities may have a negative impact on the environment. As a result, forms of sustainable tourism are now being explicitly addressed. But generally if regimes want to encourage inbound tourism, they have to make entry easy, through relaxing or abolishing visa requirements, at least for short-stay visitors, and make adjustments to regulations covering gambling, consumption of alcohol, and other potential problem areas.

Educational migrants are also generally viewed favorably. Not only is education a valued export industry, but it also creates a skilled labor force that can be recruited into the local labor market, as in Singapore (Ko 2004). The presence of foreign students may allow the expansion of universities in a period of demographic decline, as is presently the case in Japan. However, there are also problems: education may well be a cover for migrants who are actually engaged in other less welcome activities, as is a perennial fear in Japan. Nevertheless, if the corollary of the export of education is that the workforce is likely to become more diverse and multicultural, then governments will eventually have to react by bringing immigration procedures, employment regulations, pensions, and welfare entitlements into line with those of the migrants' own countries, to allow them to move across national boundaries.

With older migrants looking for alternative retirement settings, there are also clear benefits and problems for the destination countries. As people age, their costs to society generally increase, especially in terms of health care. As long as they can pay, they may well provide a useful income stream for the local medical industry, allowing the expansion of employment and infrastructure. They may also help to support the population in rural areas which are otherwise facing falling fertility and a declining population (Mock 2008). Citizenship and passports may provide opportunities for governments to make money, filtering out the poor, and only allowing in those with big bank accounts who are able to support themselves and contribute to the local economy. As with other forms of migration, those with financial resources are greatly preferred by destination countries.

4. While there is much that is different between migration in East Asia and migration in North America and Europe, there is also much about the topic that is rather similar. Many of the migrant groups are nominally the same: Vietnamese, Filipinos, Thai, Pakistanis, Brazilians, Nigerians – much less the Chinese, Japanese, and Koreans who are again now found with increasing frequency in each other's countries. Much of the dynamic of migrant life and migrant-host society interaction is also quite comparable. In particular, the situation of low-wage migrant labor is similar, including the range from fully legal (and regulated) workers to those who overstay the time limits of their visas, work despite a visa that prohibits work, or cross national borders illegally. The day-to-day realities of such migrant lives in the shadows – whether Chinese in Japan and Korea, or rural Chinese in Chinese cities – would be all too familiar to a North American audience: financial insecurity, weak unionization, limited housing, lack of medical care, poor (if any) education, harsh constraints on family life, and general cultural and social disavowal. Yet there is indeed much that is different between East Asia and North America. The scale of international migration is still, for example, far lower in East Asia. Historically, the degree of cultural diversity is also much lower. One result is that, somewhat paradoxically, the smaller numbers of migrants in East Asia are in many ways more culturally challenging.

5. In the classic English translation of the classic German translation of the Yi Jing (Baynes 1957), this comes out as "it furthers one to cross the great water." The original Chinese, however, is a little more compact (利渉大川) and less about frothy seas. It turns out, for example, that the "great water" is just a "big river" and the meaning of the metaphor thus depends a great deal on whether one imagines the Yangtze River, the Yellow River, or perhaps one of those smaller rivers that Caroline Grillot notes on the China-Vietnam border.

References

Akaha, Tsuneo, and Anna Vassilieva, eds. 2005. *Crossing National Borders: Human Migration Issues in Northeast Asia.* Tokyo: United Nations University Press.

Appadurai, Arjun. 1997. *Modernity at Large: Cultural Dimensions of Globalization.* Minneapolis and London: University of Minneapolis Press.

Bartram, David. 2000. "Japan and labor migration: Theoretical and methodological implications of negative cases." *International Migration Review* 34(1): 5–32.

Baynes, Carey F. 1967. *The I Ching or Book of Changes.* Translation of the Richard Wilhelm Translation. Princeton: Princeton University Press.

Chung, Kiseon, and Hyunho Seok. 2000. "Culture and social adjustment: Migrant workers in Korea and local workers in overseas Korean firms." *Asian and Pacific Migration Journal* 9(3): 287–309.

Cohen, Robin. 2006. *Migration and Its Enemies.* Oxford: Blackwell.

Douglass, Mike. 2009. "Global householding: Towards a multicultural age in East Asia," pp. 137–168 in *Global Movements in the Asia-Pacific*, eds. Pookong Kee and Hidetaka Yoshimatsu. Singapore: World Scientific Press.

Douglass, Mike, and Glenda S. Roberts, eds. 2003. *Japan and Global Migration: Foreign Workers and the Advent of a Multicultural Society.* Honolulu: University of Hawai'i Press.

Eades, Jerry S. 2001. "New directions in Asia Pacific studies: A summary." *Ritsumeikan Journal of Asia Pacific Studies* 7: 116–146.

———. 2004. "Dynamics of migration: Past, present and future movements of peoples in the Asia Pacific." *Ritsumeikan Journal of Asia Pacific Studies* 14: 57–74.

Faier, Lieba. 2009. *Intimate Encounters: Filipina Women and the Remaking of Rural Japan.* Berkeley: University of California Press.

Fukuoka, Yasunori. 2000. *Lives of Young Koreans in Japan.* Melbourne: Trans Pacific.

Graburn, Nelson, John Ertl, and R. Kenji Tierney, eds. 2008. *Multiculturalism in the New Japan: Crossing the Boundaries Within.* Oxford and New York: Berghahn.

Haines, David W. 2008. "Transnational migration: Some comparative considerations," pp. 15–26 in *Transnational Migration in East Asia*, eds. Shinji Yamashita, Makito Minami, David W. Haines, and Jerry Eades. Osaka, Japan: National Museum of Ethnology.

Haines, David W., Makito Minami, and Shinji Yamashita. 2007. "Transnational migration in East Asia: Japan in comparative focus." *International Migration Review* 41(4): 963–967.

Harvey, David. 1990. *The Condition of Postmodernity: An Enquiry into the Origins of Cultural Change.* Cambridge, Mass. and Oxford: Blackwell Publishers.

Kashiwazaki, Chikako, and Tsuneo Akaha. 2006. "Japanese immigration policy: Responding to conflicting pressures." *Migration Source* (2006), http://www.migrationinformation.org/Profiles/display.cfm?ID=487.

Kim, Bumsoo. 2006. "From exclusion to inclusion? The legal treatment of 'foreigners' in contemporary Japan." *Immigrants and Minorities* 24(1): 51–73.

Kim, Joon. 2003. "Insurgency and advocacy: Unauthorized foreign workers and civil society in South Korea." *Asian and Pacific Migration Journal* 12(3): 237–270.

Ko, Yiu Chung. 2004. "Singapore's 'foreign talent' policy: Development and implementation." *Ritsumeikan Journal of Asia Pacific Studies* 14: 85–98.

Komai, Hiroshi. 2001. *Foreign Migrants in Contemporary Japan.* Melbourne: Trans Pacific Press.

Lee, Hye-Kyung. 1997. "The employment of foreign workers in Korea: Issues and policy suggestions." *International Sociology* 12(3): 353–371.

———. 2003. "Gender, migration and civil activism in South Korea." *Asian and Pacific Migration Journal* 12(1/2): 127–154.

Lee, Shin-wha. 2003. "Human security aspects of international migration: The case of South Korea." *Global Economic Review* 32(3): 41–66.

Lim, Timothy C. 2003. "Racing from the bottom in South Korea? The nexus between civil society and transnational migrants." *Asian Survey* 43(3): 423–442.

———. 2004. "Commentary," pp. 514–516 in *Controlling Immigration: A Global Perspective*, eds. Wayne A. Cornelius, et al. Stanford, California: Stanford University Press.

———. 2009. "Who is Korean? Migration, immigration, and the challenge of multiculturalism in homogeneous societies." *The Asia-Pacific Journal* 30: 1–9.

Linger, Daniel Touro. 2001. *No One Home: Brazilian Selves Remade in Japan*. Stanford, California: Stanford University Press.

Lintner, Bertil. 2002. *Blood Brothers: Crime, Business, and Politics in Asia*. Bangkok: Silkworm.

Liu-Farrer, Gracia. 2010. "Between privilege and prejudice: Chinese immigrants in corporate Japan's transitional economy," pp. 123–146 in *Global Movements in the Asia-Pacific*, eds. Pookong Kee and Hidetaka Yoshimatsu. Singapore: World Scientific Press.

Mani, A. 2005. "Labor markets and migrants in Southeast Asia." *Ritsumeikan Journal of Asia Pacific Studies* 18: 71–106.

Massey, Douglas, Joaquin Arango, Graeme Hugo, Ali Kouaouci, Adela Pellegrino, and J. Edward Taylor. 1998. *Worlds in Motion: Understanding International Migration at the End of the Millennium*. Oxford: Clarendon Press.

Miyazaki, Koji. 2008. "Aging society and migration to Asia and Oceania," pp. 139–150 in *Transnational Migration in East Asia: Japan in a Comparative Focus*, eds. Shinji Yamashita, Makito Minami, David W. Haines, and Jerry S. Eades. Osaka: National Museum of Ethnology.

Mock, John. 2008. "Multicultural education," pp. 123–136 in *Transnational Migration in East Asia: Japan in a Comparative Focus*, eds. Shinji Yamashita, Makito Minami, David W. Haines, and Jerry S. Eades. Osaka: National Museum of Ethnology.

Nagy, Stephen Robert. 2009. "Multicultural coexistence policies: Responses of local governments in the Tokyo metropolitan area to the pressures of international immigration," pp. 147–180 in *Global Movements in the Asia-Pacific*, eds. Pookong Kee and Hidetaka Yoshimatsu. Singapore: World Scientific Press.

Ono, Mayumi. 2008. "Long-stay tourism and international retirement migration. Japanese retirees in Malaysia," pp. 151–162 in *Transnational Migration in East Asia: Japan in a Comparative Focus*, eds. Shinji Yamashita, Makito Minami, David W. Haines, and Jerry S. Eades. Osaka: National Museum of Ethnology.

Park, Young-bum. 2004. "Country report: Republic of Korea" in *Workshop on International Migration and Labour Market in Asia*. Tokyo: Japan Institute for Labour Policy and Training.

Picard, Michel, and Robert Everett Wood, eds. 1997. *Tourism, Ethnicity, and the State in Asian and Pacific Society*. Honolulu: University of Hawaii Press.

Ryang, Sonia. 1997. *North Koreans in Japan*. Boulder CO: Westview.

Ren, Xuefei. 2009. "Transnational architectural production in downtown Beijing," pp. 341–368 in *Global Movements in the Asia-Pacific*, eds. Pookong Kee and Hidetaka Yoshimatsu. Singapore: World Scientific Press.

Roth, Joshua Hotaka. 2002. *Brokered Homeland: Japanese Brazilian Migrants in Japan*. Ithaca, New York: Cornell University Press.

Sakanaka, Hidenori, and Akihiro Asakawa. 2007. *Iminkokka Nippon: Issenman-nin no Imin ga Nippon wo Sukuu* [Japan as a migrant state: 10 million migrants save Japan]. Tokyo: Nihonkajoshuppan.

Sasaki, Koji. 2008. "Between emigration and immigration: Japanese emigrants to Brazil and their descendants in Japan," pp. 53–66 in *Transnational Migration in East Asia: Japan in a Comparative Focus*, eds. Shinji Yamashita, Makito Minami, David W. Haines, and Jerry S. Eades. Osaka: National Museum of Ethnology.

Sassen, Saskia. 1992. *The Global City.* Princeton: Princeton University Press.

Seol, Dong-Hoon, and Geon-Soo Han. 2004. "Foreign migrant workers and social discrimination in Korea." *Harvard Asia Quarterly* 8(1): 45–50.

Seol, Dong-Hoon, and John D. Skrentny. 2004. "South Korea: Importing undocumented workers," pp. 481–513 in *Controlling Immigration: A Global Perspective*, eds. Wayne A. Cornelius, et al. Stanford, California: Stanford University Press.

Takao, Yasuo. 2003. "Foreigners' rights in Japan: Beneficiaries to participants." *Asian Survey* 43(3): 527–552.

Takenaka, Ayumi. 1997. "Towards Nikkeiism: Japanese (Nikkei)-Peruvian migrants as a new ethnic minority," pp. 82–98 in *Beyond Boundaries: Selected Papers on Refugees and Immigrants, Volume 7*, eds. Ruth Krulfeld and Diane Baxter. Arlington, Virginia: American Anthropological Association.

Toyota, Mika. 2008. "Care for the elderly: Family duty or paid service?" pp. 163–174 in *Transnational Migration in East Asia: Japan in a Comparative Focus*, eds. Shinji Yamashita, Makito Minami, David W. Haines, and Jerry S. Eades. Osaka: National Museum of Ethnology.

Tran, Mariko. 2006. "Unable or unwilling to leave the nest? An analysis and evaluation of Japanese parasite single theories." *Electronic Journal of Contemporary Japanese Studies*, 3 July 2006, http://www.japanesestudies.org.uk/discussionpapers/2006/Tran.html.

Tsuda, Takeyuki. 2003. *Strangers in the Ethnic Homeland: Japanese Brazilian Return Migration in Transnational Perspective*. New York: Columbia University Press.

———, and Wayne A. Cornelius. 2004. "Japan: Government policy, immigrant reality," pp. 439–476 in *Controlling Immigration: A Global Perspective*, eds. Wayne A. Cornelius, et al. Stanford, California: Stanford University Press.

Yamanaka, Keiko. 2007. "Increasing international marriages in East Asia: Japan, South Korea and Taiwan." Paper presented at the Panel "East Asia in Motion: A Comparative Perspective to Transnational Migration," the Annual Meeting of the Japanese Society of Cultural Anthropology, 2–3 June 2007, Nagoya, Japan.

Yamashita, Shinji. 2003. *Bali and Beyond: Explorations in the Anthropology of Tourism.* Translated by J.S. Eades. Oxford and New York: Berghahn.

———. 2008a. "Transnational migration of women: Changing boundaries of contemporary Japan," pp. 101–116 in *Multiculturalism in the New Japan: Crossing the Boundaries Within*, eds. Nelson Graburn, John Ertl, and R. Kenji Tierney. Oxford and New York: Berghahn.

———. 2008b. "Transnational migration in East Asia: Japan in a comparative focus," pp. 3–13 in *Transnational Migration in East Asia: Japan in a Comparative Focus* (Senri Ethnological Report 77), eds. Shinji Yamashita, Makito Minami, David Haines, and Jerry Eades. Osaka: National Museum of Ethnology.

Yamashita, Shinji, Kadir H. Din and Jerry S. Eades, eds. 1997. *Tourism and Cultural Development in Asia and Oceania.* Bangi: UKM Press.

Yamashita, Shinji, Makito Minami, David W. Haines, and Jerry S. Eades, eds. 2008. *Transnational Migration in East Asia: Japan in a Comparative Focus.* Osaka, Japan: National Museum of Ethnology.

Part I:
Migrants, States, and Cities

CHAPTER 1

Human Trade in Colonial Vietnam

Nicolas LAINEZ

> Our topic in this study, trafficking in persons, is being done in large scale. Pirates disembarked spontaneously, attacked villages and withdrew … taking young men and women as prisoners to sell them at the markets of the Celestial Empire. In land, they had correspondents [that] attracted Annamese girls in lovers' appointments, took their service as maids or bought children from parents. (Paulus 1885: 45)

If one looks at the archives, it is clear that history can be a useful tool in the understanding of the modern phenomena of human trafficking. These practices, widespread over the Indochinese peninsula a century ago, and so aptly described by colonial administrators, have not disappeared from contemporary Asia according to observers, researchers, and anti-trafficking campaigners. In fact, today's practices resemble what was taking place a hundred years ago to such a great extent that the arguments of those aid organizations who claim this problem is anchored in recent processes of globalization must be challenged. Instead, the similarities and parallels between the colonial period and the present one are striking, emphasizing durability as well as change.

The objective of this chapter is to map this institution of trading human beings at the intersection of the nineteenth and twentieth centuries, providing a specific Vietnamese example of the more general need to consider historical precursors to contemporary migration patterns. The chapter will begin by describing the major national and transnational trafficking routes, pointing out the details of crossing points and dispersal markets. As will be shown, those trafficked were Vietnamese, but also Cantonese, Japanese, and European. Then, the nature of this human trade will be assessed by focusing on its different resulting social forms, particularly adoption, concubinage, and prostitution. Finally, French policies to suppress piracy in Tonkin[1] and to manage prostitution – considered as a "necessary evil" – will be outlined.

The period covered by this chapter ranges from 1863, when an anonymous author published *Note sur l'Esclavage*, to 1941, date of the publication of Andre Baudrit's book *La Femme et l'Enfant dans l'Indochine Française et dans la Chine du Sud (Rapt-Vente-Infanticide)*. Secondary sources comprise published historical papers and books as well as reports from French colonial administrators. Primary sources include reports of proceedings and administrative letters from French Consuls in China from the National Archives Center No. 1 in Hà Nội. Given that the sources are disparate in nature and quality, the images drawn are necessarily partial. The goal is not to offer a definitive picture of the situation, but to explore a research perspective on human trafficking that emphasizes historical similarities and parallels. One should keep in mind that all these sources bear the stamp of colonialism (Delaye 2005), whether in justifying the system or in the interventionist intentions of narrators who hoped their testimony could relieve human injustice and "heal a wound that the flag could not cover up" (Paulus 1885: 49). One should also bear in mind that, just as in the prolific contemporary literature on trafficking from the media, aid organizations, and national agencies, the voices of those actually trafficked are usually absent. The women and children tricked, kidnapped, sold, exploited, or thrown into the Gulf of Tonkin rarely leave their own testimony. Some, then as now, disappear into the red light districts of urban centers while others succeed in finding a relatively stable new life or returning home to their villages.

Mechanisms and Routes

Numerous complaints and newspaper accounts from the colonial period tell of child abductions in the Red River delta. Children of indigent Vietnamese or Chinese families continuously disappeared without leaving a trace. Kidnappers used a wide range of techniques to abduct their prey: enticing promises for work or marriage, candies to lure young children, chloroform to put victims to sleep, brutal raids and kidnappings, bandit attacks on coastal villages. Once deceived, victims were usually moved from one intermediary place to another before being sold in border towns or northern ports like Hải Phòng. On 2 January 1936, the newspaper *Annam Nouveau* offered figures on reported disappearances: 172 in 1933, 134 in 1934, and 236 in 1935, yielding an average of 180 missing children per year. The French colonial justice system was at first inadequately equipped to deal with these offenses, although over the years it adopted a more active approach (as shall be discussed).

We lack reliable data about the prices paid for these individuals as well as stable reference points to set up comparative tables of the currencies, whether Chinese silver tael, French Indochinese Union piaster, French francs, Hong Kong dollars, or thirty gram "ounces" of gold. The price of each person was calculated according to criteria of ethnic origin, gender, age, health and physical condition, and educational level. For women, virginity was an added criterion of value. Factors related to market supply and demand also affected price. In general, women were more expensive than men because they were perceived as being more malleable and entrepreneurial as workers and because they could also become spouses or concubines. Those who were sold were often later exchanged for money, rice, salt, cattle, weapons and ammunition, opium, or for other individuals. In 1883, Taboulet (1883: 117) indicated prices in piasters as follows: a child of ten to twelve cost fifteen to eighteen piasters, at fifteen a boy's value climbed to twenty piasters and a girl's could climb to thirty or forty piasters if pretty. The markup in price was considerable. In 1906, for example, the price of a Vietnamese child bought for one piaster in Vietnam could reach one or two hundred Hong Kong dollars. In 1941, Baudrit (1941: 118) states that the price of a *Tonkinois* child was between six and fifteen dollars when first purchased, but the value could reach thirty to one hundred Hong Kong dollars on the island market. These figures indicate the substantial profits that were generated by the trade in humans at that time.

Generally, agents who abducted the women and children were not those who exploited them. Victims were commonly sold and resold through a chain of intermediaries that generated profit in each transaction. In Tonkin, the identification of potential victims was usually accomplished by local women traders who had little difficulty in identifying prey for themselves or in assisting other captors. These women, who acted as brokers, often bought children for small amounts of money and then raised them in their houses. The children destined to be sent to China, for example, were dressed with Chinese-style clothing, their hair arranged with Chinese-style braids, and their teeth were whitened if they had been previously lacquered in black. While being raised, children were prepared for the fate that awaited them. For the majority, that was domestic service, prostitution, or marriage-like unions. Generally they stayed with the brokers for a period of between six months and two years. After that, children were sent to Chinatowns in Hà Nội or Sài Gòn, or to southern China. The youngest recruits were prized by Chinese residents or Cantonese traders traveling in Indochina. Some young women might also marry French administrators. It was possible for those who benefited from the company of these women during their sojourns in Indochina to do so without knowing their companion's true origin.

In the late nineteenth century, human trafficking in northern Vietnam seems to have been in the hands of Vietnamese and Chinese bandits. Some of these worked with German or British merchants by subcontracting the shipment of the merchandise. In the South China Sea, complex alliances developed among organized criminal groups, fortune pirates, and shipping traders, all under the eyes of powerless French authorities.

The actual routes of human trafficking were multiple. *Tonkinois* recruits were transferred to China by both sea and land. By sea, women from the Red River delta were routed to Hải Phòng either by land or by small rivers that pour out into the gulf. From there they were shipped to Pakhoi in Guangxi province.

Sometimes they were hidden in bunkers or "ostensibly taken by parents of alleged Chinese which for the occasion had changed the national costume for a disguise that gave them the appearance of Chinese girls" or "with legal passports issued by the Residences where it was clearly mentioned *with their own children.*"[2] From Pakhoi, they were sent to the port of Haikou in the island province of Hainan (formerly Hoi Hao) and then transferred to Macao or Hong Kong. Arrests were frequent in Hải Phòng after the promulgation of a decree in December 1912 that strengthened controls on suspicious vessels. As a consequence, smugglers started to use more discreet sampans, carrying small numbers of persons to circumvent Hạ Long Bay, Cát Bà, or Ke Bao islands.[3] By day, children were hidden in caves, and by night they traveled on junks or were hidden in steamship holds. Given these circumstances, trips to China could last for several days; many died of hunger, exhaustion, or drowning after being thrown into the sea by the sailors. The Franco-Vietnamese press nicknamed pirates from the Gulf of Tonkin the "dogs of the sea" (*chiens de la mer*) because they never hesitated to throw victims, tied up, into the water when French sea police patrols approached.[4]

By land, convoys took isolated trails to cross the mountainous provinces of Đông Triều, Bắc Giang, and Lạng Sơn towards Guangxi. If departing from Hà Nội, convoys moved towards Tuyên Quang, then crossed the Lào Cai Chinese border with Yunnan to reach Mong Tseu. Most of the women traveling by land supplied the demand for marriages and adoptions in Guangxi province.

Trading Women for What Purposes?

Why did Chinese need to import Vietnamese women? Did China lack for females? Hải Dương Resident Massimy asserted various reasons (Baudrit 1941: 90). First, Chinese women caught on the spot knew the region and could easily escape, whereas Vietnamese women sent far from their homeland could not. Second, men preferred not to buy Chinese compatriots because they felt more sympathy for them than for their Vietnamese counterparts. Third, Chinese employers enjoyed greater freedom with Vietnamese employees than with Chinese. Fourth, Vietnamese women were easier and cheaper to acquire than Chinese women.

Although most of these arguments seem plausible, one is highly questionable. The fact that Vietnamese women were cheaper than Chinese, more easily subjected to all kinds of tasks, and less tempted to escape, all seems reasonable. But to argue that Chinese did not want to buy fellow Chinese due to sympathy or compassion seems to contradict the *mui tsai* system (literally "little sister" or "small servant" in Cantonese dialect) that developed in southern China in the late nineteenth and early twentieth century. This system was grounded in poverty and only worsened during periods of famine, epidemics and natural disasters, and after the two opium wars. The *mui tsai* system actually generated the first international campaign against what was labeled "child slavery" (Haslewood 1930). It is believed that hundreds of thousands of the young and destitute from southern China provinces were sold as wives, concubines, or prostitutes at that time. The youngest (the *mui tsai*) were sent to work as domestic employees for wealthy owners in Canton, Hong Kong, Malaysia, or Singapore. Transactions were usually subject to written contracts. A *mui tsai* could become either a servant or a concubine, and the purchaser had the right to re-sell her, marry her, or make her his concubine. The servant had to perform domestic chores and she usually received little or no financial reward (Chin 2002, Haslewood 1930, Jaschok 1988, Warren 1993).

Buying servants, wives, or concubines must be distinguished from prostitution. Silvestre's (1880) report about slavery and forms of servitude in Cochinchina, Landes's (1880) letter about prostitution in Chợ Lớn, and Hardy's article (1994) about military brothels or BMC (*Bordel Militaire de Campagne*) all portrayed a complex situation: Chinese brothels employing Cantonese children, Japanese and European prostitutes serving French troops, and trafficking of Chinese and Vietnamese women to Singapore. In 1880, Chợ Lớn Mayor Landes described the traffic of young girls being employed as maids or prostitutes in the Chinese municipality.[5] Like northern female brokers, Chợ Lớn Madams raised their recruits, mostly young Cantonese or Hongkongese girls, to become second spouses or prostitutes. The status of concubine was a godsend for Chinese human traders who disguised their victims as concubines. Vietnamese girls were dressed in Chinese clothing and received Chinese education to gradually obliterate their Vietnamese identity. Girls covered the cost of their instruction and their living expenses by working as domestic workers or singers. Madams subjected their employees to debts and tracked them if they ran away. The best alternative for a young woman to escape was to marry a wealthy Chinese. Prices depended on the candidate's age, beauty, qualities, and size of debt. Some of these women remained in brothels as boarders when, for example, a husband already had several concubines and did not want to bring an additional one into the home or when a merchant only wanted to visit the concubine occasionally when he stopped in town. If no client had expressed the desire to marry these women by the age of fifteen or sixteen, or if the price requested by the Madam was too high, they became prostitutes. When they became old, prostitutes were enlisted as domestic workers or hairdressers and could officially retire. Chợ Lớn, for example, counted sixty-five "official" retired prostitutes in 1880.

The Sài Gòn-Chợ Lớn area was a hub through which trafficked women passed and in which they worked. In addition to Vietnamese women, other prostitutes came from Southern China, Japan, or Europe. In 1880, Landes (1880) counted eleven brothels in Chợ Lớn employing 45 women and 66 girls aged from five to fourteen. In 1908 there were 216 women, a quarter of whom were under the age of fifteen. In the early 1910s, records indicate between 300 and 380 prostitutes, plus 450 declared as prostitutes but fugitive. Figures stagnated during the 1920s, but grew considerably in the early 1930s to reach 650 declared and 450 declared but fugitive. Nevertheless, these official prostitutes (meaning those who had regular medical examinations) only accounted for a fraction of all prostitutes according to French doctors. In fact most women were illegal or unreported to the Mores Brigade (*Brigade des moeurs*). Medical authorities from the 1930s believed that five thousand prostitutes were working in Hà Nội, two thousand in Hải Phòng, and "thousands" in Sài Gòn-Chợ Lớn.

Vietnamese and Chinese prostitutes worked side by side with Japanese and European women. There were the Japanese *Karayuki-san*, "women who go far away" or "women sent to China" (Roustan 2005, Warren 1993). The *Karayuki-san* implantation in Indochina began in the early 1880s and had ended by the early 1920s. The majority of them were destitute prostitutes (or pimps) whose remittances represented an important source of revenue for the Japanese government. Japanese women offered their sexual services in Southeast Asian cities like Sài Gòn, Hà Nội, Hải Phòng, Singapore, Kuala Lumpur, or even further afield in Siberia and Australia. French clients considered Japanese women as the most exotic and also the safest in terms of venereal diseases, especially compared to Vietnamese women. Japanese brothels were located in Vietnamese-style houses and had no distinctive marks at the front gate. The business was conducted discreetly and neither the facades nor the employees appealed directly to neighborhood clients. Yet *Karayuki-san* themselves were easily identifiable thanks to their exclusive dress: *kimono, obi* (wide cloth belt), *geta* (elevated wooden clogs), and bun in their hair. This dress suggested the status of luxury prostitute and ensured visual differentiation from local Vietnamese or Chinese competitors (Roustan 2005). In the late nineteenth and early twentieth centuries, Japanese international prestige was affirmed by war victories against the Chinese in 1894 and the Russians in 1904. Following these wars and commercial successes in Malaysia that enriched the Japanese economy, Japan started to repatriate *karayuki-san* in the early 1920s. With the need for remittances reduced and an increased feeling of shame towards these women "having being sent far away," the need to repatriate them was considered urgent.

Finally, a few European prostitutes also operated in Vietnam. They were brought by merchants transiting through Singapore or Hong Kong. These Europeans worked in Westernized cities in the hands of criminal networks specializing in foreign demand. The clientele included French military officers, civil servants, and rich merchants. European prostitutes worked discreetly in private houses which were not advertised as brothels. The *Valaque* women from Eastern Europe were a special category and suffered from stigmatization. French authorities expelled them from Indochina between 1915 and 1920 claiming that they were causing a deterioration in public morality. *Valaque* prostitutes were subjected to special legislation and suffered from segregation policies or spatial confinement.

French Policy against the "Yellow Trade"

The "yellow trade" was an offense that had to be suppressed in the eyes of the French colonial administration. Yet prosecutions of kidnappers were rare. Silvestre (1880: 140) gives us some figures on convictions: three in 1874, one in 1875, one in 1876, one in 1877, three in 1878, and fifteen in 1879. The trade posed numerous problems not only for the victims but also for the colonial administration. First, France observed the development of complex criminal alliances between secret societies and bandits engaged in illicit activities in the Gulf of Tonkin and, despite its indisputable noble intentions, felt unable to protect colonial subjects. This undermined its credibility. Second, the traffic created diplomatic troubles with China and European countries operating in Chinese ports, especially Germany and Britain, which did not agree with the spontaneous controls on their ships. Third, the trade caused tensions to develop between the Government of Indochina, reliant on the Ministry of the Colonies, and the French consuls in China, reliant on the Ministry of Foreign Affairs. Tensions crystallized in the case of rescues and repatriations. Vietnamese "victims" who were arrested by Chinese police were usually taken to French consular delegations in charge of organizing their repatriation. The cooperation between these consular authorities and colonial administrators inevitably caused problems. As a consequence, victims were cloistered amidst jurisdictional battles: who was to organize their repatriation, who was to fund it, and what was to be done with the women once they were back in Vietnam? (Lessard 2009).

What actions, then, did the French undertake to combat the trade in humans? First of all, prosecutions and penalties against convicted criminals rose at the beginning of the twentieth century, although they remained discreet in the pages of local newspapers. Moreover, authorities extended their vigilance at the Sino-Vietnamese border, which included strengthening controls over the delivery of travel permits to China. An agreement signed in 1895 allowed the establishment of a joint Sino-Vietnamese police force to suppress criminal activities at the frontier. Maritime shipping was also targeted and vigilance was increased over junks and vessels heading to China from Hải Phòng. These repressive policies had a few successes: dismantling criminal networks, arrests of bandits, repatriation of Vietnamese victims from China, and reinforcement of land and sea controls. However, and despite numerous efforts, the results of this campaign were limited. Indeed, the authorities even observed an increase in the trade.

Repatriations posed a number of problems. On the one hand, repatriations raised ethical questions: What should be done with women who welcomed their own migration to China and did not want to return to Vietnam? What was to be done with those who felt happy with their marriage? And what about those who had nobody awaiting them in Vietnam or had nowhere to go? "Will we again break these unions, irregular at the initial stage, but already sanctioned by time and mutual consent?" asked the Resident of Bắc Kạn in 1904.[6] If the law had to be applied with severity, newly formed families would risk separation.

On the other hand, if women were handed over without proper follow-up, were they not at risk of resale? Here is a frightening notice found on the public walls of Quang Tcheou Wan, Canton province, on July 1918:

> Tchan the battalion leader [...] informs the public that 252 young women ab-ducted and not yet repurchased are remaining. Those who wish to redeem their wives and daughters must go straight to the Hop Ky house, Lord's of Pan Pou Kuong, to convey a price, and after having paid a suitable amount, the redemp-tion will take place. There will be no more formalities [...] No one must disobey this order. (Bonnafont 1924: 776 as cited by Baudrit 1941: 117)[7]

One of the probable reasons why piracy and human trafficking escalated was the increased development of infrastructures that allowed commercial and hu-man exchanges: land roads and fluvial streams were improved, regional markets and complex commercial circuits were developed. Needless to say, the Vietnam-ese peasantry was impoverished under the French, thus providing a fertile ground for indebtedness and all kinds of exploitation. In addition, the perception of traf-ficking by colonial administrators and French Consuls in China diverged. The former never approved the trade and were constantly frustrated by their inability to put an end to it in Vietnam. Yet, Consuls were confronted by Vietnamese victims whose stories horrified them. They were also exhausted by the colonial administrative bureaucracy, and the frequent attitude of indifference when re-patriations had to be organized. Caution is therefore necessary when analyzing colonial policies emanating from different institutional bodies since the "French administration" did not form a homogenous group (Lessard 2009).

Beyond the specific issue of human trafficking, how did the French perceive prostitution and how did they regulate it? Not only was trafficking in women for prostitution a grave offense, but prostitutes also represented a "venereal danger" as they were prime suspects for conveying sexually transmitted diseases. During the French occupation, prostitution was considered a "necessary evil" that was essential to comfort the morale of the troops (Guénel 2001, Tracol 2009, 2010). The colonial administration encouraged prostitution for soldiers in specific and controlled areas. Early on, French observers were bothered by the apparent lack of administrative supervision on prostitution by Vietnamese authorities, and this policy changed dramatically under French rule. But problems remained. A ma-jority of French military and civilian personnel resided in the municipalities of Sài Gòn and Hà Nội. At the end of the nineteenth century, the ratio of French immigrants was one woman for seven men. The installation of troops in urban centers generated a particularly concentrated demand for sexual services. There was a need both to make women available and to control them. The fight against so-called illegal prostitution – beyond medical control or taxation – was directed largely toward public health. As early as 1880, the French administration set up regulatory policies. Some prostitutes working in brothels were registered, subjected to taxation, and obliged to follow regular medical check ups, whereas other prostitutes – the majority – worked unregistered and discreetly. Those women were anonymous and illegal, and were therefore uncontainable. They became an obsession for the French who sought to regularize them by implementing regulations. From 1880 onwards, an impressive list of decrees and laws prohibiting soliciting or clandestine prostitution emerged. These laws and decrees sought to control the delivery of permits to open new brothels, to apply discriminatory licenses (in 1912, opening a Vietnamese house cost 30 piasters whereas to open a Chinese or a Japanese house cost 150), to enforce segregationist policies that forbade mixing women from different origins in the same establishment, and to impose heavy taxation that could be reinvested in health centers.

One crucial part of managing prostitution was the "Mores Brigade" that was created in municipalities as early as 1880 to register prostitutes, monitor establishments, and suppress the activities of illegal prostitutes. Registered women received a card indicating their age, workplace, and the results of their weekly medical tests. Cards also described the shape of their face, nose, mouth, and chin. The main demand of the army was to establish brothels hosting "healthy" women. This would lead to "reserved quarters" (*quartiers réservés*) for the prostitutes. Yet medical centers for prostitutes were limited in number and in resources and could not provide the necessary services. Vietnamese brothels were perceived as dirty and employing "old" and "unhealthy" women. In general, Vietnamese prostitutes were perceived as having a higher risk of passing sexual diseases to clients compared to Japanese, Chinese, or European prostitutes.

Connecting the Past and the Present

The "yellow trade" emerged as an issue of significance in colonial Vietnam from the end of the nineteenth to the first half of the twentieth century. Countless sources provide evidence of this: deception and abduction complaints, cases brought to court, miscellaneous articles in the Vietnamese press, discoveries of "human convoys" crossing the Sino-Vietnamese border or heading towards China across the Gulf of Tonkin. Whether recruited voluntarily or by force, impoverished women were transported from the countryside to the major Indochinese cities that had a strong French presence (Hà Nội, Sài Gòn, Chợ Lớn and Hải Phòng), and further to Hong Kong and the Chinese provinces of Guangxi, Yunnan, and Guangdong. They were transported through a variety of networks and for a variety of reasons, mostly to become prostitutes, servants, spouses and mistresses. Movement occurred in two directions. On the one hand, Vietnamese were sent to the urban centers or to southern China; on the other, Chinese, Japanese, and European women were imported through different networks to fill the prostitution and marriage or mistress market in Vietnam for international merchants and French administrators and soldiers.

Contemporary studies about human trafficking and labor in Asia, as well as mobility for the purpose of prostitution and forms of domestic servitude, would be enriched if historical material were more often taken into consideration.

Firstly, the historical approach enables scholars to map the domestic and transnational flows of mobility for the purposes mentioned above. As in the colonial period, contemporary migrants are now transported through the same places as their predecessors, such as the land borders of Vietnam and China (Grillot 2009 and her chapter in this collection) and Cambodia (Lainez 2011a), and further to Singapore as attested by recent research (Lainez 2011b) and media reports (VNS 2008). As in the past, the majority of women now come from rural, impoverished and often indebted households in the densely populated Mekong and Red River deltas. It is undeniable that Vietnamese transnational trade and family networks continue to play a critical role in the structuring of cross-border mobility. Still largely unknown, these Vietnamese networks, often intertwined with Chinese and Cambodian networks (for Vietnam's neighboring countries), deserve more research from a sociological perspective. Grillot (2009, and her chapter in this collection) shows how Vietnamese women are easily convinced by traders and brokers from the Vietnam-China border to enter into the marriage and prostitution industry in China. As in the colonial period, Vietnamese women are imported not only to marry and to reproduce, but also to work in the petty-trade and prostitution sectors. More research is needed to evaluate the nature of these networks across the borders and their involvement in facilitating cross-border mobility. Sources from both the colonial period and the present could be combined to explore the morphology of these networks that continue to structure cross-border mobility.

Secondly, as this chapter suggests, human trafficking seems to have occurred in the past in ways that are very similar to the present: the sale of human beings, the use of deception, and the kidnapping of women and children. Media reports and complaints from the Indochinese period often mentioned the sale of young children, especially young women for adoption, domestic work and prostitution purposes. The extreme poverty of the peasantry has long been a justification for this type of sale. Colonial ethnography (Savinien 1899, Anonymous 1863, Dartiguenave 1908) and literature address this particular kind of human transaction that prevails in present-day Vietnam. The famous novel *When the Light is Out (Tắt Đèn)* by Ngô Tất Tố published in 1939 illustrates this practice remarkably well. It is a major work addressing the sale of humans in Vietnamese rural society in detail. The story takes place in an imaginary province of Tonkin in the 1930s. It describes the harsh reality of a peasant woman who is reduced to extreme poverty and is eventually forced to sell her eldest daughter, aged seven, for two piastres to a moneylender of the village who is both rich and arrogant. Her motive is simple: to pay the tax and liberate her husband who has been imprisoned after having been beaten by tax collectors. Through a gradual descent into hell, minutely described by the writer, the mechanisms that turn the unacceptable into the acceptable are exposed. These sales of young children continue in Vietnam, and the issue is regularly reported in the local and international press (Asia Pacific News 2009, BBC News 2009, Hoang Tuan and Tiên Tho 2009). The findings of my fieldwork conducted between 2008 and 2009 in Châu Đốc, a Vietnamese district on the border between An Giang and Takeo provinces, show that mothers who were raped, abandoned by their partner, or incapable of raising their child for lack of financial means, placed their children in the illegal adoption market. Brokers, generally women paid by commission, travel from Hồ Chí Minh City to Châu Đốc to take these children away from their mothers. These brokers visit the young mothers at home or go to the town square to obtain information from indigents, beggars, and street prostitutes about possible "suppliers." The children are sold for sums ranging from US $250 to US $600 and are then placed with urban families who are unable to have children. As described by Ngô Tất Tố in the late 1930s, this form of transaction becomes acceptable from a moral standpoint because of its context: a poor and desperate mother is driven into selling her child so that she can support herself and her other children. In other words, destitution and despair excuse the socially condemned act of selling one's children.

Thirdly, the family depicted in the novel *When the Light is Out* is representative of Southeast Asian families that have long been afflicted by high levels of indebtedness, cash scarcity and lack of savings, high interest rates, and widespread debt-bondage. In colonial Vietnam, the situation was exacerbated by the land and taxation policies implemented by the French government which made farmers even poorer. Pierre Gourou (1940: 277, cited by Ngo Vinh Long 1991: 84) stated that hardly any Cochinchinese farmer began the rice season without getting into debt. In addition, farmers constantly borrowed to survive and to cover costly birth, marriage, and death ceremonies (Buu Loc 1941: 9–19). For moneylenders, high interest loans were an easy, reliable and profitable way to generate wealth with a relatively small capital investment. It was often the case that borrowers were unable to repay their loans; the lenders would then seize the land as repayment of the interest and/or principal. For the majority of peasants who had nothing to mortgage, the loans were generally short term. But a small debt did not mean a low interest rate; quite the opposite, as the small loans were the ones which brought the lenders the most, up to 3650 percent per year for the *vay bạc ngày* (daily loans) or *vay cắt cổ* (cut-throat loans) types (Gourou 1940: 277, cited by Ngo Vinh Long 1991: 85). These loans were typically repaid in cash or in kind. The moneylenders were mainly Vietnamese, but Chinese and Chetty Indians from Tamil Nadu (South India) were also in the money-lending business. Informal credit had a corrosive effect on Vietnamese peasant society. After having mortgaged their few available assets such as land and crops, insolvent farmers had no choice but to use their labor, or that of their wife and children, as collateral. Indeed, according to available sources, renting out one's services, or that of one's spouse or children, to repay a loan was tolerated and regulated by law at the beginning of the Lê dynasty (1428–1788) until the end of the Nguyên dynasty (1802–1945) (Briffaut 1907, Dang Trinh Ky 1933, Buu Loc 1941). Once in debt, it was almost impossible for the farmers to escape from the vicious circle; as a consequence, they ended up borrowing again to repay interest.

Although the historical and economic context has changed dramatically, a similar pattern of household indebtedness and the persistence of a highly developed informal credit sector have been observed in present-day Vietnam, particularly in the Mekong delta where I have conducted field research. This sector strangles the debtor, as in the expression that Pierre Gourou noted back in the 1940s: *cho vay tiền cắt cổ,* which stands for "cut-throat loans." Moneylenders charge a rate of interest ranging from 20 to 150 percent a month. The amount and conditions of the loan differ according to the needs and the solvency of the debtor, the willingness of the moneylender, and the role of a broker when one is used. Poor provincial households that refrain from agricultural activity must borrow to subsist, to cover unexpected expenses, or to make expensive purchases. Understanding the economic and social bond between the debtor and the creditor is critical for an understanding of the whole socioeconomic system and its social implications, for instance why poor and heavily indebted parents resort to forcing their children into child labor or commercial sex in order to repay loans. Colonial and contemporary studies of slavery and debt-bondage are immensely useful in forming a general understanding of socioeconomic systems that seem to have transcended time.

Notes

1. Tonkin is the northernmost region of Vietnam, south of the Chinese provinces of Yunnan and Guangxi and to the east of Laos. France assumed sovereignty over Tonkin and Annam after the Franco-Chinese war (1881–1885), using the name of the capital in Vietnamese for the whole region.
2. For the two citations: Hà Nội, National Archives Center Number 1. File n. 76594, letter sent by the Resident Superior of Tonkin to the provincial Residents on 22 April 1891.
3. The Resident of Quang Yen describes these facts in a letter addressed to the Resident Superior of Tonkin: "Recently an Annamese woman presented herself in Port Wallut and declared that a Chinese, named Sa Van, delivered her and her two children to a Chinese junk. Six women, two girls and four Annamese children were on board, but she did not say anything else. The junk sailed at night, during the day; the boss

obliged them to disembark and hid them behind rocks. On the second day after departure, the junk was near the island of Vạn Vược when discovered by a postal service ship in Gow Tow Island that tried to seize it." Hà Nội, National Archives Center Number 1. File 76594, letter n. 19, 6 January 1912.

4. On 8 November 1909, the Assistant Director of the Customs Department in Hải Phòng informed the Resident Superior of Tonkin about the seizure of a junk carrying women: "The captain of the launch named Argus met during a cruise in the Hạ Long Bay a Chinese junk traveling to China and transporting five Annamese women tied up and hidden. When questioned, they declared having been shipped against their will, and accused the captain of the junk and two crewmen of having tried to get rid of them by throwing everyone into the sea when the launch was discovered." Hà Nội, National Archives Center Number 1. File n. 76594, letter n. 2140.

5. "Prostitution has created quite a slave market in Chợ Lớn, Canton, and Hong Kong. Matrons raise female infants from poor families, bring them up, train them in the infamous occupation which awaits them and, when they reach the age of consent, they are sent to Chợ Lớn, to correspondents who, according to the subjects' beauty, sell them to rich Chinese who keep them for pleasure or sell them to brothels" (Landes 1880: 138).

6. Hà Nội, National Archives Center Number 1, File n. 8857, letter n. 881, 14 May 1904.

7. The author adds, "It is conceivable that with so limited elements of appreciation, the buyers could easily mistake about the quality of those they wanted to buy."

References

Anonymous. 1863. "Note sur l'Esclavage." *Revue Maritime et Coloniale* 7: 78–80.

Asia Pacific News. 15 July 2009. "Vietnamese police bust child-trafficking ring." Online article: http://www.monstersandcritics.com/news/asiapacific/news/article_1489759. php/Vietnamese_police_bust_child-trafficking_ring_#ixzz 0LLNwXeuW&C, downloaded 31 October 2011.

Baudrit, André. 1941. "La Femme et l'Enfant dans l'Indochine Française et Dans la Chine du Sud (Rapt-Vente-Infanticide)." *Bulletin de la Société des Etudes Indochinoises* (nouvelle série) 16(3): 87-153.

BBC News. 22 September 2009. "Vietnam baby fraud trial begins." Online article: http://news.bbc.co.uk/2/hi/asia-pacific/8269121.stm, downloaded 31 October 2011.

Briffaut, Camille. 1907. "L'Engagement Pour Dettes Dans le Droit Sino-Annamite." *Questions Pratiques de Législation et d'Economie Sociale*: 1–34.

Buu Loc. 1941. *L'Usure Chez le Paysan d'Annam*. Paris: Recueil Sirey.

Chin, Angelina. 2002. "The management of women's bodies: Regulating mui tsai and prostitutes in Hong Kong under colonial rule 1841–1935." *Hong Kong Cultural and Social Studies* (e-journal, February).

Dang Trinh Ky. 1933. *L'Engagement des Personnes en Droit Annamite*. Paris: Domat-Montchrestien.

Dartiguenave, Henri. 1908. "Des Ventes d'Enfants en Indochine." *Revue Indochinoise* (January–June) 9: 239–247.

Delaye, Karine. 2005. "Slavery and colonial representations in Indochina from the second half of the nineteenth to the early twentieth century," pp: 129–142 in *The Structure of Slavery in Indian Ocean Africa and Asia*, eds. Gwyn Campbell and Frank Cass. London and Portland: Frank Cass Publishers.

Gourou, Pierre. 1940. *L'Utilisation du Sol en Indochine*. Paris: Centre d'Etudes de Politique Etrangère.

Grillot, Caroline. 2009. *Volées, Envolées, Convolées. Vendues, en Fuite ou Re-Socialisées... Les "Fiancées" Vietnamiennes en Chine*. Bangkok and Paris, IRASEC and Connaissances et Savoirs.

Guénel, Annick. 2001. "Prostitution, Maladies Vénériennes et Médecine Coloniale au Vietnam de la Conquête Française à la Guerre d'Indépendence," pp: 233–249 in *Vietnamese Society in Transition: The Daily Politics of Reform and Change*, ed. John Kleinen. Amsterdam: Het Spinhuis.

Hardy, Michel. 1994. "BMC et Prévention Sanitaire." *Revue Historique des Armées* 194: 38–43.

Haslewood, Hugh and Clara. 1930. *Child Slavery in Hong Kong: The Mui Tsai System*. London: The Sheldon Press.

Hoang Tuan and Tiên Tho. "Infant traffickers caught in southern Vietnam." *Thanh Niên*, 10 November 2009.

Jaschok, Maria. 1988. *Concubines and Bond Servants: The Social History of a Chinese Custom*. London and Hong Kong: Zed Books and Oxford University.

Lainez, Nicolas. 2011a. *A Leg In and a Leg Out. Sex Migration of Vietnamese Women to Singapore*. Ho Chi Minh City: Alliance Anti-Trafic (October).

———. 2011b. *Transacted Children and Virginity: Ethnography of Ethnic Vietnamese in Phnom Penh*. Ho Chi Minh City: Alliance Anti-Trafic (June).

Landes, Antony. 1880. "Lettre au Gouverneur Général de l'Indochine. Rapport sur la Prostitution et le Trafic des Femmes à Cholon." *Excursions et Reconnaissances* 4: 145–147.

Lessard, Micheline. 2009. "'*Cet Ignoble Trafic*': The kidnapping and sale of Vietnamese women and children in French colonial Indochina, 1873–1935." *French Colonial History* 10(1): 1–34.

Ngo Tat To. 1983 [1939]. *When the Light is Out*. Hanoi: Foreign Languages Publishing House (second ed.).

Ngo Vinh Long. 1991. *Before the Revolution. The Vietnamese Peasants Under the French*. New York: Columbia University Press.

Paulus, A. 1885. "L'Esclavage dans l'Indochine et en Particulier au Cambodge et Dans l'Annam." *Bulletin des Sciences Economiques et Sociales*: 41–50.

Roustan, Frédéric. 2005. "Français, Japonais et Société Coloniale du Tonkin: Exemple de Représentations Coloniales." *French Colonial History* 6: 179–204.

Savinien. "Bétail Humain," *L'Avenir du Tonkin* 1389, 26 October 1899.

Silvestre, Jules. 1880. "Rapport sur l'Esclavage." *Excursions et Reconnaissances* 4: 96–147.

Taboulet, Georges. 1883. "Une Mission au Tonkin. Sur la Canonnière la *Massue*." *Bulletin de la Société Bretonne de Géographie* 6: 109–143.

Tracol-Huynh, Isabelle. 2009. "La Prostitution au Tonkin Colonial: Entre Races et Genres." *Genre, Sexualité et Société* 2 (Autumn). Online article: http://gss.revues.org/index1219.html, downloaded 31 April 2010.

————. 2010. "Between stigmatization and regulation: Prostitution in colonial northern Vietnam." *Culture, Health and Sexuality* 12: 1–15.

Vietnam News (VNS). 2008. "Ho Chi Minh City police arrest duo for trafficking woman."

Warren, James Francis. 1993. *Ah-Ku and Karayuki-san: Prostitution in Singapore 1870–1940*. Singapore: Oxford University Press.

Archives

National Archives Center Number 1. Hanoi, Vietnam.

CHAPTER 2

Wind through the Woods: Ethnography of Interfaces between Migration and Institutions[1]

XIANG Biao

Migration constitutes an interesting subject for study for at least two interrelated reasons. First, migration flows appear elusive, amorphous, and constantly changing. Second, migrants are often dislodged from the established systems of how the host society is organized (e.g. trade unions or neighborhood organizations). States thus face multiple challenges in understanding, controlling, and caring for migrants. This renders migration studies particularly difficult: how can we make sense of something that is by definition unstable and exceptional?

Following the time-honored sociological metaphor that likens society to the woods, we may consider migration as gusts of wind through the woods. In the woods, all we can really see and touch are the trees, the grass, the birds – i.e., the individuals – and there is no such thing as "woods" that can be grasped physically. But it is undeniable that there is such a thing as forest – an emergent fact resulting from a large number of trees standing together throughout their lives. A society, then, is a forest of people. We can establish its collective characteristics and can talk about the average, the rate, the ratio, and subsequently the trend and the structure. If it is methodologically and theoretically challenging to figure out the woods by observing the trees, migration poses an even more difficult subject. Although the existing literature often treats migration as a mini-forest that has its own stable patterns, structures, and lifecycle, any attempts to discover universalistic determinants about the who, how, why, and when of migration have been notoriously unsuccessful.

Instead, migration flows are more like the wind. Wind is an inherent part of the life of the woods and is generated by numerous factors that defy any reductionist analysis in isolation. But the wind may render the internal life of the woods more visible. How different parts of the woods react to the wind may provide us with rare clues into important features of the larger structure of the woods: where the birds have rested, how the roots have grown like veins beneath the ground, and how the layers of leaves have overlapped with each other. The wind brings all this into sharp relief.

Migration is deeply embedded in, and fundamentally shaped by, various intertwined institutional setups. It makes little sense to extract migration from the matrix of social institutions as an object in itself with clear boundaries and internal regularities. Partly because of this, the behaviorist perspective in migration studies – aimed at understanding migration as a separable kind of behavior – may generate limited insights. This chapter probes ways in which we can turn these difficulties into sources of knowledge innovation. I advocate a mode of ethnography that goes beyond migratory experiences and instead focuses on the interface between migration flows and established social structures.

What may an ethnography of interfaces look like? And how may one practically do it? Drawing on my on-going research on labor migration in East Asia, I will reflect in this chapter on a mode of "multi-level ethnography" as a specific means toward delineating the interplays between migration and institutional arrangements.

Multi-level Ethnography

My on-going project examines labor migration from China to Japan, South Korea, and Singapore, the three leading destinations for unskilled Chinese labor migrants. I chose northeast China, particularly Liaoning province, as my main research site because of the dramatic increase in labor outmigration from the region since the early 1990s. The northeast in general, and Liaoning province in particular, was the national base of heavy and military industries since the establishment of communist rule, and represented an archetype of state socialism. The sudden surge in outmigration resulted from the massive labor lay-off, starting in 1994, which was in turn caused by state-induced privatization of large state-owned enterprises. Due to the strong socialist legacy of the region, outmigration from the northeast presents a particularly useful case for examining the interface between flows and institutions. But the northeast is by no means unique. Migration from the region is subject to the general governance structure and constitutes a typification of the general pattern. Governments, in both China and the receiving countries, regulate labor mobility by developing complex partnerships with various social actors, particularly with labor recruitment agents.

Central to my ethnography is a system of "agent chains." Almost directly mirroring the setup of the state bureaucracy, recruitment agents exist at almost all administrative levels; they coordinate with each other and constitute these agent chains. At the top of the chain are large, licensed companies in major cities. Called "window" companies, they sign contracts with foreign firms and process the legal paperwork that is necessary for outmigration. The window companies outsource the task of labor recruitment to middle-level agents in the prefectures who, in turn, subcontract to subagents in local districts or rural townships, who are referred to colloquially as "the legs." When the overseas employer complains to the recruitment agent in the destination country about a migrant, the foreign agent pressures the window company to seek quick solutions, and the "window" often passes the task on downward. The "leg" disciplines the migrant transnationally by pressuring the migrant's family in the home country.

In the everyday conversations between both agents and migrants, agents closer to foreign clients (employers) are referred to as the "upstairs" (*shangxian*, literally meaning "the string above"), and those closer to migrants are the "downstairs" (*xiaxian*, "the string below"). Handed down from the upstairs to the downstairs are orders for labor, which are called *zhibiao* (quotas). They are so called because the orders are seen as analogous to the quotas for resource allocation imposed from the top down in the pre-reform, centralized command economy. The quotas determine the relations between agents. The higher upstairs the agents are, the closer they are to the origin of quotas, and the more powerful, reliable, and profitable their business becomes. Government officials and senior staff at window companies, however, explain the recruitment process quite differently. They call the upstairs the "downstream" (*xiayou*) and the downstairs the "upstream" (*shangyou*). In this narrative, migrant labor moves from the upstream (origin village) to the downstream (destination) like a river.

The physical movement of the migrant figures centrally in this official presentation because this is what government officials and window company staff are supposed to monitor. From the point of view of the government of the receiving country, it is necessary to prevent the downstream from being polluted by illegal or unruly migrants; the upstream must therefore be sanitized. Indeed, "root cause" has become a standard keyword in the global discourse of international migration management. While the migrants see quotas from above as determining their migratory projects, the destination countries, sitting on the top floor, regard themselves as innocent potential victims of the actions of the migrants. The co-existence of these two oppositional narratives reveals exactly what agent chains are all about. They help migrants navigate through the upstairs-downstairs hierarchy and at the same time assist states in monitoring upstream-downstream flows. In other words, they mediate between the fixed state bureaucracy that attempts to control mobility from above, and the fluid migration flows that tend to transgress administrative lines from below.

Although researchers and policy makers often talk about "migration policies" as a coherent body of regulations, migration is in reality governed by a wide range of disparate institutions and practices. The methodological implications can be difficult. In tracing the governance of mobility, I found myself not only traveling back and forth between the places of origin, transit, and destination, but also running up and down along the upstairs/downstream – downstairs/upstream hierarchy. My fieldwork in China was carried out in five places: (1) Beijing, where a large number of "windows" are located; (2) Shenyang, the capital city of Liaoning province and the host of five foreign consular offices for the northeast region, thus a strategic location for large agents; (3) FS prefecture, an active migrant sending place in Liaoning; (4) QY county under FS prefecture; and finally (5) a few townships and villages in QY. On the destination side, fieldwork was carried out in Singapore, South Korea, Japan, and the United Kingdom.[2] Over a period of almost four years (from July 2004 to November 2007), I interviewed more than two hundred informants including migrants, officials, agents, employers, NGO activists, and others. Although the constant traveling was demanding, the "super-"multi-sited fieldwork was not particularly disorienting. The connections between these places at different levels, both within China and beyond, collectively constitute a more or less coherent transnational order of migration. As a result, this work presents a "multi-level" ethnography.

Level is related to, yet different from, scale. Scale, as human geographers use it, is an emergent, provisional fix of territorial scope of social actions or relations. (In a sense, scale in the human geography literature is similar to Appadurai's [1990] concept of "scape.") Proposing the concepts of "scale jumping" and "re-scaling," recent human geography literature interprets globalization as a process in which the national scale of the state is decentered, corporate operations jump both upward to the supra-national scale and downward to the sub-national level, and social institutions are constantly de-territorialized at one scale but re-territorialized at another (e.g. Smith 2002; Swyngedouw 1996; Brenner 1999). But for my informants, the "pluri-territorial, polycentric and multi-scalar geographies" of globalization (Brenner 1999: 69), and the "collapse" of the global and household scales in migrants' transnational life, are neither terribly exciting nor particularly worrying. They are far more concerned about the opposite: why do they have to go through so many levels of agents and bureaucracy in order to go overseas? It is not a big deal to chat with your children transnationally everyday through Skype; it is a big deal to have to pay so much money to the agents and not be able to cut the route short. Many migrants would be more than satisfied if their only child could one day work for the recruitment agent in the town, sitting in the air-conditioned office all the time, and not need to bother with the transnational scale at all.

The rescaling imperatives of capital and everyday life are apparent, but we have to distinguish the water currents, no matter how spectacular, from the underlying riverbed that determines how and where the river goes. Consider how companies in Japan and South Korea hire unskilled foreign workers. In contrast to what is usually imagined, few employers are large transnational corporations in global cities; instead, most are small, low-end enterprises located in remote areas.[3] Facing increasing international competition, local capital has to rely on transnationally recruited labor for survival. But instead of jumping scales, the recruitment operation may be more accurately described as "climbing" levels. To start, employers need to submit their hiring plans to local industry associations, who apply for quotas on their behalf from the national association, which in turn applies to the government. After approval, the quotas are sent to designated Chinese window companies and subsequently "climb" down. It is true that agents also attempt to transgress the scalar structure in order to maximize profits. A group of freelance middlemen in Shenyang and FS, for example, have wide international connections and often cut deals with overseas partners directly. Their business is sometimes dubbed *kongshoudao*, Chinese for karate, literally meaning "the art of empty hands" because the middlemen seldom register companies but are skillful in maneuvering between scales. As capable as they are, these middlemen still have to rely on "legs" for recruitment (otherwise the migrants won't trust them) and, more importantly, have to appease, often bribe, staff in window companies to manage the exit procedure. "Window fees," ranging from RMB 2,000 to 20,000 for processing each migrant's document (excluding the bribes for the individual staff), is a main income source for window companies. Structured in a multi-level manner, agent chains deal with the bureaucracy efficiently to get the business done, and at the same time reinforce the deeply territorialized scales of control in order to secure their own gatekeeper positions.

The state structures and the agent chains, both of which are hierarchically organized but fraught with internal tensions, intersect with each other at all levels. As noted, agent chains are themselves a product of the chain of command of the pre-reform era. Most agency staff in China have connections with government, and the "legs" are often actual government institutions such as labor bureaus or villagers' committees (*cunmin weiyuanhui*). Furthermore, recruitment agents have more commonalities and deeper connections with government agencies at the same level than they do with their partners in the labor recruitment chains either "downstairs" or "upstairs." This had led to a "vertical division of labor" that cuts across the public and private sectors in mobilizing and controlling labor. (This vertical division of labor produces the image of the state as a rational, unified entity that is above and encompasses the society.) It is in the intersections between the bureaucracy and agent chains, as well as in the cross-level interactions, that the order of transnational migration is maintained. In delineating these institutional matrices, multi-level ethnography not merely extends the multi-sited approach along a new dimension, but also acquires new ethnographic coherence and analytic power. The multi-level perspective turns physical sites into exemplary nodes in an institutional setup, and therefore renders specific observations more generalizable – generalizing not by imagining particular places as microcosms of a self-fulfilling system, but by teasing out the actual linkages between the nodes.

Multi-level ethnography is also an explanatory ethnography. I take the multi-level structure so seriously because the structure provides answers to some of the questions that bother me and especially my informants. My fieldwork was that of a "detective" in the sense that it was aimed at working out puzzles, especially: (1) why the agent fees are so high, a question about which migrants are greatly worried and (2) how migration is controlled in practice, a question which concerns the officials. As they are asking the same questions, my informants have of course done their own thorough analyses and developed their own articulated explanations. I build my ethnography on their ethnographic constructions and, at the same time, turn their interpretations into my conceptual resources and material for analysis. The explanatory ethnography is thus an ethnography born out of dialogues. Furthermore, in the field, dialogue is the only way to hold long conversations with busy officials and agents. Ma Wei, a typical "karate player" (freelance agent) and one of my key interlocutors, told me that he was so forthcoming because our conversations brought him back to the "lie-down debates" (*wo tan*) of his college time. (College dormitories in China cut off electricity at 10 or 11 p.m.; the six or eight roommates have to go to bed and they engage in heated debates on all topics they can think of, often till dawn.) Conversely, when my informants deemed my questions irrelevant, they simply refused to answer. Thinking back, I never actually used the word "interview" (*caifang* or *fangtan*) when approaching my informants-interlocutors; I instead proposed to *tantao* (literally meaning to explore and discuss). When all is said and done, I was ultimately interested more in the system than their "way of life" and that brought us together in questions that were important to both of us. Exchanging our explanations of various problems was thus a natural way of interacting with each other.

In sum, my work on migrants is simultaneously "studying up" to interrogate the center of power (Nader 1972), "studying down" to examine everyday interactions, and most importantly "studying through" (Reinhold 1994: 477-479 as cited in Shore and Wright 1997: 14) to "trace ways in which power creates webs and relations between actors, institutions and discourses across time and space." This kind of multi-level ethnography provides an example of an "institutional ethnography" (Smith 2005) that aims to delineate the life of institutions and to reveal large power structures.

The Ethnographer in Multi-level Ethnography

Agent chains must make moral sense, especially to the migrants, in order to be sustainable. In a boldly decorated and nearly suffocating Karaoke bar, I asked Liu Fang and two of his fellow would-be migrants what they thought of the amount of profit – astonishing for me (a minimum of RMB 5,000 per head and up to 30,000) – that each agent made out of them. Apart from the standard reply of "what can you do," Liu, a skinny chain smoker with permanently uncombed hair, argued that agents deserve it:

> Anyone can see this business makes money. But why haven't I become an agent?
> This is not a business that anyone can do! [*XB: Why can't everyone do it?*] This
> needs capacity! You must have the connections… If it is not difficult, why hasn't
> everyone gone into the business? They charge so much money because they are
> *not* ordinary people!

Later, Liu Fang and his friends asked me about my future plans. Liu said I could
consider becoming an agent; his friend added that the position of university
lecturers and civil servants are nowadays also good. Grouping academics, bureaucrats, and private business people together like this, unthinkable until the late
1990s, represents a view now prevalent in China. Academics, bureaucrats, and
business people are all "capable people." They share similar lifestyles and out-
looks, they are described as the main modernizers, and they gain the most from
the reforms.[4] The morality of the agent business is thus not only based on fulfilled
promises and reciprocity (see Li Minghuan 2006), but is also linked to a new
ideology of "capacity" (*nengli*) which combines the neoliberal notions of human
capital and individual success on one hand, and Chinese elitism on the other.

This is also how agents perceive themselves. Lan Lan is the manager general of
a middle-level agency in FS that was set up by the son of a local official in charge
of foreign affairs for the prefecture. A stunningly pretty former actress, Lan Lan
seldom shows any expression, but she was visibly angry when mentioning three
workers who went underground in Japan. Lan Lan's counterparts in Japan were
fined by the Japanese government, and the counterparts sent the bill, as well as
a stern warning, to them. Her shiny, ivory-colored nails were tapping the red
leather pad on her desk:

> I couldn't believe it. How could we be cheated by *them*? These peasants know
> so little, we developed such a good system, but in the end *we* were cheated! […]
> We told the border police and customs bureau [of China] immediately, if they
> [the migrants] came back, they must be detained and punished! […] We had
> people run away before [when the agent was sending out business visitors]. But
> these are peasants! You tell me how angry I should be?!

Thus, the agents control migrants not only for political safety and profit maxi-
mization, but also because they place themselves in the position of commanding
and controlling in the larger society. In sum, the rapid social stratification, the
emergence of a "total elite" bloc, and the re-strengthening of the legitimacy of the
Chinese state among its population, renders agent chains socially apprehensible
and morally acceptable.

I, a polite, neat-looking Oxford researcher, transnational and professional, was
seen as belonging to a top social stratum in the imagined social hierarchy. In
retrospect, this perceived position and my unconscious downward appropriation

of inter-scalar relations shaped the way in which I entered the system. I started with the level that is most familiar to me – the national. Through my personal connections, especially my Beijing University alumni networks, I got in touch with the labor ministry; by presenting my research in terms of national issues, I was quickly accepted by the officials. But I soon discovered that my transnational position was much more attractive. Jin Lu, a young, rising, enthusiastic official in the ministry, wanted me to conduct a survey about overseas demand for Chinese labor. He hoped that this "Oxford report" would generate more attention from the senior levels at the ministry and beyond to this emerging field, and at the same time demonstrate the professionalism of his department, and thus enhance its authority among the agents. The survey was never started, but our rapport developed. Jin made me part of his department's advisory board. He referred to me jokingly as "foreign aid" at the inaugural meeting of the board. In 2006 I worked as a short-term consultant of the Geneva-based International Organization for Migration (IOM) for a project that was commissioned by the government of Korea on labor outmigration from China and Mongolia. This position brought me limited access to the tightly guarded commerce ministry. The commerce ministry was at that time deadlocked in competition with the labor ministry over who should take charge of labor migration to South Korea after the substantial policy reforms in Korea; they both expected the IOM report to have some impact on the Korean side. My connections with the central government opened the door for me to the large window companies in Beijing and Shenyang, who in turn brought me to their "downstairs" agents. (But the chain of introduction works one way only: no downstairs agent agreed to introduce me to an upstairs counterpart.) My connections with the United Kingdom and Singapore raised much interest among the agents. I was constantly approached for information about these countries and for help in assessing the authenticity of documents from overseas.

It was much harder to establish rapport with government officials. Zhou Tong, the cadre in charge of labor outmigration at the Liaoning provincial labor bureau, received me with ambiguity. Zhou said he would be happy to talk, but his supervisor warned him not to say too much, possibly fearing that I might report to the ministry negatively. I met the FS prefecture official at a national conference organized by the ministry, and I thus established contact with her without following the bureaucratic hierarchy. My transnational position, an advantage at the national and provincial level, became a definite liability in approaching the QY county government. Both the provincial and prefecture officials hesitated in helping me as they were wary that government departments at the lower level were already fed up with the numerous tasks imposed from above. (In this regard, the FS official was very critical of the provincial bureau.) I asked an acquaintance in Shenyang, a former school classmate of an outgoing deputy mayor of QY, to pull some strings. The deputy mayor was away and his assistant, who was also in charge of state security, took me to a couple of government departments. On the second day the assistant said to me: "Little Xiang, you received high education, but you came here without an introduction letter, you work overseas although your nationality is Chinese, and you ask for so much information." She suggested I have a good rest in the hotel. That night when I was chatting with the head of the QY government-run recruitment company, he received a mobile phone message and went to the toilet. He looked nervous when emerging again, took all the documents and left.

I subsequently pinned my hopes on a cadre in the provincial propaganda department who was seeking my advice about his son's studying in the United Kingdom. He set up a banquet in a fancy restaurant in Shenyang and invited a few veteran officials working in propaganda or research departments. He said at the first round of toasts that he was pleased to bring "theoretical authorities" in the province to discuss – *tantao* – my research. When he raised the glass again, he asked for help on my behalf. The former head of the provincial academy of social sciences followed by saying that since the propaganda official "begged" him, he would have to beg his subordinate, the deputy head of FS academy, to help me. The deputy head pledged on the phone that she would "fulfill any task assigned." But when she discovered that I had a job overseas, she asked me to come back in two days. The moment she saw me again, she pointed to her throat and said she had a bad cold and wouldn't be able to speak for the coming weeks. My third visit failed again due to my "overseas status" (*haiwai shenfen*). I concluded that I had to resort to my Beijing University networks and start climbing across levels from the very beginning again. A few phone calls to Beijing put me in touch with Huang Ai, a cadre at the rank of prefecture governor and one of the youngest senior officials in Liaoning province. Huang saw me as an "international scholar" (*guoji xuezhe*) who had come to do serious research instead of repeating official clichés. She discussed with me the "fundamental challenges" that the Chinese government faces, praised my persistence, and encouraged me to "dare to identify problems and expose problems!" Two days later, through the mediation of a FS official, I met literally all the officials with whom I wanted to talk in QY.

My fieldwork experiences show again the complexity of levels. On the one hand, the hierarchy is uncompromisingly rigid but, on the other, the superiority of the higher level should never be taken for granted. Huang Ai offered help due to her appreciation of my transnational, independent status, but the FS and QY officials finally accepted me purely because of Huang's request, which was regarded as an intra-governmental directive. What serves as a powerful currency at one level may be regarded as irrelevant at another. This renders jumping or skipping levels difficult, but "climbing" allows one to convert the currency step by step. The difficulty in skipping over certain levels is an important aspect of the order-making project. For instance, just as high-level government officials blame the lower level for corruption while still relying on them for everyday functioning, government and window companies often blame agents of the low levels for exploiting migrants although in reality they depend on them for controlling the migrants. This game of blaming, a result of the differentiated concerns and rationalities across levels, is indispensable for the states and high-level companies in maintaining their legitimacy and moral authority in case of failure in protecting migrants' rights or enforcing laws. But this kind of game also provides opportunities for researchers who are trying to understand the varying goals and ideologies of these different levels and how they nevertheless form an effective working system for labor migration.

Notes

1. I wish to thank Professor David Haines at George Mason University for his generous help with an earlier draft of this chapter.
2. More than half of the informants are recruitment agents or related, and the rest are would-be migrants and government officials. Participatory observation was made in agents' offices where I helped agents to fill out forms and translate documents, or when I accompanied would-be migrants in their visits. As this project deals to a great extent with state bureaucracy, I conducted extensive documentary research on government polices and reports. I also conducted some brief field research in the People's Republic of Mongolia and in Thailand, two other labor-sending countries in Asia.
3. In 2004, 40 percent of all Chinese migrant workers overseas were working in manufacturing industries, 26 percent in construction, and 14 percent in agriculture, forestry, and fishing industries (CHINCA 2004: 10–11).
4. The "three represents" theory developed by Jiang Zemin in 2000, supposedly the defining doctrine for the Communist Party of China (CPC) today, is widely interpreted as an explicit attempt to legitimize an alliance between the party state and the newly emerged elites. The theory argues that the party should always represent advanced productive forces, advanced culture, and only thirdly, the fundamental interests of the broadest masses of the people. In November 2006, the CPC Central Committee issued an important document entitled "Opinions on Consolidating and Expanding United Front in New Century and New Stage." The sole objective of the document is to urge the entire party to recognize the importance of business people in private sectors and freelance professionals as the CPC's potential allies.

References

Appadurai, Arjun. 1990. "Disjuncture and difference in the global cultural economy." *Theory, Culture and Society* 7: 295–310.

Brenner, Neil. 1999. "Beyond state-centrism? Space, territoriality, and geographical scale in globalization studies." *Theory and Society* 28(1): 39–78.

CHINCA (China International Contractors Association). 2004. *Annual Report on China's International Labor Collaboration* [Zhongguo Duiwai Laowu Hezuo Niandu Baobao 2004]. Beijing: China's International Contractors' Association. December.

Li Minghuan. 2006. "Transnational migration brokerage in southern China." *IIAS Newsletter* 42: 12–13. Special Issue: Are You A Criminal? On The Illegality of Daily Life. Amsterdam: Institute of International Asia Studies.

Nader, Laura. 1972. "Up the anthropologist – Perspectives gained from studying up," pp. 284–311 in *Reinventing Anthropology*, ed. Dell H. Hymes. New York: Pantheon Books.

Reinhold, Susan. 1994. *Local Conflict and Ideological Struggle: "Positive Image" and Section 28.* D.Phil thesis, Department of Anthropology, University of Sussex.

Shore, Chris and Susan Wright. 1997. "Policy: A new field of anthropology," pp. 1–39 in *Anthropology of Policy*, eds. Chris Shore and Susan Wright. London: Routledge.

Smith, Dorothy E. 2005. *Institutional Ethnography: A Sociology for People.* Toronto: AltaMira Press.

Smith, Neil. 2002, "Remaking scale: competition and cooperation in prenational and postnational Europe," pp. 227–238 in *State/Space: A Reader*, eds. Neil Brenner, Bob Jessop, Martin Jones, and Gordon MacLeod. Oxford: Blackwell.

Swyngedouw, Erik. 1996. "Reconstructing citizenship, the re-scaling of the state and the new authoritarianism: Closing the Belgian mines." *Urban Studies* 33(8): 1499–1521.

CHAPTER 3

Migrant Social Networks: Ethnic Minorities in the Cities of China

ZHANG Jijiao

The year 2008 marks the thirtieth anniversary of China's economic reform. According to China's National Bureau of Statistics, by 2005 about 150 million migrant workers had moved to cities from rural areas in search of jobs, and the number will reach 200 million by 2015 and 250 million by 2025 (Fan 2008). It is not well known that a large proportion of these urban migrants are from China's ethnic minority communities. However, it is worth noting that, according to an incomplete census at the end of 2008, the population of resident and migrant minorities in China's nearly seven hundred cities is about 20 million.[1]

With this growing number of minority migrants, most major cities of China have been drastically transformed as the urban demographic landscape has been ethnically diversified (Zhang 2009b). Guizhou province, for instance, had 520,000 people of various ethnic groups who left as migrant workers by the year 1997, of whom over 90 percent went to cities in east China (Zhang 2003). According to the national census in 2000, the population of minorities had reached 590,000 in Beijing alone. Other major ethnic migrant destinations included Tianjin (over 260,000), Shenzhen (over 210,000),[2] Guangzhou (over 130,000), and Nanjing (over 80,000).[3] In effect, then, a multiethnic society has emerged in urban China based on internal, rather than international, migration. This chapter reports on a study examining the urban experience of these ethnic migrants in China, especially with respect to the relation between their social networks and their work experience (Zhang 2007, 2009a).

Rethinking Networks in a Chinese Context

In his book *From the Soil*, Fei Xiaotong pointed out that the traditional Chinese social network was formed by blood, kinship, and geographical proximity. He observed that everyone in a social network is a center, and that the social impact produced by them is like the ripples spread out from a rock thrown into water.

Wherever the ripples extend, not only are social relations generated, but also in those ripples the closeness of such relations can be fathomed. That is the essence of the well-known theory of *chaxu geju* (Fei Xiaotong 1941).[4]

Influenced by this theory, previous studies of migrants to cities in China have focused on the social networks formed by such populations, their self-identity, and their group relations, taking into consideration such homogeneous contingencies as blood, geographic proximity, occupation, and such aspects of hierarchical relations as social roles, social status, and personal identity. For example, the studies done by Wang Chunguang (1995) and Xiang Biao (2000) on "Zhejiang Village" in Beijing revealed that the groups of migrants living in a particular area not only generated a mutual community identity and social networks based on blood, geographic proximity, and occupation, but also created a kind of autonomous community life. Such studies are clearly structural in nature, assuming that a specified individual or group possesses some special properties, according to which they can be correspondingly categorized. Such studies give prominence to the hierarchical relations in the social structure, putting the subjects into position according to such contingencies as their social status, identity, and roles.

Ideas about networks, however, have evolved greatly in recent decades with the work of J.C. Mitchell and A.L. Epstein on social networks (Mitchell 1958, 1966, 1969; Epstein 1961), Mark Granovetter on embeddedness and weak ties (Granovetter 1973, 1974, 1985), Alejandro Portes on relationship embeddedness and structure embeddedness (Portes 1995, 1998), Bian Yanjie on strong ties (Bian 1997), James S. Coleman on social capital (Coleman 1990), Elizabeth Bott on close-knit kin (Bott 1957), Ronald Burt on structural holes (Burt 1992), and Stanley Lieberson on ethnic acculturation (Lieberson 1963). Such work suggests a need in China to shift from the classic *chaxu geju* model to a more fully developed network analysis. Just as Bian Yanjie's network analysis is a refined Chinese version of Granovetter's work, network analysis for urban communities should also be an improved model of *chaxu geju*. However, many practitioners' interpretation of *chaxu geju* remains too mechanical for the study of urban floating populations.

As a matter of fact, the point of departure of both *chaxu geju* and contemporary network analysis is basically the same: both aim at an interpretation of the wider social network and the rules thereof through the analysis of personal networks. Both therefore tend to be ego-centered analytical techniques. The difference lies in the fact that the Chinese rural version of *chaxu geju*, derived from structuralist-functionalist analysis, is applicable to the analysis of a specific community's internal relations in a static rural society, and is rarely used in the study of cross-cultural (or inter-clan) relations. Now based on the quintessence of *chaxu geju*, the employment of network analysis is valid for cross-cultural (and inter-clan) relations and for the constantly changing social relations in the Chinese urban communities, particularly in transient urban communities whose social relations are often very unstable. It might therefore be safe to conclude that our analytical tool is more flexible and effective.

The superiority of a more developed network analysis over the rural version of *chaxu geju* can be found in the following aspects. First, network analysis pays attention not only to existing ties, but also to newly developed ties, while *chaxu geju* focuses on the fixed relations in an established society. Second, network analysis treats the network ties as social capital, rather than only describing the status quo of a society's social relations. Third, network analysis takes into account the factors of time and space, recognizing the fact that urban social relations are different from those in the rural areas, and that the strength of the ties also varies with time. Fourth, network analysis, particularly by drawing on the theory of "structural holes," identifies relatively scarce information and its maneuverability in social relations, the control of which can bring about personal benefit.

The Chinese urban version of network analysis, derived in part from the Chinese rural version of *chaxu geju*, can assist not only in the description of the condition and characteristics of the various social network ties, such as the different features and roles of strong embeddedness and weak embeddedness, but also in the analysis of the rules of such social network ties, including trust, exchange, and allocation of resources, whether that involves the functions of network ties in employment-seeking, adaptation to an urban way of life, or the allocation of resources for family businesses.

In a nutshell, the current urban Chinese version of network analysis is a more comprehensive analytical framework, under the inspiration of the refined version of Granovetter's network analysis by Bian Yanjie who takes into consideration China's actual conditions, on the basis of the rural version of *chaxu geju* by Fei Xiaotong, by theoretically making reference to the theories of social capital and structural holes, and by factoring in the variables of time and space and existing and newly developed social ties.

Study Approach

For the purposes of this chapter, urban migrants can be defined simply as people born outside the city in which they now live. Defining their social networks, however, is much harder. In a general sense, one can indicate the components of networks on two levels: first, a relatively personal one of family, clan, relatives, friends, colleagues, teachers, and classmates; and, second, a somewhat broader level of hometown people, people of the same ethnic group, and others with whom people interact directly or indirectly, such as government officials, company bosses, or even investors.

The data used in this chapter derive from two studies. The first one focused on four minorities (Dai, Korean, Mongolian, and Tibetan) and was conducted from 2001 to 2002 in two selected cities: Beijing in the north and Shenzhen in the south. However, the particular questionnaire that will be discussed here was not used in Shenzhen, so the discussion of this study refers only to the 207 persons in Beijing from whom valid responses were obtained. The second study focused on six minorities (Dai, Korean, Mongolian, Bai, Hui, and Yi) and was conducted from 2007 to 2008 in four selected cities in four different directions of China: Huhhot in the north, Qingdao in the east, Kunming in the west, and again Shenzhen in the south. The two studies included personal life histories, in-depth interviews, focus group discussions, and participant observation, as well as the formal questionnaire. Here, the emphasis will be on the quantitative data, since it is especially helpful in sketching the overall situation of urban minorities and the general differences among migrants of different geographical and ethnic origins.

The Social Networks of Urban Migrants

In our research, we examined how the social networks of ethnic migrants to cities affected their employment situation. Employment is a readily available variable and thus provides a good focus for an initial assessment of migrant networks and how they change over time in a new urban environment. To understand how the networks operated, however, it is necessary to start with the kinds of employment that these migrants found. Our 2001–2002 survey in Beijing showed that the two main industries in which they were currently working were food services (59.4 percent) and entertainment (26.6 percent). ("Entertainment" here includes work in leisure and recreational businesses.) Furthermore, there had been a 12.6 percent increase for the former and a 0.8 percent increase for the latter from the period before this survey until the time of the survey itself. These job proportions varied somewhat among the four interviewed ethnic groups. Before the survey, more Mongolian (41.7 percent) and Tibetan (50 percent) migrants worked in entertainment and more Korean (63.4 percent) and Dai (50 percent) migrants worked in food services. At the time of the survey, the proportions had increased: yet more Mongolian (46.8 percent) and Tibetan (68.8 percent) migrants worked in entertainment and yet more Korean (82. 6 percent) and Dai (80 percent) migrants worked in food services. Nearly half of the migrants in Beijing (47.3 percent) worked at these jobs for private businesses and most (83.1 percent) were ordinary staff or clerks. Wages were low: 73 percent of the migrants earned less than RMB 1,000 per month; 25.2 percent earned less than RBM 500 per month.

Our 2007–2008 survey in four cities (Huhhot, Qingdao, Kunming, and Shenzhen) showed the majority of migrants working either in food services (45.2 percent) or in manufacturing (12.3 percent). We also compared their current employment with that before the survey. There was (as in the Beijing survey) a notable increase in those working in food services (13.2 percent) but only a marginal increase (0.2 percent) in those working in manufacturing. A majority of the migrants (60.2 percent) worked for private businesses and the largest group of them (42.9 percent) reported that they were ordinary staff or clerks. The nature of their work had determined that their salary was low, with the majority (51.7 percent) earning less than RMB 1,000 per month, and 13.7 percent earned less than RMB 500 per month. As with the Beijing survey, these income figures support Solinger's view that a new urban underclass of migrant workers is developing (Solinger 2008: 251–266).

But how do the migrants come to the city and find these jobs? Regarding the channels used to find a first job and live in the city, 56 percent of the 207 interviewees in the 2001–2002 survey in Beijing were aided by relatives or friends, 31.1 percent used their own efforts, and 10.6 were linked to jobs by the government or private companies. The four minority groups had somewhat different response patterns. The most common answer of Korean migrants was their social network of relatives or friends (69 percent), while the second most common answer was "try by one's own efforts" (24.1 percent), leaving 6.9 percent with other approaches. The same pattern held for Tibetan migrants (62.5 percent relying on relatives and friends and 31.3 percent relying on their own efforts). For Dai migrants, 86.7 percent relied on relatives and friends, none on their own efforts, leaving 13.3 percent linked to jobs by the government or private organizations. For Mongolian migrants, in sharp contrast, the most common answer was "try by one's own efforts" (48.1 percent), while the second most common was the help of relatives or friends (35.1 percent).

Table 3.1 • Summary of Reliance on Social Networks: First Job (in Percent)

	Own Efforts	Social Network			Others
		Overall	Relatives	Friends	
Beijing					
Korean	24.1	69.0			6.9
Dai	00.0	86.7			13.3
Mongolian	48.1	35.1			16.8
Tibetan	31.3	62.5			6.2
Total	*31.1*	*56.0*			*10.9*
Four cities					
Korean	22.7	47.4	29.9	17.5	29.9
Dai	19.4	54.8	29.0	25.8	25.8
Mongolian	39.5	43.0	21.1	21.9	17.5
Yi	22.2	58.3	19.4	38.9	29.5
Bai	41.3	43.5	28.3	15.2	15.2
Hui	46.2	43.5	25.6	17.9	10.3
Total	*31.3*	*40.1*	*22.8*	*17.3*	*28.6*

Notes: For the Beijing survey on this particular question, there was only the joint category of "relatives and friends." For the four cities survey, classmates and teachers are included in the total for "friends."

In the 2007–2008 survey in four cities, there were six interviewed minorities, three matching those in the Beijing survey (Dai, Korean, Mongolian) and three different ones (Bai, Hui, and Yi). Overall in the survey, 22.8 percent of the 573 interviewees were aided by their relatives and 17.3 percent of them by friends – thus 40.1 percent for the combined social network of relatives and friends – while 31.3 percent of the migrants relied on their own efforts.

However, the patterns varied according to ethnic minority. For the three ethnic minorities that were also interviewed in the Beijing survey, the situation was as follows. For Korean migrants, 29.9 percent relied on relatives, 13.4 percent on friends, and 4.1 percent on teachers or classmates, yielding a total of 47.4 percent relying on their social network. The second most common response was "by one's own efforts" (22.7 percent). For Mongolians, 21.1 percent relied on relatives, 18.4 percent on friends, and 3.5 percent on teachers and classmates, yielding a total of 43.0 percent relying on their social network. Yet, as with the data from Beijing, Mongolians showed a very high level of reliance on their own efforts (39.5 percent). Among Dai migrants, 29.0 percent relied on relatives and 25.8 percent on friends, yielding a total of 54.8 percent relying on their social network. Only 19.4 percent relied on their own efforts.

For the minorities not represented in the earlier Beijing survey, reliance on personal networks was high for the Yi, although with a preference for friends over relatives. Thus 19.4 percent relied on relatives, 33.3 percent relied on friends, and 5.6 percent on teachers or classmates, yielding a total of 58.3 percent relying on their social network. In addition, 22.2 percent relied on their own efforts. For the Bai and Hui, however, it was individual efforts that were most crucial. Of the Bai, 28.3 percent relied on relatives and 15.2 percent on friends, yielding a total of less than half (43.5 percent) relying on social network ties, with nearly as many (41.3 percent) relying on their own efforts. Of the Hui, 25.6 percent relied on relatives and 17.9 percent on friends, yielding a total relying on social network ties of 43.5 percent. As with the Bai, nearly the same number (41.3 percent) relied on their own efforts.

These survey results suggest, not surprisingly, the importance of social network ties in the initial movement of ethnic minority migrants to Chinese cities. However, they also show great variability between different ethnic minorities. There is, for example, the quite distinctive pattern of Mongolian, Bai, and Hui migrants, for whom relying on one's own efforts is roughly as important as relying on social networks. Even among the other groups, for whom social network ties are clearly predominant, their relative importance varies considerably from very high figures from Beijing for the Dai (86.7 percent), Koreans (69 percent), and Tibetans (62.5) to lower but still variable figures from the four-city survey: 58.3 percent for the Yi, 54.8 percent for the Dai (31.9 percent lower than their Beijing figure), and 47.4 percent for Koreans (21.6 percent lower than their Beijing figure). So there is clearly both variation among the ethnic minorities and variation in the environments in which they find themselves in different Chinese cities. But is there also change over time that reflects the need to consider social networks as reflecting both migrant origins and the new contexts in which the urban migrants live?

Changing Social Networks

The two surveys discussed here did not have a longitudinal component so cannot directly address how migrant social networks changed over time. But they did include questions both about how migrants found their first jobs on coming to the city (seen in the immediately preceding discussion) and migrants' subsequent lives. In particular, a question about how migrants found their current job provides a useful comparison, since most of these migrants had been in the city for at least a few years. In the Beijing survey, for example, 35.3 percent of the migrants relied on relatives and 25.1 percent on friends, giving a total of 60.4 percent relying on their existing social network. This figure is slightly higher that the figure for reliance on social network ties at the time of first moving to the city.

Table 3.2 • Summary of Reliance on Social Networks: Current Job (in Percent)

	Own Efforts	Social Network			Others
		Overall	Relatives	Friends	
Beijing					
Korean	21.8	70.1	36.8	33.3	8.1
Dai	6.7	80.0	73.3	6.7	13.3
Mongolian	39.0	39.0	19.5	19.5	22.0
Tibetan	6.3	87.5	50.0	37.5	6.2
Total	*29.5*	*60.4*	*35.3*	*25.1*	*10.1*
Four cities					
Korean	38.4	28.8	13.7	15.1	31.8
Dai	23.3	54.8	26.7	23.3	21.9
Mongolian	49.1	36.8	16.7	20.1	14.1
Yi	33.3	55.6	18.1	36.1	11.1
Bai	41.3	43.5	21.7	19.6	15.2
Hui	60.0	32.5	22.5	10.0	7.5
Total	*43.4*	*32.5*	*17.1*	*15.4*	*24.1*

Note: For the four cities survey, classmates and teachers are included in the total for "friends."

Again, there was variation among the four Beijing groups. The most common source of help for Korean migrant interviewees was relatives (36.8 percent) and the second was friends (33.3 percent), yielding 70.1 percent overall relying on their social network – again a slightly higher figure than that for their first job on moving to the city. For Tibetan migrants, the most common answer was also relatives (50 percent) and the second was friends (37.5 percent), yielding a total for social networks of 87.5 percent – much higher than the figure on first moving to the city. Likewise for the Dai migrants, the most common answer was relatives (73.3 percent) and the distant second was friends (6.7 percent), yielding 80 percent relying on social networks – again a much higher figure than for reliance on social networks at the time of first moving to Beijing. Finally, as before, the most common answer for Mongolian migrants was "by one's own efforts" (39 percent). Their second and third most common answers were (respectively) relatives (19.5 percent) and friends (also 19.5 percent), yielding a total of 39 percent relying on social network ties.

In Beijing then, this consideration of aid in obtaining the current job suggests that there are potentially three patterns with which to contend: (1) a relative stability in reliance on social networks (seen overall and in the case of Korean migrants); (2) an increasing reliance on social networks among groups already relying very heavily on social networks (seen with the Tibetans and Dai); and (3) possibly an increasing reliance on social networks by those who did not originally rely greatly on them (seen in the case of the Mongolians). There are thus some intriguing variations in the Beijing data, but the relatively small sample size of 207 suggests the need for caution.

Caution is also needed because the implications of the four-city 2007–2008 survey are somewhat different. In the four-city survey overall, 43.4 percent of the 573 migrant indicated they had found their job by their own efforts. The percentages relying on relatives (17.1 percent) and friends (15.4 percent) yield a total of 32.5 percent depending on social networks. This is a significant shift from the case at initial arrival in the city, an increase of nearly 10 percentage points. But, as with Beijing, there were variations among the different groups. Of Korean migrants, 47.4 percent relied on social network ties, almost exactly the same figure as relied on social networks for initial contacts when coming to the city. Of Dai migrants, 54.8 percent relied on social network ties, again almost exactly the same percentage as relied on social networks for original contacts when coming to the city. For Mongolians, as usual, greatest reliance was on one's own efforts (49.1 percent), leaving only 36.8 percent relying on social network ties. (This showed an increased reliance on one's own efforts by Mongolian migrants in this four-city survey, compared to a decreased reliance on one's own efforts in Beijing.)

Finally, for the three groups not represented in the Beijing survey (Yi, Bai, and Hui), the situation was as follows. Of the Yi, 18.1 percent relied on relatives and 36.1 percent relied on friends, for a total of 55.6 percent relying on social network ties, roughly the same figure as for initial contacts in the city, and with the same preference for friends over relatives. Of the Bai, 21.7 percent relied on relatives and 19.6 on friends, yielding a total of 43.5 percent relying on social networks versus 41.3 percent relying on "one's own efforts." These figures too are roughly similar to those for initial contact in the city. Finally, of the Hui, 22.5 percent relied on relatives and 10 percent on friends, yielding a total of 32.5 percent relying on social network ties. Here the percentage relying on social network ties was greatly lower. Fully 60 percent relied on their own efforts to obtain their current job, up from 41.3 percent relying on their own efforts for initial contacts in the city.

Results from the four-city survey thus further complicate this analysis of social networks and employment. The overall situation in different cities seems to vary both in the aggregate and for even the same ethnic minorities in the different cities. Furthermore, specific ethnic minorities differ in their reliance on social networks and in the way that reliance changes from initial arrival to most recent employment. The groups also clearly differ in the most important components within social networks ranging from the strong reliance on kin rather than friends among the Bai and Koreans, to the clear preference for friends over kin by the Yi. The two surveys discussed here cannot resolve these issues, but at the very least they show the importance of social network ties and the variability in their nature and importance among different ethnic minorities in different cities at different stages of migrant adjustment to a new urban China.

Further Analysis

Without a doubt, the theory of *chaxu geju* is pertinent in the description of the social networks built upon the primary relations among the transient population from outside urban areas. However, in the context of economic and social transition, blindly copying the theory of *chaxu geju* may render an overly simplistic analysis. Starting with hierarchical relations (such as identity and social hierarchy) may to some extent illuminate the status and role of the transient population in the social structure and market arrangement, but may also run the risk of neglecting the rules and other factors in the hierarchical relations. There are four key factors to consider.

First, the migrants, as newcomers, may experience so-called "culture shock" and feel nervous when first encountering the "unfamiliar" and "novel" urban environment. For migrants from rural areas or small towns, the metropolis is an uncharted and unpredictable world. The bonds built upon the ties of blood, geographic proximity, and occupation are the most intimate and reliable social foundation, providing them with a minimum subsistence in urban areas. Nevertheless, they cannot simply "scrounge for food" among their acquaintances;

instead, they need to establish new relations for employment, investment, and business operation, making new friends, starting a family, and engaging in exchange, by following the "urban rules."

Second, the migrant population is faced with a cross-cultural and cross-regional social network that is complex, heterogeneous, and changeable – quite unlike the relatively uniform, homogeneous, and stable rural social relations in their native places. Their original social relations are mostly left far away in their hometowns, and the values and ethical standards they followed there become increasing impractical. For reasons of survival, adaptation, and development, they have to deal with strangers and establish new social connections and networks. Our investigations have revealed a change in how ethnic minorities assessed the value of social and economic association before and after migrating. For example, in their native place, Mongolians attached the greatest importance to "friendship." However, once in Beijing, they found greatest importance in "the relationship between superiors and subordinates." "Friendship" fell to second place on their lists. In contrast, the Tibetan and Dai migrants placed the highest valuation on "kinship relations" when in their original residence but, once in the city, shifted that highest valuation to "friendship." The Koreans differed from both of these patterns, maintaining across migration the primary importance of "friendship."

Third, ethnic minorities seeking employment in urban areas must participate in cross-ethnic interactions. In the cities, where the Han majority has the dominant position, the bonds formed among official governmental systems, commercial interactions, and individual relations constitute a network that includes the Han and other ethnic nationalities. Such networks are a sort of intangible resource, from which information, funding, and opportunity can be obtained. Ethnic minorities seeking progress in urban areas are compelled to become part of these networks. No matter where you are from or what nationality you are, you have to subject yourself to the rules by which these networks operate. These rules include the practices of officialdom, how contracts work in the economic realm, the importance of standard Chinese for communication, and the way in which life is lived on a daily, local basis. These rules often differ from the customs of the ethnic groups, so they must change. In order to change migrants must constantly become better acquainted with these rules.

Fourth, social structures have enormous room and elasticity for change (Li 1992). As migrant populations adapt themselves to the constantly changing urban social structure, they avail themselves of the enormous room and elasticity of this social structure to build new network ties. Such networks are neither confined to their own community nor solely derived from the new groups with whom they now interact. Instead, these networks are open and utilitarian in nature, serving as a force which not only pushes forward social and economic development but also affects modes of resource allocation and directions in industrial restructuring and economic reform. Migrants in urban areas are thus not merely stuck in a specified structure of a specific community, but part of a dynamic network of social relations. We need to further examine such relations and the rules thereof.

Conclusion

In this chapter I have advocated the analytical use of network theories, and have pointed out that different social networks are utilized by different migrants at different job-seeking stages. When employment seeking by migrant job-seekers becomes a practice followed by a sufficient number of people, social capital associated with various kinds of social network will be available. That will provide a clearer picture of the seemingly disorganized job-seeking situation of migrants when we look upon each and every one of them as a member of the social network, when we see their migration as part of the networking, and when we recognize the structure and function of the network. An additional section of the two surveys discussed earlier, for example, also asked questions about who migrants would turn to for help. In responses to that question, a more complicated network emerged that partially comprised relatives and friends – the social network discussed earlier – but also local government and people at work (both bosses and colleagues).[5]

It is precisely with respect to migrants' constant development and exploitation of network ties that modifications in network analysis are needed to extend Fei's classic *chaxu geju*. Such extended network analysis not only addresses the existence and current use of networks, but also sheds light on the potential of networks for change. Social capital reflects both the resources contained in a social network and the ability to mobilize those resources. Migrant job-seekers, upon entering urban areas, must thus go beyond their original social networks to expand their social capital. They need access to new resources and often new ways of accessing those resources. Only those who have succeeded in doing this can hope to have a higher income and enjoy a higher social status. The preliminary survey data presented here cannot fully answer those questions, but the great variability in reliance on networks by different ethnic minorities in different cities at different points in their integration suggests how rich a context for these questions are the waves of ethnic minority migrants finding their way into a new urban China.

Notes

1. There are more than 1.3 billion people in China. The minority population of 20 million in the cities is thus a relatively small one.
2. The minority population in Shenzhen increased rapidly to over 361,500 by the end of 2005 (Shenzhen Municipal Bureau of Statistics).

3. The census of the year 2000 included people who had lived in the city more than half a year, but did not take into account registered permanent residence.

4. See Fei Xiaotong's *From the Soil* (First Edition 1941; Reprinted by Sanlian Bookstore in 1985). In the book, Fei argued that Chinese society organizes itself by principles different from those in the "West." For Fei , the central feature of Chinese society was *chaxu geju* (differential mode of association) based on *shehui guanxi* (ranked categories of social connections). Fei focused on comparisons between "Western" society and Chinese society, using two metaphors to convey the difference between the two: "Western" organization is formed by straws collected to form a haystack, whereas Chinese society consists of the waves generated by the splash of rocks thrown into water.

5. The responses to that question are too complicated to summarize here. But it is worth noting that, like the data reported in the text, the pattern of responses in the Beijing and four-city surveys was quite different, even for the same ethnic minority. For example, Korean migrants looked first to friends in Beijing (31.9 percent) but to local government (21.5 percent) in the four-city survey, with friends noted at only 13.4 percent.

References

Bian, Yanjie. 1997. "Bringing strong ties back in: Indirect ties, network bridges, and job searches in China." *American Sociological Review* 62(3): 366–386.

Bott, Elizabeth. 1957. *Family and Social Network*. London: Tavistock Publications.

Burt, Ronald. 1992. *Structural Holes: The Social Structure of Competition*. Cambridge: Harvard University Press.

Coleman, James S. 1990. *Foundations of Social Theory*. Boston: Harvard University Press.

Epstein, A.L. 1961. "The network of urban social organization." *Rhodes-Livingstone Journal* 29: 29–62.

Fan, C. 2008. "Migration, *hukou*, and the city," pp. 65–89 in *China Urbanizes: Consequences, Strategies, and Policies*, eds. S. Yusuf and T. Saich. Washington, D.C.: The World Bank.

Fei, Xiaotong. 1941 (First Edition). *From the Soil*. Reprinted by Sanlian Bookstore (Shanghai) in 1985.

Granovetter, Mark. 1973. "The strength of weak ties." *American Journal of Sociology* 78(6): 1360–1380.

———. 1974. *Getting a Job: A Study of Contract and Careers*. Cambridge: Harvard University Press.

———. 1985. "Economic action and social structure: The problem of embeddedness." *American Journal of Sociology* 91(3): 481–510.

Li, Peilin. 1992. *Another Invisible Hand: The Transformation of Social Structure. Chinese Social Sciences*, Vol.5.

Lieberson, Stanley. 1963. *Ethnic Patterns in American Cities*. New York: The Free Press of Glencoe.

Mitchell, J.C. 1958. "Types of urban social relationships," pp. 84–87 in *Present Inter-Relations in Central African Rural and Urban Life*, ed. R. Apthorpe. Lusaka: Rhodes-Livingstone Institute.

———. 1966. "Theoretical orientations in African urban studies," pp. 37– in *The Social Anthropology of Complex Societies,* ed. Michael Banton. London: Tavistock Publications.

———. 1969. *Social Networks in Urban Situations: Analyses of Personal Relationships in Central African Towns.* Manchester: Manchester University Press.

Portes, Alejandro. 1995. "Economic sociology and the sociology of immigration: A conceptual overview," pp. 1–41 in *The Economic Sociology of Immigration: Essays on Networks, Ethnicity, and Entrepreneurship,* ed. Alejandro Portes. New York: Russell Sage Foundation.

———. 1998. "Social capital: Its origins and applications in modern sociology." *Annual Review of Sociology* 24: 1–24.

Solinger, D. 2008. "The political implications of China's social future: Complacency, scorn, and the forlorn," pp. 251–266 in *China's Changing Political Landscape: Prospects for Democracy,* ed. L. Cheng. Washington, D.C.: Brookings Institution Press.

Wang, Chunguang. 1995. *Social Mobility and Social Restructuring.* Hangzhou: Zejiang Remin Press.

Xiang, Biao. 2000. *A Village beyond Borders* [In Chinese]. Beijing: Sanlian Press.

Zhang, Jijiao. 2003. "Ethnic minority labor out-migrants from Guizhou Province and their impact on sending areas," pp. 141–154 in *China's Minorities on the Move: Selected Case Studies,* eds. Robyn Iredale et al. New York: M. E. Sharpe,

———. 2007. "Migrants' social network used in seeking employment in urban areas," pp. 427–466 in *Urbanization and Multi-Ethnic Society,* eds. Buddhadeb Chaudhuri and Sumita Chaudhuri. New Delhi, India: Inter-India Publications.

———. 2009a. "The orientation of urban migrants' social network: A comparative survey on six minorities in the cities of China," pp. 127–139 in "China Networks," Special Issue of *Chinese History and Society Vol. 35,* eds, Jens Damm and Mechthild Leutner, Berliner China-Hefte, Germany.

———. 2009b. "Migration, the emergence of multi-ethnic cities and ethnic relations in China," pp. 173–188 in *Beyond Multiculturalism: Views from Anthropology,* ed. Giuliana B. Prato. Surrey, England: Ashgate Publishing.

CHAPTER 4

Migration and DiverseCity:[1] Singapore's Changing Demography, Identity, and Landscape

Brenda S.A. YEOH and Theodora LAM

A city-state with explicit globalizing ambitions and orientations, Singapore in many respects continues to be "rooted in the condition of colonial pluralism" (Goh 2008: 236). Since the city's birth as a trading emporium in the nineteenth century, Singapore has been associated with a cosmopolitan demography, culture, and landscape first engendered by a liberal open-door policy on immigration during the colonial regime, and later re-engineered to fuel a planned program of economic growth and nation-building after independence. At the turn of the nineteenth century, the population residing within the municipal boundaries of the colonial city comprised a 74 percent Chinese majority from various dialect groups (the main five being Hokkiens, Teochews, Cantonese, Hylams, and Hakkas) and "sizeable minorities of 'natives of the Malay Archipelago' (14 percent, made up chiefly by Peninsular Malays, Javanese, Boyanese and Bugis), 'natives of India' (8 percent, comprising mainly Tamils, Bengalis and Parsees), Eurasians (2 percent), Europeans (1 percent), and 'other nationalities' (1 percent, principally Arabs, Jews, Sinhalese and Japanese)" (Yeoh 1996: 38). Observers – particularly Western travel writers – of the city's "street scenery" populated by the diverse mix of people groups were often moved to heights of descriptive prose in an attempt to capture the cosmopolitan flavor of Singapore, albeit through the lens of colonial mindsets that tend to conflate diversity with "chaos," "promiscuity," "Oriental quaintness," and a lack of discipline and order (Yeoh 1996).

A century later, at the beginning of the twenty-first century, popular accounts describing the city to outsiders continue to highlight the distinctiveness of its demographic and cultural diversity (without the gloss of colonial idioms) as exemplified in tourist websites such as:

> Singapore is truly cosmopolitan, a fascinating mixture of people and culture: officially Chinese, Indian and Malay, but also with a huge foreign resident

and transit population of Americans, Burmese, Europeans, Indonesians, Japanese and fellow Asians, making it one of the most diverse centers in Asia. (http://www.amadeus.net/home/new/destinations/en/guides/singapore/wts. htm, accessed on 3 May 2012)

Often portrayed as a successful non-Western city subject to economic and social engineering by a strong state operating in an illiberal democracy, postcolonial Singapore continues to bear the hallmarks of diversity. While the demographic profile of Singapore as preserved in the first post-independence national census in 1970 registered a total population of just over two million comprising an overwhelming majority of citizens (90.4 percent) and much smaller proportions of permanent residents or PRs (6.7 percent) and non-residents[2] (2.9 percent), declining fertility rates among the citizen population – total fertility rate was only 1.15 in 2010 (Singapore Department of Statistics 2011a) – coupled with labor augmentation programs through aggressive (but also selective) immigration policies have produced within less than four decades a very different social and demographic complexion. In 2010, out of a total population of 5.08 million, less than two-thirds (63.6 percent) were citizens, 10.7 percent were PRs and 25.7 percent were non-residents (Singapore Department of Statistics 2011a).

The increasing proportion of the non-resident/non-citizen population is a direct consequence of Singapore's policy of attracting and relying on "foreign manpower" – at both the high and low ends of the spectrum – to overcome the limits of local resources. Indeed, foreigners constituted around 35 percent or slightly more than one million of the nation's 3.14 million-strong workforce in 2010, possibly making Singapore the country with the highest proportion of foreign workers in Asia (Ministry of Manpower 2011). Such openness to foreign others is seen to be an essential strategy if Singapore is to compete successfully in the current round of globalization, as is made clear in the following exhortation from one of the nation's top political leaders – in this case the then Senior Minister Lee Kuan Yew – invoking the need to become "cosmopolitan" to secure a key role in the globalized economy:

> To succeed, Singapore must be a cosmopolitan centre, able to attract, retain and absorb talent from all over the world. We cannot keep the big companies out of the local league. Whether we like it or not, they are entering the region. … Now in a globalised economy, we are in competition against other cities in the First World. Hence we have to become a cosmopolitan city that attracts and welcomes talent in business, academia, or in the performing arts. They will add to Singapore's vibrancy and secure our place in a global network of cities of excellence. (http://members.lycos.co.uk/Collin/SM_Speech.html, accessed on 15 February 2000)

While these two snapshots of Singapore's cultural-demographic mix a hundred years apart share a superficial similarity in their emphasis on population diversity as a hallmark of the city's cosmopolitan character, there are significant differences. Singapore's cosmopolitan trajectory is not underpinned by a smooth or consistent master logic but instead by twists and turns. The colonial cosmopolitan society was a product of the way in which "plural societies" developed under colonialism, where "different sections of the community live side by side, but separately … each group hold[ing] by its own religion, its own culture and language, its own ideas and ways" and where "even in the economic sphere there is a division of labor along racial lines" (Furnivall 1948: 304-305). In the immediate postcolonial nation-building phase, and against the backdrop of a plural society with racialized categories hardened by colonial policy, the new national leaders had little choice but to advocate the welding of heterogeneous groups into "one people" on the premise of an ideology of a "separate but equal" multiracialism (Benjamin 1976; Siddique 1989). Nation-building in the early decades of independence placed primary emphasis on economic nationalism as well as on the management of race within the strictures of Singapore's founding philosophy – the logic of the 4Ms+M (Multiracialism, Multiculturalism, Multilingualism, Multireligiosity plus Meritocracy). Government formulations about the Singapore nation right into the twenty-first century continue to invoke a multiethnicity based on the four "founding races" (i.e. the so-called Chinese-Malay-Indian-Others [CMIO] model)[3] as the stuff of which nations are made. In his vision of "building a multiracial nation through integration," for example, then Prime Minister Goh Chok Tong (2000: 16) made clear that the way forward for Singapore:

> … is not mosaic pieces, but four overlapping circles. Each circle represents one community. The area where the circles overlap is the common area where we live, play and work together and where we feel truly Singaporean with minimal consciousness of our ethnicity. This pragmatic arrangement of seeking integration through overlapping circles has underwritten the racial and religious harmony that Singapore enjoys today.

Such formulations privilege fixed categories (tied to ancestral cultures) and ignore the more mobile "others," numbering over a million and a quarter of the Singapore population, who are present in the city yet do not belong to the "CMIO races" constituting the Singapore citizenry. Indeed, the same construction of the national self is characteristic of the collection of official statistics in Singapore (at least in terms of statistics released into the public domain). Ethnicity is almost always used as an organizing principle in the categorization and analysis of data on the Singapore citizenry while an impenetrable silence surrounds the fate of the over one million "non-resident" others (and in fact the "PRs" as well).[4] Ranging from "foreign workers" in construction, domestic service, and other "dirty, dangerous and difficult" (the 3Ds) sectors, to "foreign talents" belonging to the professional and managerial classes, these mobile individuals are outside state constructions of the national population and do not appear in any form of census-taking. What census categories also fail to fully capture are the increasingly complex social formations resulting from the rapid rise of cross-nationality marriages, stirring into the city diversity in the form of marriage migrants, "foreign spouses" and "children of mixed marriages."

Until recently, most scholarly writings on post-independence Singapore have also treated Singapore as a bounded nation-state, with few references to the untidy tapestry of Singapore's migrant past, or the increasing presence of mobile others with the potential to trouble notions of the national self. More recent scholarship is coming to grips with the porosity of national borders and the immense diversity of people – of different degrees of transience and permanence – who inhabit a city with an increasingly high density of transnational flows and linkages. The influence of transnationalism, which gained momentum in the last two decades, not only highlighted the intensity and velocity of movements of people and objects across national boundaries but also thrust upon nation-states the role of facilitating, managing, and responding to the networks of people movements (Urry 2000). On the policy front, even as more attempts are made to socialize "new immigrants" into Singapore's multicultural society through cross-national and cross-racial exposure, the awareness that mobility will increasingly be the quintessential experience of the twenty-first century is becoming more consciously acknowledged.

As Sandercock (2006: 43) notes, the contemporary phenomena of "immigration and ethnicity" are "constitutive of globalization and are reconfiguring the spaces of and social relations in cities in new ways." In this chapter, we examine the way in which rapid and highly diverse transnational immigration is reconfiguring the social and spatial fabric of global-city Singapore in terms of three related aspects: first, demography (particularly how it relates to a "multiracial" nation); second, identity (particularly the ambivalence about hyphenated identities); and, third, landscapes (particularly how they reflect different kinds of immigration).

Immigration and the Changing Demography of a "Multiracial Nation"

Persisting in its efforts to win the race to become a global city, the Singapore government has geared up its development and planning strategies to cater to a population scenario of 5.5 million over the next forty to fifty years. Given that its population is already 5.18 million (in 2011), this target does not seem too remote (Singapore Department of Statistics 2011a). However, growing the population to attain global-city goals cannot simply depend on the indigenous citizenry since the number of citizen births was only 30,131 in 2010, producing a growth rate of

Table 4.1 • Singapore's Population and Annual Growth

	Number as at June (Mid-Year) ('000)					Average Annual Growth[a] (%)				
		Singapore Residents[d]					Singapore Residents[d]			
Year	Total Population[b,d]	Total	Singapore Citizens	Permanent Residents	Non-Residents	Total Population[b,d]	Total	Singapore Citizens	Permanent Residents	Non-Residents
1970	2,074.5	2,013.6	1,874.8	138.8	60.9	2.8	na			
1980	2,413.9	2,282.1	2,194.3	87.8	131.8	1.5	1.3			
1990	3,047.1	2,735.9	2,623.7	112.1	311.3	2.3c	1.7c	1.7c	2.3c	9.0
2000	4,027.9	3,273.4	2,985.9	287.5	754.5	2.8	1.8	1.3	9.9	9.3
2004	4,166.7	3,413.3	3,057.1	356.2	753.4	1.3	1.4	0.8	6.5	0.7
2005	4,265.8	3,467.8	3,081.0	386.8	797.9	2.4	1.6	0.8	8.6	5.9
2006	4,401.4	3,525.9	3,107.9	418.0	875.5	3.2	1.7	0.9	8.1	9.7
2007	4,588.6	3,583.1	3,133.8	449.2	1,005.5	4.3	1.6	0.8	7.5	14.9
2008	4,839.4	3,642.7	3,164.4	478.2	1,196.7	5.5	1.7	1.0	6.5	19.0
2009	4,987.6	3,733.9	3,200.7	533.2	1,253.7	3.1	2.5	1.1	11.5	4.8
2010	5,076.7	3,771.7	3,230.7	541.0	1,305.0	1.8	1.0	0.9	1.5c	4.1
2011	5,183.7	3,789.3	3,257.2	532.0	1,394.4	2.1	0.5	0.8	-1.7	6.9

a) For 1970, 1980, 1990 and 2000, growth rate refers to average annual growth over the last ten years. For 2004–2008, growth rate refers to growth over the previous year.

b) Total population comprises Singapore residents and non-residents. Resident population comprises Singapore citizens and permanent residents.

c) Average annual growth rate between 1980 and 1990 are computed based on 1980 and 1990 using de facto concept.

d) Data for 2004–2007 have been revised with reference from Feb 2008.

e) The growth in the permanent resident population started to slow down from 2010 due to the tightened immigration framework.

Source: Compiled from Singapore Department of Statistics 2008: 1; 2009; 2011a.

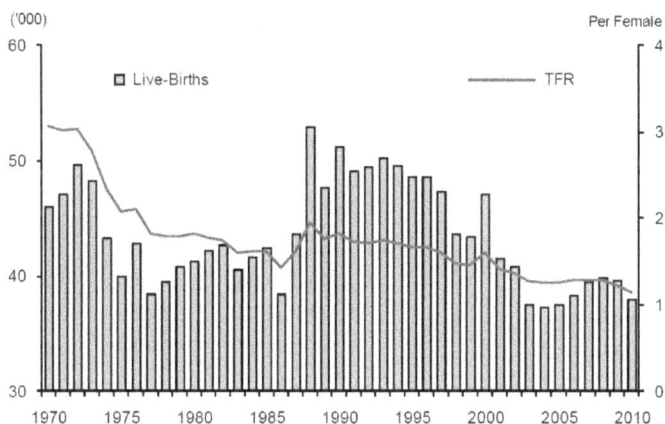

('000)   Per Female
60   4

   □ Live-Births   ——— TFR

                                                                      3
50

                                                                      2

40

                                                                      1

30   0
   1970   1975   1980   1985   1990   1995   2000   2005   2010

Figure 4.1 • Total Live Births and Total Fertility Rate (Singapore)

Note: Before 1980, rate refers to total live births and total population. From 1980, TFR is based on resident live births and resident population (i.e. Singapore citizens and permanent residents).

Source: Singapore Department of Statistics 2011a: 20.

only 0.8 percent (Singapore Department of Statistics 2011b) (see Table 4.1). As is the case in several rapidly developing or developed countries in East and Southeast Asia, fertility rates have declined rapidly in the post-independence decades, plummeting to below-replacement levels in a much shorter time period than in most Western countries. Figure 4.1 shows the declining total live births and total fertility rate in Singapore. Measures implemented by the Singapore government to boost fertility have met with limited success (Straughan, Chan, and Jones 2009: 187).

Aware of the difficulties in reversing very low fertility rates among the citizenry, the state has since turned to other strategies – specifically attracting "foreign manpower," regardless of nationality – to augment its population size (Koh 2003). This strategy has proven much more immediately effective: the increases in Singapore's population and its labor workforce in recent decades are largely accounted for by the burgeoning pool of PRs and non-residents who grew by varying percentages over the years (Table 4.1).

Foreign manpower enters Singapore through different immigrant channels and in different categories (see Yeoh 2006), including "foreign talents" (skilled labor or employees holding positions at the professional and managerial levels); "foreign workers" (unskilled/low skilled labor in the construction, manual labor, and domestic industries); workers with mid-level skills (such as technicians, chefs, and health care workers); international students (from the primary to tertiary levels); entrepreneurs; trainees; confinement nannies; athletes and sporting talent; and family (spouses, parents or unmarried children of Singapore citizens/

Table 4.2 • Estimated Numbers of Major Foreign Nationals in Singapore (Various Years)

Nationality	Number	Year
Chinese	200,000	*na*
Malaysian	200,000	2009
Indonesian	150,000	*na*
Filipino	136,489	2004
Indian	90,000-100,000	2006
Bangladeshi	80,000-90,000	2009
Myanmarese	50,000-60,000	2008
Thai	45,000	*na*
Japanese	26,370	2007
Sri Lankan	20,000	*na*
British	20,000	2008
American	15,000	2008
Australian	15,000	2007
South Korean	13,509	2009
German	6,500	2009
French	5,000	2007

Sources:

China, Indonesia, Thailand and Sri Lanka: http://www.starzesthometuition.com.sg/aboutsingapore.html, date accessed 12 July 2009.

Malaysia: Ministry of Human Resources, http://www.mohr.gov.my/pemberhentian/index.php?option=com _content&task=view&id=47&Itemid=6, date accessed 12 August 2009.

Philippines: Philippine Overseas Employment Administration (POEA), http://www.poea.gov.ph/docs/STOCK %20ESTIMATE%202004.xls, date accessed 12 August 2009.

India: Lal, Reeves, and Rai (2006).

Bangladesh: High Commission of Bangladesh, Singapore, http://bangladesh.org.sg/cms/index.php?option= com_content&task=view&id=36&Itemid=29, date accessed 12 August 2009.

Myanmar: Daniel Lwin cited in *The Sunday Times* (9 March 2008).

Japan: Ministry of Foreign Affairs of Japan, http://www.mofa.go.jp/region/asia-paci/singapore/index.html, date accessed 12 August 2009.

Britain: British Chamber of Commerce cited in *The Business Times* (8 April 2008).

America: American Chamber of Commerce cited in *The Business Times* (8 April 2008).

South Korea: Ministry of Foreign Affairs and Trade, http://www.mofat.go.kr/consul/overseascitizen/ compatriotcondition/index6.jsp?TabMenu=TabMenu6, date accessed 12 August 2009.

Australia: *The Business Times* (1 August 2007).

Germany: Embassy of the Federal Republic of Germany, http://www.discover-germany.sg/, date accessed 12 August 2009.

France: *The Straits Times* (24 April 2007).

PRs, as well as mothers accompanying their children to Singapore schools who stay in Singapore as dependents or on long-term visit passes). According to reports from various ministries, the breakdown of these foreigners by categories was 871,000 unskilled work permit holders (foreign workers) in 2011, and in 2010, 240,000 employment (foreign talents) and S-pass[5] holders (catering to those with mid-level skills), and 91,500 foreign students (*The Straits Times*, 16 November 2010; 10 March 2011; 15 August 2011). Though a detailed breakdown of these foreigners by nationality and ethnicity is not available, estimates on the numbers of major foreign nationals in Singapore can be found in Table 4.2.

Of the growing numbers of foreigners in Singapore, a significant percentage take on Permanent Residency (figures were at an all-time high of 79,167 in 2008 but have dropped to 29,265 in 2010 due to tighter immigration policies) and a smaller percentage become new citizens (18,758 in 2010). Along with differential birth rates among local racial categories, immigration has been an important dynamic shaping the resident population mix and CMIO proportions over the years. Comparing the racial arithmetic of increased immigration in the period after independence, the proportions of "Others" (from 1.2 percent to 3.3 percent) and "Indians" (from 7.0 percent to 9.2 percent) have increased from 1970 to 2011 respectively while those of "Malays" (from 14.8 percent to 13.4 percent) and "Chinese" (from 77.0 percent to 74.1 percent) have declined within the same period (Table 4.3).[6] Another facet of increased immigration which has a bearing on the multiracial complexion of the nation-state is associated with the rapid increase in cross-nationality and inter-ethnicity marriages. In 2010, cross-nationality marriages involving a citizen spouse and a foreign spouse[7] accounted for 40.6 percent of all marriages registered in Singapore, while marriages across ethnic categories made up 20.2 percent of all marriages (17.5 percent under Women's Charter and 33.3 percent under Muslim Law Act) (Singapore Department of Statistics 2011b, 2011c).

The influx of foreign spouses affects CMIO arithmetic in at least two ways. First, foreign spouses represent a wide range of ethnicities (for example, "foreign brides" tend to be Chinese, Vietnamese, or from South and Southeast Asia). Though they initially enter Singapore under the non-resident category, they may eventually make the transition to PR status before becoming new citizens.[8] Second, these cross-ethnic marriages yield children of mixed ethnicity. While by Singapore law these children will automatically adopt their father's ethnicity at birth (Chua 2003), they may not, in fact, fit easily into any of the CMIO categories, even the catch-all "Others." As a disgruntled new citizen, a Caucasian man with a Malaysian wife of Indian heritage and three children (two from a previous marriage to a Chinese woman and one from this marriage) who was unable to purchase public housing due to racial quotas (Ooi, Siddique, and Soh 1993), lamented: "We don't fit a cookie-cutter definition of race and to simply categorize us as 'Other' overlooks our unique blend of race and culture" (*The Straits Times*, 31 January 2008).

Table 4.3 • Distribution of Singapore's Resident Population by Citizenship Status and Race

Year	Residential Status	Chinese	%	Malay	%	Indian	%	Others	%	Total	%
1957	Singapore Resident[a]	1,090,596	75.4	197,059[b]	13.6	124,084[c]	8.6	34,190	2.4	1,445,929	100
1970	Citizen	1,478,200	78.8	264,361	14.1	112,683	6.0	19,534	1.0	1,874,778	100
	PR	73,246	52.8	33,647	24.2	28,208	20.3	3,684	2.7	138,785	100
	Singapore Resident	1,551,446	77.0	298,008	14.8	140,891	7.0	23,218	1.2	2,013,563	100
1980[d]	Citizen	1,740,862	79.3	306,027	13.9	128,969	5.9	18,422	0.8	2,194,280	100
	PR	46,954	53.5	22,691	25.8	14,435	16.4	3,765	4.3	87,845	100
	Singapore Resident	1,787,816	78.3	328,718	14.4	143,404	6.3	22,187	1.0	2,282,125	100
1990	Citizen	2,023,138	78.0	372,192	14.3	175,680	6.8	24,233	0.9	2,595,243	100
	PR	79,657	72.5	10,464	9.5	15,227	13.9	4,524	4.1	109,872	100
	Singapore Resident	2,102,795	77.7	382,656	14.1	190,907	7.1	28,757	1.1	2,705,115	100
2000	Citizen	2,284,617	76.8	441,737	14.9	214,642	7.2	32,095	1.1	2,973,091	100
	PR	220,762	76.1	11,896	4.1	43,149	14.9	14,311	4.9	290,118	100
	Singapore Resident	2,505,379	76.8	453,633	13.9	257,791	7.9	46,406	1.4	3,263,209	100
2005	Citizen	2,684,900	75.6	484,600	13.6	309,300	8.7	74,700	1.4	3,113,000	100
	PR									440,500	100
2008	Citizen	2,721,800	74.7	495,100	13.6	323,400	8.9	102,300	2.8	3,164,400	100
	PR									478,200	100
2009	Citizen	2,770,300	74.2	500,100	13.4	343,500	9.2	120,000	3.2	3,200,700	100
	PR									533,200	100
2010	Citizen	2,794,000	74.1	503,900	13.4	348,100	9.2	125,800	3.3	3,230,700	100
	PR									541,000	100
2011	Citizen	2,808,300	74.1	506,600	13.4	349,000	9.2	125,300	3.3	3,257,200	100
	PR									532,000	100

Compiled from various sources: 1957 (Chua 1964: 43), 1970 and 1980 (Saw 2007: 53), 1990 (Singapore Department of Statistics 1992: 37–38) and 2000 (Singapore Department of Statistics 2001: np.). The breakdowns by citizenship status and race are not available for 1957, 2005 and 2008 to 2011. The figures for Singapore's resident population (includes both Singapore citizens and permanent residents [PRs]) in 2005, and 2008 to 2011 are included for reference purposes only, and are taken from Singapore Department of Statistics (2006, 2008, 2010, 2011a).

a) The population resident in Singapore includes persons classified as belonging to private households; persons classified as belonging to institutional households; wayfarers on land, and persons, other than in transit, enumerated on board ships and boats within Port Limits (Chua 1964: 1).

b) Written as Malaysians in Chua (1964: 43).

c) Written as Indians and Pakistanis in Chua (1964: 43).

d) In 1980, citizenship and residential status are defined as:

Citizenship refers to the legal nationality of the person acquired by birth, registration or naturalization. Persons who were citizens of Australia and New Zealand are classified with citizen of the European countries. Persons who did not acquire the citizenship of any country are classified with those whose citizenship status was unknown.

Persons are grouped into two categories of residential status, namely, Singapore Residents and Non-residents. All Singapore citizens and non-citizens who have been granted permanent residence in Singapore are classified as Singapore Residents. Non-citizens who claimed Singapore permanent residence by virtue of their long stay in Singapore are also classified as Singapore Residents.

Persons who are not Singapore permanent residents are classified as Non-residents. They include foreign students studying in Singapore, work permit holders, employment pass holders and their dependents. (Singapore Department of Statistics 1981: 64)

Immigration and the Hyphenation of Identities

According to a study on ethnicity, national identity, and sense of rootedness among Singaporeans, conducted by the Institute of Public Policy, the majority of Singaporeans prefer to identify themselves in terms of national identity (Singaporeans) than by ethnic identity following CMIO prescriptions (*The Straits Times*, 18 June 2002). At the same time, while the state promotes the development of a national identity, it does not advocate the erasure of ethnic markers; in fact not only does state policy support and accommodate a diversity of ethnic identities (*The Straits Times*, 18 June 2002), it ties many of its programs on housing, heritage, education, language, and community building to a foundational understanding of "race" in the context of an even-handed multiracialism. As a journalist put it, "no one is required to abjure his race in order to be a Singaporean" *(The Straits Times,* 22 July 2001).

While ethnic categories continue to have significant traction in Singapore society, under the weight of transnational immigration pressures they are likely to become less bounded to allow for more complex forms of identification. The complexities of social identification were overtly recognized (possibly for the first time in a national speech) in Prime Minister Lee Hsien Loong's 2006 National Day Rally Speech (cited in *The Straits Times*, 22 August 2006). In his appeal to Singaporeans to welcome "new immigrants," he not only argued for a recognition of difference ("A Chinese-Chinese is different from a Singapore-Chinese. An Indian-Indian is different from a Singapore-Indian"), but proposed that this could be done by allowing for "hyphenated" national-racial identities at least for the first few generations:[9]

> … we will hyphenate, Australian-Singaporean, Chinese-Singaporeans, Chinese-Chinese Singaporeans. But make them one of us and if we meet one of them, let's be friendly, let's go out of our way to show them around, help them, make them feel at home…. So even if the first generation is not completely

Singaporean, the second generation growing up here will be and will contribute to Singapore.

It appears that while CMIO-multiracialism has not been abandoned as a systematic framework for race relations in Singapore, the presence of a wide diversity of immigrants with different degrees of similarity and difference to the citizenry is beginning to move understandings of racial categorization beyond the fixity of four "homogeneous but overlapping" circles toward an acceptance of hyphenated identities as legitimate, even as the hope remains that the "hyphens" are transient phenomena that will dissolve with subsequent generations. It should, however, be noted that hyphenation may not necessarily provide a framework appropriate for the rescue and restoration of former creolized cultures ("transethnic solidarities") such as the *Peranakan* culture;[10] neither does hyphenation as a means of accommodating "foreign others transiting to becoming part of national self" apply to the case of foreign workers (a large proportion of the non-resident category) who are not permitted to settle in Singapore. Nevertheless, for a nation-state forged out of racial categories derived from a colonial history of racial prejudice, and from postcolonial developments based on the preservation and management of racial difference, active recognition of hyphenated identities is a major step towards more flexible thinking about race, the cultivation of cosmopolitan sensibilities, and the accommodation of difference. As has been argued elsewhere, "much of the host-migrant identity politics in Singapore at this time is confrontational and ridden with derogatory undertones" (Yeoh and Yap 2008: 201). Yet fostering an identity politics based on flexible as opposed to rigid, pre-defined categories would allow globalizing cities to capitalize more creatively and positively on sameness and difference.

Immigration and Transformations of the Everyday Landscape

The impact of immigration on the everyday landscape of cities has attracted considerable debate. On the one hand, Turner (2007) argues against a post-national version of "flexible citizenship" in an age of increased mobility and instead follows Shamir (2005: 199) in proposing a reconceptualization of globalization "not as a system of liquid mobility" but one that also produces "closure, entrapment and containment." He notes that anxieties over terrorism and urban violence have created a "fear of diversity," triggering processes of "enclavement" and "new forms of enclosure" involving complex and sophisticated systems ranging from bureaucratic barriers, legal exclusions, and registrations to the use of forensic medicine and bio-profiling. On the other hand, more optimistic accounts of the impact of rapid immigration on the urban landscape show that "immigrant-led spaces also function as important economic generators in the urban economy and contribute to the sense of cultural diversity and cosmopolitanism" (Price and Benton-Short 2008: 36–37). Li (1998), for example, describes "ethnoburbs" as suburban ethnic spaces characterized by both vibrant ethnic economies and strong ties to the globalizing economy, while Chacko (2008) uses the term "sociocommerscape" to denote ethnic commercial centers instrumental in the revitalization of declining urban areas in post-industrial cities.

In the context of Singapore, the "new pluralism" noticeable in the everyday landscape reflects the complexity of class, race, nationality, and residency status that shape the conditions under which transnational migrants remain in and experience the city. Goh (2008), for example, observes that:

> … the new pluralism is reinforcing the old conjunction of race and class in the new globalized economy. Thus, in Singapore, while the largely Chinese professional class competes with hastily naturalized immigrant Chinese and Indian professionals to hobnob with white expatriates possessing privileged residency status, these groups are serviced by working-class Chinese, Indian, and Malay Singaporeans in different economic sectors, and everyone live in spaces built and maintained by Indian, Indonesian, and Filipino immigrant workers with minimal legal protection.

The unskilled or low-skilled migrant workers admitted into the city-state on short-term work permits – as disposable labor without any residency rights (Yeoh 2006) – are most prominent in the everyday landscape in the form of "weekend enclaves," transient social and commercial landscapes containing migrant concentrations. Confined largely to their workplaces during the working week (such as construction sites or Singaporean homes in the case of foreign domestic workers), large numbers of migrant contract workers congregate temporarily in strongly ethnicized enclaves over the weekend. Some examples include Little India/Serangoon Road, which attracts Indian and Bangladeshi workers; Little Manila in Lucky Plaza, right in the heart of the Orchard Road shopping belt, for Filipina domestic workers; and Little Thailand for Thai workers at the Golden Mile Complex on Beach Road. Certain landscapes are also changeable within the span of a day; for example, a residential and commercial district in the day, Joo Chiat turns into a vibrant Little Vietnam by night. Foreign worker gatherings have also sprung up in open spaces near shopping centers and Mass Rapid Transit (MRT) stations in the Housing and Development Board (HDB) estates, the residential heartlands where the majority of Singaporeans live.

These weekend enclaves and foreign worker gatherings are often viewed negatively or with unease by Singaporeans who consider them a form of "intrusion" into "their own backyards." Some have openly expressed their displeasure and asked the authorities to step up security measures in these places; others wondered whether these workers could be relocated to out-of-sight locations such as offshore islands (*The Straits Times,* 12 October 2008). Residents of HDB flats located in Little India have put up steel barricades around their blocks to keep foreign workers out and when the state announced plans to situate a foreign work-ers' dormitory in Serangoon Gardens, a middle-class residential estate, 1,600 resi-dents signed a petition in protest[11] (*The Straits Times,* 12 October 2008). These voices reflect a "use and discard" sentiment among the general population who want foreign workers to do the work that citizens shun, but at the same time wish that these workers could be erased from the landscape.

At the other end of the skills spectrum, professional and managerial migrants are also making their mark on the landscape. Nationality- or ethnicity-based enclaves have sprouted in private residential and HDB heartland areas such as Woodlands (Americans), Serangoon Gardens (French and Australians), Tanjong Rhu and Meyer Road (Indians), West Coast (Japanese), and East Coast (Kore-ans), often in the vicinity of their respective country's international schools (*The Sunday Times,* 17 August 2008). Their presence has significantly altered the retail landscape in the residential estates, transforming "old-school shops selling joss sticks and simple grocery items" into alfresco eateries, upmarket specialist shops, modern convenience stores or supermarkets, wine shops, and new beauty and wellness services that attract a "more diverse 'globe-trotting' crowd" or serve a "cosmopolitan clientele" (*The Straits Times,* 25 October 2008).

While there is a certain degree of resentment that these so-called foreign tal-ents take away jobs, are paid too much, and enjoy all the privileges of living in Singapore with none of the responsibilities that citizens bear, there is also an acknowledgment that the Singapore economy currently needs foreign talent to enhance its global competitiveness and to keep pace with global changes (Yeoh and Huang 2003). The influx of well-heeled expatriates boosts property prices and rental yields reaped by homeowners. It also increases exposure to other cul-tures, including the welcomed addition of a wide range of international cuisines into Singapore's restaurant scene: "next to their contributions to the economy, the best thing about expats is the authentic food which follows them here" (*The Sunday Times,* 17 August 2008). Not only does the social heterogeneity resulting from multiple streams of migration have a transformative effect on the tapestry of everyday spaces such as shopping malls, hospitals, offices, campuses, places of worship, and street-life in general, it also opens up opportunities for the new and spectacular. As Prime Minister Lee Hsien Loong elaborated:

> …Today we get people from all over the world too. We have people from Tur-key, there are Portuguese, somebody from Venezuela, somebody from Morocco, even a Korean or two, some Russians. And they add colour and diversity to this society. So our cuisine is something special. Singaporeans love food. You want Korean ginseng chicken, you can get the real thing cooked by a Korean. You want Arab food, you go to Arab Street, you can eat shawarma, which is shish

kebabs. You can smoke the hubble-bubble, the waterpipe. Now harder because new rules on no smoking. But it's something different for Singapore.... And we have other customs too. Recently there was a splendid wedding in Singapore. The groom came riding on a white horse. He was a Marwari, it's an Indian group, Indian businessman, very successful caste. So the zoo is now thinking of going into the service of providing horses and elephants for weddings. (quoted in *The Straits Times*, 22 August 2006)

Singapore as DiverseCity

What we have tried to show in this chapter is that contemporary migration is a compelling force for increased diversity in Singapore, introducing new and complex forms of diversity into an already plural city. A nation-city-state like Singapore that is inextricably plugged into globalization processes can no longer be constructed solely on the basis of a nationality-bound demography, but must now selectively incorporate a wide range of non-citizens of different skill levels, occupation, ethnicity, nationality, and gender. One especially provocative change is the rapid increase in cross-national and cross-ethnic marriages, a phenomenon that is significant in terms of the current demographic mix of this global city but that also plants seeds of further variability in the profile of future generations of Singaporeans. In terms of identity, it is clear that the CMIO template that has formed the basis of the imagined community of Singaporeans since independence is being transformed in the face of diverse immigration flows. The ensuing identity politics of difference and sameness organized around ethnicity and nationality require more flexible management of race while still capitalizing on the intrinsic strengths of an already plural society. In the everyday landscapes that mirror the complexities of this increasing social diversity, there are processes of enclosure and enclavement along self/other divides, but there are also processes of selective acculturation and negotiated co-existence as people with different histories and geographies meet and take stock of one another in the constant (re) making of this city of diversities.

Acknowledgments

We are grateful for funding support (Grant No: T208A4103) from the Ministry of Education for some of the research on which this chapter is based.

Notes

1. The term "DiverseCity" was first used in a joint project by Toronto City Summit Alliance and Maytree Foundation entitled "DiverseCity: The Greater Toronto Leadership Project." Comprising eight linked initiatives, the project aims to promote diversity among Toronto's leadership (http://www.diversecitytoronto.ca/, accessed on 13 August 2009).
2. The "non-resident population" refers to individuals who hold passes for short-term stays in Singapore; these include the Employment Pass, Work Permit, Dependant's Pass, and Long-term Social Visit Pass. This category excludes tourists and "transients."
3. Singapore-style multiracialism is based on the arithmetic formula of four "separate" but "equal" races in a nation of "one people." The philosophy propounds the need to submerge ethnic identity to the larger purposes of nation-building and national identity construction, while at the same time providing space for each of the four founding ethnic groups to promote, valorize, and reclaim ethnic links and identity. This form of multiculturalism continues the colonial classificatory schemas drawn under British rule and underlies ethnic policies governing inter- and intra-ethnic relations in different spheres of life.
4. In addition, basic information regarding nationality, ethnicity, gender, and other characterizations of the non-citizens is not available in the public domain.
5. There are around 98,000 S-pass holders according to *The Straits Times* (10 March 2011).
6. Unfortunately, no data are available for the non-resident population which is likely to contain much higher proportions of "Others."
7. Foreign spouses tend to be mainly from Asia: in 2010, 95.9 percent of non-citizen brides and 64.7 percent of non-citizen grooms were of Asian origin (Singapore Department of Statistics 2011b).
8. Over the past ten years, an average of about 8,500 Singaporean Permanent Residents (SPRs) have become Singapore citizens annually (Wong 2007).
9. In the context of Japanese emigrants and their generationally identified successors such as the Nisei, Sansei, and Yonsei after the Issei left Japan and settled in the United States, Tetsuden Kashima (personal communication, 22 October 2008) explained that the hyphenated form "Japanese-American" would suggest the equal coexistence of "Japanese" and "American" identities whereas "Japanese American" (the term used for the second generation onwards) would put the emphasis on "American" and reduce "Japanese" to a modifier.
10. *Peranakan*, meaning descendent in the Malay language, is a form of new creolized culture resulting from inter-marriage between Malays and those of Chinese descent (Goh 2008).
11. Reasons for their objection included "fears that the workers would commit crimes in the area, seduce their maids and dampen property prices." The state relented by relocating the entrance of the dormitory to another street that would be built to order and which faced away from the residential estate, and by housing mainly Malaysian and Chinese workers (male and female) from the manufacturing and service industries in the dormitory instead of foreign workers from the construction sector (who are mainly of South Asian origin). This prompted the observation that while

the "Serangoon Gardens saga" is as much a class issue as it is a racial one, a "veiled racism" is clearly at work in shaping the spatial politics of exclusion.

References

Anonymous. 2001. "All in the race." *The Straits Times*. 22 July.

Anonymous. 2011. "A proper way to leave." *The Straits Times*. 15 August.

Arshad, Arlina and Chong Chee Kin. 2008. "Myanmar illegals risk life and limb to enter Singapore." *The Sunday Times*. 9 March.

Benjamin, Geoffrey. 1976. "The cultural logic of Singapore's multiculturalism," pp. 115–133 in *Singapore: Society in Transition*, ed. Riaz Hassan. Kuala Lumpur: Oxford University Press.

Chacko, Elizabeth. 2008. "Washington, D.C.: From biracial city to multiethnic gateway," pp. 203–225 in *Migrants to the Metropolis*, eds. M. Price and L. Benton-Short. Syracuse: Syracuse University Press.

Cheam, Jessica. 2008. "The changing face of the heartland." *The Straits Times*. 25 October.

Chua, Beng Huat. 2003. "Multiculturalism in Singapore: An instrument of social control." *Race and Class* 44(3): 58–77.

Chua, Seng Chew. 1964. *Report on the Census of Population, 1957*. Singapore: Lim Bian Han, Government Printer.

Davie, Sandra. 2010. "Private schools: A question of quality." *The Straits Times*. 16 November.

Furnivall, John Sydenham. 1948. *Colonial Policy and Practice: A Comparative Study of Burma and the Netherland Indies*. Cambridge: Cambridge University Press.

Goh, Chok Tong. 2000. "Building a multi-racial nation through integration (speech at the Second Convention of Singapore Malay/Muslim Professionals, 5 November 2000)," pp. 13–21 in *Speeches: A Bimonthly Selection of Ministerial Speeches [November–December]*. Singapore: Ministry of Information and the Arts.

Goh, Daniel. 2008. "From colonial pluralism to postcolonial multiculturalism: Race, state formation and the question of cultural diversity in Malaysia and Singapore." *Sociology Compass* 2(1): 232-252.

Koh, Aaron. 2003. "Global flows of foreign talents: Identity anxieties in Singapore's ethnoscape." *Sojourn* 18(2): 230-256.

Kok, Melissa. 2011. "Tighter criteria for work-pass applicants." *The Straits Times*. 10 March.

Lackey, John M. 2008. "Door shuts on flat applicant of 'other' race." *The Straits Times*. 31 January.

Lal, Brij V., Peter Reeves and Rajesh Rai. 2006. *The Encyclopedia of the Indian Diaspora*. Singapore: Editions Didier Millet and National University of Singapore.

Lee, Hsien Loong. 2006. "Growing the S'pore family." *The Straits Times*. 22 August.

Li, Wei. 1998. "Anatomy of a new ethnic settlement: The Chinese ethnoburb in Los Angeles." *Urban Studies* 35(3): 479–501.

Ministry of Manpower. 2011. *Report on Labour Force in Singapore, 2010*. Singapore: Ministry of Manpower.

Ooi, Giok Ling. 2002. "Allowing for ethnic diversity boosts national identity." *The Straits Times*. 18 June.

Ooi, Giok Ling, Sharon Siddique, and Kay Cheng Soh. 1993. *The Management of Ethnic Relations in Public Housing Estates*. Singapore: Times Academic Press for Institute of Public Policy Studies.

Price, Marie, and Lisa Benton-Short. 2008. "Urban immigrant gateways in a globalizing world," pp. 23–50 in *Migrants to the Metropolis*, eds. M. Price and L. Benton-Short. Syracuse: Syracuse University Press.

Sandercock, Leonie. 2006. "Cosmopolitan urbanism: A love song to our mongrel cities," pp. 37–52 in *Cosmopolitan Urbanism*, eds. J. Binnie, J. Holloway, S. Millington and C. Young. London and New York: Routledge.

Saw, Swee Hock. 2007. *The Population of Singapore: Second Edition*. Singapore: Institute of Southeast Asian Studies.

Sengupta, Nilanjana. 2007. "Strong turnout among French voters in S'pore." *The Straits Times*. 24 April.

Shamir, Ronen. 2005. "Without borders? Notes on globalization as a mobility regime." *Sociological Theory* 23(2): 197–217.

Siddique, Sharon. 1989. "Singaporean identity," pp. 563–577 in *Management of Success: The Moulding of Modern Singapore*, eds. K.S. Sandhu and P. Wheatley. Singapore: Institute of Southeast Asian Studies.

Sim, Arthur. 2008. "Home leases stagnant for 2 years, still looking soft." *The Business Times*. 8 April.

Singapore Department of Statistics. 1981. *Census of Population 1980, Release no. 2*. Singapore: Singapore Department of Statistics.

————. 1992. *Singapore Census of Population 1990: Demographic Characteristics*. Singapore: Singapore National Printers.

————. 2001. *Census of Population 2000: Advance Data Release*. Singapore: Singapore Department of Statistics.

————. 2006. *General Household Survey 2005: Statistical Release 1: Socio-Demographic and Economic Characteristics*. Singapore: Singapore Department of Statistics.

————. 2008. *Population Trends 2008*. Singapore: Singapore Department of Statistics.

————. 2009. *Yearbook of Statistics Singapore 2009*. Singapore: Singapore Department of Statistics.

————. 2010. *Population Trends 2010*. Singapore: Singapore Department of Statistics.

————. 2011a. *Population Trends 2011*. Singapore: Singapore Department of Statistics.

————. 2011b. *Population in Brief 2011*. Singapore: Singapore Department of Statistics.

————. 2011c. *Yearbook of Statistics Singapore 2011*. Singapore: Singapore Department of Statistics.

Straughan, Paulin, Angelique Chan and Gavin Jones. 2009. "From population control to fertility promotion – a case study of family policies and fertility trends in Singapore," pp. 181–203 in *Ultra-low Fertility in Pacific Asia*, eds. G. Jones, P. Straughan and A. Chan. Oxford and New York: Routledge.

Tan, Conrad. 2007. "Stanchart private banking unit woos Aussie Expats." *The Business Times*. 1 August.

Tan, Dawn Wei. 2008. "The 'them and us' divide." *The Straits Times*. 12 October.

Tan, Theresa and Melissa Sim. 2008. "Havens away from home." *The Sunday Times.* 17 August.

Turner, Bryan. 2007. "The enclave society: Towards a sociology of immobility." *European Journal of Social Theory* 10(2): 287–303.

Urry, John. 2000. *Sociology beyond Societies: Mobilities for the Twenty-first Century.* London and New York: Routledge.

Wong, Kan Seng. 2007. "Written Answer to Parliamentary Question on (a) how many persons were granted permanent residency in Singapore; (b) what were the 20 most common nationalities of such persons granted permanent residency; and (c) how many Singapore Permanent Residents became Singapore citizens for each of the last ten years." Press Release 21 May 2007. Available online http://www.mha.gov.sg/news_details.aspx?nid=MTAwNw %3d%3d-Y2zskoJuHE0%3d, accessed on 12 August 2009.

Yeoh, Brenda SA. 1996. *Contesting Space: Power Relations and the Urban Built Environment in Colonial Singapore.* Kuala Lumpur: Oxford University Press.

Yeoh, Brenda. 2006. "Bifurcated labour: The unequal incorporation of transmigrants in Singapore." *Tijdschrift voor Economische en Sociale Geografie* (Journal of Economic and Social Geography) 97(1): 26–37.

Yeoh, Brenda, and Shirlena Huang. 2003. "Civil space in a city-state: The place of foreign domestic workers in Singapore," pp. 341–354 in *Migration in the Asia Pacific: Population, Settlement and Citizenship Issues*, eds. R. Iredale, C. Hawksley, and S. Castles. Cheltenham: Edward Elgar.

Yeoh, Brenda, and Natalie Yap. 2008. "'Gateway Singapore': Immigration policies, differential (non)incorporation and identity politics," pp. 177–202 in *Migrants to the Metropolis*, eds. M. Price and L. Benton-Short. Syracuse: Syracuse University Press.

CHAPTER 5

A Transnational Community and Its Impact on Local Power Relations in Urban China: The Case of Beijing's "Koreatown" in the Early 2000s[1]

Kwang-Kyoon YEO

"Wangjing Road" (*wangjingjie*: 望京街), a newly built eight-lane street around the center of the Wangjing area, is one of the symbols of "New Wangjing," a suburb of Beijing. On both sides of the road are rows of giant billboards just above the neatly arranged concrete walk for pedestrians. One sign shows an enlarged colorful picture of the blue sky and white skyscrapers rising behind a meadow with a crystal blue pond. Red Chinese characters over the picture say, "Construct New Beijing, Welcome New Olympics, Develop New Chaoyang, Build New Wangjing" (建设新北京, 迎接新奥运, 发展新潮阳, 打造新望京). Another sign displays white Chinese characters over a bird's eye view of high-rise condos, with the words: "Digital Wangjing, Green Wangjing, Humane Wangjing, Modern Wangjing" (数字望京, 绿色望京, 人文望京, 现代望京). These signs seem to proclaim the future of Beijing, proud host city of the 2008 Olympics, and also the future of Wangjing, a new model community for twenty-first century China. Behind these colorful signs installed by the local government office, however, there are remnants of the old Wangjing, with dilapidated brick houses in abandoned open spaces, some unearthed and others occupied by unattended farmland. These billboards not only declare the future of "New Beijing" and "New Wangjing" but also shroud the residues of the old Mao-era Wangjing.

What makes this new Wangjing different from the old one is not only the collection of high-rise buildings and transnational chain stores like KFC, Walmart, and IKEA but, more significantly, the cultural, economic, and political diversity of the people who live and work in the area. According to the Street Office of Wangjing (*wangjing jiedaobanshichu*: 望京街道办事处), there were an estimated 210,000 people living in the Greater Wangjing area (*dawangjing*:大望京) in 2008. Among them, the office recognized a "floating population" of 50,000, one quarter of the total residents.[2] Unspecified in these figures are South Korean citizens, Han Chinese rural migrants, and ethnic minority migrants. Two decades of reform since the 1980s and the accelerated integration with the global economy since the 1990s have not only changed the economy and skyline of Wangjing, but also have brought people with different political, economic, and cultural backgrounds into it. Embracing these changes, the Street Office quickly added "International Wangjing" to its original motto of "Digital, Humane, Green, and Modern Wangjing" (Han and Lian 2005).

This chapter focuses on Wangjing New Town (*wangjingxincheng*: 望京新城), one of the earliest developments in the overall Wangjing Project, and its transformation into a transnational community in the early 2000s.[3] This particular condo-community has been known as "Koreatown" or "Wangjing Koreatown" (*hanguocheng* or *wangjing hanguocheng*: 韩国城 or 望京韩国城) with its large number of South Korean residents and businesses. Since 2000, the community has witnessed a rapidly growing number of foreign residents. According to an unofficial local estimate in the summer of 2002, there were already at least 5,000 South Korean residents in Wangjing New Town, one third of the total residents of the condo community. Including those who lived around the New Town, the number of South Koreans was estimated at over 10,000 in 2002. However, it was illegal, until September 2003, for any foreigners to live in Wangjing New Town or other local Chinese communities outside "foreigner designated areas." Even with these early legal prohibitions, South Korean expatriates have changed this government model community into a "Koreatown," the largest foreigner concentration in post-Mao Beijing (Ding and Song 2005; Seo 2007). By 2008, an estimated 60,000 South Koreans lived and worked in this area.

Based on participant observation and interviews in Wangjing and Beijing, this chapter explores one critical period of Wangjing's transformation, between 2002 and 2004, when "New Wangjing" was struggling to build its own identity separate from its old farmland image and from other new developments in late socialist China (Zhang 2001: 2–3). Focusing on the Wangjing New Town community (Area Four), I will examine the political, economic, and social conditions that have made a local Chinese community into a "Koreatown." How could these then "illegal" migrants from South Korea live in a local Chinese neighborhood and transform the area into Beijing's largest foreign expatriate community within several years? Why have South Korean citizens moved on such a large scale to urban China in general and to this part of the Chinese capital in particular? How have local Chinese with contesting political, economic, and cultural interests responded to the increasing population and influence of South Korean residents in the area? By examining the formation of Wangjing Koreatown in Beijing from 2002 to 2004, this chapter illuminates not only the process of early settlement of South Korean citizens in urban China, but also the changes in the power dynamics among the local government, the Chinese residents, and the foreign expatriates, all responding to the increasing integration of the Chinese economy into the global economy.

South Korean Residents in Urban China

The current wave of migration of South Korean citizens to urban China started in 1992, with the normalization of diplomatic relations between China and South Korea, and increased throughout the decade. Before 1992, there were few formal political, economic, or cultural exchanges between the two countries.[4] According to statistics from the Korea Trade Investment Promotion Agency (KOTRA), there were already some 112,000 Koreans who visited China in 1993, just one year after normalization. After that, the number increased continuously to 588,000 in 1997. After a sudden drop (to 306,000) in 1998 when the South Korean economy was hit by the Asian Economic Crisis, the number dramatically increased to 824,000 in 1999, almost eight times more than in 1993. In 2000, the number surpassed a million for the first time, rising to 1,345,000 (KOTRA 2008). Although there are no statistics on how many are of these were long-term residents, the patterns seen in these numbers correspond to the time when large numbers of Koreans were noticed in Wangjing by the local Chinese.

What made such a large number of South Koreans decide to come to China, a former enemy state and economically less developed country? Considering there had been virtually no interactions between the two countries for nearly four decades since they fought in the Korean War in 1953, it is important to examine the political, economic, and cultural factors behind the growing migration of South Koreans to China.

Political, Economic, and Cultural Factors for South Korean Migration to Urban China

Around the late 1980s, when the Soviet Bloc was starting to be dismantled, "globalization" (*segyehwa*: 세계화) became a dominant discourse among the South Korean public. Since the end of the Korean War in 1953, the government of South Korea had mostly depended upon the United States and Japan, its two most influential allies during the Cold War, for its political stability and economic development. With signs of the end of the Cold War, however, the Roh Tae Woo regime (1987–1992), the last military dictatorship in modern Korea, anxiously rushed into a series of diplomatic normalization talks with former enemies like the Soviet Union and China, aiming to build its own political legacy. Instead of being labeled as "Red Soviet Union" and "Communist China," these two former enemies were promoted as new frontiers through which to explore the economic and political interests of a "globalized" South Korea. China, with its long political and cultural influence on the Korean peninsula and its future economic potential, has been particularly at the center of this globalization discourse in South Korean society (Kim 2000; Bergsten and Choi 2003).

On 24 August 1992, despite furious opposition from Taiwan (Republic of China) and North Korea (Democratic People's Republic of Korea), the South Korean and Chinese governments signed a normalization treaty ending almost forty years of political hostility and economic vacuum between the two countries. Cautious yet ambitious Korean companies and students ventured into China for new economic and educational opportunities. As China successfully developed its economy during the 1990s, more Koreans visited, some deciding to stay in China to capitalize on the "China Opportunity."[5] Increasing competition in the global market also forced South Korean conglomerates to explore the rapidly growing China market. The economic and social instability in South Korea, created by the "structural adjustment policy" imposed by the International Monetary Fund (IMF) during the Asian Economic Crisis since 1997, has pressured more small- or mid-sized companies to think of the "China Opportunity" as an alternative. Since then, the increasing proportion of South Korean migrants to China has included small business owners or individual investors who are looking for new business opportunities in China after experiencing hardship in their businesses in Korea.

The geographical closeness of Korea and China also contributes to increasing Korean migration to China. It is only a one-and-a-half hour flight between Incheon International Airport (outside Seoul) and Beijing International Airport. Several hours on a ferry can bring Korean tourists and small traders to the east coast of China (Tianjin, Qingdao, Dalian, etc.) from the west coast of Korea (Incheon and Mokpo). In addition to the brief traveling time, there is only one hour's time difference between South Korea and China.[6] That makes it possible for the life of South Korean residents in China to be closely synchronized with the rhythms of daily life in Korea. For example, South Korean residents in Wangjing start the day by watching live Korean morning news and Seoul traffic information on satellite television. They make phone calls to business partners and family members in South Korea without concern about waking them up in the middle of the night. The closeness of space and time zone between South Korea and China has been a major factor contributing to the rapid increase of South Korean migration to China.

A cultural closeness, part real and part imagined, also facilitates the current migration of South Koreans to China. The two countries, despite sharing many cultural customs and moral values from Confucianism, have developed very different social and cultural systems during the forty-year virtual absence of interaction. However, the China imagined in the minds of many South Koreans is still a place with a traditional Confucian culture that permeates the lives of local

Chinese people. This imagination by the South Korean public of contemporary China has made many South Koreans more comfortable in deciding to migrate to China rather than to other countries. This imagined cultural familiarity is often stressed in the sharing of physical appearance, Chinese characters, and basic foods. Early on during their stay in China, most of them discover how different socialist China has become from their imagined traditional China, yet they often respond by continuing their search for evidence of the survival of traditional China in socialist China.

Another important factor for the rapid migration of South Koreans to China is the presence of a large number of Korean Chinese who can function as cultural brokers in China. They are descendants of Korean migrants who moved to northeast China between the late nineteenth century and the mid-1940s. After the founding of the PRC in 1949, Koreans in China became Chinese citizens and were recognized as one of the fifty-five official ethnic minorities in China (Gladney 2004; Park 1996; Iredale et al. 2001, 2003; Rack 2005). According to a recent population survey by the Chinese government, there are about two million Korean Chinese, most of them living in three northeast provinces, Liaoning (辽宁省), Heilongjiang (黑龙江省), and Jilin (吉林省) provinces (Yoo 2002; Park 1996; Suh and Shultz 1990). Until the beginning of the 1980s, few Korean Chinese lived in Beijing as government officials, students, or professors. During the 1990s, however, more Korean Chinese ventured into the capital, in part because of a loosened *hukou* (household registration system) policy and in part because of the increasing economic opportunities with South Korean businesses in Beijing (Rui 2010). With their maintenance of Korean culture (language, food, family values), Korean Chinese have become effective cultural brokers and a labor resource for South Korean businessmen and women who, often without much understanding of Chinese culture or language, have tried to undertake business opportunities in China. For example, there are rows of Korean restaurants, bars, and clothing stores in Wangjing and Wudaokou in Beijing. Mostly funded by South Korean investors, these businesses hire Korean Chinese as managers, waitresses, and clerks. Without these Korean Chinese, the daily operation of the stores would not be possible. Other Korean restaurants owned by Han Chinese in Beijing also often employ a few Korean Chinese who, with their bilingual ability, can serve Korean as well as Chinese customers. Throughout the formation and expansion of Korea-towns in urban China, Korean Chinese have helped South Koreans avoid many obstacles in maintaining their businesses and daily lives in a foreign land. While there are increasing tensions and conflicts between the two groups, it is undeniable that Korean Chinese have been a rich cultural, economic, and emotional resource for the early South Korean expatriates in China.[7]

The difference in living expenses between the two countries has also encouraged South Koreans to venture into urban China. According to the World Bank, South Korea's per capita GNI (Gross National Income) of US $13,980 is more than ten times higher than that of China, only US $1,290 in 2005 (World Bank 2005). Compared to the sky-rocketing housing and education expenses in urban South Korea, Beijing is still considered an inexpensive place to live and raise children. When South Korean expatriates came to China for the first time, many of them focused on business opportunities rather than making China a second home. The low financial risks enabled South Koreans to visit and stay in China with relative comfort. Over time, some have returned to Korea, but others have decided to bring their family members to China. This comparative economic status of South Korea also makes it easier for South Koreans to obtain entry visas to China. The Chinese government does not require extensive financial and legal documents from South Koreans who wish to travel to China. Although there is no practical permanent residence system for long-staying foreigners in China, many South Koreans have become *de facto* migrants who renew their temporary visas without much problem. The low level of economic and legal barriers for South Koreans helps to bring China closer to the minds of Korean citizens than other countries, particularly the United States and Japan.

The Making of Wangjing Koreatown

Since the diplomatic normalization between China and South Korea in 1992, there have been a few places where large numbers of South Korean citizens have lived in Beijing, especially the Asian Games Village (*yayuncun:* 亚运村) and Wudaokou (*wudaokou:* 五道口). Most of these South Koreans were employees (and their families) of large- or middle-scale South Korean companies or Korean students enrolled in Chinese universities. With housing subsidies from their transnational companies, the employees could afford to rent rather expensive housing (at least US $2,500 per month for two or three bedrooms) in foreign gated communities such as the East Changan area (*Dongchangan:* 东长安), the Third Embassy area (*sanlitun:* 三里屯), and the Asian Games Village (Gu and Shen 2003; Wu and Webber 2004). The student groups usually lived either in school dormitories or, with the permission of the school if they had children, in apartments rented from Chinese landlords near the university.

The rest of the South Koreans, mostly private business owners and investors, were scattered in many local Chinese communities. They could neither afford expensive houses in one of the foreigner gated communities nor enroll in universities to live in dormitories. Although it was illegal to live outside foreigner-designated areas or university dormitories, they were often ignored by Chinese authorities and local residents' committees because of their relatively small numbers, indistinguishable appearance from local Chinese, and personal relationships (*guanxi*) with Chinese landlords and local authorities (Kipnis 1997; Yan 1996; Yang 1994). However, at the same time, they were fearful of inspections by the

Chinese police and felt they were being watched by the ubiquitous eyes of the members of the work units (*danwei*: 单位) and the neighborhood committee (*juminweiyuanhui*: 居民委员会). They also felt concern in these relatively poor and crowded residential areas for their young family members. Seen as wealthy foreigners by the locals, some parents worried that their children could be bullied by Chinese children due to language and cultural differences. They even feared that the children might become easy targets of kidnapers seeking ransom.

When Wangjing New Town opened in 1999, it seemed to represent a good alternative for Koreans looking for inexpensive, safe, and familiar living quarters in Beijing. A few Koreans with several years of living experience in China first moved into this new development with their families. Although inconvenient because of the lack of roads, public transportation, shops, and restaurants, Wangjing's new buildings seemed to provide a safe place for these new South Korean tenants and their young children. The lack of daily surveillance by the work unit system also made them feel freer than in other neighborhoods. As the initial settlement of these tenants went well, more South Koreans decided to move into Wangjing. South Koreans were also attracted to Wangjing New Town's emphasis on security with twenty-four-hour guards in each building and electronic entrance keys provided only to the residents. Life in high-rise apartment complexes has become familiar to many South Koreans since the 1970s and was an appealing aspect of Wangjing New Town (Gelézeau 2003). The price, security, and familiar lifestyle in Wangjing New Town thus drew more of these individual and business owners who had young family members.

Wangjing's location was another attraction for South Koreans. Wangjing is very close to the Beijing International Airport – only about a half-hour taxi ride. This was convenient for many South Koreans who often traveled several times a year between China and Korea for business trips or to visit their families in Korea. Wangjing is also close to the Asian Games Village to the west and to the Third Embassy area to the south, both of which are populated with numerous foreigner-oriented businesses, including many with Korean involvement. Unlike the situation for Beijing urbanites whose work places are near the center of the city, Wangjing provided convenient access to these more suburban Korean businesses.

According to some early Korean settlers, it was around early 2000 when a sizable number of Koreans in Wangjing New Town was first noticed. Mr. Kim, a businessman in his late forties, has lived in Beijing since 1994 and now lives in Wangjing New Town. He remembered:

> When I first came to Beijing [1994], there were only a small number of Korean students studying Chinese language or Chinese medicine living near the schools in Wangjing. It was in 2000 when I noticed a large increase of Koreans in this area. It's about that time when the first building of Wangjing New Town started to accommodate its residents.

A Korean business woman who has lived in Beijing since 1996 and moved to Wangjing in 2000 shared her surprise at the large number of South Korean residents in Wangjing:

> My husband came to China in 1992 and lived in Wangfujing [王府井] by renting a room from a retired Chinese couple. Whenever I visited my husband and stayed there, the landlord always warned me not to speak Korean in public and not to dress like a foreigner. There were few foreigners not to mention Koreans [in Beijing]. When I moved to Wangjing in April of 2000, however, it was the opposite. It was difficult not to hang out with other Koreans here. So, it was difficult to make friends with Chinese [because of Koreans].

Wangjing New Town, once ridiculed as a "sleeping city" with its unkept promises and delayed development, suddenly found a new group of tenants. They were willing to pay a comparatively high rent without complaining about the inconvenience of living in an isolated location. Foreigners from South Korea moved into once empty apartment units in the community. Besides filling in apartment buildings, some of them also started to open businesses such as restaurants, beauty salons, and convenience stores in unofficial partnerships with Chinese citizens. Korean Chinese, some of whom had lived in the neighboring Huajiade area before the development of Wangjing, noticed the new opportunities and also started to open restaurants, real estate offices, and travel agencies to serve the new residents and their large disposable incomes. Wangjing New Town, once on the verge of being a failed project, seemed to revive its dream of being a Chinese twenty-first century model community. But this time the dream had an unexpected twist: the crucial importance of South Koreans and Korean Chinese rural migrants to that dream.

The Meanings of the Making of Koreatown: Changing Dynamics of Urban Local Politics

In a larger context, the formation of Koreatown in Beijing is a consequence of the contesting powers between the state and the market in late socialist China. Since 1978, the Chinese Communist government has initiated market reform (Whyte and Parish 1984; Perry and Wong 1985). Encouraged by initial success in the 1980s, the government has accelerated reform with the privatization of state-owned enterprises, the modification of the *hukou* system, and the integration of the Chinese economy into the global economy (Davin 1999; Solinger 1999; Jacka 2005; Zhang 2001; Cook 2006; Wu and Webber 2004; Smart 2004; Smart and Zhang 2006).

On the one hand, these changes have strengthened the competitiveness of the Chinese economy with an increasing supply of cheap labor from rural China and unprecedented levels of foreign investment in urban China. On the other hand, however, these reforms have also increased the diversity of the urban population with large numbers of private entrepreneurs, rural migrants, and foreign workers. As a consequence, the daily influence of the state has been diminished on a diverse city population unbounded by the former *danwei* work unit system (Davis et al. 1995; Lü and Perry 1997; Bray 2005). Witnessing the ineffectiveness of that system on urban populations, the central government has cautiously tried to replace it with the *shequ* management system (Kojima and Kokubun 2002). Based on residential areas, the *shequ* system can be more inclusive of a diverse population that may work in different parts of the city (Tomba 2009).

In an attempt to maintain its dwindling control on city dwellers in a market economy, the state has expanded this *shequ* management system in many new developments in urban China (Bray 2005; Xu 2000). Wangjing New Town is one such development that is managed by the *shequ* system. Unlike the old management system where every resident belonged to a work unit, the community under the *shequ* system consists of several competing organizations representing different political and economic interest groups (WJJD 2002). In Wangjing New Town, for example, there are the Street Office (*wangjing jiedao banshequ*: 望京街道办社区), the Police Station (*paichusuo*: 派出所), the Residents' Committee (*juminweiyuanhui*: 居民委员会), the Management Office (*wangjingxincheng guanlisuo*: 望京新城管理所), and the Apartment Owners' Association (*yezhuyuanhui*: 业主委员会). The Street Office of Wangjing is the highest local governmental authority. Under the supervision of the Street Office, the Residents' Committee functions as the eyes and ears to observe any unusual activities among the residents and report to the higher office. It is also the mouth of the government, responsible for organizing, executing and reviewing most political campaigns. The Police Station in Wangjing works with the Street Office, but is not under its direct supervision. The Wangjing Management Office has responsibility for all resident services and maintenance of the buildings, as well as supervising thousands of security guards and receptionists. Finally, the Owners' Association is an unofficial representative body for those who purchase apartments in Wangjing New Town (Wang 2002).

In order to maintain effective control of the daily life of the residents, these various official and unofficial institutions have to coordinate with each other. In reality, however, they differ from each other – and often compete – based on the different interests that they represent (Fleischer 2005, 2007). When South Koreans started to move into Wangjing New Town in 2000, these organizations had different reactions to the new residents. While the Police Station carried out occasional inspections to find illegal foreign residents, the Residents' Committee and the Owners' Association, including Chinese landlords and investors, worked to protect their lucrative South Korean tenants. The Street Office was also reluctant to enforce the law which would deflate the demand for empty apartments, as this could fuel the already growing discontent among the Chinese residents in Wangjing. These differing welcomes and reactions made possible the continuing concentration of South Koreans in Wangjing New Town.

South Korean migrants in Wangjing have, in turn, had a significant influence on the local economy and, thus, on the dynamics of local power politics. With ample economic capital by local standards, they have filled once empty apartments and rented commercial spaces which were unattractive to the local Chinese at that time. Although it was illegal to live in a local Chinese community until September 2003, they not only opened many businesses with Korean Chinese or Han Chinese partners, but also created many jobs for local Chinese. Given the restrictions of Chinese financial laws, they also had to reinvest most of their profits within China. Many Korean businessmen and women have chosen to reinvest in the Wangjing area itself because of the large number of potential customers, including South Koreans and Korean Chinese. Once considered a "sleeping city" with an uncertain future, Wangjing has been recreated as a dynamic transnational space due, at least in part, to the influx of South Korean people and capital (Xu 2004).

Since 2003, local authorities have tried to recognize the increasing economic influence of South Koreans in Wangjing. For example, the bi-weekly local gazette, *Wangjingshequ* (望京社区), published and distributed by the Street Office, has started to include Korean-language pages. Although mostly focusing on advertisements with a few invited essays by Korean residents, it is still a significant sign of official recognition of the presence of South Korean residents. The local police station also modified its implementation of the foreigner registration rule in Wangjing. According to the rule, all foreign nationals staying in any local Chinese community must register at the local police station within twenty-four hours of arrival. Instead of enforcing this rule, however, the local police station in Wangjing simply encouraged foreigners to register at a convenient time. In 2004, they also opened a satellite police station inside Wangjing New Town where foreigners can register without making a trip to the local police station.[8] Since 2003, the Residents' Committee of Wangjing New Town has also invited South Korean representatives to attend their regular meetings. Although they have no right to vote, five particular South Korean residents who have lived in the community for years have been able to build personal networks with some members of the Residents' Committee.[9] These changes by local government organizations have come from both internal debates and discussions with South Korean residents in the community.

By 2006 Wangjing was well positioned as one of the hottest real estate markets in Beijing, able to compete with communities at the center of the city. For example, the apartment price in new buildings in Wangjing, up to 14,000–18,000 yuan (US$ 2,000–2,600) per square meter, became as expensive as apartments in Xidan, one of busiest shopping districts in the center of the city. Transnational corporations such as Walmart, IKEA, and E-Mart (South Korea) opened branches in Wangjing to attract the growing number of transnational consumers and middle-class Chinese citizens with large disposable incomes. In the spotlight of the 2008 Beijing Summer Olympics and its explosive transformation into a transnational suburb, most people forgot about the struggle of new Wangjing as a "sleeping city" in the early 2000s (Zhang 2006; Ying 2008).

Despite Wangjing's newfound glory and confidence, there were many outsiders unregistered and unrecognized in its official history. Construction workers, security guards, and maids from rural villages built the foundation of new Wangjing, but their contribution to the current development of Wangjing has never been recognized. In a similar sense, the early South Korean residents in Wangjing contributed to turning a "sleeping city" into a prosperous transnational neighborhood. Of course, they did not come to Beijing to build Wangjing and they are also beneficiaries of Wangjing's success and of a generally positive early welcome from residents and government officials working toward that success. Yet, considering the rising national and ethnic tensions among Han Chinese, Korean Chinese, and South Korean citizens – both in China and Korea – this history of Wangjing Koreatown is a useful reminder that transnational and cross-ethnic ties can be mutually beneficial. The Wangjing case suggests that such ties are perhaps most positive when there are common economic goals and flexible urban government structures.

Notes

1. This is an abridged version of an original paper. The fieldwork for the paper was supported by a research grant (2002–2004) from the Weatherhead East Asian Institute of Columbia University and a Doorae scholarship for the social sciences. The revision of the paper was supported by a postdoctoral fellowship from the East Asian Studies Center, Ohio State University, from 2007 to 2008.
2. Wangjing Shequ Public Affair Information Network (望京社区公共服务信息网), October 2008.
3. The official name of Wangjing New Town is Wangjing West Garden; it consists of two high-rise condo communities, Area Three and Area Four, separated by Wangjing Road. Wangjing New Town is a general name for the Greater Wangjing area developed by the Wangjing Project but Wangjing West Garden is often referred to as Wangjing New Town, in part because it is one of the earliest and most symbolic developments by the Project. The fact that the Chinese billboard signs of "Wangjing New Town" are installed at the top of the buildings of the community helps to reinforce this confusion. For this chapter, I focus on Wangjing West Garden Area Four

(*wangjingxiyuan 4 qu*: 望京西园 4 区), which is considered the center of the Korean community in Beijing.

4. There was a very limited degree of informal economic trade between the two countries beginning in 1979 (Cheon 2004).

5. The "China Opportunity" includes all the optimistic discourses which circulated on the development of China in the public sphere of South Korea. For example, considering the future of China, the media often describe it as "the world's largest market" for businessmen and women and "the frontier for the twenty-first century" for students and young Koreans. However, these hopeful narratives are often based on rosy macro-economic projections that ignore the volatile political environment in China and East Asia.

6. Despite the vastness of its territory, the third largest in the world by the most inclusive definitions, the People's Republic of China imposes only one time-zone, Beijing Time, in all its regions.

7. As time moved on, however, there were increasing tensions between South Koreans and Korean Chinese in China. During the 1990s, an increasing number of Korean Chinese accumulated financial capital and business experience either while working with South Korean businesses in China or while working in South Korea as migrant laborers (Yoo 2002; Park 1996; Rui 2010). Separated from their former bosses or starting new business with their own money, Korean Chinese have often found themselves competing with South Korean businesses for a limited market of South Korean and Korean Chinese residents in urban China.

8. From an interview with an executive member of the Beijing office of Korean Association in China (15 March 2006).

9. From an interview with a long-time South Korean resident in Wangjing (22 March 2006).

References

Bergsten, C. Fred, and Inbon Choi. 2003. *The Korean Diaspora in the World Economy.* Washington, DC: Institute for International Economics.

Bray, David. 2005. *Social Space and Governance in Urban China: The Danwei System from Origins to Reform.* Stanford: Stanford University Press.

Cheon, Kyung-Hee. 2004. "South Korea-China Relations, 1979–1992: The Normalization Process in Transnational Perspective." Ph.D. dissertation. University of California, Irvine.

Cook, Ian G. 2006. "Beijing as an 'internationalized metropolis'," pp. 63–84 in *Globalization and the Chinese City*, ed. Fulong Wu. Abingdon: Routledge.

Davin, Delia. 1999. *Internal Migration in Contemporary China.* New York: St. Martin's Press.

Davis, Deborah S., Richard Kraus, Barry Naughton, and Elizabeth Perry, eds. 1995. *Urban Spaces in Contemporary China: The Potential for Autonomy and Community in Post-Mao China.* Woodrow Wilson Center series. Washington, DC.

Ding, Chengri, and Yan Song. 2005. *Emerging Land and Housing Markets in China.* Cambridge, MA: Lincoln Institute of Land Policy.

Fleischer, Friederike. 2005. "Housing China's Emerging Classes: Competing Interests in a Beijing Suburb." Ph.D. dissertation. City University of New York, Anthropology.
———. 2007. "To choose a house means to choose a lifestyle: The consumption of housing and class-structuration in urban China." *City & Society* 19(2): 287–311.
Gelézeau, Valerie. 2003. *Séoul, Ville Géante, Cités Radieuses*. Paris: CNRS Editions.
Gladney, Dru C. 2004. *Dislocating China: Reflections on Muslims, Minorities, and other Subaltern Subjects*. London: C. Hurst.
Gu, Chaolin, and Jianafa Shen. 2003. "Transformation of urban socio-spatial structure in socialist market economies: The case of Beijing." *Habitat International* 27: 107–122.
Han, Zirong [韩子荣] and Lian, Yuming [连玉明]. eds. 2005. 中国社区发展模式: 安全型社区. [Zhongguoshequfazhanmoshi: Anquanxingshequ – Chinese shequ development model: Safety model shequ]. 北京: 中国时代经济出版社. Beijing: Zhongguoshidaijingjichubanshe [China Times Economy Publishing].
Iredale, Robyn R., Bilik Naran, and Fei Guo. 2003. *China's Minorities on the Move: Selected Case Studies*. Armonk: M.E. Sharpe.
Iredale, Robyn R., Bilik Naran, Wang Su, Fei Guo, and Caroline Hoy. 2001. *Contemporary Minority Migration, Education, and Ethnicity in China*. Cheltenham, UK and Northampton, MA: Edward Elgar Publishing.
Jacka, Tamara. 2005. *Rural Women in Urban China: Gender, Migration, and Social Change*. Armonk: M.E. Sharpe.
Kim, Samuel S. 2000. *Korea's Globalization*. New York: Cambridge University Press.
Kipnis, Andrew B. 1997. *Producing Guanxi: Sentiment, Self, and Subculture in a North China Village*. Durham, NC: Duke University Press.
Kojima, Kazuko, and Ryosei Kokubun. 2002. "The 'shequ construction' programme and the Chinese Communist Party." *Copenhagen Journal of Asian Studies* 16: 86–105.
KOTRA (Korea Trade Investment Promotion Agency). 2008. http://www.kotra.co.kr.
Lü, Xiaobo, and Elizabeth J. Perry. 1997. *Danwei: The Changing Chinese Workplace in Historical and Comparative Perspective*. Armonk: M.E. Sharpe.
Park, Heh-Rahn. 1996. "Narratives of migration: From the formation of Korean Chinese nationality in the PRC to the emergence of Korean Chinese migrants in South Korea." Ph.D. dissertation. University of Washington.
Perry, Elizabeth J. and Christine Wong. 1985. *The Political economy of reform in post-Mao China*. Cambridge, MA: Council on East Asian Studies/Harvard University Press.
Rack, Mary. 2005. *Ethnic Distinctions, Local Meanings: Negotiating Cultural Identities in China*. London and Ann Arbor: Pluto Press.
Rui, Dong-Gen. 2010. "Reclamation of ethnicity and reconfiguration of urban ethnic community – focused on associations of Chaoxianzu at Wangjing Korean Town in Beijing." *Journal of North-east Asian Cultures* 25: 531–547.
Seo, Jung Min. 2007. "Interpreting Wangjing: Ordinary foreigners in a globalizing town." *Korean Observer* 38(3): 469–500.
Smart, Alan. 2004. "The Chinese diaspora, foreign investment and economic development in China." *The Review of International Affairs* 3(4): 544–566.
Smart, Alan, and Li Zhang. 2006. "From the mountains and the fields: The urban transition in the anthropology of China." *China Information* 20(3): 481–518.
Solinger, Dorothy J. 1999. *Contesting Citizenship in Urban China: Peasant Migrants, the State, and the Logic of the Market*. Berkeley: University of California Press.

Suh, Dae-Sook, and Edward. J. Shultz. 1990. *Koreans in China*. Honolulu, Hawaii: Center for Korean Studies, University of Hawaii.

Tomba, Luigi. 2009. "Of quality, harmony, and community: Civilization and the middle class in urban China." *Positions* 17: 591–616.

Wang, Hongying [王红英]. 2002. "The Investigation of New Urban Community Autonomous Organization" [新型城市社区自治组织的研究--以国家与社会关系中的业主委员会为例], Renmin University [中国人民大学].

Whyte, Martin King, and William L. Parish. 1984. *Urban Life in Contemporary China*. Chicago: University of Chicago Press.

WJJD [Wangjing Jiedao: 望京街道]. 2002. "望京街道办事处简介" [Wangjingjiedaobanshichujianjie – Summary of the Wangjing Street Office]. http://wjjd.bjchy.gov.cn.

World Bank. 2005. "World Development Indicators Database." World Bank.

Wu, Fulong, and Klaire Webber. 2004. "The rise of 'foreign gated communities' in Beijing: Between economic globalization and local institutions." *Cities* 21: 203–213.

Xu, Dongping [舒东平]. 2004. "Wangjing 'sleeping city' will change in two years" [望京"卧城"两年有望翻身]. *Beijing Youth Daily* [北京青年报], 13 May.

Xu, Youngxiang [徐永祥]. 2000. *Community Development in China* [社区发展论]. Shanghai: Huadong Ligong University Press [华东理工大学出版社].

Yan, Yunxiang. 1996. *The Flow of Gifts: Reciprocity and Social Networks in a Chinese Village*. Stanford: Stanford University Press.

Yang, Mayfair Mei-hui. 1994. *Gifts, Favors, and Banquets: The Art of Social Relationships in China*. Ithaca: Cornell University Press.

Ying, Ding. 2008. "The Korean mergence." *Beijing Review*. 4 March.

Yoo, M.K. 2002. "Between ethnicity and citizenship: Identity of Korean Chinese workers in South Korea" [민족과 국민 사이에서: 한국 체류 조선족들의 정체성 인식에 관하여]. *Journal of Korean Cultural Anthropology* [한국문화인류학] 35: 73–100.

Zhang, Jiaqi [张家齐]. 2006. "Wangjing: A path from 'sleeping city' to 'largest residential shequ in Asia'" [望京 : 从"卧城"到亚洲最大社区的变迁路]. *New Beijing Daily* [新京报]. 11 May.

Zhang, Li. 2001. *Strangers in the City: Reconfigurations of Space, Power, and Social Networks within China's Floating Population*. Stanford: Stanford University Press.

———. 2006. "Contesting spatial modernity in late-socialist China." *Current Anthropology* 47(3): 461–476.

CHAPTER 6

Immigration, Policies, and Civil Society in Hamamatsu, Central Japan

Keiko YAMANAKA

The literature on Japan's civil society has recently grown in volume, broadened in scope, and deepened in analysis. Scholars have discussed the history, social organization, and relationships between the state and Japanese voluntarism in such areas as the environment, consumerism, religion, and social welfare (see Schwartz and Pharr 2003). Transnational migration, immigrants' rights, and multiculturalism are topics that have been added to this list since the late 1980s, when an influx of foreign migrant workers arrived in Japan.[1] Increasing incidents of industrial accidents, unpaid wages, and human rights violations met by undocumented immigrant workers, many of whom were victimized by clandestine traffickers, have triggered civil activism on their behalf (Roberts 2003; Shipper 2008).

With the emergence of a multicultural society, many socially concerned Japanese citizens have seized the opportunity to act on their belief that non-citizen workers are endowed with basic rights to equality and justice regardless of their nationality. These activists believe that the Japanese state has been overly preoccupied with labor shortages, national security, and crime prevention, while neglecting the rights and wellbeing of immigrant workers in Japan. The lack of interest by the state in protecting immigrants' rights gives rise to an unregulated labor market, thereby subjecting immigrants to exploitation and discrimination based on their nationality, ethnicity, gender, and legal status.

The blatant contradictions inherent in economic globalization have elicited resistance from the grassroots worldwide (e.g., Portes 1999). The daily experience of oppression has spurred immigrants, ethnic minorities, and other socially disadvantaged groups to mobilize collective identities with shared interests, leading them to rally for change. Immigrants and citizen activists in Japan are no exception to these processes. By the early 1990s, dedicated citizens throughout Japan had organized numerous groups to assist immigrants in demanding that public agencies relax the rigid administrative rules that prevented immigrants' access to public services (Shipper 2008). In response, local governments of many industrial cities, where large numbers of immigrant populations were concentrated, implemented their own policies designed to alleviate the disadvantages suffered by their immigrant residents in such areas as language, education, health, and housing (Tegtmeyer Pak 2003; Haig 2008).

The Japanese national government has not been unaware of the growing contradictions built into its immigration policies. In addition to rampant discrimination against immigrants, a number of major macro-structural changes, such as low fertility, an aging population, and intensified global competition, have forced governmental agencies to address immigration as critical to any agenda for the next few decades. Since the early 2000s, flurries of study reports and policy proposals by leading ministries, politicians, and research institutes have proposed a variety of new ideas, programs, and plans for immigration reform in response to emerging multiculturalism (Roberts 2008; Yamanaka 2008; Tai 2009).

Recent heightened attention to these issues by national organizations has constituted a major shift and step forward compared to twenty years ago, when local citizen activists and municipal administrators were the only actors responding to immigration problems and multicultural issues (Takao 2003). Despite changing perceptions at the national level, however, at the time of writing the Japanese government has not yet come up with comprehensive immigration policies and visions for a multicultural society that would ensure equality and justice to everyone, regardless of ethnicity, gender, or nationality (Yamanaka 2010).

In this chapter, I will focus on civil society organizations and the actions they have taken on behalf of transnational migrant workers in Hamamatsu City in Shizuoka Prefecture, central Japan, since the early 1990s. Civil society and social movements are important factors influencing political processes of immigration policy making in any highly industrialized country. Other major factors contributing to these processes commonly include economic and demographic changes, the specific history of nation-building in the country, its political structures, media, public opinion, and international relations (Cornelius et al. 2004). Among these factors, civil society serves needs and interests of immigrants in their daily lives that are often systematically ignored by domestic lawmakers and bureaucracies. Civil groups and their social movements represent the voice of immigrants, advocate their rights, and ensure that their viewpoints are included in policy making processes.

Such political processes on behalf of immigrants usually begin with an incident in a local setting in which a lack of citizenship has generated rigid barriers to immigrants, preventing them from solving problems on their own. With few cultural and institutional resources, immigrants in need often seek assistance from established organizations known for their charity, such as the Catholic church, or volunteers, such as social workers. In response, a group of concerned citizens often forms an informal association to serve the needs of unprotected immigrants more systematically and effectively than could any individual.

This process of organizing a civic association for specific public goals is shaped heavily by two major sociopolitical factors. At the national level, governmental rules concerning the formation of civic organizations determine their legal status, regulations, and privileges. At the local level, community support for the agendas of civil groups contributes substantially to their success in achieving their goals. I will describe the formation, organization, and activities of three pro-immigrant groups in Hamamatsu in order to demonstrate how the governmental rules concerning civic groups on the one hand, and the presence or absence of local support for the agendas of the three organizations on the other, influence their chances for success in achieving their goals.

This chapter comprises four sections: (1) a theoretical discussion of the characteristics of Japanese civil society; (2) a description of Japan's immigration policies regarding unskilled immigrant workers; (3) a discussion of the impact of the arrival of immigrant workers in Hamamatsu and the local government's response to it; and (4) analyses of three grassroots citizens' groups that support immigrants in Hamamatsu.

Japan's Civil Society: "Members without Advocacy"

According to Pekkanen (2006), Japanese civil society constitutes a dual structure. It has a myriad of small local groups that help citizens develop social capital. (Some examples are Neighborhood Associations, Women's Clubs, and Children's Clubs, all of which are aimed at self-help, communication, and socialization.) On the other hand, Japan lacks independent professionalized organizations that advocate a cause, conduct research, or campaign for policy change. (Analogous examples of this type of civil society to be found in the West include Amnesty International, Greenpeace, and the American Association of Retired Persons.) In Japan, lacking such professionalized national organizations that specialize in mobilizing resources for social change, civil society constitutes what Pekkanen (2004a: 243) calls "members without advocacy."

The dual nature of Japan's civil society finds its origin in the developmental state politics of the Meiji period (1868–1912). In their efforts to build a modern nation, national leaders of the time forcefully promoted industrialization and militarization (rich nation, strong army). Under this policy, the government placed strict limits on the formation of civil society groups (Pekkanen 2004a: 229–230). The legacy of governmental control of citizen's public activities continued into the post-WWII period. Successive conservative governments also maintained strict regulations, although they relaxed restrictions for social welfare, religious, medical, and educational organizations. Laws governing formal civil groups granted the bureaucracy enormous power to monitor and sanction the formation of groups, and their financial and public activities (Pekkanen 2004b: 369). As a result, despite Japan's rapid economic development, the growth of civil society remained slow throughout the postwar period.

Major change came in 1998 when parliament passed the "Special Non-Profit Activities Law" (the NPO Law). That law simplified application procedures for members of citizens' groups to obtain NPO legal-person status, thus broadening the range of their civil activities. Several years later, revisions of the tax code enabled specified categories of groups to extend tax benefits to charitable contributors (Pekkanen 2004b). Official legal status enabled NPOs to enjoy such privileges as owning offices, telephones, and bank accounts. Encouraged by these legal changes, by 2004 some 16,000 legal NPOs had emerged. This greatly invigorated Japanese civil society (Kingston 2004: 75).

The 1998 NPO Law has, however, retained bureaucratic power over NPO groups' autonomy and financial independence, enabling the overseeing agency to monitor and punish any group that does not follow the agency's guidance. Fearing interference by the state, many independent groups have chosen to remain informal, without the benefit of legal NPO status. At the national level, a dearth of large professionalized advocacy organizations has prevented Japan's civil society from generating a dynamic and responsive public discourse in support of their agenda.

The dual structure of Japan's civil society shapes social and political contexts against which numerous pro-immigrant groups must struggle for survival. As the examples of Hamamatsu citizens' groups will show (see below), most groups acting on behalf of immigrants in Japan are small and lack adequate funding, manpower, and facilities to expand their activities (Shipper 2008). At the national level, the absence of highly professionalized advocacy organizations greatly hinders the development of effective nation-wide campaigns for immigrant rights (Milly 2006). These organizational and structural difficulties force Japan's civil society to endure an uphill battle in challenging policy makers who prioritize border control and labor supply over the human rights of immigrant workers (Yamanaka 2010).

Japan's Immigration Policies and Unskilled Workers

In 1990 the Japanese government revised its Immigration Control and Refugee Recognition Law to institute three major changes affecting unskilled labor. First, the law confirmed the state's stance against the employment of unskilled foreigners, defining such employment as a criminal offense. Second, the same law created a new "long-term residence visa" category for foreign nationals of Japanese ancestry (*Nikkeijin*), up to the third generation, to enter and reside in the country with few restrictions. Third, the law also created a new visa category for "industrial trainees." Accordingly, in the same year, a governmental decree instituted a new "Industrial Trainee System" (ITS, *Sangyo Kenshusei Seido*). This permitted foreign trainees to receive "on-the-job training" for two years in companies with fewer than fifty employees. Because by definition trainees were not regular workers, they were conventionally paid less than market wages and were excluded from protection by the Labor Standards Law (Kawakami 2006).[2] In 1993, the government enacted the "Technical and Practical Trainee System" (TPTS, *Gino Jisshusei Seido*), by which, upon completion of one year's training, trainees would engage for a second year in "job performance," with the protection of the "Labor Standards Law." In 1997, the period of technical and practical training was extended to two years.

These reforms in immigration policy, from the early to mid-1990s, resulted in a situation that contradicted Japan's law prohibiting employment of unskilled foreigners (Tsuda and Cornelius 2004). After the reforms, Japan's foreign population, including foreigners who had arrived before 1990 (most of whom were former colonial citizens and their descendants from the Korean Peninsula) grew rapidly each year, surpassing two million by 2005. They accounted for 1.57 percent of the nation's population, which included a diverse collection of both skilled and unskilled foreigners who entered and worked under a variety of constraints and conditions for various periods of time.

Of all categories of foreigners, the ones of greatest concern to government and industry were unskilled workers. These immigrants arrived under a variety of non-working visas, including *Nikkeijin*, industrial trainees, and "illegal" visa-overstayers. Due to Japan's sluggish economy throughout the 1990s and 2000s, labor demands for foreign workers have fluctuated greatly. However, numbers of *Nikkeijin* (mostly from Brazil and many fewer from Peru) continued to increase, surpassing 300,000 in the year 2000 and reaching 376,000 by the end of 2007 (see Figure 6.1). In the fall of 2008, the global economic recession hit *Nikkeijin* workers hard, sharply plunging the number of *Nikkeijin* to 325,000 in 2009 and to 285,000 in 2010.

In sharp contrast, the number of unauthorized workers decreased steadily during the same period, especially after 2001, the year in which the terrorist attack on New York's World Trade Center occurred. Thereafter, Japanese authorities strengthened law enforcement against unauthorized residents, as a result of which their numbers dwindled from 252,000 in 2000 to 171,000 in 2007. The economic recession since the fall of 2008 also affected the unauthorized workers, causing a steep decline in their numbers to 78,000 in 2010. During the same period, there was a rapid increase in the number of industrial trainees in Japan, almost doubling from 36,000 in 2000 to 88,000 in 2007. Because the trainees' employers often allowed them to engage in actual job performance, immigrant rights advocates called industrial trainees "workers in disguise" (Kawakami 2006).

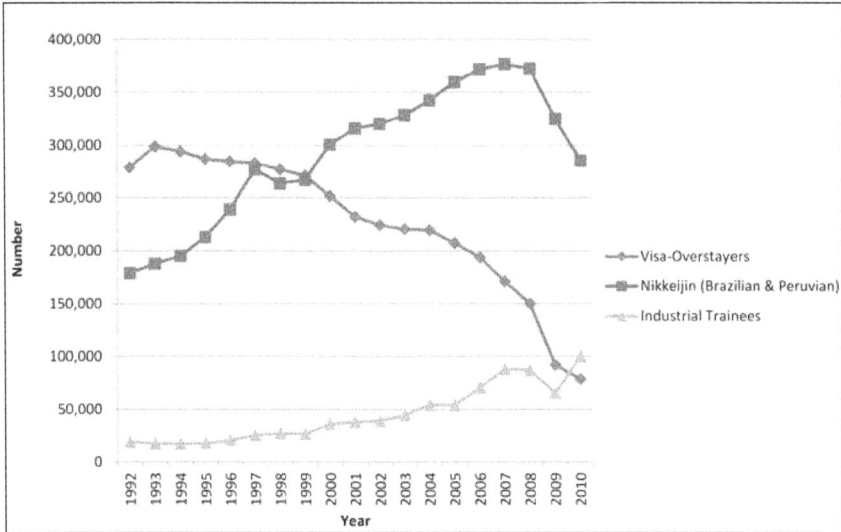

Figure 6.1 • Changes in Numbers of Japan's Unskilled Foreign Workers

Hamamatsu City's Responses to Transnational Immigration

As people of Japanese ancestry, *Nikkeijin* are distinguished from the other two categories of unskilled workers (industrial trainees and unauthorized workers) by their long-term resident status. Once the 1990 Revised Law legitimized the *Nikkeijin* as residents and workers, a demand for labor in manufacturing industries shunned by Japanese drew them to Japan in large numbers. Over the past two decades, they have settled with their families in the Kanto and Tokai Regions, both of which have high concentrations of manufacturing industries.

The Kanto Region comprises the capital, Tokyo, and its surrounding six prefectures: Ibaragi, Tochigi, Gunma, Saitama, Chiba, and Kanagawa. In 1997, these seven administrative units accounted for 34 percent of the registered Brazilians and Peruvians in the nation (Japan Immigration Association 1998). The Tokai Region, located in central Japan west of the Kanto Region, includes six prefectures: Aichi, Gifu, Mie, Nagano, Shizuoka, and Yamanashi. In 1997, these six prefectures accounted for 47 percent of the total *Nikkeijin* population in Japan.

Hamamatsu, a city of more than 700,000, and its neighboring cities Kosai and Iwata in western Shizuoka Prefecture, are the headquarters of several major automobile, motorcycle, and musical instrument corporations, including Suzuki, Yamaha, and Honda. Thousands of subcontractors supply the parts to be assembled by these corporations to become vehicles and musical instruments.[3] Contiguous and to the west of these cities lie Toyohashi, a city of 350,000, and its neighbors Toyokawa, Toyota, and others in the eastern part of adjacent Aichi Prefecture along the Pacific Coast.

Immigrant workers, both documented and undocumented, find this area (Tokai) attractive because of chronic labor shortages among small-scale subcontractors. In addition, the mild climate of Tokai and easy access to its major cities draw large numbers of immigrant workers, including industrial trainees and unauthorized employees.[4] In 2004, five of Tokai's six prefectures (excluding Yamanashi) entered the list of the ten prefectures with the largest numbers of industrial trainees (Kawakami 2006: 77). In the same year, all six prefectures of the Tokai Region entered the list of the top fifteen prefectures where arrested immigrants were employed at the time of arrest (Japan Immigration Association 2006: 47).

Since the beginning of the 1990s, Hamamatsu has witnessed a rapid increase in the population of *Nikkeijin* from Brazil and Peru (Yamanaka 2003a). In March 1987, there were only 10 registered Brazilians living in Hamamatsu. Five years later, in March 1992, the city's Brazilian population multiplied by 613 times to 6,132 (Hamamatsu City 1993: 29). During the same period, the Peruvian population increased from 1 to 698. By the end of 2006, a total of 21,702 (19,402 Brazilians and 2,300 Peruvians) registered as residents in Hamamatsu, accounting for 67 percent of the city's foreign population (Japan Immigration Association 2007: 111).

Such an increase in the *Nikkeijin* population has posed severe difficulties for Hamamatsu's local government. In earlier years, administrators attempted to overcome linguistic and cultural gaps by providing consultation and information on public services in Portuguese and Spanish (Tegtmeyer Pak 2003). However, increasing incidents of cultural friction between immigrants and citizens, aggravated by frequent media reports of ethnic discrimination and high drop-out rates for immigrant children in high school, led the local government to focus on institutional problems (Yamanaka 2003b, 2003c). By 2000, the city had established a Foreign Citizens Forum as a board advisory to the Mayor. It had also organized Japanese language classes for Brazilian children who were not enrolled in school and a bilingual school that instructed them in both Japanese and Portuguese (Yamanaka 2003b, 2006).[5]

Despite the good intentions of city administrators, the task of meeting every need of a large and diverse immigrant population was overwhelming. By the early 1990s, there had been many incidents of immigrant workers who were seriously injured, became sick, or even died. In other cases, immigrant employees suddenly lost their jobs without receiving the wages they had earned. Legally unprotected, some victims brought their cases to Japanese citizens known for their sympathy and community service. These citizens often organized an informal association in order to assist immigrants more systematically and effectively, while addressing the root causes of their troubles.

In the following section, I discuss three such organizations in Hamamatsu that represent the voices of immigrants in the areas of employment, human rights, and health.

Three Citizens' Groups in Support of Immigrants

Hamamatsu Overseas Laborers Solidarity (Herusu no Kai)

In November 1989, an incident in which a Filipino industrial trainee killed her newborn baby shook the conscience of some Hamamatsu citizens. In response, Hamamatsu Overseas Laborers Solidarity (called *Herusu no kai*, hereafter *Herusu*) was organized in July 1990 (*Herusu no Kai* Newsletter 1990). The leading members numbered ten, including religious workers, social workers, labor unionists, teachers, and other professionals. Based in a Catholic church in the city, this group of citizen volunteers accepted telephone calls from immigrant workers who needed help to solve their problems, regardless of their nationality or legal status. Because the problems often involved clients with unauthorized status, serious injuries, illnesses, or unscrupulous employers, the problems were often complicated and time consuming.

Because of its conscientious work, *Herusu* soon earned a favorable reputation among immigrant workers, which kept the members busy. However, the group faced severe problems of its own. One was shortage of manpower. There were only a handful of members with expert knowledge who could function during weekdays. The group also suffered from a lack of funding. As an independent volunteer group, the organization relied heavily on donations and annual member fees. Consequently, the group was never able to establish its own office or even to have a telephone line, but borrowed these from other organizations. In 2008, after almost twenty years, the active members were aging or were otherwise unavailable, so that their number dwindled. In 2007, its total cash flow (annual income and expenses) amounted to less than 300,000 yen ($2,500), with an emergency reserve fund of 400,000 yen ($3,333) (*Herusu no Kai* News Letter 2008a). Yet despite the small-scale nature of its operation, *Herusu* has been instrumental in the creation of other similar citizens' groups that are dedicated to the rights of immigrant workers.

Medical Aid for Foreigners (MAF)

The Medical Aid for Foreigners organization began its first annual medical checkup program in October 1996. Dr. T., a heart surgeon and supporter of *Herusu*, became well aware of the complex problems faced by uninsured patients when a young Nepali man sought help for an illness that would require costly heart surgery and lengthy post-operative treatment (Yamanaka 2005b). The patient was an unauthorized visa overstayer with no access to any kind of health care plan. After many discussions with citizen activists and the local Nepalese community, Dr. T. operated on the patient. His surgery was successful but it left unpaid a total of 6 million yen ($54,000). This difficult experience prompted Dr. T. and *Herusu* to recruit hundreds of citizen volunteers in order to organize an annual medical checkup program for uninsured immigrants.

With the sponsorship of a Hamamatsu Rotary Club and other charity-minded organizations, in October 1996 the "First Annual Free Medical Checkup for Foreigners" took place in a public hall near the Hamamatsu central train station. Despite the absence of medical facilities at that location, and with no experience of such services, 209 volunteers with diverse capacities (doctors, dentists, nurses, technicians, and interpreters in many languages) successfully carried out the medical screening of 259 foreigners, both adults and children, authorized and unauthorized.

Since then, MAF has continued its annual checkup program every October. Amid the controversy regarding immigrants' access to inexpensive health care at both national and local levels (see below), MAF's contribution to immigrant health has attracted widespread publicity in the local and Tokai media. As a result, each year MAF has expanded its activities by adding new medical services and specialties for testing, more professionals, volunteers, and sponsors, all serving many more uninsured immigrants, the majority of whom are increasingly *Nikkeijin* families.

Encouraged by its success, in 2005 MAF expanded its annual health checkup to *Nikkeijin* schoolchildren in Brazilian and Peruvian schools (which are seriously underfunded). MAF launched the children's program in response to the fact that many of the children lacked basic health care because their immigrant parents lacked access to good health care. Between August and November 2008, sixteen physicians with fifteen interpreters volunteered to examine a total of 850 children in six Brazilian and Peruvian schools (*Herusu no Kai* 2008b). These checkups were made possible through donations by the city's two medical testing laboratories.

Despite its success, MAF has faced severe problems in serving uninsured foreigners, particularly in the lack of financial resources. As a voluntary association, it has not received public subsidies. Instead, it has had to rely on private donations to cover all the expenses of the medical checkup program, and on a large number of volunteers to carry out all of the related tasks. Another problem has been that of responses of examinees to the medical services. After each checkup, MAF has reported the results to each examinee. Over the years, MAF has learned that a majority of the examinees do not follow up on the treatment indicated by the results of their examinations. This has been primarily because of the difficulties immigrant workers face in taking time off from work and the absence of insurance that could pay for the treatment.

In 2008, for the first time in its twelve-year history, MAF failed to offer an annual checkup. This was because Dr. T., the charismatic engine of the group, had a personal health problem which prevented him from participating. Furthermore, the general hospital that had hosted the program during the previous few years was unable to provide the space to accommodate it. According to a *Herusu no Kai* Newsletter (2009), that year's hiatus was expected to be temporary – and indeed MAF resumed the program the following year.

Grupo Justiça e Paz

Lack of access to inexpensive health care has been a source of serious concern among immigrant populations, as well as community activists, as has been described above. This has been because the volume of uninsured immigrants in Hamamatsu has increased rapidly since 1992, when the Ministry of Health and Welfare issued a decree prohibiting immigrant workers from enrolling in the National Health Insurance Program (NHIP) (Roth 2002). After the Hamamatsu administration adopted the Ministry's decree, Ms. Y., a social worker and former member of *Herusu*, recognized the increasing pain and distress felt by many uninsured immigrants in the city (Yamanaka 2005b). Father H., the Brazilian *Nikkeijin* Catholic priest who had been serving the city's *Nikkeijin* community, was also deeply concerned about the absence of health insurance among his compatriots.

In March 1997, Ms. Y. and Father H. and his followers organized the *Grupo Justiça e Paz* (Group of Justice and Peace, hereafter *Grupo*) and initiated a public campaign urging the Hamamatsu municipal government and the Shizuoka Prefectural government, and the Assembly of each of them, to expand membership in the NHIP to include the city's legal foreign residents. In its petition, addressed to the head of each of these organizations, *Grupo* discussed the difficulties experienced by uninsured immigrant patients and demanded that: (1) the city government create a new health insurance plan designed specifically for immigrant worker populations; (2) the prefectural government launch a medical emergency relief fund for uninsured immigrants; and (3) the city government establish a new department responsible for providing immigrants with public services.

Grupo's proposal met with indifferent, sometimes hostile, responses from the local governments of Hamamatsu and Shizuoka Prefecture and their Assemblies. All of them replied to *Grupo* that their policies would follow the national government's guidance, which was to bar immigrant workers from membership in the NHIP. With regard to the remaining demands, local policy makers made it clear that they had no intention of implementing any part of *Grupo*'s proposal. Such a flat rejection by local governments and their assemblies clearly reflected the fact that non-citizens are not allowed to vote, so the former had no motive to respond to *Grupo*'s proposal. It also mirrored the fact that Hamamatsu relies heavily on tax revenues from the big manufacturing corporations that dominate the local labor market. Therefore, local administrators and politicians were more concerned with supplying labor to them than with protecting the rights of the migrants who supply the labor.

Despite the official rejections, *Grupo* continued its campaign for the next few months by collecting 5,500 signatures from Hamamatsu citizens. With little sympathy from local administrators and politicians, the group ended its campaign with few achievements. *Grupo*'s efforts, however, had made Hamamatsu citizens widely aware of the lack of health care insurance for immigrant workers in the city.

Conclusion

The three examples of citizens' voluntary associations that acted in support of immigrants in Hamamatsu – *Herusu no Kai*, Medical Aid for Foreigners, and *Grupo Justiça e Paz* – share a number of organizational characteristics. All three are informal, small, and local. Each operates on a meager budget while valuing its independence. As a result of these financial and political circumstances, none of them has applied for the legal NPO status that would enable them to improve their facilities and enhance their public image. The meager budget has also forced each group to rely heavily on private donations and the personal resources of dedicated members, preventing each from becoming a viable and institutionalized association for the advocacy of immigration policy change.

While sharing many similarities, the three groups differ widely in their orientations, goals, and ability to achieve their goals. Since its beginning, *Herusu no Kai* has been concerned about human rights for immigrant workers and for their overall wellbeing. The high proportion of Catholics in the membership probably accounts for its humanist inclination and the strong activist commitment of its long-term members. Medical Aid for Foreigners (MAF) has relied heavily on the professional resources and networks of Dr. T. and members of *Herusu* for carrying out the annual checkup program for more than ten years. The goal of MAF is to remedy inequality in health care. As such, it appeals to a wide range of local citizens, enabling the group to expand its scale of operation year after year. In contrast to these two groups (*Herusu* and MAF) that have served the urgent humanitarian needs of migrants, the *Grupo Justiça e Paz* has addressed the longer-term political goals of enhancing the rights of immigrants. As mentioned above, with little support from local administrators and politicians, *Grupo*'s campaigns have achieved few successes and the group soon disbanded.

In conclusion, these accounts of three Hamamatsu grassroots citizens' groups demonstrate the results of the strict regulatory framework of Japan's civil society (Pekkanen 2006: 16–19). That framework severely constrains the administrative and financial capability of civic groups to develop firm and permanent resources for growth and expansion. Transnational migration and the rights of the migrants are recent additions to the agenda of Japan's civil society. Such unfamiliar goals have not yet garnered strong support from local and national policy makers, who value economic development over human rights for non-citizens. How and to what extent Japanese grassroots initiatives are able to influence immigration policy toward humanitarian and egalitarian goals will affect profoundly Japan's commitment to the realization of a true democracy and a multiethnic society with increasingly diverse needs.

Notes

1. Prior to the arrival of transnational immigrants in the late 1980s, 700,000 Koreans and 200,000 Chinese lived in Japan as permanent residents. The majority of these immigrant populations were former colonial citizens and their descendants who had arrived in Japan before and during WWII. For literature on the circumstances of the "oldcomer" populations, see Lie (2001, 2008), and Chung (2010).
2. The Labor Standards Law is applied to all workers regardless of nationality.
3. Beginning in 1992, using interviews, survey questionnaires and participatory observations, I conducted research on immigration and community formation among Brazilian *Nikkeijin* populations in Hamamatsu, Shizuoka Prefecture. The research focused on *Nikkeijin* migratory processes, employment and community activities, and local governments' policies regarding their settlement in the city. The data upon which this chapter is based were collected between the mid-1990s and the mid-2000s.
4. For studies of a group of unauthorized immigrant workers in Tokai, see Yamanaka (2000, 2005a).
5. Within Brazilian communities in the city, immigrants also formed numerous groups and clubs for hobbies, sports, leisure, and entertainment. Most of these organizations were informal, intended to create common interests and expand social networks. Some of them grew to pool their resources for collective goals. For an example of such group activities among a group of Brazilian parents whose children were enrolled in one public school, see Yamanaka (2003b, 2006).

References

Chung, Erin Aeran. 2010. *Immigration and Citizenship in Japan*. Cambridge: Cambridge University Press.

Cornelius, Wayne A., Takeyuki Tsuda, Philip L. Martin and James F. Hollifield, eds. 2004. *Controlling Immigration: A Global Perspective*. Second Edition. Stanford: Stanford University Press.

Haig, Ken. 2008. "National Aliens, Local Citizens: The Politics of Immigrant Integration in Japan in a Comparative Perspective." Ph.D. dissertation, Department of Political Science, University of California, Berkeley.

Hamamatsu City. 1993. *Hamamatsu-shi ni okeru Gaikokujin no Seikatsu Jittai, Ishiki Chosa* [Survey on life facts and consciousness of foreign residents in Hamamatsu City]. Hamamatsu: Hamamatsu-shi Kikakubu, Kokusai Koryushitsu.

Herusu no Kai. 1990. *Herusu no Kai Newsletter.* July (1). Hamamatsu: Gaikokujin Rodosha to tomoni Ikiru Kai [Hamamatsu Overseas Laborers Solidarity].

———. 2008a. *Herusu no Kai Newsletter.* August (160). Hamamatsu: Gaikokujin Rodosha to tomoni Ikiru Kai.

———. 2008b. *Herusu no Kai Newsletter.* December (161). Hamamatsu: Gaikokujin Rodosha to tomoni Ikiru Kai.

———. 2009. *Herusu no Kai Newsletter.* March (162). Hamamatsu: Gaikokujin Rodosha to tomoni Ikiru Kai.

Japan Immigration Association. 1998. *Zairyu Gaikokujin Tokei, Heisei 10 nendoban* [Foreign resident statistics, 1998]. Tokyo: Japan Immigration Association.

———. 2006. *Shutsunyukoku Kanri Kankei Tokei Gaiyo, Heisei 17 nendoban* [Statistics on immigration control, 2005]. Tokyo: Japan Immigration Association.

———. 2007. *Zairyu Gaikokujin Tokei, Heisei 18 nendoban* [Foreign resident statistics, 2006]. Tokyo: Japan Immigration Association.

Japanese Ministry of Justice. 1993 to 2011. "Toroku Gaikokujin Tokei" [Registered foreigners statistics]. http://www.moj.go.jp/nyuukokukanri/kouhou/nyukan_index.html.

Kawakami, Sonoko. 2006. "Suji kara miru Gaikokujin Kenshusei, Gino Jisshusei" [Examination of statistics on foreign trainees and practical trainees]. In Gaikokujin Kenshusei Network, ed. *Gaikokujin Kenshusei: Jikyu 300 yen no Rodosha* [Foreign trainees: workers paid 300 yen per hour]. Tokyo: Akashi Shoten.

Kingston, Jeff. 2004. *Japan's Quiet Transformation: Social Change and Civil Society in the Twenty-First Century.* London: RoutledgeCurzon.

Lie, John. 2001. *Multi-Ethnic Japan.* Cambridge: Harvard University Press.

———. 2008. *Zainichi (Koreans in Japan): Diasporic Nationalism and Postcolonial Identity.* Berkeley: University of California Press.

Milly, Deborah J. 2006. "Policy advocacy for foreign residents in Japan," pp. 123–151 in *Local Citizenship in Recent Countries of Immigration: Japan in Comparative Perspective,* ed. Takeyuki Tsuda. Lanham, MD: Lexington Books.

Pekkanen, Robert. 2004a. "Japan: Social capital without advocacy," pp. 223–255 in *Civil Society and Political Change in Asia: Expanding and Contracting Democratic Space,* ed. M. Alagappa. Stanford: Stanford University Press.

———. 2004b. "After the developmental state: Civil society in Japan." *Journal of East Asia Studies* 4(3): 363-388.

———. 2006. *Japan's Dual Civil Society: Members Without Advocates.* Stanford: Stanford University Press.

Portes, Alejandro. 1999. "Conclusion: Towards a new world - the origin and effects of transnational activities." *Ethnic and Racial Studies* 22(2): 463–477.

Roberts, Glenda S. 2003. "NGO support for migrant labor in Japan," pp. 275–300 in *Japan and Global Migration: Foreign Workers and the Advent of a Multicultural Society,* eds. Mike Douglass and Glenda S. Roberts. Honolulu: University of Hawai'i Press.

———. 2008. "Immigration policy: Frameworks and challenges," pp. 765–779 in *The Demographic Challenges: A Handbook about Japan,* eds. Florian Coulmas, Harald Conrad, Annette Schad-Seifert, and Gabriele Vogt. Leiden: Brill.

Roth, Joshua. 2002. *Brokered Homeland: Japanese Brazilian Migrants in Japan*. Ithaca, NY: Cornell University Press.

Schwartz, Frank J. and Susan Pharr, eds. 2003. *The State of Civil Society in Japan*. Cambridge: University of Cambridge Press.

Shipper, Apichai W. 2008. *Fighting for Foreigners: Immigration and Its Impact on Japanese Democracy*. Ithaca, NY: Cornell University Press.

Tai, Eika. 2009. "Japanese immigration policy at a turning point." *Asian and Pacific Migration Journal* 18(3): 315–344.

Takao, Yasuo. 2003. "Foreigners' rights in Japan: Beneficiaries to participants." *Asian Survey* 43 (3): 527–552.

Tegtmeyer Pak, Katherine. 2003. "Foreigners are local citizens, too: Local governments respond to international migration in Japan," pp. 244–274 in *Japan and Global Migration: Foreign Workers and the Advent of a Multicultural Society*, eds. Mike Douglass and Glenda S. Roberts. Honolulu: University of Hawai'i Press.

Tsuda, Takeyuki and Wayne A. Cornelius. 2004. "Japan: Government policy, immigrant reality," pp. 439–478 in *Controlling Immigration: A Global Perspective*, eds. Wayne. A. Cornelius, Takeyuki Tsuda, Philip L. Martin, and James F. Hollifield. Second Edition. Stanford: Stanford University Press.

Yamanaka, Keiko. 2000. "Nepalese labour migration to Japan: From global warriors to global workers." *Ethnic and Racial Studies* 23(1): 62–93.

———. 2003a. "'I will go home, but when?' Labor migration and circular diaspora formation by Japanese Brazilians in Japan," pp. 123–152 in *Japan and Global Migration: Foreign Workers and the Advent of a Multicultural Society*, eds. Mike Douglass and Glenda S. Roberts. Honolulu: University of Hawai'i Press.

———. 2003b. "Feminized migration, community activism and grassroots transnationalization in Japan." *Asian and Pacific Migration Journal* 12(1-2): 155–187.

———. 2003c. "A Breakthrough for ethnic minority rights in Japan: Ana Bortz's courageous challenge," pp. 231–259 in *Crossing Borders and Shifting Boundaries*, eds. Mirjana Morokvasic-Müller, Umut Erel, and Kyoko Shinozaki. Opladen, Germany: Leske+Budrich.

———. 2005a. "Changing family structures of Nepali transmigrants in Japan: Split-households and dual-wage earners." *Global Networks: A Journal of Transnational Affairs* 5(4): 337–358.

———. 2005b. "Migration, differential access to health services and civil society's responses in Japan," pp. 141–160 in *Migration and Health in Asia*, eds. Santosh Jatrana, Mika Toyota, and Brenda S.A. Yeoh. London: Routledge.

———. 2006. "Immigrant incorporation and women's community activities in Japan: Local NGOs and public education for immigrant children," pp. 97–117 in *Local Citizenship in Recent Countries of Immigration: Japan in Comparative Perspective*, ed. Takeyuki Tsuda. Lanham, MD: Lexington Books.

———. 2008. "Immigration, population and multiculturalism in Japan." Woodrow Wilson International Center for Scholars, *Asia Program Special Report* 141 (July): 11–28.

———. 2010. "Civil society and social movements for immigrant rights in Japan and South Korea: Convergence and divergence in unskilled immigration policy." *Korea Observer* 41(4): 615–647.

Part II:
Family, Gender, Lifestyle, and Culture

CHAPTER 7

Multiple Narratives on Migration in Vietnam and Their Methodological Implications

Hy V. LUONG

Since the end of the command economy with its system of subsidized food rationing in cities, rural-to-urban migration in Vietnam has quickly accelerated. According to official censuses, the net migration inflow to Hồ Chí Minh City, the largest urban center and the biggest magnet for migrants all over Vietnam, increased from 14,872 a year from 1984 to 1989, to about 100,000 a year in the 1989–1999 period, and over 200,000 a year from 1999 to 2004 (see Luong 2009a). By 2004, those who were classified as migrants numbered 1.6 million and officially made up 30 percent of the urban population in Hồ Chí Minh City.[1] The increasing rural-to-urban migration in Vietnam is a part of the global trend of generally greater mobility both within and across national boundaries.

Field research on migration tends to be carried out either with migrants or with their staying-behind relatives. Despite the increasingly shared understanding that multi-site fieldwork, conducted in both sending and receiving areas, will provide a fuller understanding of migration as well as many other phenomena (see Marcus 1995: 105-110), multi-site fieldwork in both sending and receiving areas is not frequently undertaken because it involves more complex research logistics. This chapter, based upon a multi-site study of rural-to-urban migration in Vietnam, seeks to highlight the methodological value of multi-site field research on migration through an analysis of the multiplicity of narratives on migration by both migrants in migrant-receiving areas and their family members staying behind in rural communities. In the majority of cases, narratives by migrants and their family members on the circumstances and motives for migration are partially divergent. My analysis starts with these partially divergent narratives because they constitute the majority of cases in our sample and because of their methodological significance for the study of migration. On another level, however, the partially divergent narratives are underlain by a shared model and moral framework for family life. It is a model of filial children and caring parents for whom separation through migration is undesirable. I would suggest that studies of migration, no matter whether internal or international, would be methodologically enriched by research at both the sending and receiving ends, as well as conceptually by paying closer attention not only to the political economy of migration but also to the moral framework within which are embedded migration decisions and negotiation among family members on these decisions.

Rural Migration to Hồ Chí Minh City: An Overview

Research on internal migration in Vietnam tends to be conducted either with migrants (e.g., Vietnam-GSO and UNFPA 2005), or occasionally with their family members in the sending communities (e.g., Tessier 2002, 2003). To date, there are only two studies on internal migration in Vietnam that involve research in both sending and receiving communities (Vũ Thị Hồng, Gubry, and Lê Văn Thành 2003; Nguyễn Thế Nghĩa, Mặc Đường and Nguyễn Quang Vinh 2005; Luong 2009b). The latter study, conducted from 1997 to 2001 as a collaborative project between the U.S. Social Science Research Council and the Institute of Social Sciences in Hồ Chí Minh City, is the only study that utilizes both survey and open-ended interview methods and involves research in both the receiving area and multiple sending communities, in this case four communities in two different regions of Vietnam (the Mekong delta and the central coast).

The four sending communities in our study on migration to Hồ Chí Minh City were chosen from the two most important provinces sending migrants to the city in the 1994-1999 period: Long An province in the Mekong delta in the south, and Quảng Ngãi province in the central coast. In each province, we chose one commune sending a larger number of migrants to our three studied sites in Hồ Chí Minh City, and another in the same district standing in a different socioeconomic cluster from the first chosen commune, in order to ensure a more representative sample from the same district (see Luong 2005: 178-187).

Migrants came in disproportionate numbers from the ranks of young villagers aged 15 to 35. Very few children below the age of 15 in our rural household sample are migrants. Of the members of those households aged 15 to 24, 42 percent in Long An province and 29 percent in Quảng Ngãi were migrants at the time of our study in 2000. Of people aged 25 to 34, 24 percent in Long An and 27 percent in Quảng Ngãi were migrants. As a result, the strong majority of migrants were aged 15 to 34. 89 percent (209 out of 235) of Long An migrants were in this age range at the time of our study in 2000, while over three quarters (140 out of 181) of Quảng Ngãi migrants were in this age range (Table 7.1).[2]

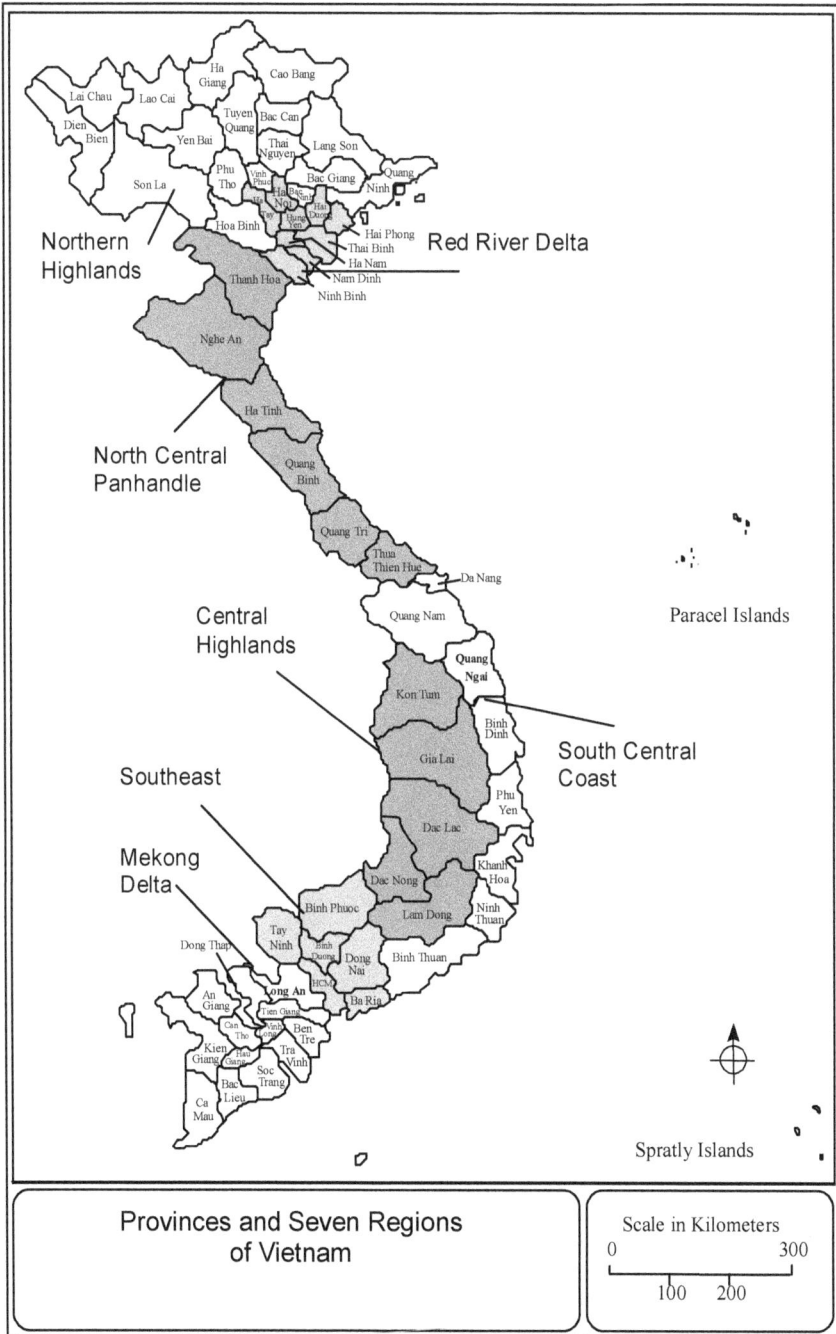

Figure 7.1 ◆ Provinces and Seven Regions of Vietnam

Table 7.1 ◆ Percentages of Migrants and Non-Migrants in Different Age Groups in Long An and Quảng Ngãi

Age group	Long An		Quảng Ngãi	
	Non-migrant	Migrant	Non-migrant	Migrant
6 or less	106 (100%)	0	125 (98%)	2 (2%)
7–14	229 (99%)	2 (1%)	330 (100%)	0
15–24	216 (58%)	156 (42%)	220 (71%)	88 (29%)
25–34	164 (76%)	51 (24%)	138 (73%)	50 (27%)
35–44	188 (93%)	15 (7%)	150 (82%)	32 (18%)
45–54	127 (95%)	7 (5%)	100 (92%)	9 (8%)
above 54	192 (98%)	4 (2%)	213 (100%)	0
Total	*1,222 (84%)*	*235 (16%)*	*1,276 (88%)*	*181 (12%)*

The overwhelming majority (83 percent) of migrants from the studied households in Long An chose Hồ Chí Minh City as their destination due to the fact that Long An is next to Hồ Chí Minh City. For Quảng Ngãi, which is approximately 800 kilometers from Hồ Chí Minh City, only 42 percent of the migrants from the studied households chose Hồ Chí Minh City (Table 7.2).

Table 7.2 ◆ Places of Residence of Long An and Quảng Ngãi Migrants in 2000

	Long An		Quảng Ngãi	
South central coast	1		42 (23%)	
Central highlands	0		36 (20%)	
Hồ Chí Minh City	196 (83%)		76 (42%)	
Rest of southeast	16 (7%)		24 (13%)	
Mekong delta	21 (9%)		0	
Other	1		3 (2%)	
Total	*234 (100%)*		*181 (100%)*	

Of the total number of surveyed households (N=600) in the four sending communities in two regions of Vietnam, we conducted in-depth interviews with twenty percent (N=120) Of the sixty-nine migrants from the surveyed households whom we were able to find in Hồ Chí Minh City, only twenty-two came from households with which we had conducted in-depth interviews and, because of duplicate migrants from some households, they came from only seventeen of those in-depth interviewed households. A few narratives were unusable,[3] so the following analysis relies on sixteen narratives by "tracked-down" migrants; these migrants were from thirteen households in the sending communities. More specifically, this final set of cases included eight households in Long An (which were home to ten migrants) and five households in Quảng Ngãi (which were home to six migrants). All the narratives, both of migrants and home community house-holds, were collected in 2000–2001.

Narrative Convergence and Divergence

The following analysis focuses on the circumstances and motives for migration, since both family members residing at home and the migrants themselves experienced them first-hand. While the narratives of both migrants and their family members had some other topics in common, such as the experiences of the former in Hồ Chí Minh City, the discussion of these issues by family members at home was not based on first-hand knowledge, and the comparison of narratives is thus not as meaningful.

In general, out of ten migration cases from the Mekong delta for which both migrants and family members at home gave narratives, three cases gave rise to highly similar narratives from both migrants and family members, and seven cases, partly divergent narratives. Of the six cases from the central coast, three involved considerable convergence in narratives, while three involved a partial divergence. Thus, ten of the sixteen cases in both regions involved partial divergence in narratives. There were no significant gender differences: seven of the eleven sets of narratives about/by female migrants and three of the five about/by male ones were divergent.

On one level, the divergence in narratives involves one of the three following scenarios:

1. The parent/caretaker's encouragement of migration as a solution to the migrant's (potential) wayward behavior.
2. The migrant's personal dream or aspiration or peculiar circumstances not acknowledged by his/her parent.
3. The migrant's emphasis on his/her decision to migrate as a sacrifice to help solve economic difficulties in the family, in contrast to parents' de-emphasis on family difficulties and stress on accepting migration for the good of the migrant.

On another level, all three types of narrative divergence, as well as most cases of narrative convergence, center on a dominant moral framework for family life. It is a model of filial children and caring parents, all of whom are supposed to consider the welfare of other family members to be of foremost importance, and the separation through migration to be undesirable.

In the following analysis, I will present examples of the three types of narrative divergence, and then discuss the sociocultural bases for narrative divergence.

1. Potentially wayward child (three cases)

In cases 1a and 1b, it was not the young migrants but their parents in the rural sending communities who commented on the young migrants as wayward children and who mentioned the young migrants' socially embarrassing behavior at home as one reason for migration.

Case 1a: Thái, aged 26 and having completed grade 9, migrated from Quảng Ngãi to Hồ Chí Minh City for a soldering job. He cited his need for an income as well as a desire to help his family:

> Interviewer: Why did you go to the City to look for work?
>
> Thái: Economic conditions were such that I had no income. *I work here* [in Hồ Chí Minh City] *to earn money to help my family.*
>
> Interviewer: Did your family face difficulties due to its strong reliance on agricultural work?
>
> Thái: Occasionally. When there was a crop loss, we ate manioc [instead of rice].... We did not have much cash income.
>
> (Excerpt from an interview by Lê Quang Minh and Trương Quang Đạt)

Thái's father, however, talked about Thái's limited educational success, the unacceptability of idleness, and the value of migration to Thái. The father downplayed the importance of the family's economic difficulties and their importance in the decision-making process on migration.

> Interviewer: How were your family circumstances before Thái migrated?
>
> Thái's father: We did not really face economic difficulties. But living standards were not as high as now. He wanted to go. We let him go because he was no longer in school and if he just hung around [here] for fun, nothing was achieved... *If he went to the city, urban socio-cultural conditions were superior, and he could learn something useful.*
>
> Interviewer: Why did Thái leave?
>
> Thái's father: Frankly, he did fine in school at an earlier age. But in grade 10 and then grade 11, his performance deteriorated... There were subjects he did not like to study. I scolded him and reminded him [to study]. He became a bit pessimistic. *He asked to quit schooling. I told him that if he quit, it could not be just for playing around.* If he quit, he had to do something. *If he could not achieve something in his study, then he had to do something on the economic front...* I told

him that I wanted him to finish at least grade 12, and that if he wanted to quit [earlier], it was his right but he had to write me a piece of paper saying that it was his desire. Otherwise, his wife and children later on might question why I had not let him continue his schooling.... He first left for Đà Lạt, but I was concerned about his health in the Central Highlands. He left for Hồ Chí Minh City four months later.

(Excerpt from an interview by Võ Công Nguyện and Nguyễn Ngọc Anh)

Case 1b: A female migrant Linh, aged 18 and completing grade 4, migrated from Long An to Hồ Chí Minh City to work in a restaurant. Like Thái in (1a), Linh cited her desire to help her family and presented herself as a filial daughter:

Linh: My family conditions were difficult. We were short of many things.. Income from agriculture was quite limited... I left for work to provide some money for my family....

Interviewer: Was it you who had the idea of working in Hồ Chí Minh City or somebody in your family decided to have you go?

Linh: It was my decision. My parents agreed to it.

(Excerpt from an interview by Phạm Ngọc Đĩnh and Phạm Thành Duy)

Linh's mother confirmed the family's economic difficulties, but also mentioned Linh's wayward behavior and their parent-child tension toward the end of the interview:

Interviewer: How was your family circumstance when she left [for work elsewhere?]

Linh's mother: We faced economic difficulties. My husband and I were not on good terms with each other. Being sad, we scolded our child. I was sadder when she left.

....

Linh's mother: When she left, we had a lot of economic difficulties... We lived hand to mouth, buying rice only after selling the products of our labor... We had neither rice in storage for daily use, ... nor money to deal with sickness. We were in debt. We have been paying back the debt over the past few years and even worked for [the creditor for] no wage to pay back the debt.

I scolded my daughter because she dated a married man… if that relation of hers continued, his wife and children would be miserable… and then he would abandon her anyway. She was sad and left.

(Excerpt from an interview by Phạm Ngọc Đĩnh and Phạm Thành Duy)

2. Migration out of personal dream or aspiration or due to peculiar circumstances not acknowledged by parents (four cases)

In cases 2a and 2b, migrants reported on major disappointments in their social lives at home as being one important reason for departure, while their relatives in rural sending communities did not mention these reasons at all.

Case 2a: Female migrant Danh, aged 30 in 2001, moved from Quảng Ngãi to Hồ Chí Minh City about five years earlier to work as a garment worker. Her parent's narrative mentioned the family's economic difficulties and her inability to do agricultural work:

Interviewer: How were your family conditions before Danh's departure?

Danh's parent: She migrated because we faced economic difficulties. She said: "I think that we do not have enough to eat from agricultural work. You have a difficult life. Neither you nor I fare well."… She saw many migrating.

Interviewer: Did you have debts?

Danh's parent: I was afraid of debts. We lived within our means.

Interviewer: Were there natural disasters or crop losses then?

Danh's parent: Crop losses, yes. One year, wind caused paddy to be so thin…

Interviewer: Why did she migrate to work far away?

Danh's parent: Because at home, she was weak and unable to do agricultural work.

(Excerpt from an interview by Võ Công Nguyện and Nguyễn Ngọc Anh)

Danh's parent thus highlighted that her migration would benefit not only the family but also Danh herself. These benefits and these circumstances for migration were acknowledged in Danh's narrative. However, Danh also mentioned a complex set of factors at work, including her mother's initial objection to her migration and the relation with her boyfriend which her parent did not bring up at all. She emphasized the migration decision as being her own.

Interviewer: Why did you like to work far away from home?

Danh: My family had economic difficulties. Secondly, I was weak and unable to do agricultural work. I can only work in the shade.

....

Interviewer: Was your family in debt?

Danh: We earned enough from agriculture for our livelihood. When I was small, I went to school. The school required some physical labor work. My mother did not agree because I was small. The teacher expelled me. No more school for me. Furthermore, we faced a labor shortage at home. My elder brother continued schooling, but the reasoning in my family was that as a girl, I did not need schooling.

Interviewer: Did any family member object to your departure?

Danh: My mother said that the house would be empty and objected. But I felt sad because many friends of mine had got married. *I was still single and sad because of a love affair leading nowhere. I decided to go.* My brother did not object because I had grown up then.

Interviewer: You left for two reasons, for your own livelihood due to inability to work in agriculture, and some sadness about your boyfriend. Which was the primary reason?

Danh: My own life was more important. The other factor [sadness about the boyfriend] made me sad for a while only.

(Excerpt from an interview by Nguyễn Thị Hoà and Nguyễn Thị Minh Châu)

Case 2b: Female migrant Cẩn, who had stopped schooling after grade 6 due to a shortage of labor at home, moved from Long An to Hồ Chí Minh City to work as a domestic worker and cook assistant. When asked about the reasons for Cẩn's migration, her mother cited the family's economic difficulties. More specifically, her mother reported that she had been allocated two hectares of rice fields by the government in a new agricultural frontier, had repeatedly lost her crops and a total of .7 tael of gold in agricultural investments, and faced economic difficulties.

Interviewer: Did her (Cẩn's) migration help to improve your family's conditions?

Cẩn's mother: We faced economic difficulties. Otherwise, no reason for her migration.

(Excerpt from an interview by Lê Quang Minh and Trương Quang Đạt)

Cẩn left for work in Hồ Chí Minh City, as her mother had to stay in the home village in order to take care of her elderly maternal grandmother. Cẩn reportedly sent home VND 500,000–700,000 (US \$35–\$50) every two or three months. However, Cẩn mentioned an additional and more personal reason for her departure: the tension in her relation with her mother.

> Cẩn: [I left for work in Hồ Chí Minh City 10 years ago] because my family had [economic] difficulties.
>
> Interviewer: Did you decide on your own or your mother or maternal grand-mother had their input?
>
> Cẩn: Because I was sad.
>
> Interviewer: Why was that?
>
> Cẩn: [My] mother scolded and insulted me constantly… I was angry and left without much planning…
>
> (Excerpt from interview by Lê văn Minh and Trương Quang Đạt)

3. Filial child and caring parent (three cases)

In cases 3a and 3b, the divergence between the narratives of migrants and their back-home parents' increased. Migrants emphasized how they, as filial children, decided to migrate in order to alleviate their parents' economic difficulties. In contrast, parents stressed that as caring parents, they would not have let children migrate simply for the latter's remittances, and that their families did not face (major) economic difficulties at the time of their family members' migration.

Case 3a: Female migrant Thúy, aged 24 in 2001, migrated from Long An to Hồ Chí Minh City in March 1996 to work as a home-based embroidery subcontractor. She returned home one year later, reportedly to help her parents with farm work during a peak agricultural period. She left again in September 1997 for a factory job in Hồ Chí Minh City. She reportedly earned VND 800,000 (US \$56) a month, and remitted 300,000–400,000 (\$21–\$28) monthly at the time of an interview carried out in 2001. In her narrative, Thúy emphasized her strong desire to help her family as being the reason for her migration, presenting herself as a highly filial daughter:

> Interviewer: Can you tell me why you migrated to Hồ Chí Minh City from March 1996 to March 1997?
>
> Thuý: My family did not have enough money. I wanted to help my family.

Thúy reported that in 1996–1997, although her family had about 7,000–8,000 square meters of ricefields, they yielded only one crop a year, and the harvest before her first departure had been poor. When she left for the second time for Hồ Chí Minh City in August 1997 for a factory job, Thúy said that such a job fulfilled her dream.

> Interviewer: Why did you migrate again in August 1997, after returning home in March 1997?
>
> Thuý: The harvest was over. I had helped my family with the harvest. I also dreamed of working in a factory. It was a dream fulfilled.
>
> (Excerpt from an interview by Quách Thu Cúc and Trần Anh Tiến)

Thúy's father, however, reported that their family circumstances had been normal at the time of her migration, and that he had let her go to Hồ Chí Minh City for her own benefit (interview of Thuý's father by Trần Minh Tân and Phan Thị Thùy Trâm). This narrative is at least partly congruent with Thúy's discussion of her second migration to Hồ Chí Minh City, but not with Thúy's narrative on her first trip when she reportedly left the village in order to help her parents financially.

Case 3b: Female migrant Nhung, who had completed junior high school (grade 9), moved from her home village in Long An province to work in a paper factory in Hồ Chí Minh City. When asked about the reason for her migration, she stated:

> Nhung: At home, after farm work, there was not much to do. I had to work to earn additional income to help my family.
>
> (Excerpt from an interview by Quách Thu Cúc and Trần Anh Tiến)

Nhung's father downplayed the economic needs of their family as the reason for Nhung's migration:

> Interviewer: Did your family face economic difficulties when Nhung migrated?
> Nhung's father: We faced some difficulties, but not to the extent that she had to migrate. Her migration is to provide extra money for her shopping whenever she wants to. [Also] when she gets married, she may have a [gold] ring. [Such a ring serves] as a souvenir and to provide for her own protection when she may be in need [of money once married].
>
> (Excerpt from an interview by Phan Văn Dốp and Đào Quang Bình)

In cases 3a and 3b, parents emphasized that they had agreed to their daughters' migration for the latter's benefits. The self presented is thus that of a caring parent who would put a child's benefits first and foremost and whose need for financial contributions from the child is insignificant or non-existent at the time of the latter's migration. In contrast, the two daughters in cases 3a and 3b emphasized their desire to help their parents financially and their concern for family welfare as the reasons for migration. In other words, the daughters presented themselves as filial children. Notwithstanding the divergence in the narratives about the reasons for the children's migration, all the narratives in cases 3a and 3b emphasized on another level the family members' care for one another. This common discursive emphasis is congruent with the long-existing and dominant moral framework in Vietnam that stresses the solidarity, mutual care, and hierarchy among the members of the same household (see Luong 1990: ch. 3).

In the context of the dominance of the aforementioned moral framework, wayward behavior on the part of children or moving away for one's own benefit, as in cases 1a, 1b, 2a, and 2b, is considered as an embarrassing moral failure or morally questionable. Most Vietnamese consider that quitting school due to deteriorating school performance (1a) is a moral failure. Another kind of moral failure is dating a married man (1b). Being constantly scolded by a parent (2b) is a sign of an embarrassing problem either on the part of the child or the parent. A dead-end love affair (2a) is not necessarily a moral failure but it does not reflect well on the parties involved. And in the Vietnamese context, moral failures or questionable behavior reflect poorly, not simply on those individuals directly involved, but also on their family members, especially on parents who are normally held responsible for educating children. Cases 1a, 1b, 2a, and 2b all highlight tension and conflicts within a Vietnamese family, tension and conflicts which are far from being uncommon. A child who disappointed parents by not studying, not working hard, dating a married person or somebody not approved by parents might implicitly espouse an alternative moral framework that allowed for more independent behavior among family members. However, no narrator in our study on migration explicitly articulated and advocated such an alternative model. All the young migrants in these cases emphasized the economic difficulties faced by their families and the importance of this factor in their migration decisions. They presented themselves as filial children, at least in the decision-making processes regarding migration, and thus did not challenge the dominant moral framework for family life.

Within such a dominant framework for family life in Vietnam, family tension and conflicts reflect poorly on both children and parents who are expected to behave, respectively, as filial children and caring parents. It is far from surprising from a methodological perspective that such moral failures or questionable behavior are not consistently reported in narratives by migrants residing in Hồ Chí Minh City or their family members at home. What is more surprising is that they were reported at all, especially as narrators did not know interviewers well. After all, narratives involve the construction and presentation of self by narrators to their interlocutors. Embarrassing behavior could be revealed to people within a small and close circle where selves are potentially seen in fuller, or more intimate terms, but seldom to the public. Thus, even when there is a total convergence in the narratives given by migrants and their family members to researchers on the reasons for migration, it is possible that in some cases narrators did not discuss all the reasons for migration (especially morally questionable behavior) and did not fully present the context of migration.[4] While the hiding of moral failures or the under-reporting of morally questionable behavior in the presentation of self to the public is common in numerous societies, this behavioral tendency is accentuated in the Vietnamese sociocultural system due to the Vietnamese discursive socialization process.

At an early age, Vietnamese are taught to use not pronouns but ideally kinship terms when addressing others and when referring to themselves. In speaking to a parent, for example, even a sixty-year-old Vietnamese speaker is expected to refer to themselves not with any personal pronoun, but with the kinship term *con* ("child"). For another example, children are regularly scolded for using the personal pronoun *nó* ("he/she/him/her/it") in reference to slightly older siblings, as this term implies the speaker's lack of deference to the third-party referent. The *I*, the *you*, and the *he/she/they* of English have as their counterparts in the Vietnamese system dozens of linguistic forms of various grammatical subclasses (kinship terms; proper nouns; personal pronouns; and "status" terms) which are alternatively used to refer to the addressor, the addressee, as well as third parties in social interactions. Common and proper nouns are used with considerably greater frequency than personal pronouns, not only for third-party references, but also pervasively for address and self reference in Vietnam (Luong 1990). While personal pronouns highlight the constantly shifting addressor and addressee roles in immediate interactional contexts, the pervasive use of kinship and other role terms renders salient the lasting behavioral and contextual implications of these terms ("mother", "child", "cadre", "subject"). The common self-referring term *tôi* in Vietnamese is not a neutral form, but is prototypically used to structure a more distant relation among acquaintances.[5] Personal pronouns simply do not constitute the pivotal point of person reference among Vietnamese as they do in Western languages. As a result, a Vietnamese speaker's discursive practices in the interaction with one's father must differ from those in one's interaction with a sibling or a mere acquaintance (see Luong 1990). In Vietnamese speech interaction, speakers are acutely aware of the two-way relation between contexts/relations on the one hand and discursive forms and what can or cannot be said on the other. A speaker's narrative on certain issues with moral implications may differ, depending on whether one is talking to a parent or a close friend, or to a group insider or outsider (cf. Bachnik and Quinn 1994). The multiplicity of narratives on the reasons for migration is thus not surprising. Any Vietnamese narrative invokes both a shared moral framework and a more individualized reflection of one's own referential position within that framework.

Methodological Implications of Narrative Divergence

No matter what underlies the divergence in narratives on the reasons for migration, given the fact that almost two thirds of narratives by migrants and their relatives show partial divergence, research only with migrants or only with their family members at home runs a high risk of oversimplifying reality. The potential divergence between migrants' and family members' narratives on the reasons for migration suggests that, from a methodological standpoint, we need to conduct research with as many involved actors as possible and in both migrant-receiving and sending communities. Multiple narratives need to be elicited in order to have a fuller picture of the migration process (cf. Linde 1993: 5-7, 135-140, 144-147). Even in a survey in which migrants and/or their family members can list multiple causes for migration and rank the relative importance of these causes (Vietnam-GSO and UNPFA 2005), it is likely that such information presents only the partial truth of a complex process.[6] In emphasizing the need for multiple and multi-sited narratives on migration, I do not wish to deny in methodological terms the value of survey data and quantitative analyses on the demographic, temporal, and spatial dimensions of migration (e.g., age and gender of migrants, duration of migration trips, their current and past residences). However, certain aspects of migration, like the contexts and reasons behind it, are highly complex and embedded in local moral frameworks. They need to be studied with great sensitivity to the multiplicity of narratives on the same process. In conceptual and theoretical terms, the political economic inequalities between urban and rural areas or between the capitalist core and hinterlands undoubtedly play important roles in shaping the microscopic decisions of migrants and their families (Wallerstein 1979; cf. Stark 1991). However, these decisions on migration, and the negotiation between prospective young migrants and their families on whether to migrate or not, are also deeply embedded in moral, local frameworks. Without the consideration of such shared moral frameworks, our analysis will remain incomplete.

Notes

1. Hồ Chí Minh City still has five primarily rural districts at the time of writing. Their number and surface area have been rapidly decreasing for two decades due to rapid urbanization. The official figure given for migrants in Hồ Chí Minh City in the 2004 census also underestimates the actual number since it does not include mi-

grants who have gained permanent registration in the city and who were no longer counted as migrants in the Vietnamese administrative classification.

2. In Vietnam, children normally start grade 1 in elementary school at the age of 6, and finish compulsory junior high school education at the age of 15. Many informal-sector employers in destination areas normally feel more comfortable hiring migrants aged 15 or older than those below the age of 15 although, needless to say, this varies among employers. For people in the official workforce (including migrants working in medium and large enterprises), the retirement age is 55 for women and 60 for men. These are the reasons for selecting the first two age categories in Table 7.1 (6 or below, 7–14), and the last one (above 54).

3. I do not include interviews with six migrants in Hồ Chí Minh City in my analysis for two reasons. In most cases, our interviews with their parents at home did not deal with their migration because they left their home villages for the first time after our interviews with their parents had taken place. Those interviews did not deal with the departures of those migrants. In one case, the interview with parents was conducted in the presence of the two siblings who had migrated to Hồ Chí Minh City and were visiting home at the time of the interview.

4, Of the six sets of convergent narratives, four shared an emphasis on low or unstable incomes, economic difficulties in the migrant's family and migrant's future remittances as the reasons for migration; one an emphasis on the migrant's desire for financial independence and exploration of urban life; and one an emphasis on both sets of reasons.

5. The implication of a distant relation in the use of the personal pronoun *tôi* for self reference can be mitigated or changed by a solidarity-presupposing address term (*cậu, em*, or personal name).

6. The reasons listed in the survey questionnaire included: unemployment in the sending area, a job in the receiving area, completion of study, further education, marriage, proximity to close associates, no close associates in the sending area, health care, better physical environment, better life, better social and spiritual conditions, business, end of employment contract, children's future, and other reasons (to be listed) (Vietnam-GSO and UNFPA 2005: 153).

References

Bachnik, Jane and Charles Quinn, eds. 1994. *Situated Meaning: Inside and Outside in Japanese Self, Society, and Language.* Princeton: Princeton University Press.

Linde, Charlotte. 1993. *Life Stories: The Creation of Coherence.* Oxford: Oxford University Press.

Luong, Hy V. 1990. *Discursive Practices and Linguistic Meanings: The Vietnamese System of Person Reference.* Amsterdam and Philadelphia: John Benjamins.

———. 2005. "Thành phố Hồ Chí Minh: Vấn đề tăng trưởng kinh tế, di dân, và đô thị hoá" [Hồ Chí Minh City: Economic growth, migration, and urbanization], pp. 163–200 in *Đô thị hoá và vấn đề giảm nghèo ở thành phố Hồ Chí Minh: Lý luận và thực tiễn* [Urbanization and the Issue of Poverty Reduction in Hồ Chí Minh City:

Theory and Reality], eds. Nguyễn Thế Nghĩa, Mặc Đường, and Nguyễn Quang Vinh. Hanoi: Nhà xuất bản Khoa học xã hội.

———. 2009a. "Rural migration to Hồ Chí Minh City: A tale of two regions," pp. 77–102 in *Urbanization, Migration, and Poverty in a Vietnamese Metropolis*, ed. H.V. Luong. Singapore: National University of Singapore Press.

———, ed. 2009b. *Urbanization, Migration, and Poverty in a Vietnamese Metropolis*. Singapore: National University of Singapore Press.

Marcus, George. 1995. "Ethnography in/of the world system: The emergence of multi-sited ethnography." *Annual Review of Anthropology* 24: 95–117.

Nguyễn Thế Nghĩa, Mặc Đường, and Nguyễn Quang Vinh, eds. 2005. *Đô thị hoá và vấn đề giảm nghèo ở Thành phố Hồ Chí Minh: Lý luận và thực tiễn* [Urbanization and the Issue of Poverty Reduction in Hồ Chí Minh City: Theory and Reality]. Hanoi: Nhà xuất bản Khoa học xã hội.

Stark, Oded. 1991. *The Migration of Labor*. Cambridge, MA.: Basil Blackwell.

Tessier, Olivier. 2002. "Commuting from the village to the city: Analyzing the pattern of migration of the people of the northern village of Hay to Hanoi," pp. 387-420 in *Vietnam Exposé: French Scholarship on Twentieth-Century Vietnamese Society*, eds. Gisèle Bousquet and Pierre Bourdieu. Ann Arbor: University of Michigan Press.

———. 2003. "Ra đi để cải thiện cuộc sống và tình cảm gắn bó với làng quê" [Departures for better livelihood and attachment to home village], in *Làng ở vùng châu thổ sông Hồng: Vấn đề còn bỏ ngỏ* [The Village in the Red River Delta: Open Questions]. Hanoi: Ecole Francaise d'Extrême-Orient, National Center of Social Sciences, and National University of Vietnam in Hanoi.

Vietnam-General Statistical Office and United Nations Population Fund-UNFPA. 2005. *Vietnam Migration Survey 2004: Major Findings*. Hanoi: General Statistical Office and UNFPA.

Vũ Thị Hồng, Patrick Gubry, and Lê Văn Thành. 2003. *Những con đường về thành phố: Di dân đến thành phố Hồ Chí Minh từ một vùng đồng bằng sông Cửu Long* [The Routes to the City: Migration to Hồ Chí Minh City from a Region in the Mekong Delta]. Hồ Chí Minh City: Nhà xuất bản Thành phố Hồ Chí Minh.

Wallerstein, Immanuel. 1979. *The Capitalist World Economy*. Cambridge: Cambridge University Press.

CHAPTER 8

Cross-Border Marriages between Vietnamese Women and Chinese Men: The Integration of Otherness and the Impact of Popular Representations

Caroline GRILLOT

When one talks about cross-border marriages between Vietnamese women and Chinese men in southern China, economic conditions and demography are often, if not always, emphasized to explain the frequency of such unions in modern history and, more specifically, in recent decades. However, many aspects of this phenomenon are rarely, if ever, considered, such as the way in which communities along each side of the Chinese-Vietnamese frontier view their neighbors; their degree of appreciation and understanding of one another; their representation of women, men, romance, and marriage; and the impact of these factors on the phenomenon of cross-community alliances, status, and individual choice. In addition, spouses' voices are not often heard, outside the framework of human-trafficking testimonies. From a human trafficking perspective, there is also a tendency to view cross-border marriages as unfortunate migration cases, or as a local "response" to social problems. The shortage of potential brides, for example, is often presumed to increase the trade in women in rural and border areas. During my field research on mixed-marriage couples on the Sino-Vietnamese border, I found the reality to be much more complex. I propose in this chapter a different approach to these international marriages through hearing how the women involved in them explained, in their own words, their experiences and life changes since leaving their original communities, whatever form that departure took.

The research results described here are based on five months of intermittent fieldwork conducted between 2006 and 2009 in the border cities of Hekou (Yunnan province) and Dongxing (Guangxi province), and in their Vietnamese twin cities in Vietnam, respectively Lào Cai (Lào Cai province) and Móng Cái (Quảng

Ninh province), each separated from China by a narrow river. Due to the political sensitivity of this research topic, I sought a few initial local connections and then used a snowball sampling method to access informants.[1] This approach allowed the interviewees, when introduced by trustworthy acquaintances, to disclose their private affairs away from the scrutiny of public authorities or other community members. The resulting participant observation, interviews, and informal discussions with Vietnamese women, Sino-Vietnamese couples, and other local people provide the materials for an analysis of a phenomenon that is often approached without considering the personal experiences and perspectives of all the participants.

Self and Others

Both these sets of twin gateway cities have throughout history been dedicated to border trade, and have experienced considerable economic development since the reopening of the China-Vietnam border in 1989. As a result, cross-border migration is very active in both directions. The way in which Vietnamese people in general are perceived in border areas depends on which Chinese communities interact with them.[2] Local people's points of view differ from those of Chinese internal migrants who have recently settled in border cities like Hekou or Dongxing. The local people, generally speaking, are more open-minded and tolerant because they share with their neighbors across the border a common history and similar evolution that affects their lives. Chinese migrants appear more reluctant to interact, apart from in strictly business-oriented transactions; they also appear more suspicious and indifferent, even condescending, toward people with whom they share a common space but not necessarily common visions and interests.

As business partners, tourists, prostitutes, translators, or workers, Vietnamese women voice perspectives that are also specific: some acknowledge the reluctance of the Chinese migrants to interact and prefer it to the prejudice of local people towards them. Others feel that they are perceived by the migrants as foreigners with whom there cannot be any common language. With locals, however, they manage to build a relatively stable relationship based on trust and a common understanding of the border's realities. No matter what the perception, Vietnamese women living in Chinese border towns still must endure undisguised prejudice, from unfavorable comments about their compatriots to unsavory stares; at the same time, they must slowly gain the trust of their Chinese neighbors by adapting to different social codes. Mutual social representations are a complex combination of points of view, which deeply affect local relationships – and thus marital exchanges.

Questions of Terminology

A close examination of the terminology employed in the languages of these communities represents an interesting way to discover in conversations and in the media the reflections of these social representations. Which words are used not only depends on which nationality an individual belongs to, but also on his or her historical background, ethnic origin, social interactions, education level, social status, and even physical condition. In any given society, people behave in a certain way toward one another, revealing social inequities and placing each individual in a certain frame.

Additionally, the media operates as the perfect channel for the promotion of these social representations. In articles and news reports, the terms most often used for Vietnamese women are *Yuenan mei* [Vietnamese little sister], *Yuenan xifu* [Vietnamese bride] or *Yuenan laopo* [Vietnamese wife] – the same terms employed by local Chinese people for Vietnamese women in Chinese border towns. In an echo of past decades when Chinese women went to Taiwan to find a life partner, and thus were caught up in external perceptions as "foreign brides," the Chinese media today offers a nearly exact repetition in the stigmatization used to describe Vietnamese brides. This time, businessmen or lonely husbands are mainland Chinese, and the poor fiancée or venal prostitute is Vietnamese, identified by the general but slightly condescending term, *Yuenan mei*.

However, a closer look at the terminology used to characterize Vietnamese people in general, and Vietnamese women in particular, reveals a certain contradiction in representation. For instance, these women are perceived as very respectful of family in the domestic sphere, but they are believed to act without scruples outside of family life in the public sphere, thereby bolstering suspicions.

Ambiguous Vietnamese Women

How does all this work? In border areas, Vietnamese women represent a certain type of person in the collective imagination. Although considered exotic above all, they also embody the attributes of the peasantry, such as poverty, lack of education, and inappropriate attitudes. These and other disparaging stereotypical features are also commonly used when referring to ethnic minority groups, especially in southern China. The only positive qualities attributed to them are ambiguous insinuations concerning their virtues: they are beautiful and have light skin, a thin waist or big eyes – physical features also much appreciated in local prostitution work. So, when locals comment on Vietnamese women, one can easily connect these comments with sexually valued attributes, especially in a border town like Hekou, well known for its sex industry. In people's minds, the distinction between the different categories of Vietnamese women seems as narrow as the river that separates the two countries. However, other recognized characterizations of these women include their physical strength and endurance at work, and their expression of filial piety within the marital sphere. But here again, the emphasis which is placed on women's ability to work and their commitment to their families appears to be another way of justifying a certain form of exploitation – hard work and low pay – and also of depreciating Vietnamese men's competence. In both perspectives, the general point of view could be summed up as follows: "Lucky for them, Vietnamese women are tough, because they don't have much else to rely on and, with a Vietnamese man for a husband, some have no other choice." This kind of formulation is the key to understanding the underlying reasons for cross-border marital exchanges.

Interactions between the local Chinese population and Vietnamese women migrants are limited to a few types. They are generally based on common or competitive interests and the "investment" in a shared space dedicated to the exchanges of all kinds of agents: clients, tourists, porters, shop and street vendors, money changers, translators, and prostitutes. In sum, contact between Vietnamese women and the local Chinese population is mainly funneled into a framework in which each individual has a specific role determined by business and the exchange of money, and in which each individual embodies well-maintained stereotypes and prejudices. As they all share a very limited physical and social space in which they interact, impressions are multiple and complex, and tend to be applied indiscriminately to all Vietnamese women. It becomes difficult to distinguish which specific feature or criticism is related to which particular women. The so-called "Vietnamese market" in Hekou is one example. The second floor is the territory of brothels where Vietnamese prostitutes work. An inside balcony allows them to call directly on potential customers who are busy buying souvenirs on the first floor from Vietnamese women vendors trying their best to offer an exotic image of their country and culture embodied in the fruit, coffee, sandals, or lacquer wood items they sell. The very same space is thus used by two groups of women who convey similar images.

According to those living on the Chinese border, Vietnamese women are often seducers with a troubled past, able to fake a temporary relationship with an honest man in order to gain funds to feed a family back home, and to return to Vietnam in the end. Needless to say, these mercantile visions of venal and manipulative "husband hunters" come from a population that lives near the Vietnam border and who accumulate money from commercial activities often at the expense of a Vietnamese clientele that is easily deceived with cheap, low-quality items. Yet it is often heard that one cannot trust what Vietnamese people say, as "they are neither honest nor sincere, share few moral values, and have bad intentions." My informants sometimes warned me: "Don't look for these women, they won't tell you the truth about their purpose, origin or status, but tales so that you will pity them… for most of them, there is no need to be compassionate."

These representations do not entirely lie outside the facts, since the relationship between the two communities is largely based on trade, with money as the common language. Dongxing and Hekou traders mostly come from cities in Guangxi and Yunnan provinces or from eastern China. They are not necessarily familiar with or interested in local history or the nature of the relationship between Chinese and Vietnamese in this specific social space along the border. Indeed, those who settled in Hekou and its surrounding areas before the conflicts between the two countries arose during the 1970s may still express some resentment and suspicion toward former enemies whose government threatened Vietnam's Chinese community and fought fiercely during the border war that ensued in the winter of 1979. Personal loss and pain, as well as nationalist humiliation, during this short but traumatic experience remain vivid in the local memory. But nowadays, Chinese migrants' perception of Vietnamese is more based on the impressions their clients have left during negotiations, deals, and contracts, and on their respect for the tacit understandings underlying the exchange of goods and cash. There is thus great suspicion toward the Vietnamese population on the part of the Chinese migrants who ignore the language, social conduct, and historical background that underlie local community interactions. The Vietnamese themselves admit that they need to improve their skills, trade abilities, and adaptation to the market economy to establish relationships based on trust and a better reputation with their partners. Meanwhile, Chinese merchants continue to complain about the difficulties and disappointing experiences of trading with Vietnamese people.

Given these conditions, how can one be surprised by the vision left behind by some Vietnamese women when their remembered identity elements are poverty, cultural backwardness, and venality? Examples of opportunistic women who have shamelessly exploited generous and naïve partners feature in many local conversations. Such stories prevent the establishment of relationships between the communities based on trust, especially when they are related to personal (and sometimes illegal) affairs for which there is no legal recourse in cases where trust is breached.

This lack of trust underlies the lack of concern that locals express about the misfortune of Vietnamese women and the apathy toward Chinese men who need them to solve sexual, family, or domestic issues. Therefore, the mediocre impression that Vietnamese people in general, and Vietnamese women more specifically, leave on their Chinese neighbors limits not only efficient economic partnerships but also the solidarity or compassion that people might have for victims of deception (among whom are many prostitutes and sold brides), or for those who simply cross the border trying to find a new (if not always better) life in what is perceived as a more open society. Indeed, if I believed my Chinese informants in Hekou, the majority of Vietnamese prostitutes are pleased with their work because their gains are better than in any other activity in their native country and, more generally, ambitious Vietnamese women all wish to find rich Chinese husbands to steal money from, or any male partner to father a child. Using such a frame of interpretation to analyze attitudes does not help greatly in understanding the complex factors that explain the presence of Vietnamese women in China, but it does help to explain the relative failure of campaigns to fight human trafficking and prostitution at the Sino-Vietnamese border. Locals suggest that: "people in Vietnam deceive each other"; "some women deserve their situation – they do not complain about staying here, and they do whatever they do"; "it is worse in their country anyway"; "do not exaggerate their fate"; and "those who have tried to help [these women] have been deceived."

Community Suspicion

In China, as in Vietnam, societal suspicion can be a heavy burden for mixed families. My experience in Móng Cái attests to such difficulties and how they emerge in the behavior and comments of those around mixed couples. To be able to meet such a couple, usually a Chinese trader and his local wife, one needs to penetrate a certain network of friends who share the same experience and lifestyle. In the field, I have almost always learned more about Vietnamese wives' lives through their friends than through their own direct confidence. This hiding of the truth reflects the real stigma that affects young women who choose to live with Chinese men. Whatever the nature of the relationship, its origin and its sincerity, they are often suspected of being concubines, second wives, or unscrupulous profiteers. Being assigned such a status in a society where marriage has such a high value influences couples' attitudes. Their reluctance to reveal the nature of their own relationship – or that of their acquaintances – suggests the difficulty of a life that wanders off the beaten track, and the consequent need to cover up its inherent ambiguities. That reluctance then gives rise to additional suspicion. The main reason for this cautious behavior comes from a fear of social judgment.

In Móng Cái, these women, sometimes *er'nai* (concubine or second-wife), sometimes marginalized individuals in their own society, are often seen as opportunists trying to sell themselves to a potential Chinese husband, and afraid of losing their chance to have a family. Protecting aspects of their life through optimistic narratives becomes a necessity in the absence of a clear distinction on the part of the community between a Chinese man's spouse and a prostitute. The ambiguous term "concubine" may be voiced directly, or may be implied by a complicity of silence or reprobation by insinuation. Most women try to protect themselves behind an acceptable, public version of their story that can forestall or disarm slander about their past situation, current position, or future intentions. One must remember how the nature and success of these marriages can affect the general reputation of Vietnamese women, including those about to accept a fiancé's offer of such a mixed marriage. For the secondary wives of Chinese, or for those young women with a hidden past they cannot talk about, everything must remain unseen so that they can protect their public face and preserve their dignity.

The Fantasy of the Model Wife

If the Chinese maintain such reserve vis-à-vis their Vietnamese neighbors in general, then why would they take Vietnamese women as wives, and continue to do so over long periods of time? Arguing that it comes down to the poverty factor, and thus pragmatism on both sides, does not offer a fully satisfactory answer. An alternative explanation emerges from local conversations, which base this behavior on the expectations of the men. In contemporary China, after years of Maoism that significantly changed women's position and a post-reform era that saw this position replaced by a more complex balance between men and women's status on the market and in the family realm (Hershatter 2007), the resulting – rather equal – participation of both spouses in the family economy tends to sustain an impression of the relative emancipation of Chinese women compared to their Vietnamese neighbors. Additionally, the limited number of women leads them to become more demanding when marriage opportunities arise. For men who have been educated in a certain traditional vision of family where each member's role is precisely defined, these changes can be distressing. Even though many of these men grew up in the late Maoist and early post-reform periods, they are still influenced by the traditions their parents passed on to them. The resulting confusion about societal changes and new patterns within the household realm (Yan Yunxiang 2003) has led some of these men to seek conventional family values and the related model of femininity: the traditional, subservient housewife. Torn between nostalgia and fantasy, these ordinary Chinese men seek refuge in an imagined conjugality – and one that seems to drive men from other countries to seek their wives in this part of the world, and in Vietnam in particular (Constable 2004; Thai 2008).

It is precisely in this context that Vietnamese women appear as the ideal alternative, the obvious saviors of a weakening patriarchal power. The Vietnamese housewife seems radically opposed to her Chinese counterpart: she is entirely devoted to her family, to her husband whom she must obey, to her children for whom she cares. She never requires material compensation for this devotion. She works hard and would never dare to gamble away her income. She embodies all the precious traits and qualities a man might require from a wife. At least this is how she is represented. A Chinese woman, for example, can dare to look down on her husband if he does not earn enough income. This loss of respect in the domestic sphere is often mentioned and inflicts psychological pressure on men who must work harder to meet the increasing financial needs of their families.

Vietnamese women, by contrast, are often described as having characteristics which are the exact opposite of those attributed to such Chinese women who "are only interested in money," "like to waste their money on games," "are tough and dominant at home," "not tender enough," "do not respect their husbands, toward whom they are more and more demanding," and so on. Vietnamese women thus emerge as more traditional, less emancipated, less demanding.

Therefore, one can appreciate the appeal that Vietnamese women may have in the eyes of disappointed Chinese men, whether the latter are older bachelors, men previously married to Chinese women, younger candidates for marriage, or those currently married who emphasize how tyrannical Chinese wives can be. When these same men have the opportunity to observe, to interact, or to personally get to know some of their Vietnamese female neighbors, this contrast can be exaggerated as their fantasy is embodied in these women, whom they perceive to be alternative partners. This preference for Vietnamese women can be interpreted as an appreciation of a different social/familial/affective bond established between spouses, based on an imagined relationship that better fits the image of a traditional marriage that preserves men's pride and dignity. A Vietnamese wife, at least in popular discourse, is thus the source of much less trouble and disappointment than a Chinese one, and this makes for a more peaceful marriage.

Nevertheless, when it comes to talking about Vietnamese prostitutes who live in China, the opposite attributes are often found. Here Vietnamese women are seen as emancipated, promiscuous, venal, profiteers. This unflattering portrait is also used to describe those women who are suspected of seeking a Chinese husband to get out of a life of prostitution or a marginalized social position in Vietnam, and thus are not as "pure" as their supposedly untouched sisters. Money and wealth are often mentioned as the reasons why these women come to China, as if they all wished only to enjoy the advantages of Chinese economic advancement. According to this view, the opportunism of Vietnamese women contrasts with the way in which local Chinese people portray themselves. The latter like to describe themselves as generous, hospitable, almost naïve. Men give their trust and welcome to foreign women in distress; but subsequently deceived, neglected, and robbed, they find their pride, dignity, and self-esteem damaged by unscrupulous and disrespectful women. Indeed, some Vietnamese women are accused of stealing from their Chinese partner the child they conceived together. This can do terrible harm to the self-esteem of Chinese men.

The Perfect Husband

Surprisingly, and in stark opposition to Chinese representations of them, Vietnamese people – at least in these border areas – praise their Chinese neighbors when it comes to appreciating their business skills. Historical events have not been forgotten but are rarely brought up. Chinese people are respected as traders if not as people. These impressions influence the image of Chinese men that circulates among Vietnamese women, especially those who may be ready to cross the border to find their ideal partner, whether personal or economic. In contrast to this favorable portrait of honest and reformist Chinese men, Vietnamese men often appear to them as more dishonest and closed-minded. This affects the vision Vietnamese women have of Chinese men as potential husbands, both for those who deliberately choose to meet such men and for those who experience life with them, whatever the circumstances of their marriages. Whether voluntary or not, immersion into Chinese society and family life allows Vietnamese women to form comparisons with what they know about conjugality in their own community. Many married women in Vietnam complain about their husbands, and those who are not yet married, or are divorced or widowed, explain how difficult being married to a Vietnamese man can be. In southern Vietnam, overseas Vietnamese, Taiwanese, Koreans or Singaporeans provide an alternative but in northern Vietnam, where such international alliances have not been so mainstream, mainland Chinese men are a geographically closer and more personally interesting option.

The social and economic conditions in China, supposedly better than in Vietnam, are one factor pushing women to consider potential partners in China. But they are not the only reason. An ideal husband fantasy has been projected onto Chinese men, who are seen as culturally similar but more open-minded due to the influence of social modernization in China. This image of Chinese men stands in contrast to the frequently unflattering description of potential Vietnamese husbands. But for women from rural areas, choosing a Chinese man who may meet their expectations and who is far away, rather than a local Vietnamese man, is not easy. Many of the Vietnamese women who find a Chinese partner have, in fact, already escaped their former lives. They have also often broken community rules. The female virtues of tolerance and compassion, which in reality mean dealing with an authoritarian husband, are part of marital life for most of these wives. This often includes putting up with abuse from husbands in the forms of laziness, gambling, drugs, domestic violence, adultery, polygamy and other issues. A woman's desire to be free, to survive, to protect her children, or simply to have a better personal life may lead her to leave, as the only way to carry on with her life. However, the act of leaving is subject to social condemnation. Women who leave may be considered as neglectful or weak, or as unconventional women unable to fulfill their duties or handle their husbands, and may subsequently have difficulties obtaining official divorces. They need great courage to make the decision to leave, and to consider their new situation as anything other than the end of their personal and social lives. Although solidarity and compassion towards those who suffer from domestic and family abuse exists among local Vietnamese communities, little support is given to those who decide to leave the household.

The most disappointed and determined of these women try to find an idealized new partner on the other side of the border. But what sort of man are they looking for? On the whole, Vietnamese women look for a Chinese husband who is everything that a Vietnamese husband is not, someone who will consider an equal sharing of domestic tasks and income-earning activities, a more egalitarian relationship, a more limited number of children, and respect. While idealized, these hopes are not entirely unrealistic. On the Chinese side of the border, after all, economic changes have brought about some of those characteristics of equality and sharing in the domestic realm. During their migration to urban centers (which is an initiation into adulthood as well as an economic necessity for most Chinese rural families at some point), young Chinese women acquire working experience as well as maturity. Often forced to live alone while they find a job, their personality, strength, and instincts for protection are put to the test. They learn to struggle in a tricky environment. Eventually, the economic power they accrue by meeting their family's needs, and by taking charge of their own future, dramatically changes the roles traditionally reserved for them as women, even though this process may be contested at both the individual and societal levels.

For years now, this situation has changed the social face of the rural world in China. Men have learned to recognize the importance of the contribution of women's work to the family and the community, and to accept women's new ambitions. When it is the men who leave home to sell their labor to urban construction sites, mines, or infrastructure projects during the agricultural off-season, the women are left behind to take care of the family, fields, and live-stock. Therefore women acquire a certain decision-making power in domestic and local affairs. The "feminization" of the countryside reflects the changes taking place in a society whose traditional values, including the distinct allocation of gender roles, are being overthrown.

Therefore, when looking for a Vietnamese wife, Chinese men hope to find the conventional family values to which they attach importance and an ideal marital relationship that, despite social changes, includes a wife who demonstrates obedience, work efficiency, care of the home and of the children's education, fidelity, modesty, and absence of material demands. A "traditional" Vietnamese wife is thus appealing as a refuge from change. Paradoxically, however, that "traditional" Vietnamese wife is herself seeking to escape tradition by looking for a modernized – or at least modernizing – Chinese husband.

Life after Marriage

Not surprisingly, then, what Chinese men discover in their Vietnamese partner does not always correspond to their original fantasy. They are correct that the education of Vietnamese women and their perception of the duties of a wife prepare them to be devoted housewives. But those specific Vietnamese women who migrate to China expect something more from their Chinese partner and his family and community: freedom of movement and action, respect, a certain level of comfort, and the opportunity to improve their living conditions and domestic status. They have these expectations because this is how they have imagined China.

After marriage, many Chinese husbands seem confused by the behavior of their Vietnamese partners, who appear less docile than they had expected. Some decide to give in to their new wife's determination; some impose their views through authority; some abandon their wives after a short life together; others allow them to travel back to Vietnam. Such reactions are partly, although not entirely, the consequence of disillusionment vis-à-vis their expectations. Some husbands cope with their disappointment by avoiding responsibilities, or by becoming indifferent or mean, or by unsuccessfully trying to gain their wife's affection.

From the wife's point of view, there can also be disillusionment, but there is also some hope. Listening to Vietnamese women talk about their experiences at home in Vietnam brings to light the difficulties of life for a wife there. Whatever their family and private situation is, the women all talk of exhaustion, a sense of loneliness within their family, an absence of recognition for their daily work, control by their husband, economic pressure, and other burdens. Therefore, for those women who settle in China, willingly or unwillingly, a new life presents useful opportunities. Vietnamese women soon become aware of women's status in Chinese society and of what is expected from them as they enter their new home. They soon realize that they might have an opportunity for emancipation. Among those who marry Chinese men, some are surprised not to be asked to work hard outside the home; others observe that their husband helps with housework, cooking, and child care. One may feel glad that her own child is being accepted as a family member while another may enjoy a few years of marital life before choosing to become a mother. In any case, family life, at least in the first months or years, opens a new perspective and a different approach to the duties of wife and mother.

From the perspective of Vietnamese women, the lives of Chinese women, although tough, symbolize a certain degree of emancipation and thus provide motivation for finding a Chinese husband. The view is often an exaggerated one based on other people's experience and a very sharp comparison with marriage in Vietnam. That exaggerated view reflects both the lack of detailed knowledge by Vietnamese women of Chinese women's lives and also the lure of a tempting fantasy: material comfort, greater recognition of women's status, an open-minded spouse, social improvement, less physical work, and an egalitarian sharing of daily tasks.

Imagination and Ignored Realities

Some gap will always remain between what was imagined before these marriages and what is experienced afterwards. Expectations based on imaginings rather than actual facts cannot help but lead to disappointment, once the river has actually been crossed. Not all Vietnamese women are perfect housewives and not all Chinese men fit the ideal husband model. Furthermore, the images of these ideal partners are themselves subject to change, especially given the pace of social change in these two societies. Some of these imaginings are based on the media. Television in Vietnam, for example, broadcasts a large number of Chinese TV shows and plays a crucial role in how Vietnamese think about China. In addition, imagination finds inspiration in observation and interaction between Chinese men and Vietnamese women in border towns. For example, Vietnamese women hear about the personal, often very convincing experiences of "elder sisters," who have married Chinese. These stories can have a decisive impact on Vietnamese women who are already considering an alternative life. Mass culture and such individual narratives together create a form of fantasy about the nature of China, Chinese people, and Chinese life,[3] within which the character of a Chinese husband is one particular collective imagining.

Geographical frontiers are often not as strong as social frontiers, and the way in which communities interact with each other, how they appreciate, construct, express, and identify themselves in opposition to others, affects their life choices and status in specific social spaces such as border areas. In the case of the Sino-Vietnamese border, poverty and demographic issues cannot fully explain why Vietnamese women and Chinese men choose to share their lives. As is strongly indicated in local narratives of those living along the Honghe or Beilun rivers, people on both sides are influenced by images, representations, and rumors about each other. These visions may lead them to conclude alliances across these borders, whether they are official or not, mutually desired or not.

Notes

1. The number of interviewees ultimately reached fifty men and women directly involved in some form of cross-border relationship, and an equivalent number of other community members.
2. For additional general information on the China-Vietnam border, see Darwin, Wattie, and Yuarsi (2003), Evans, Hutton, and Eng (2000), Zhang (2010), and Zhou (2002). For additional information specifically on marriage along that border, see Grillot (2010) and Le, Belanger, and Khuat (2007).
3. After the Sino-Vietnamese war, the first women who left for China at the end of the 1980s with the border's reopening – most of whom were deceived and sold – often came back to visit their parents once their independence was negotiated with their new family.

References

Constable, Nicole, ed. 2004. *Cross-Border Marriages: Gender and Mobility in Transnational Asia*. Philadelphia: University of Pennsylvania Press.

Darwin, Muhadjir, Anna-Marie Wattie, and Susi Eja Yuarsi, eds. 2003. *Living on the Edges: Cross-Border Mobility and Sexual Exploitation in the Greater Southeast Asia Sub-Region*. Yogyakarta: Gadjah Mada University, Center for Population and Policy Studies.

Evans, Grant, Christopher Hutton, and Kuah Khun Eng, eds. 2000. *Where China Meets Southeast Asia: Social and Cultural Change in the Border Regions*. New York/Singapore: St. Martin's Press/Institute of Southeast Asian Studies.

Grillot, Caroline. 2010. *Volées, envolées, convolées... Vendues, en fuite ou re-socialisées: les "fiancées" vietnamiennes en Chine* [Stolen, Vanished, Wedded. Sold, Runaway, or Re-socialized: the Vietnamese "Brides" in China]. Paris: Connaissances & Savoirs.

Hershatter, Gail. 2007. *Women in China's Long Twentieth Century*. Berkeley: University of California Press.

Le Bach Duong, Danièle Belanger, and Khuat Thu Hong. 2007. "Transnational migration, marriage and trafficking at the China-Vietnam border," pp. 393–425 in *Watering the Neighbour's Garden: The Growing Demographic Female Deficit in Asia,* eds. Isabelle Attané and Christophe Z. Guilmoto. Paris: Committee for International Cooperation in National Research in Demography.

Thai, Hung Cam. 2008. *For Better or for Worse: Vietnamese International Marriages in the New Global Economy*. New Brunswick, NJ: Rutgers University Press.

Yan Yunxiang. 2003. *Private Life under Socialism: Love, Intimacy, and Family Change in a Chinese Village, 1949-1999*. Stanford, CA: Stanford University Press.

Zhang Juan. 2010. *Border opened up: Everyday Business in a China-Vietnam Frontier*. Sydney: Macquarie University, Ph.D. dissertation (unpublished).

Zhou Jianxin. 2002. *Zhong Yue Zhong Lao Kuaguo minzu jiqi zuqun guanxi yanjiu* [Sino-Vietnam and Sino-Laos Cross-Border Ethnic Groups and Ethnic Relationship]. Beijing: Renmin Chubanshe.

CHAPTER 9

Achieving and Restoring Masculinity through Homeland Return Visits

Hung Cam THAI

This chapter deals with the varied ways in which Vietnamese working class immigrant men remake class and masculinity by returning to visit their homeland. I contend that while research on transnationalism has become increasingly important since the early 1990s in guiding much of the current research on international migration, little has been theorized about the significance and consequences of return visits by migrants to the community of origin, especially how such visits are notably gendered social moments and processes. The subjects of this chapter are Vietnamese immigrant men who were part of a larger study on the emergence of a Vietnamese transpacific marriage market that has been gathering momentum in recent years (Thai 2008). During fourteen months of fieldwork carried out in distinct intervals in Vietnam and in the United States from 1997 to 2001, I got to know a total of 69 transpacific couples in the Vietnamese diaspora. In this distinct and emergent global marriage market, the immigrant Vietnamese men typically go to Vietnam to marry by arrangement, subsequently returning to their places of residence in the Vietnamese diaspora (most are from the United States, Canada, France, and Australia) to initiate paperwork to sponsor their wives. I came to know them during this waiting period by first entering the lives of the brides in Vietnam and later the lives of the U.S.-based grooms (Thai 2008). For the most part, because I did not interview transnational couples – both wives and husbands – when they were in the same place, I am providing an analysis about a specific period, a "snapshot" of marriage and migration during the waiting period. The data analysis presented here centers on some of the men's experiences during their return visits before taking up shared residence with their wives.

These transpacific marriages involve complex arrangements by networks of kin across the diaspora and, during the process of these marital arrangements, most of the grooms had returned to Vietnam for the first time since their emigration from Vietnam. That is, the first time they met their wives was also the first time that many of them had returned to their home country after some years of being away from it. Through probability sampling procedures, I discovered that nearly 80 percent of the men who returned from the Vietnamese diaspora to marry worked in low-wage employment. Focusing on these low-wage immigrant men, who are beginning to build and sustain transnational ties to their homeland, helps to shed light on the effects of global and transnational forces on gender relations in immigrant communities and in the homeland. This task is a particularly important one because immigrants are turning more and more frequently to their home countries for social, economic, and political activities. Furthermore, as Robert Courtney Smith argues, immigrant men "are seen to want to return home or to imagine themselves returning, whereas women want to settle or imagine themselves settling, because men lose status and power in the United States and women gain them" (2006: 13). The narratives of the men in this study reveal how low-wage immigrant men construct their masculinity given that their lives are placed "at the intersection and interstices of vast systems of power: patriarchy, racism, colonialism, and capitalism, to name a few" (Chen 1999: 589).

At the most basic level of cultural ideology, masculinity is a "personal and collective project" that often assumes an association between breadwinning and manhood (Donaldson 1993: 645). In the mid-1980s, a "new sociology of masculinity" (Carrigan, Connell, and Lee 1985) was proposed in order to critically examine power relations among men and between men and women. Since that framework was introduced, much of the scholarly work on the topic has invoked the plural *masculinities* to account for the diverse range of men's experiences. Although most scholars agree that masculinity does not constitute a singular ideology or practice, it is clustered around what Connell (1995) calls "hegemonic masculinity" which "asserts the naturalness of male domination, based on solidarities between men as well as on the subordination of women" (Jackson 1999: 201). While the notion of hegemonic masculinity is directly linked to the institution of male dominance, few men actually embody it, although most men "benefit from the patriarchal dividend of dominance over women" (Kendall 2000: 261). And although hegemonic masculinity operates across the spectrum, most scholars agree that it often marginalizes working-class men, while excluding men of color and gay men. While some scholars have argued that the concept of hegemonic masculinity is of limited use in a non-Western context, I pay attention to the transnational dimension of masculinities. An analysis of masculinity involving transnational migrants must, in my view, account for meanings of social class across international borders. As Donaldson (1993) points out, the relationship between social class and masculinity is an under-studied aspect of research on contemporary manhood. This focus is important because class privilege, for some men, sometimes makes up for other kinds of marginality (such as racial marginality). Here, I view masculinity as a process, rather than an outcome for low-wage Vietnamese immigrant men. Return activities, even if they are temporary, constitute important moments of redefining manhood.

This chapter therefore discusses the first return visit to Vietnam that the men took to meet their wives as well as subsequent trips undertaken while their wives waited in Vietnam for paper clearance to migrate. These are not just moments of meeting their wives-to-be, but extraordinary moments of a transnational journey for the men since most of them were immigrants to the West, and had only returned to Vietnam for the first time; some returned for the sole purpose of marriage, but for others, the first return visit may have prompted a desire for a transpacific marriage. I will show that homeland return visits constitute a defining moment for immigrants and their social relations across transnational social fields. Yet, it is not simply a practice based on nostalgic notions such as "home" and "roots." It is a complicated emotional desire, to be sure, but is also a contestable duty that can have powerful effects, destabilizing and altering social relations in the community of origin, producing new social hierarchies along class and gender lines, and restoring traditions that had apparently been abolished over time. Rather than analyzing specific marriages or the relatively recent formation of this contemporary transpacific market as I have done elsewhere (Thai 2003, 2008), I take this opportunity to analyze return visits as an analytical category in the larger discussion on contemporary transnational cultures.

At the outset, it is important to note that the notion of return has been conceptualized in the scholarly literature primarily as return migration, which refers to "the movement of emigrants back to their homelands to resettle" (Gmelch 1980: 136). Return visits, by contrast, do not require a permanent move but still allow migrants to "maintain multiple, yet socially meaningful, identities in both their current place of residence and their external homeland" (Duval 2004: 51). For overseas Vietnamese, return migration in order to resettle in the homeland is rare (Long 2004). It is difficult, compared to the situations of other Asian immigrants, for Vietnamese to reintegrate and resettle back in a country that they left as political refugees during the last quarter of the twentieth century. For potential return migrants to Vietnam, buying land and property is a complicated process, as is obtaining paperwork for long-term residence. Return visits, therefore, are an especially important social practice for Vietnamese desiring to sustain transnational family ties.

In fact, even such return visits have only recently become possible, due to changes in Vietnamese government policy and international diplomatic relations, particularly between the United States and Vietnam.[1] In 1986, after having no contact with most of the outside world for over a decade, the government of Vietnam adopted a new socioeconomic policy called *Doi Moi* (renovation) which did not end state ownership or central planning, but moved the country from complete state-sponsored socialism to partial free market capitalism (Ebashi 1997; Morley and Nishihara 1997). The normalization of economic and social ties by 1995, the year when U.S. President Bill Clinton established full diplomatic relations with the country (Morley and Nishihara 1997), gradually increased the number of individuals from the Vietnamese diaspora who returned to Vietnam to visit family members or to vacation. The Vietnamese government estimates that there are currently more than one million overseas Vietnamese who return to visit annually, a dramatic increase from 87,000 in 1992 and 8,000 in 1988 (Thomas 1997).

A fundamental concern here is the question of how transnational mobilities can simultaneously challenge as well as reinforce patriarchy. "Instead of being a social equalizer that empowers all migrants alike," as Luis Guarnizo argues, "transnational migration tends to reproduce and even exacerbate class, gender, and regional inequalities" (Guarnizo and Smith 1998: 281). As Yen Le Espiritu notes in her study of Filipino transnational communities, the idealization of the home "becomes problematic when it elicits a nostalgia for a glorious past that never was, a nostalgia that elides exclusion, power relations, and difference or when it elicits a desire to replicate these inequities as a means to buttress lost status and identities in the adopted country" (2003: 15). The fact that men in my study returned to Vietnam for a spouse says much about gender relations in their transnational journey from Vietnam to the West and back to their homeland. In my interviews with informants about their transnational networks and during the more than twenty-five trips I have made to Vietnam since 1997 to carry out fieldwork, I always heard people telling me that return visits were usually made first by men, followed by women and children in later return visits. But in general, single men were among the first group of people who returned to Vietnam, some for the sole purpose of finding a wife.

In terms of the macro determinants of this specific transnational marriage market, it is demographically gendered because very few overseas women return to Vietnam for husbands, as I have discovered in my investigation of case studies and in my confirmation with marriage registration lists at the Department of Justice in Vietnam. The basis of this gendered pattern is that a high male mortality rate during the Vietnam War, together with the fact that more men than women emigrated during the last quarter of the twentieth century, has produced what demographer Daniel Goodkind (1997) calls the "Vietnamese double marriage squeeze," a situation resulting in a "surplus" of women of marriageable age in Vietnam and a "surplus" of men of marriageable age in Vietnamese overseas communities, especially in Australia and in the United States. In an addition to the problem of the double marriage squeeze, Vietnamese immigrant men are much less likely than Vietnamese immigrant women to marry interracially, which reduces their chance of finding marital partners in immigrant-receiving societies (Qian 1997, 1999; Qian et al. 2001).

In what follows, I consider intersecting aspects of the lives of these Vietnamese low-wage immigrant men that precede and follow their return visits to their communities of origin. For analytical clarity, I provide the narratives of Chanh and Loc to show how these men take on, redefine, and challenge meanings of masculinity as they move through the categories of refugee, immigrant, and transmigrant in the course of return visits to the homeland.[2] The stories of these two men offer an exploratory look at how men can either "achieve" or "restore" masculinity across transnational social fields. Examining the interview data revealed these two distinct patterns among Vietnamese immigrant men as they begin to develop transnational identities. I should note that some men undergo multiple, sometimes overlapping, patterns of change so that these two patterns of achieving and restoring masculinity should be viewed as Weberian ideal types.

Achieving Masculinity

Among men who achieve masculinity through return visits, most migrated as children and generally had no experience of the labor market prior to their emigration from Vietnam. These men had varied socioeconomic backgrounds as children, but for the most part, they were now low-wage working adults. With the exception of a few men who worked in ethnic enterprises such as nail salons, where average hourly wages ranged from $8 to $12 per hour, the men in this study generally earned from $6 to $8 per hour. They usually worked in hourly wage, secondary labor-market jobs that offered them little stability (Sakamoto and Chen 1991). For the most part, they worked long hours for low pay. Their yearly salaries ranged between $8,000 and $24,000, and many of them fell below the U.S. poverty level at the time I conducted fieldwork (Dalaker 2001). For many of these men, as I have pointed out elsewhere (Thai 2003), low-wage status frequently translated into low chances of marriageability, which directly related to their sense of masculinity. Many of the men in this study pointed out that lack of financial resources in Vietnamese immigrant communities made them less desirable as marriage partners. Moreover, many of them also talked about their low-wage jobs as unrespectable, which they felt was connected to their sense of being a man. My findings reflect other findings that have shown that men are more likely than women to view their work lives as the most central aspect of their identity (Lamont 1992, 2000; Rubin 1976). Return visits to their homeland frequently offered these men, both temporarily and in the long run, an opportunity to achieve masculinity by translating wages that seem low from a U.S. perspective to wages that seem high when viewed from Vietnam. Many spoke of how this "wage convertibility" offered them a sense of emotional belonging.

The story of Chanh Tran, a thirty-two-year-old jewelry repairman who lived near Seattle when I met him, illustrates how return visits allow some men to remake social class in order to "achieve" masculinity as they take up transnational identities. For example, when I asked Chanh how he felt the first time he made a return visit to Vietnam, he quickly explained to me, "As soon as the plane touched the airport, I knew there was something there for me. I definitely had the feeling that I was home." One of the ways in which class identity becomes so poignantly evident for the men in this study is how they talk about the affordability of consumables in Vietnam, an indicator of how their low economic status took on a different meaning as they returned to Vietnam. In other words, achieving masculinity is directly related to these men's increased financial power, especially in their roles as providers. As a case in point, when I asked Chanh why he felt there was "something there" for him when the plane touched the airport, he explained:

> Before I decided to come to Vietnam, I wanted to know what to expect, and so I talked to some of my friends who had gone, and to my cousin who made visits to Vietnam. Most of the men told me how everything in Saigon is catered to men, that everywhere you go, it's really cheap and you can have a good time without having much money, and everyone treats you very nicely.

Chanh's family migrated to the United States when he was seven, part of the first large group of Vietnamese refugees who were evacuated directly out of Vietnam in the days before the fall of Saigon on 30 April 1975.[3] Chanh came of age in a family of four, living in a suburban town two hours outside of Seattle. His father worked on the assembly line at a factory when they arrived in the United States, eventually becoming a manager of the plant, while his mother took up nursing as an occupation. Chanh said he was an ambitious student in high school, excelling in math and sports. He wanted to "confess," as he expressed it, that from early on he was enamored with the idea of having money because one of his uncles owned a lucrative jewelry store near where they lived. "I wanted to earn as much money as I could, to help my parents, and to provide for my future family," he explained. Many of the immigrant men I spoke to in this study emphasized the importance of making money and providing for their families, including their wives and parents, to their identity as men. For this reason, and although he graduated in the top ten of his high school class, Chanh decided not to attend college immediately after high school, but instead took on an apprenticeship with his prosperous uncle. Chanh earned more than his friends after high school but, over time, his income stagnated as his friends who went on to college eventually earned more than he did. When I met him, Chanh had not been able to open up his own jewelry store as he had hoped, and he was still working for his uncle for an hourly wage. Reflecting on his choice of work, Chanh told me he had strong regrets about not having gone to college. He said he felt extremely marginal in his circle of friends, especially in the Vietnamese communities and networks in which he and his family were embedded:

> I definitely think that there is a stigma for not having a college degree, and most people in the Vietnamese community I know who came to the United States the same time I did went to college. I regret not having gone to college because it definitely gave me less status in the community. At the time that I decided on not going [to college], I thought that I would eventually open a jewelry store like my uncle and would make a lot of money.

Some scholars have argued that the homeland "is not only a physical place that immigrants return to for temporary and intermittent visits, but also a concept and a desire – a place that immigrants visit through the imagination" (Espiritu 2003: 10). I contend that it is precisely the return visit that allows some immigrants to realize their social status, and to take on an economic privilege relative to the people in their homeland. In short, crossing physical boundaries also results in the crossing of social boundaries. For instance, when I asked Chanh to elaborate on the moment his plane landed when he took his first visit in 1998, he explained:

> When we landed, the moment we stepped outside the airport and got a taxi to drive to my uncle's house, everything was cheap. I could afford to pay for taxis and other things that I couldn't pay in the U.S. The rest of the trip was awesome because I was able to pay for many of the times we went out.

Restoring Masculinity

Of all the men in this study, only 30 percent (n = 21/69) migrated when they were under the age of eighteen. This means that the vast majority – 70 percent – of the men in this study were adult migrants, having come of age in their homeland. It is these men for whom, through return visits, restoring masculinity was made possible by developing transnational ties to their homeland. Thus, I use the term "restore" to capture an experience of social class directly linked to masculinity that was lost due to migration, and perhaps regained upon making return visits. Men who restore masculinity differed from men who achieve masculinity primarily because the former group had reached adulthood in their homeland before emigration and had either entered or finished secondary education before they arrived on Western soil; many of them had already entered the labor market prior to migrating abroad. Moreover, most of them were unable to transfer either their skills or social status once they migrated to the West. In other words, these men had "achieved" masculinity, if they had done so at all, in their homeland before they migrated, but had experienced tremendous downward mobility and a resulting diminution of their sense of masculinity as a result of migration. The visits to their homeland served to restore their masculinity.

The story of forty-four-year-old Loc Phan highlights how, rather than increasing one's status, migration could in fact bring substantial loss to one's sense of status, especially when the homeland is used as a reference point for understanding one's position in the global status hierarchy. As part of the urban middle class in Saigon, Loc aspired to become a doctor after he graduated from high school in 1974, but his parents told him that he could not attend college because they wanted to start making preparations to leave Vietnam when the war ended. His father had connections in the Mekong delta with someone who organized boat trips for potential refugees to go to another Southeast Asian country so they could be "processed" by various Western countries as political refugees. Eventually, Loc's family became boat refugees and arrived in a suburb of Orange County where his parents had family ties. At the time that I met him, Loc was working for minimum wage in the produce department at a large ethnic supermarket near the ethnic enclave of Little Saigon in Orange County. He had been working there for nearly fifteen years, after a number of odd jobs in various ethnic enterprises, and had been living with his parents in government subsidized housing since 1979, when they arrived in the United States after spending a few years in a refugee camp in Malaysia. Loc had hoped that, over time, he could start his own business. But working at such low wages meant that he could not save enough capital to start any kind of business.

In talking about the pre-migration years, Loc revealed that his childhood was one of privilege by any standard – he grew up in a household with successful parents who owned a factory that produced office furniture for the domestic market. As an adolescent, Loc had luxuries he never encountered as a young adult: domestic servants, chauffeurs, and the best education available. It was this childhood affluence that shaped how Loc understood his social standing as a young man coming of age in his cultural context in Vietnam. As a high school graduate in 1974, towards the end of the war in Vietnam, Loc had already formed a romantic relationship with a classmate to whom he had promised marriage prior to his family's migration. When I asked him what happened to that first romantic relationship, Loc explained:

> Well, of course, I told her that I would return in a few years and marry her. But that didn't happen. The bad part of it is that I couldn't afford to go back there until two years ago, and of course I don't expect her to wait for me for that long. I thought I would be sad, but when I came back to Vietnam for the first time, there were so many people I met, so many old friends. So I wanted to make new relationships, meet new people, maybe find a wife on that trip.

For these men, restoring masculinity was usually made possible because they were able to develop a triangular relationship based on identifiable historical and geographical places that connect them, the community to which they migrated, and the community from which they originated (Guarnizo and Smith 1998: 13). In other words, the men in my study were able to restore masculinity only because they had built a transnational status system through their migration that linked their community of origin and community of destination. The effect is that such men are able to restore masculinity upon their return to the homeland precisely because of the economic divide between their homeland and their immigrant communities; this offers them the opportunity to "convert" their low wages from the West to high wages as they make return visits to Vietnam (Thai 2005). Partly because of the lack of knowledge about life in the United States, Loc's relatives and friends in Vietnam frequently thought of migration as desirable, which enhanced his status when he returned home. As Loc explained:

> I saw many people of my youth, some of them became very successful in Saigon, but they did not judge me for what I do in the United States. Some really wanted to find ways to go to the United States. I don't know why they want to. I think they have much better lives in Saigon. But they always think the United States is a land of opportunity. They don't know that it's hard to make money unless you have a lot of money.

Yet it is precisely this perception of the United States among locals in Vietnam and Loc's ability to convert low wages to high wages in Vietnam that gave him the opportunity to remake notions of social class in the context of a transnational status system. This is because wage disparities between Vietnam and the United States made even the lowest wages, such as what Loc earned, appear to be a large amount of money. When I asked Loc to recount how he felt during the first visit back, he described his feelings:

> When I returned to Vietnam for the first time, I didn't know for sure if I was going to tell people that I worked at the supermarket all these years. But when I went there, I remember not feeling as poor as I do in America! So even for many people I knew in Saigon, my job at the supermarket was a dream job. I remember this very clearly because the first time I went back in 1998, they opened up one of the first Western style supermarkets in Saigon and I took some of my friends there and I told them with this feeling of shame that I work at one of those places in the United States. And some of them told me they thought it was a great job! [laughs] I didn't feel like I was this poor man like I do in the United States working in a job that no one cares about.

Remaking Class and Masculinity through Return Visits and Transnational Ties

For many immigrant men in this study, return visits to Vietnam evoked deep emotions and a strong sense of belonging to the homeland. I suggest that return visits produce and fashion such emotions in ways that remake class and masculinity in the context of transnational ties. Through the stories of the transnational migrants in this study, I suggest that it is insufficient in this era of globalization to approach a class analysis of immigrants' lives within a bounded national scope or other bounded territorial spaces, as often occurs in the sociological literature on social class (Wright 1997). Moreover, this chapter echoes the scholarly research highlighting the fact that migration powerfully reshapes gender relations in post-migration communities (Espiritu 1997; Hondagneu-Sotelo 1994, 2003; Kibria 1993). This chapter adds to this ongoing effort by showing how return visits to the homeland can alter or amplify gender relations during the post-migration years, especially how men take on new gender ideologies and meanings of social class after making return visits to the homeland.

The broad purpose of this chapter is to show that return visits are an integral part of the transnational experience among Vietnamese immigrant men. These moments help to build and sustain transnational ties that offer an important geographical identity for taking on and challenging their class positionings. In her research on Italian migrants in Australia, anthropologist Loretta Baldassar (1997, 1998, 2001) observes that the return visit "reveals that migration is not simply about departure and establishing one's home in a new country." I see return visits as one manifestation or expression of the "multiple ties and interactions linking people or institutions across the borders of nation-states" (Vertovec 1999: 448) and that can powerfully help migrants negotiate their roots and routes (Gilroy 1993).

Notes

1. When one speaks of postwar Vietnamese men returning to their homeland, it should be understood in the context of the origin of mass refugee migration when the Vietnamese represented the core group of refugees who fled Southeast Asia shortly after the withdrawal of American troops from Vietnam and the fall of Saigon on 30 April 1975.

2. To protect the privacy of informants, all names have been changed. In addition, I have changed the names of villages in Vietnam and small towns in the United States. I have kept the real names of all metropolitan areas. And while full Vietnamese names are usually indicated in the order of last, middle, and first names, I will use "American" standards of referencing names since I used this format when I got to know informants.

3. Although Saigon's name was changed to Ho Chi Minh City when the South surrendered to Northern Vietnamese military troops in 1975, most people I met in contemporary Vietnam still refer to the city as "Saigon," or simply "Thanh Pho" [The City]. I echo their frames of reference by using the name "Saigon," and "Saigonese" to refer to the locals there.

References

Baldassar, Loretta. 1997. "Home and away: Migration, the return visit and 'transnational' identity." *Communal Plural* 5: 69–94.

———. 1998. "The return visit as pilgrimage: Secular redemption and cultural renewal in the migration process," pp. 127–156 in *The Australian Immigrant in the 20th Century: Searching Neglected Sources*, eds. Eric Richards and Jacqueline Templeton. Canberra: Australian National University Press.

———. 2001. *Visits Home: Migration Experiences between Italy and Australia*. Melbourne: Melbourne University Press.

Carrigan, Tim, Bob Connell, and John Lee. 1985. "Toward a new sociology of masculinity." *Theory and Society* 14: 551–604.

Chen, Anthony S. 1999. "Lives at the center of the periphery, lives at the periphery of the center." *Gender & Society* 13: 584–607.

Connell, R.W. 1995. *Masculinities*. Berkeley, CA: University of California Press.

Dalaker, Joseph. 2001. "U.S. Census Bureau, Current Population Reports, Series P60–214, Poverty in the United States: 2000." Washington, D.C.: U.S. Government Printing Office.

Donaldson, Michael. 1993. "What is hegemonic masculinity?" *Theory & Society* 22: 643–657.

Duval, David Timothy. 2004. "Linking return visits and return migration among Commonwealth eastern Caribbean migrants in Toronto." *Global Networks* 4: 51–67.

Ebashi, Masahiko. 1997. "The economic take-off," pp. 37-65 in *Vietnam Joins the World*, eds. James Morley and Masashi Nishihara. Armonk, NY: M.E. Sharpe.

Espiritu, Yen Le. 1997. *Asian American Women and Men: Labor, Laws and Love*. Thousand Oaks, CA: Sage Publications.

———. 2003. *Home Bound: Filipino American Lives across Cultures, Communities, and Countries*. Berkeley: University of California Press.

Gilroy, Paul. 1993. *The Black Atlantic: Modernity and Double Consciousness*. London: Hutchinson.

Gmelch, George. 1980. "Return migration." *Annual Review of Anthropology* 9: 135–159.

Goodkind, Daniel. 1997. "The Vietnamese double marriage squeeze." *International Migration Review* 31: 108–128.

Guarnizo, Luis E. and Michael Peter Smith. 1998. "The location of transnationalism," pp. 3–34 in *Transnationalism from Below*, eds. Michael Peter Smith and Luis E. Guarnizo. New Brunswick, NJ: Transaction.

Hondagneu-Sotelo, Pierrette. 1994. *Gendered Transitions: Mexican Experiences of Immigration*. Berkeley: University of California Press.

——. 2003. *Gender and U.S. Immigration: Contemporary Trends*. Berkeley: University of California Press.

Jackson, Cecile. 1999. "Men's work, masculinities and gender division of labour." *Journal of Development Studies* 36: 89–108.

Kendall, Lori. 2000. "'Oh no! I'm a nerd!': Hegemonic masculinity on an online forum." *Gender and Society* 14: 256–274.

Kibria, Nazli. 1993. *Family Tightrope: The Changing Lives of Vietnamese Americans*. Princeton: Princeton University Press.

Lamont, Michele. 1992. *Money, Morals, & Manners: The Culture of the French and the American Upper-Middle Class*. Chicago: University of Chicago Press.

——. 2000. *The Dignity of Working Men: Morality and the Boundaries of Race, Class, and Immigration*. New York: Russell Sage Foundation.

Long, Lynellyn D. 2004. "Viet Kieu on a fast track back," pp. 65–89 in *Coming Home?: Refugees, Migrants, and Those Who Stayed Behind*, eds. Ellen Oxfeld and Lynellyn D. Long. Philadelphia: University of Pennsylvania Press.

Morley, James W., and Masashi Nishihara. 1997. "Vietnam joins the world," pp. 3–14 in *Vietnam Joins the World*, eds. James W. Morley and Masashi Nishihara. Armonk, NY: M.E. Sharpe.

Qian, Zhenchao. 1997. "Breaking the racial barriers: Variations in interracial marriage between 1980–1990." *Demography* 34: 263–276.

——. 1999. "Who intermarries? Education, nativity, region, and interracial marriage, 1980 and 1990." *Journal of Comparative Family Studies* 30: 579–597.

Qian, Zhenchao, Sampson Lee Blair, and Stacey D. Ruf. 2001. "Asian American interracial and interethnic marriages: Differences by education and nativity." *International Migration Review* 35: 557–586.

Rubin, Lillian Breslow. 1976. *Worlds of Pain: Life in the Working-Class Family*. New York: Basic Books, Inc.

Sakamoto, Arthur, and Meichu D. Chen. 1991. "Inequality and attainment in a dual labor market." *American Sociological Review* 56: 295–308.

Smith, Robert Courtney. 2006. *Mexican New York: Transnational Lives of New Immigrants*. Berkeley: University of California Press.

Thai, Hung Cam. 2003. "Clashing dreams: Highly educated overseas brides and low-wage U.S. husbands," pp. 230–253 in *Global Woman: Nannies, Maids and Sex Workers in the New Economy*, eds. Barbara Ehrenreich and Arlie Russell Hochschild. New York: Metropolitan Books.

——. 2005. "Globalization as a gender strategy: Respectability, masculinity, and convertibility across the Vietnamese diaspora," pp. 76–92 in *Critical Globalization Studies*, eds. Richard. P. Appelbaum and William I. Robinson. New York: Routledge.

——. 2008. *For Better or for Worse: Vietnamese International Marriages in the New Global Economy*. Rutgers, NJ and London: Rutgers University Press.

Thomas, Mandy. 1997. "Crossing over: The relationship between overseas Vietnamese and their homeland." *Journal of Intercultural Studies* 18: 153–176.

Vertovec, Steven. 1999. "Conceiving and researching transnationalism." *Ethnic and Racial Studies* 22: 447–473.

Wright, Eric Olin. 1997. *Class Counts: Comparative Studies in Class Analysis*. Cambridge: Cambridge University Press.

CHAPTER 10

Mothers on the Move: Transnational Child-Rearing by Japanese Women Married to Pakistani Migrants

Masako KUDO

This chapter explores a newly emerging pattern of transnational living among Japanese-Pakistani mixed marriages. This pattern is one in which the Pakistani husband continues to be based in Japan, while the Japanese wife and their children move to the husband's natal household in Pakistan or to a third country. The family members then frequently cross national borders to visit each other. The majority of these mixed couples were married during the 1990s. In many cases, the husbands had already overstayed their visas at the time they met their future wives. For these men, marrying local women was one of the few ways they could escape precarious lives as undocumented migrants.[1] Currently, the majority of the children from these marriages are in their early to late teens. Judging from the situation of my informants, most of the husbands are on permanent visas and some have even acquired Japanese citizenship, which appears to indicate that they have settled down in their host country. Why, then, do some of the Japanese spouses move out of Japan with their children and leave their migrant husbands behind? Was putting down roots in a "rich country" the actual goal for these economic migrants? In this chapter, I explore the meaning behind the transnational family and try to understand what kind of "relatedness" has been imagined or constructed within the socioeconomic environment in which the family members find themselves.

The discussion that follows draws mainly on in-depth interviews I have been carrying out since 1998 with forty Japanese women married to Pakistani migrants. Most of the interviews took place in Tokyo and its surrounding areas, while some were in Pakistan. Among my informants, eleven experienced living in Pakistan where their children went to local schools while their husbands remained in Japan.

At the time of the first interviews, four of the women were based in Pakistan, while the remaining seven moved to Pakistan at a later date. Currently, six have returned to Japan with their children and five are still living in Pakistan.[2] This indicates that the scattering of families over national boundaries can be temporary even though it was initially meant to be a long-term arrangement. Moving to Pakistan is still a potential option in the future for many of my informants.[3] By examining the transnational living arrangements, we can discern a shifting notion of "family," as well as the hopes projected on future generations by the couples involved. The experiences of the Japanese wives in particular reveal conflicting desires and images concerning "family" within this newly emerging pattern in transnational families.

My discussion is divided into three sections. The first section highlights the increase in the number of Pakistani-Japanese couples and situates this phenomenon within new patterns of international marriage observed in Japan over the last two decades. Also included is a brief description of how the Pakistani husbands maintain existing ties with their natal families from the early stages of marriage and also develop new ones. The second section explores the complex factors that lead to the emergence of this new form of transnational family, including religion, education, family connections, and economics. The third section then focuses on the personal experiences of displacement that the Japanese women undergo when they cross national boundaries with their children and examines their status and role in transnational space.

Forming the Family through International Marriage: Keeping or Rebuilding Ties across National Boundaries

In Japan, couples consisting of Pakistani husbands and Japanese wives became increasingly prevalent during the 1980s and 1990s. Between 1984 and 2000, the number of Pakistani nationals registered under the visa category "Spouse or Child of Japanese National" jumped from 112 to 1,630.[4] In 2006, the population of Pakistanis registered in Japan totaled 9,086, of whom 1,225 held the "Spouse or Child of Japanese National" visa and 2,120 held the "Permanent Resident" visa (JIA 2007). Apparently, many of the men acquired permanent residency after staying in Japan with a spousal visa. Consequently, a large percentage of Pakistani male migrants in Japan are likely to be married to Japanese nationals.

This type of mixed marriage is part of a general increase in international marriages that occurred during the 1980s and 1990s. Not only has the number of international marriages in Japan risen dramatically during these two decades,[5] the data show a new, emerging "marriage scape" (Constable 2005). During the 1980s and 1990s, Japanese males who became married to non-Japanese tended to have partners within a narrow range of nationalities such as Chinese, Filipino, and Thai, while the nationalities of the spouses of Japanese females appeared to have varied more significantly.[6] This new pattern of international marriage probably reflects the influx of foreign male workers who have arrived in Japan since the 1980s to seek economic opportunities under the tight control of Japanese immigration policy.

In order to better understand the reasons behind the increase of mixed couples in Japan, it is necessary to examine the socioeconomic status of the Japanese wives as well as their aspirations and desires concerning marriage and family. Regarding the educational background of the forty Japanese women I interviewed, apart from one who finished her education after secondary school at the age of 15, ten were high school educated, eleven continued their studies at vocational college, four at junior college, nine at university, and one completed a postgraduate degree. (This information was not obtained in the remaining four cases.) As for the women's occupations prior to marriage, two were students, five were working part-time, eighteen were working full-time as office clerks, five were in medical professions such as nutritionist, and the rest had various occupations including school teacher and receptionist.

How did these women become attracted to their future husbands? The key to this question may be found in their personal narratives. On one hand, many women admitted that in the initial stage, they felt some prejudice toward "Asian foreign workers," whose low status contrasts sharply with the high status enjoyed by Westerners within the hierarchically structured image of the "other" in Japan. On the other hand, several women remarked that in comparison with Japanese men, their husbands were "kind," "sincere," and moreover "took care of and showed concern for the family." What impressed these women was both the "warm family relationships" they experienced in Pakistan in the early stages of their marriages and also the idea that their future husband represented a new type of husband and father – one who not only supports his family economically, but is also personally involved in family affairs. This concept of father and husband was novel to some of the women in that the existing image of Japanese males is of men who work long hours and leave most domestic matters to their wives. Meeting Pakistani migrants, therefore, offered an alternative form of partnership to some of the women.

How have these Japanese women built a family with their Pakistani husbands since getting married? From the very beginning, these mixed families were spread over national boundaries in three ways. First, most of the husbands continued to send varying amounts of remittances to their kin in their own country. Sending remittances is a symbolic act that proves their emotional attachment to, and moral responsibility for, their other family members back home. However, many Japanese wives considered the remittances to Pakistan as a major problem in their married life. Second, once the migrant husbands acquired a spousal visa in Japan, they tended to start their own businesses, often with the help of male siblings or relatives. Moreover, transnational kin networks became an essential factor in globalizing their businesses. Third, from a very early stage in their marriage, the husband, wife, and any children may travel to the husband's home country for various occasions, such as a sibling's marriage or *Eid* (Islamic festival). It is at these times that the husband's joint family may become involved, to a varying extent, in socializing the children as Muslims. For example, young children may be taught how to recite from the Quran by relatives they stay with.[7]

Complexities behind the Relocation of the Family

As noted, then, the increase in Pakistani-Japanese marriages does not mean that male migrants are settling down permanently in Japan; rather, their lives stretch over national boundaries. Kinship ties are maintained and renewed through the flow of remittances to their home country, the traveling to and fro among family members, and the active roles the migrants' families play in bringing up children as Muslims. In addition, these Pakistani-Japanese couples may sometimes physically relocate. It is worth examining why Japanese spouses move to another country while their Pakistani husbands continue to work in Japan.

Before exploring the factors and forces causing the relocation of the Japanese women and their children, it is necessary to understand the changes that took place in the mixed couples' lives after marriage. Most of the husbands started their own businesses after marriage. Among my forty interviewees, the husbands of twenty-eight ran their own businesses (Kudo 2007, 2009). It is noteworthy that all eleven informants who experienced living in Pakistan had a husband who was self-employed at the time of relocation. That is to say, there may be a link between the relocation of the wife and children and the husband's status of self-employment. Being self-employed, the husbands can use their time more flexibly and travel more easily across national borders than those who are employed by Japanese companies. The husbands can also stay with their wives and children when they travel to Pakistan or a third country for business purposes.

Among the eleven female informants who experienced living in Pakistan, two quit their jobs in order to move to Pakistan and the other nine had already stopped working by the time they relocated. For the most part, the women in my study became "housewives" after marriage although many informally helped their husbands' businesses while looking after children. The women's tendency to quit working outside the home became particularly strong after they had children; in fact, only seven out of the forty women kept full-time jobs. The women's decision to stay at home was in part influenced by their husband's religio-culturally derived value of gender segregation. However, it is also important to note that there has been a persistent trend among Japanese women to leave their careers during the period of child-rearing and return to work later on in life, often as part-time workers; this is borne out by the well-known "M-shaped Curve" which shows that the rate of labor participation of Japanese women in their early thirties drops sharply.[8]

Having described the socioeconomic conditions of the couples after marriage, I now return to examine the rationale for the relocation to Pakistan of the Japanese women and their children even as their husbands remain in Japan.

One of the reasons for relocation involves religion. My interviews revealed that many husbands were apprehensive about the "influences from a corrupt Japanese society" and felt a strong need to shelter their children, especially their daughters, within the "Islamic" environment of their home country. The husbands' desires to bring up their daughters in Pakistan is linked to Pakistani notions of female modesty, which require women after puberty to cover their bodies or be physically segregated from males who are unrelated to them. How they bring up their daughters is important in the long term. For example, their daughters can benefit in the Pakistani marriage market if raised in an Islamic environment where sexual segregation is practiced. A woman who was rearing her daughters in Pakistan commented, "Some Pakistani men in Japan choose to send their daughters here because girls brought up in Pakistan are perceived as sexually protected and hence ideal brides."[9]

The Japanese mothers do not necessarily agree with their husbands' view that Pakistan is the best place to nurture their children's Muslim identity. One of the main reasons for this, as I have discussed elsewhere (Kudo 2007), is that Japanese women who have converted to Islam upon marriage tend to see "Islamic" practices in Pakistan as a set of local customs that Pakistani Muslims follow without reflecting on what "true Islam" is.[10] However, Japanese wives of Pakistani migrants face various difficulties when they try to shape their children's Muslim identities in non-Islamic Japan. For instance, they feel great pressure to comply with the prevailing notions of Japanese "cultural homogeneity." This ideology makes it quite difficult for the women and their children to practice Islam in their daily lives while in Japan (Maruyama 2007: 66; Kudo 2008: 117-118). Moreover, because the Japanese educational system has not taken steps to meet the needs of children with different religious backgrounds, and also because there are no full-time Islamic schools as an alternative, the burden of developing a Muslim identity for the children falls mainly on the shoulders of the Japanese mothers. This is a responsibility that many of the women feel strongly about; thus, they may agree, albeit sometimes reluctantly, to migrate to Pakistan despite the many problems they know they will face there.

Another reason for family relocation involves educational goals, in particular, the desire to acquire the English language. Many of those who move to Pakistan send their children to prestigious schools that offer an English-mediated learning environment. As Vuorela (2002: 80) notes, "For the aspiring elite, or the people with upwardly mobile interests, education became the most valuable symbolic and social capital, worth investing in even at the expense of home life and a family environment, which would see children grow up in its confines." Having their children become fluent in English is a priority for many husbands because it bestows prestige and provides a means of economic survival in the future. Although there are international schools in Tokyo, attending these is not an option for most of the children for a number of reasons, including the economic situation of the family.[11] For the migrants, sending their children to prestigious schools in Pakistan is a much more affordable option, because the family can make the most of the favorable exchange rate between the two countries.[12]

Another factor that influences the decision to relocate is an aspiration for "relatedness." Some husbands want their children to grow up with close family relationships and to inherit their family's values, such as respecting elders.[13] A strong feeling of obligation towards one's parents is also felt by the husbands whose parents are still alive in Pakistan. Furthermore, the men's notion of fatherhood does not necessarily consist of having to live with their children and share daily experiences. That is, being "away" does not make a man less of a father. For example, one husband who was absent from his family much of the time due to his transnational business said that he sees his role as providing for his family and passing on financial resources to his child.[14] Finally, the creation of a transnational family is a way for the migrants to overcome the various kinds of marginalities they experience in Japan, such as any racial discrimination their children may face.

The factors giving rise to transnational families are therefore complex. They involve a desire on the part of the Pakistani migrants to reproduce Muslim-ness, in particular an ideal form of femininity, as well as a strong ambition for upward social mobility through education. The feelings of their Japanese wives, however, are more ambiguous. While many of them do feel it is important to bring up their children as Muslim, they face various predicaments as their transnational lives evolve, as will be explained next.

Mothers in Displacement: The Experiences of Japanese Women in Transnational Space

In Pakistan, the daily experiences of the Japanese wives are shaped by local norms and practices relating to family and gender. In most cases, the wife stays in her husband's household, which ideally will consist of the husband's parents, his married brothers with their wives and children, and his unmarried siblings.[15] The husband's family provides the Japanese wife and her children with language support and a sense of security, especially during the early stage of life in Pakistan. Still, the wife faces various difficulties in this type of joint household, in which she will spend most of her time while in Pakistan.

One cultural practice that greatly affects the Japanese wives is *parda*, a form of sexual segregation widely observed in South Asia.[16] Although the attitude toward this idea is undergoing a dynamic transformation in Pakistan, for many of the women I interviewed *parda* is still a reality that constrains their physical mobility. The power structure of the households in which they live also has an impact on the Japanese women's lives. A Pakistani household is one based on seniority and gender, and the wives are expected to act accordingly. This affects the economic autonomy of the Japanese wives. For example, the remittances from their husbands are often controlled by a senior member of the household[17] who decides how the money will be distributed among household members. The experiences of the Japanese wives in Pakistan may also be affected by the way in which they are marginalized within their husbands' households because they are outsiders not having come from their husbands' kin groups.[18] Furthermore – and particularly at the early stage of their marriages – they may be viewed as having been raised in a "corrupt" non-Islamic environment. Their cultural incompetence may also mark them negatively. As one Japanese wife who lived in Pakistan in her husband's joint household explained, "My son does not like me to visit his school because I am not good at Urdu. Also, when there is an important issue to discuss within the household, he tells me not to voice my opinion. It is not because I am a woman, but Japanese."

The position of these Japanese wives within their husbands' natal households is, however, more complex than it may seem. While the wives tend to be perceived as foreign "others" and thus appear to be at the margin of the domestic arena where local cultural values and practices are reproduced, they do take on the role of caregivers for the children and the elderly in their husbands' households. Moreover, some Japanese wives feel that compared to the wives of their brothers-in-law, they are given a higher status as women in that they contribute economically to the household as a result of the regular remittances of their husbands who acquired legal status by marrying them. The global hierarchy between Japan and Pakistan privileges the Japanese wives and gives them a certain degree of power within the domestic power structure that is otherwise determined by gender and seniority.[19]

Further complicating the lives of the Japanese women is that upon relocating to Pakistan, they may take on new burdens. Although their participation in their husbands' businesses decreases to some degree compared with their involvement in the initial stages of its establishment, they may still have to deal with business documents or renew housing contracts written in Japanese when they return to Japan with their children during the summer months. In addition, the wives may become worried about how to take care of their own aging parents who are still living in Japan. Thus, the Japanese women may feel they have to live up to expectations of them as mothers, wives, daughters, and daughters-in-law, even as their kin are scattered across national boundaries.

Conclusion

The emergence of transnational families among Japanese-Pakistani mixed couples indicates that marrying local women does not automatically lead to settling down in the country to which the men migrated. Rather, what we see are the complex trajectories of transnational families in the making, which cannot be solely attributed to the desires of Muslim migrants to develop the religious identities of their offspring in order to reproduce their own Muslim-ness. As this chapter discusses, transnational living arrangements are an outcome of complex factors including ambition for upward social mobility, the desire that Pakistani migrants have to become "related" as family, and economic strategies designed to maximize their social networks across national boundaries. Even though the migrant husbands have acquired legal status in Japan that enables them to be highly mobile, Pakistan still remains a morally and emotionally charged space for many of them.

It should be noted, however, that once dispersed across national boundaries the families may reunite and live in Japan after some years. The unstable nature of this type of transnational arrangement has advantages and disadvantages. Although the Pakistani-Japanese couples can make the best of their transnational social networks in order to form a family across national boundaries, their move is also constrained by their socioeconomic marginalities such as discrimination and the difficulties in obtaining a visa to a third country.

The process of forming and rebuilding the family in transnational space involves negotiating the meaning of "family." For the Pakistani-Japanese couples, "family" is not a closed entity composed of the nuclear unit, but also includes the joint household in Pakistan. The Japanese wives, however, may struggle with the notion of family during their displacement overseas. Through their ongoing negotiation of transnational family practices, the mixed couples challenge the commonplace notion of the family as a unit sharing food and space on a daily basis with a common language and within a homogeneous culture.

Notes

1. Japan has still not yet officially opened its doors to "unskilled" workers, but the 1990 immigration reform law granted foreign nationals with Japanese ancestry the right to reside and work in Japan. This resulted in a wave of labor migrants from South American countries. The trainee scheme has been seen as another form of "back door" to provide Japanese employers with cheap and flexible labor.
2. The trajectories of transnational family-making are quite complex. In addition, there are considerable variations in the ways in which families are scattered over national boundaries. In two out of the eleven cases in which the wife and children moved to Pakistan, the husband later moved to Pakistan as well. Out of the forty total cases I studied, there are two in which the children were sent to Pakistan to live in the natal

household of their father while the mother lives in Japan. Three of the six women who returned to Japan from Pakistan then relocated to a third country and one subsequently returned to Japan. Finally, among the six women who returned to Japan from Pakistan, three are now divorced.

3. It should be also mentioned that in three of the forty cases, the Japanese wife presently lives with her children in a third country such as the U.A.E and New Zealand where the husband has a business base (Kudo 2010). In this chapter, I limit my discussion to only those who have relocated to Pakistan.

4. Although the sex and age of the residents in this category are not provided in the statistics, it is probable that they consist predominantly of men who married Japanese women for reasons noted in Kudo (2007: 7).

5. The percentage of marriages in Japan in which one member of the couple is of foreign nationality has increased from 0.9 percent in 1980 to 4.5 percent in 2000 (MOHLW 2002).

6. This contrasts with the 1960s when over 90 percent of international marriages involving Japanese females were to Americans, South and North Koreans, and Chinese (MOHLW 2002).

7. Also, during such visits boys may be circumcised and animal sacrifices for the birth of a child (*aqiqa*) may take place.

8. The M-shaped Curve reflects a complex set of factors including social norms which prioritize caregiving roles for married women, the lack of sufficient institutional provisions for child care, and various forms of gender discrimination in employment that discourage married women with family responsibilities from continuing to work.

9. This woman added that Pakistanis tend to think of overseas Pakistanis in Western societies like England and America as "different" (in a moral sense) from themselves.

10. The majority of the women married to Pakistanis converted to Islam upon marriage. This is because in order for the husband to obtain a spousal visa, the couple must complete marital procedures in accordance with the laws of both countries concerned. The procedures include the bride's conversion to Islam which must take place before the required Pakistani religious marriage contract can be issued. Although male Muslims are permitted by Islam to marry "people of the Book," generally meaning Christians and Jews, two Japanese women who were Christians both converted to Islam upon marriage. However, cases in which Japanese Christian women did not convert to Islam upon marriage may also exist.

11. Most of these schools are also located in Central Tokyo and would require a difficult commute for the children of families that live outside Tokyo.

12. However, the meaning of a "good education" differs slightly depending on the family and the sex of the children. One woman who was living in Pakistan at the time of the first interview told me that she and her husband were thinking of sending their son to an international school, but not their daughters as they were apprehensive about "bad Western influences." Nonetheless, sending a daughter to a prestigious school is important because being educated is one of the conditions that make one's daughter an ideal bride. The families with daughters feel it is necessary to carefully balance their daughters' sexual modesty with their education.

13. In most cases, the language spoken at home in Japan is Japanese; however, some families do speak, at least to some degree, Urdu or other languages used in the husband's household in Pakistan. Some Japanese-Pakistani couples consider learning the language spoken within the husband's natal family to be important for the children in order to retain and develop intimate ties with their father and the other members of the joint household.

14. The views of this husband, however, contrast with that of some of the wives who have lived with their children away from their husbands. One woman who lived in a third country with her children but without her husband, for example, told me that she believed that their children lack discipline because of the absence of a male authority figure. Another woman who lived in Pakistan with her children while her husband continued his business in Japan wished she could have shared the joy of watching her children grow up with her husband, and added that it is a great pity her husband was not able to be with their children on a daily basis.

15. Behind the form of the joint household is an ideal that brothers should remain together (Lyon and Fischer 1997: 174). In practice, though, a household may be affected not only by the life cycle of the family, but also by other factors such as urbanization and labor migration (Dube 1997: 25; Donnan 1997).

16. Among Muslims in South Asia *parda* tends to be legitimized in terms of Islam. The different emphasis placed on the notion and practice of *parda* between Muslims and Hindus should also be noted (Mandelbaum 1988: 76-97; Dube 1997: 67). Within Pakistan, the practice of *parda* may vary according to class, region, ethnicity, and other factors. Importantly, the practice of *parda* is considered crucial in maintaining the honor of the family, which largely depends on the conduct of the women of the house.

17. One woman told me that an important key to living in harmony in the joint household is never to intervene in financial matters.

18. Ideally speaking, marriage is arranged between families within the same *biraderi*, the extended kin group. However, the ideals and practices concerning marriage among Pakistanis are undergoing a dynamic transformation both within and beyond Pakistan.

19. For instance, one woman said that her husband's joint family tolerated her living in a separate household independent of the family only because she had contributed considerably to the household economy. In this way, the Japanese wife's status in her husband's joint household is the result of the interaction of various factors, including economics, gender, and nationality.

References

Constable, Nicole. 2005. "Introduction: Cross-border marriages, gendered mobility, and global hypergamy," pp. 1–16 in *Cross-Border Marriages: Gender and Mobility in Transnational Asia*, ed. Nicole Constable. Philadelphia: University of Pennsylvania Press.

Donnan, Hastings. 1997. "Family and household in Pakistan," pp. 1–24 in *Family and Gender in Pakistan: Domestic Organization in a Muslim Society,* eds. Hastings Donnan and Frits Selier. New Delhi: Hindustan Publishing Corporation.

Dube, Leela. 1997. *Women and Kinship: Comparative Perspectives on Gender in South and South-East Asia.* Tokyo: United Nations University Press.

JIA (Japan Immigration Association). 2007. *Zairyu Gaikoku-jin Tokei* [Statistics on the Foreigners Registered in Japan]. Tokyo: Japan Immigration Association.

Kudo, Masako. 2007. "Becoming the other in one's own homeland? The processes of self-construction among Japanese Muslim women." *Japanese Review of Cultural Anthropology* 8: 3–27.

———. 2008. "Negotiation of difference in 'multicultural' Japan: Japanese women converted to Islam through international marriage," pp. 113–122 in *Transnational Migration in East Asia: Japan in a Comparative Focus,* eds. Shinji Yamashita, Makito Minami, David Haines, and Jerry Eades. Senri Ethnological Reports, No.77, Osaka: National Museum of Ethnology.

———. 2009. "Pakistani husbands, Japanese wives: A new presence in Tokyo and beyond." *Asian Anthropology* 8: 109–123.

———. 2010. "Making use of religio-cultural resources in global circulation: A case of Pakistani-Japanese Muslim couples." Paper presented at the 109th Annual Meeting of the American Anthropological Association, New Orleans, LA, 17–21 November 2010.

Lyon, Wenonah, and Michael Fischer. 1997. "Household structure and household income in Lahore," pp. 171–188 in *Family and Gender in Pakistan: Domestic Organization in a Muslim Society,* eds. Hastings Donnan and Frits Selier. New Delhi: Hindustan Publishing Corporation.

Mandelbaum, David G. 1988. *Women's Seclusion and Men's Honor: Sex Roles in North India, Bangladesh and Pakistan.* Tucson: University of Arizona Press.

Maruyama, Hideki. 2007. "Diversity as advantage in a 'homogeneous' society: The educational environment for Muslims in Japan." *Shingetsu Electronic Journal of Japanese-Islamic Relations* Vol. 1, March 2007.

MOHLW (Ministry of Health, Labour and Welfare). 2002. *Jinko Dotai Tokei* [Vital Statistics of Japan]. Tokyo: Health and Welfare Statistics Association.

Vuorela, Ulla. 2002. "Transnational families: Imagined and real communities," pp. 63–102 in *The Transnational Family: New European Frontiers and Global Networks,* eds. Deborah Bryceson and Ulla Vuorela. Oxford: Berg.

CHAPTER 11

Here, There, and In-between: Lifestyle Migrants from Japan

Shinji YAMASHITA

"Long-stay," the term Japanese use for international retirement migration/tourism, has been coming to the fore in the recent Japanese international tourist market. Against the background of an aging society with a falling birthrate and increasing life expectation, and the high cost of living in Japan, people worried about their lives after retirement have been increasingly moving abroad to places such as Hawaii, Australia, and particularly Southeast Asian countries. There they seek more meaningful lives with a lower cost of living and a warmer climate. This chapter examines this recent trend in Japanese international tourism/migration, dealing particularly with the Japanese elderly who move to Malaysia and Indonesia, on the basis of my research during the period from 2004 to 2008.[1] In so doing, the chapter attempts to link tourism and migration studies, while acknowledging the importance of contemporary lifestyles in which people increasingly live transnational lives.

Background and Development of Long-stay Tourism/Migration in Contemporary Japan

Let us begin by looking at the background and development of the long-stay phenomenon in Japan. Japan is likely to experience increasing social problems due to an aging society. It is estimated that the percentage of the population over 65 years will increase to 33.7 percent by 2035, and 40.5 percent by 2055,[2] compared to 23.1 percent in 2010.[3] This demographic change has generated anxiety about the social welfare system in contemporary Japan. The current pension system and social welfare policies will not be able to deal with the entire population of elderly people in the future, and these problems have become serious issues for individuals as well as for the government. Moreover, the burden of medical and social welfare expenses is increasing for the elderly, while the size of pensions is static or even being reduced due to the crisis in the Japanese pension system. Under such socioeconomic conditions caused by changes in demographic structure, some pensioners and retirees are likely to consider living abroad, where the cost of living is lower than in Japan, as a strategy to secure their own quality of life in retirement.

The term "long-stay" is a registered trademark of the Long Stay Foundation which was established in 1992 as a public interest corporation authorized by the then Japanese Ministry of International Trade and Industry. According to the Foundation, long-stay is explained as "a style of staying abroad for a relatively long time in order to experience the life and culture in a place of destination and contribute to the local society while leaving the economic resources in Japan."[4] The history of the Long Stay Foundation goes back to the "Silver Columbia Plan 1992" of 1986. This was a government-led project to help overseas Japanese residents live prosperous second lives in retirement. The project aimed to build an "overseas *ikigai* town" or "Japanese village" for retirees with a lower cost of living, a nicer climate, and a better living environment. However, the plan received criticism on the grounds that Japan was trying to "export" its elderly in the collapse of the Japanese bubble economy.

After the establishment of the Long Stay Foundation, "long-stay" began to put more emphasis on tourism. Since most of the supporting members of the Long Stay Foundation are from the tourism industry, they stress tourism rather than permanent migration in their marketing strategies. In recent years the tourism industry has started to commercialize long-stay tourism as well. The size of the current market is still small but if we remember that 6.14 million Japanese aged over fifty – 36.9 percent of the total outbound tourists – traveled overseas in 2010,[5] and that the percentage will increase due to the progressively aging society in Japan, this type of tourism could have great potential for the international tourism market.

Mass media also play an important role in promoting long-stay tourism. Television companies have broadcast shows about retirement life abroad. There are also many publications on Japanese international retirement migration. One publishing company, Ikarosu Ltd., a supporting member of the Long Stay Foundation, has published books specializing in long-stay tourism. Diamond Inc., known for its series of popular travel guidebooks called *Chikyû no Arukikata* (Globe Trotters Travel Guide), has started to publish a new series of guidebooks featuring long-stay tourism called *Chikyû no Kurashikata* (Globe Residents Travel Guide).

NPOs or volunteer circles for the mutual exchange of information for this purpose have also been formed, among which World Stay Club (established in 1995), *Kyameron Kai* or Cameron Long Stay Club (established in 1993), and *Nangoku Kurashi no Kai,* or Tropical Lives Club, which promotes retirement in *nangoku* or "southern countries" (established as an NPO in 1998), are well known.

Malaysia as the Most Popular Long-stay Destination

According to a survey carried out by the Long Stay Foundation in 2006, the most popular place for long-stay tourism was Malaysia,[6] followed by Australia (the most popular destination until 2005), Thailand, New Zealand, and Hawaii. The Foundation explains as follows: "Areas such as Australia, Hawaii, New Zealand and Canada were popular due to their appeal as English-speaking destinations, their high level of safety and comfortable weather. However, South Asian countries have grown increasingly popular as is the case with Malaysia and other tourist destinations such as Thailand and the Philippines, pointing to the growing demand among consumers. Some of the reasons for their increased popularity are the relatively low cost of living, the short flight time, and the warm weather. These elements are referred to as 'Cheap, Near, Warm'" (*TJI* on line, 14 November 2007).

The Malaysian government is also quite active in hosting retired people and provides a special kind of visa, "Malaysia my second home program" (MM2H). It started in 2002, although a "silver-hair program" for retirement visas had existed since 1987. The MM2H program allows foreigners who qualify by meeting certain financial and other criteria to reside in the country on a long-stay visa of up to ten years. According to statistical data from the Ministry of Tourism, Malaysia, by the end of 2006, the number of those who obtained this visa reached 9,551 people, including Chinese (2,021), Bangladeshis (1,429), British (1,049), Taiwanese (621), Singaporeans (604), and Japanese (513) (Ono 2008: 155). Shôtaro Ishihara, the managing director of Tropical Resort Lifestyle, indicated in 2007 that he expected the number of Japanese staying in Malaysia under the program to double within three years from 700 people to 1,400, due to the exodus of baby-boomers. He suggested that "there are about seven million Baby Boomers retiring this year and statistics show that twenty percent of them, or 1.4 million people, will seek a retirement home outside Japan" (*The Star*, 24 March 2007).

Yasuhiko Sakamoto, the chairman of the MM2H program promoting committee of the Japan Club of Kuala Lumpur, answered the question "why Malaysia?" as follows: "In Japan it costs at least 260,000 yen a month for retired elderly couple to lead a standard retirement life, and 370,000 yen to have a good quality of life. On the other hand, the average provision of pension for the couple is only 190,000 yen a month. This means pensioners in Japan are quite tough economically…. If you move to Malaysia, you can make the most use of the pension money up to three times, because the cost of living here is one-third. In other words, you can enjoy 600,000 yen life in Malaysia with 200,000 yen in Japan!" (*MM2H Newsletter* No.2, 2007).

In Malaysia one has various options for long-stay destinations: metropolitan Kuala Lumpur, the seaside resort of Penang, the cool Cameron Highlands, and Kota Kinabalu of Sabah, Malaysian Borneo. According to Ishihara in the newspaper article mentioned above, "Penang and Kuala Lumpur are among the most preferred states for MM2H participants as they both offer good security and healthcare facilities." But in a recent trend, people who choose Kuala Lumpur are increasing, surpassing Penang for the Japanese pensioner population. I conducted field research on Japanese long-stay elderly in Kota Kianbalu in 2004 and 2006, Penang in 2005, and Kuala Lumpur and the Cameron Highlands in 2007. In the following, I will sketch three cases on the basis of my observations in Malaysia.[7]

Case I. Enjoying the High Quality Retirement Life in Kuala Lumpur

Kuala Lumpur, the capital of Malaysia, is a developing modern city with a population approaching two million people. By 2007 the city had about 5,000 Japanese residents of whom about 700 were under the MM2H program. Mr. A provides an example. After his retirement from a trading company in 1999, he moved to Kuala Lumpur in 2000 at the age of 65 with a retirement visa, then provided by the "silver hair program." As a trading company employee, he had been posted to various places in the world such as Singapore, London, Frankfurt, Paris, and Kuala Lumpur where he stayed for seven years from 1961 to 1968. After moving to Kuala Lumpur, he and his wife have been enjoying the city life, and particularly the high quality of retirement life with Japan's one-third price. Both of them actively participate in hobbies such as golf, glee club, dancing, and aerobics organized by the Japan Club. They have bought a flat in Kuala Lumpur and sold their house in Japan. They are so satisfied with life in Kuala Lumpur that they are enthusiastically involved in promoting the MM2H program as volunteer helpers. They are now thinking that they will die in Kuala Lumpur.

Case 2. Seasonal Long-stay in the Cameron Highlands

The Cameron Highlands, famous for the Boo tea plantations since the British colonial days, are located 200 kilometers north of Kuala Lumpur. This is a cool highland resort with a temperature of 18 to 20 degrees centigrade at 1,500 meters above sea level. Because of a description in a newspaper article, Mr. B from Kitakyushu City came to the Cameron Highlands in 2004 for the first time after his retirement from a steel company at the age of 62. He was fascinated by the comfortable weather of the tropical highlands. By the time I met him in September 2007, he had visited the Highlands seven times: four times with his wife and three times alone. He usually stays in the Highlands for three months at every visit. During his stay, he plays tennis four times a week and golf twice a week. Sometimes he enjoys trekking. He comes as a tourist, rather than with the MM2H program, and belongs to *Kyameron Kai* (Cameron Long Stay Club). Most of the members come to enjoy seasonal long-stay in the summer (July to

August) and winter (February to March) seasons. In the high season Japanese long-stay residents in Cameron Highlands number about 200 to 250.

Case 3. Escaping from the Japanese Community to Malaysian Borneo

Kota Kinabalu is the capital city of the state of Sabah, Malaysian Borneo, with tropical rain forest hinterlands and coral seas. The city has approximately 540,000 people with 300 Japanese residents. However, there are only 20 people or so who stay through the MM2H program. Mr. C, with his wife and daughter, began to stay in Kota Kinabalu in 2003 in his fifties as one of the earliest applicants for this program in this region. As a member of *Nangoku Kutashi no Kai* (Tropical Lives Club), they visited Chiangmai in Thailand, Davao in the Philippines, Kuala Lumpur, Penang, and the Cameron Highlands in Malaysia to look for a good long-stay destination. However, they felt constrained by destinations that had a strong Japanese community and therefore bothersome social relationships with other Japanese residents. Instead they chose Kota Kinabalu because there was a smaller Japanese population. They preferred not to associate with a Japanese community, interacting instead with local people. They are retired in Kota Kinabalu, having escaped from Japanese society. Retirement can also be a way of releasing oneself from one's own society.

Overall, from Kuala Lumpur to Kota Kinabalu, there are a variety of ways in which Japanese pensioners can live their retirement lives in Malaysia. That variety itself is one of the attractions of long-stay in Malaysia. In addition, as the Malaysian society is based on multiculturalism, Japanese people can keep their way of living without abandoning their cultural values.

A Japanized Paradise: Pensioners in Bali, Indonesia

Bali is a well known international tourist destination in Indonesia which first developed in the 1920s. It has been a successful tourist place as "the last paradise" resort and cultural tourism. In recent years, however, the number of visitors has fluctuated because of various negative incidents such as the Asian economic crisis in 1997, the collapse of the Suharto regime in 1998, the September 11th terrorist attacks in New York in 2001, the spread of SARS and bird flus in Asia, and particularly the bombings by Muslim terrorists in the Balinese resorts of Kuta in 2002 and Jimbaran in 2005. As a result, tourism in Bali has entered a period of instability in its development cycle (Darma Putra and Hitchcock 2006).[8]

As for the nationality of foreign tourists in Bali, visitors from Japan have dominated Bali's recent international tourism landscape. Of 1.66 million direct foreign visitors to Bali in 2007, 350,000 (21 percent) were from Japan, while 200,000 (12 percent) were from Australia, 140,000 (8.4 percent) from Taiwan, and 130,000 (7.8 percent) from Korea.[9] The number of Japanese visitors to Bali rose in the early 1990s with the introduction of Japan Airlines direct flights.[10] Therefore, present-day tourism in Bali cannot be discussed without taking Japanese tourists into account. "The last paradise" created by the Western tourist gaze is now being Japanized (Yamashita 2003: 89–94).

There is also a change in the style of Japanese international tourism. Formerly Japanese tourists were well known for their group tourism and busy tour schedules. However, in recent years Japanese, particularly the young, are traveling not in groups but as individual travelers. In addition, a recent tourist brochure in Japan describes Bali as "the island which touches your heart" with a stress on the word "heart" or *kokoro* in Japanese. Also Bali is presented as a "second homeland" (Yamashita 2003: 93). Actually, the Balinese landscapes, rather than being "exotic," sometimes make Japanese people feel "nostalgic": to them the *barong* dance is reminiscent of the Japanese lion dance (*shishimai*), and rice terraces are quite familiar from Japanese rural areas.

With the increase in Japanese visitors to Bali, Japanese residents in Bali have also increased. According to the Japanese Consulate General in Denpasar, there were 1,449 Japanese residents registered at the Consulate in 2004.[11] In terms of age, 469 (32 percent) belonged to the 25 to 40 age group, 467 persons (32 percent) were less than 10 years old, and 182 (13 percent) were aged over 50. Interestingly, the biggest group by gender and age were females aged 25 to 40, who numbered 381 persons (82 percent of the age group). These are principally women who have married Balinese men after repeated trips as tourists (Yamashita 2003: Chapter 7; Yamashita 2008a). They are now giving birth and rearing their children there: that is why children below the age of 10 make up such a large portion (32 percent) of the Japanese residents in Bali – they are actually children of mixed parentage.

Among the more elderly people, those in their fifties number 101 (55 percent), followed by 65 (36 percent) in their sixties, 18 (10 percent) in their seventies and at least three (2 percent) in their eighties. Thus 91 percent of the older residents are in their fifties and sixties, and among these males (66 percent) predominate. Of the interviews I conducted with retirees from 2006 to 2008, I present three cases to illustrate the lives of pensioners in Bali.

Case 4. A Work-free Life: Early Retirement and Migration

Mr. D came to Bali in 2004, with Mrs. D, after his early retirement from a pharmaceutical company in Tokyo at the age of 55. When Mr. D turned 50 years old, he wondered if he could live abroad after retirement. His wife found an advertisement for "villas in Bali," according to which one could build a house in Bali for the seemingly very low cost of three million yen. So they visited Bali and immediately leased a piece of land in Ubud to build a house. He found the Ubud landscape nostalgic; it reminded him of the landscape in Japan in the 1960s when he was a child. The house was built a year later (it actually cost fifteen million yen) but they did not have time to visit Bali because of his work. When he was 54 years old, he decided to take early retirement from the company. He felt that he had worked hard enough and now wanted to enjoy life and his hobbies while he was still young and healthy. He rented out his house in Tokyo. In Bali he enjoys golf, fishing, and good food. His wife enjoys Balinese dance. Recently he came back to Tokyo and watched the people walking busily with "bad looking faces." He felt sorry for them and wanted to return to Bali immediately. In 2007, Mr. D took his mother to Bali. She had had a stroke (cerebral hemorrhage) and her doctor suggested taking her to Bali to stay with him. When I met her in 2008, she had recovered to the extent that she was able to have dinner outside. Providing care is much easier in Bali than in Japan because one can hire care givers at a low cost. The warm climate in Bali also helped her to recover from the stroke.

Case 5. "Japan is Over": A New Life on One's Own

Mr. E came to Bali as a tourist for the first time in 1990. Staying overnight at a hotel in Sanur, he got up in the morning sunshine to the sound of birds chirping, and felt that this was the place for him to die. After his retirement from a publishing company in Tokyo in 2001, he came to Sanur again to start his new life (and maybe to die there) when he was 61 years old. He thinks that "Japan is over," and that there is no need for him to live there anymore. His wife, however, did not follow him. She chose, instead, to live in Japan. They live separately, though they are not divorced. He is of the opinion that a husband and wife should live separately in pursuit of their own reasons for living once they have finished with child rearing and work. He enjoys his single life in Bali, playing tennis in the morning, taking a siesta in the afternoon, reading books over coffee at the seaside café at sunset, and listening to live jazz in the evening. Long-stay tourists are usually couples but there are single people like him who enjoy this kind of separate lifestyle away from their spouses.

Case 6. Escaping from a Life "Soaked with Medicines"

The F family – Mr. F, aged 69, Mrs. F, aged 67, and their daughter, in her thirties at the time of my 2006 research – came to Bali in 2004 from Mie Prefecture. Mrs. F had had several operations and her health problems resulted in a life "soaked with medicines." Through her younger daughter, they became acquainted with a Balinese visiting Japan. Hearing about Bali, Mrs. F wondered whether she could recover her health in this "paradise." So she made her first trip to Bali in March 2004 with her husband and daughter, visiting the Balinese friend who had already returned there. She liked Bali so much that she decided to move there; the

Balinese friend helped them find a house in Ubud. Four months later in July 2004, they moved to Bali. Mrs. F brought many medicines from Japan but a Balinese doctor suggested that she need not take so many. So began a life without medicine. She recovered her health, enjoyed her life, and suffered from less stress. She was able to offload the housework by hiring domestic workers cheaply. They now have visas for retirees and were thinking about selling their house in Japan, because they seldom go back there.

Compared with the Malaysian cases, pensioners in Bali seem much more individualistic: most of them are single, not couples. Even when they are married, it is often the case that they come alone, as shown in Case 5 above. They also seem to be less wealthy in general than pensioners in Malaysia, reflecting the fact that the cost of living in Bali is much lower.

International Retirement Tourism/Migration from a Japanese Perspective

Long-stay is a Japanese version of international retirement migration. Feeling anxious about the future of the Japanese pension and social welfare system, Japanese retirees seem to be more interested in enjoying a better quality of life in a foreign place with a nicer climate and lower cost of living within the range of their pensions. Here I will make some general observations of this phenomenon on the basis of the cases described so far.

First, life takes on a new meaning in retirement. Before retirement, working towards promotion on a career track and/or raising children are typically the major goals in life for most Japanese people. In retirement, people search for something that can provide them with an *ikigai* or "reason for living," such as a hobby or volunteer work. In this way they pursue their own lives, which may include being free from spouses and even from Japanese society itself. This can cause a Japanese type of transnational householding (Toyota 2006). Long-stay provides these retirees with an opportunity to pursue a new kind of life according to new value orientations. In this sense, long-stay is part of what Machiko Sato (2001) has called "lifestyle migration." It is, therefore, a new phenomenon in which tourism and migration have merged in the contemporary globalized world.

Second, there is also some continuity with lives before retirement, because retirees usually choose their long-stay destinations based on their previous experiences as employees posted abroad or as international travelers. So the long-stay destination is not necessarily an entirely new world for pensioners. Rather, people tend to move to places they know, as we have seen in Cases 1 and 5. The popularity of playing golf among the Japanese retirees in long-stay destinations is also due to the habitus acquired through their participation in the Japanese corporate culture, in which playing golf is part of their business.

Third, in the choice of long-stay destinations, economic factors play a prominent role. People want to use the purchasing power of the Japanese yen more efficiently in destinations abroad where living costs are lower than Japan. This is particularly the case in Southeast Asian countries, including Malaysia and Indonesia as examined in this chapter. Also many people prefer Asian destinations because they feel at home there; they find a familiarity with Japan, and even rediscover an "old, nostalgic Japan,"[12] as has been observed in Bali. In this way, Japanese pensioners enjoy a second home in the southern countries with lower costs. However, this may lead to the criticism that "countries in Southeast Asia are counting on their sunny climates to sell themselves to wealthy people looking for a place to spend their sunset years."[13]

Fourth, looking at their visa status, some people obtain a retirement visa but the majority have a social visit visa or a tourist visa. Therefore, they usually do not stay longer than two or three months. This is particularly the case with long-stay in the Cameron Highlands. Therefore, we should specify that long-stay is not migration in the usual sense but a sort of "multi-habitation" in an age of transnationalization. People are living here, there, and in-between.

Fifth, with regard to language, retirees usually speak Japanese, while they can use English or local tongues if necessary. As their association is mostly limited to the local Japanese society, language does not seem to cause serious problems in their daily life. Transnational living does not necessarily require the ability to speak multiple languages. Nor do they abandon their Japanese identity.

Sixth, long-stay is being popularized as a style of living rather than one of dying. Retirees move to a place where they can spend their retirement as long as they are still healthy and active. However, the increasing cost of medical care in Japan may force them to move for medical reasons in the future, leading to an increase in medical tourism to countries that promote medical services. In fact, as shown in Case 6, some people already move for health or care reasons, or even to die in a place they like, as in Case 5. In this regard I should mention that countries such as Singapore, Thailand, and Malaysia have been eagerly promoting medical tourism.[14] Moreover, Yasuhiko Sakamoto, the chairman of the MM2H program promoting committee of the Japan Club of Kuala Lumpur, mentioned earlier, suggests on his website making wills for those preparing to die abroad.[15]

Conclusion

As has been stated above, long-stay is a form of both tourism and migration. An American anthropologist, Valene Smith, defines a tourist as "a temporarily leisured person who voluntarily visits a place away from home for the purpose of experiencing a change" (Smith 1989: 1). Following this definition, tourism is a non-routine experience away from the everyday life to which tourists will return.

However, this definition cannot necessarily be applied to "long-stay" in which the distinction between tourism and migration has become blurred (Hall and Williams 2002; Oliver 2006). Therefore, in studying this new kind of tourism/ migration it is necessary to link tourism and migration studies while acknowledging the importance of contemporary lifestyles in a globalized world in which people are increasingly living in a transnational way. This linkage, based on the distinctive Japanese long-stay experience discussed in this chapter, may broaden our knowledge of transnational mobility, leading to new horizons for an anthropology of migration that emphasizes this new kind of living in-between.

Notes

1. This chapter is a revised version of earlier papers (Yamashita and Ono 2006; Yamashita 2007). For the current version, I have updated the data from my fieldwork carried out in Singapore and Malaysia in 2007 and Bali in 2007 and 2008. The field research was done as part of the research project "Aging Society and International Migration: An Anthropological Study with a Special Reference to Southeast Asia and Oceania" (JSPS Grants-in-Aid for Scientific Research for 2005-2009).
2. *Naikakufu* (the Cabinet Office of Japan). *Heisei 20 Nen Ban Korei Shakai Hakusho* (White Paper on Aging Society 2008): http://www8.cao.go.jp/kourei/ whitepaper/w-2008/zenbun/20index.html.
3. *Naikakufu* (the Cabinet Office of Japan). *Heisei 23 Nen Ban Korei Shakai Hakusho* (White Paper on Aging Society 2010): http://www8.cao.go.jp/kourei/ whitepaper/w-2011/gaiyou/23pdf_indexg.html.
4. Long Stay Foundation: http://www.longstay.or.jp/.
5. *Kokudokôtsûshô* (the Japanese Ministry of Land, Infrastructure, Transport and Tourism). *Heisei 23 Nen Ban Kanko Hakusho* (White Paper on Tourism 2011): http:// www.mlit.go.jp/statistics/file000008.html.
6. Since 2006 Malaysia has been the number one destination of Japanese long-stay tourism.
7. In Malaysia, I carried out research jointly with Mayumi Ono. We share the data on Japanese retirees obtained in our research. Ono has also published her own paper (Ono 2008).
8. According to the latest data available, however, tourists are coming back to Bali. As of 2010, direct foreign visitors to Bali numbered 2.58 million, the highest record in the history of Balinese tourism. Badan Pusat Statistik Propinssi Bali (Central Agency of Statistics, Province of Bali): http://bali.bps.go.id/
9. Direct Foreign Tourist Arrivals to Bali by Nationality in 2007. According to 2010 statistics, however, of the 2.58 million total foreign tourist arrivals to Bali, Australia (642,000, or 24.9 percent) became number one, while Japan (245,000, or 9.5 percent) slipped down to number two. Badan Pusat Statistik Propinssi Bali (Central Agency of Statistics, Province of Bali): http://bali.bps.go.id/
10. Japan Airlines abolished its direct flights between Tokyo and Bali in 2010, due to the company's rationalization of operations.

11. In 2010, the number of Japanese residents registered at the Japanese Consulate in Denpasar increased to 2,109.

12. This may be related to what one might call "Japanese Orientalism" (Yamashita 2008b).

13. This criticism was actually directed at Korean pensioners in Singapore (*The Strait Times*, 29 August 2005).

14. In recent times, not only regional patients from Indonesia or Myanmar but also Western patients have been visiting hospitals in Singapore, Malaysia, and Thailand due to the low cost of medical surgery and treatment (*South China Morning Post*, 15 December 2006). In addition, Middle Eastern patients visit Singapore or Malaysian hospitals because of Muslim connections since it is becoming more difficult for them to obtain medical treatment in Western hospitals since the September 11th terrorist incident.

15. http://www.geocities.jp./hikosakamotojp/index.html.

References

Darma Putra, I Nyoman, and Michael Hitchcock. 2006. "The Bali bombs and the tourism development cycle." *Progress in Development Studies* 6: 157–166.

Hall, C. Michael and Allan M. Williams. eds. 2002. *Tourism and Migration: New Relationships between Production and Consumption*. Dordrecht, Boston and London: Kluwer Academic Publishers.

Oliver, Caroline. 2006. "More than just a tourist: Distinction, old age and the selective consumption of tourist space," pp. 196-216 in *Tourism Consumption and Representation*, eds. Kevin Meethan, Alison Anderson, and Steve Miles. Wallingford, Oxfordshire: CAB International.

Ono, Mayumi. 2008. "Long-stay tourism and international retirement migration: Japanese retirees in Malaysia," pp. 151–162 in *Transnational Migration in East Asia: Japan in a Comparative Focus* (Senri Ethnological Reports 77), eds. Shinji Yamashita, Makito Minami, David W. Haines and Jerry S. Eades. Osaka: The National Museum of Ethnology.

Sato, Machiko. 2001. *Farewell to Nippon: Japanese Lifestyle Migrants in Australia*. Melbourne: Trans Pacific Press.

Smith, Valene. 1989. "Introduction," pp. 1–17 in *Hosts and Guests: The Anthropology of Tourism* (Second Edition), ed. Valene Smith. Philadelphia: University of Pennsylvania Press.

Toyota, Mika. 2006. "Ageing and transnational householding: Japanese retirees in Southeast Asia." *International Development Planning Review* 28: 515–531.

Yamashita, Shinji. 2003. *Bali and Beyond: Explorations in the Anthropology of Tourism*. Translated by J.S. Eades. Oxford and New York: Berghahn Books.

———. 2007. "'Long-stay': A new trend in Japanese outbound tourism." Paper presented at the 10th Biennial Conference of the International Academy for the Study of Tourism, 15-20 May, Fethye, Turkey.

————. 2008a. "Transnational migration of women from and to Japan," pp. 101–116 in *Multiculturalism in the New Japan: Crossing the Boundaries Within*, eds. Nelson Graburn, John Ertl and R. Kenji Tierney. Oxford and New York: Berghahn Books.

————. 2008b. "The Japanese encounter with the South: Japanese tourists in Palau," pp. 172–192 in *Japanese Tourism and Travel Culture*, eds. Sylvie Guichard-Anguis and Okpyo Moon. London and New York: Routledge.

Yamashita, Shinji, and Mayumi Ono. 2006. "'Long-stay' tourism and international retirement migration: A Japanese perspective." Paper presented at the workshop on "Pensioners on the Move: Social Security and Trans-border Retirement Migration in Asia and Europe," 5–7 January, Singapore.

CHAPTER 12

Moving and Touring in Time and Place: Korean National History Tourism to Northeast China[1]

Okpyo MOON

Tourism increasingly provides a major context for people's movement, culture contact, and social change. As migration research has broadened its scope to include the mobility of not only people and objects but also cultures, more and more tourism researchers are witnessing the realities of how the movements of peoples, objects, and cultures interact, even during relatively short sojourns (Rojek and Urry 1997; Lindquist 2009). Furthermore, many longer-term migrants, or those who will visit again for other purposes, initially enter a foreign country with a tourist visa. As they travel and tour the host culture, they are in many ways in the early stages of assimilating into it. The host country locals who come in contact with tourists participate in a transnational tourist industry network between the host and guest societies that may also eventually lead to their own transnational mobility. Today, then, it is plausible to think that tourism and migration (or human mobility more generally) overlap with no precise boundary between the two.

It might seem that these tourist visits have the potential to foster positive interactions between two countries, laying the basis for better relations overall. However, tourist encounters do not always enhance peace, reconciliation, or inter-cultural understandings (D'Amore 1988; Higgins-Desbiolles 2003). Just as migrants in a foreign land sometimes find themselves in a situation in which their ethnic and cultural boundaries become more clearly demarcated and consolidated, rather than becoming blurred and fluid, so too does this occur for some tourists crossing borders. This kind of phenomenon counters the arguments of more optimistic globalization theorists who see greater movement of people and opportunities for contact as contributing toward the blurring of boundaries and de-territorialization that, in turn, can lead to the creation of a global community. At times, however, "tourism works towards the re-trenchment of identities in a territory, a system of filiation and patrimony" (Park 2005: 116).

In this chapter, I will examine one such case with reference to what I term Korean "national history tourism" to northeast China. The term "ethnic tourism" usually means traveling to experience, to learn about, or to consume the history, culture, and customs of ethnic minority groups within a modern nation-state (Smith 1989: 4). This kind of tourism is growing rapidly in China, a country that possesses fifty-five officially recognized ethnic minority groups in addition to the majority Han people (Wen 1997; Sofield and Fung 1998; Tan, Cheung, and Yang 2001; Kim 2006). Some two million Korean Chinese constitute one of the largest of these ethnic minority groups within China and are becoming one object of such ethnic tourism. Compared to the more exotic minority groups, however, Korean Chinese have similar physical and cultural traits to the majority Han people and occupy a relatively less prominent position in the landscape of Chinese domestic tourism.

What I refer to here as national history tourism refers not to this domestic ethnic tourism but to Korean travelers visiting China in search of their own national, cultural, and historical connections. It should therefore be distinguished from ethnic tourism in the ordinary sense in that it is the historic and national connections on the guest side rather than on the host side that are pursued as objects of tourism. This chapter will examine the process of production and consumption of this particular type of tourism and will attempt an analysis of its implications in understanding the nature of tourist encounters and their impact upon the relations between host and guest societies.

In terms of destination, there are two different types of Korean national history tourism in northeast China: one searching for the traces of Koguryô (BC 37–668 AD) and Palhae (698–926 AD), the two ancient kingdoms of Korea that once occupied much of present-day northeast China (Koguryô Research Foundation 2004, 2005); and the other discovering and visiting the sites of the Independence Movement and anti-Japanese struggles during the colonial period (1910-1945). Although the two are often combined into a single package tour nowadays, the former raises more sensitive contestations regarding heritage ownership in which the interests of the two countries sharply diverge while, in the case of the latter, the Chinese are often featured as comrades who shared the common cause of fighting against Japanese expansionism and colonialism. Consequently, the process and meaning of history-making and its tourist consumption are quite different for the two types. If it is painful national suffering and colonial oppression that are remembered at the sites of anti-Japanese struggles, the ancient historic sites of Koguryô and Palhae offer a place to remember and consume, if only in imagination, the past, albeit lost, glories of Korean history, and thus confirm Korean national pride. The discussion here will be confined to the latter type, i.e., that focusing upon the ancient period. The analysis is based on participant observations of tours taken in the summers of 2006, 2007, and

2008, supplemented by media reports, tourist materials, and interviews of tourists as well as related tourism personnel.

Background

Although China and Korea have kept the most intimate ties politically, economically, and culturally for more than two thousand years, official contact between the two countries came to an abrupt end with the establishment of the socialist regime in China in 1949 and with the division of the Korean Peninsula into a socialist North and a democratic South. After that, it was not possible for South Koreans to travel to China freely for nearly half a century. Once diplomatic ties were resumed in 1992, however, the number of Koreans visiting China in the forms of tourism, business, and study abroad increased dramatically.

The liberalization of overseas travel regulations in 1989 had already laid the basis for an unprecedented growth of international tourism from South Korea. As can be seen in Table 12.1, just over two million South Koreans traveled overseas in 1992, which rose to over twelve million in 2010, comprising 25.8 percent of the total population of 48.8 million. The increase in Koreans traveling abroad is thus steeper even than for the Japanese, famed for their prolific travelers (Gichard-Anguis and Moon 2009). In Japan, the liberalization of overseas travel occurred in 1964, twenty-five years earlier than in Korea, but it is reported that some seventeen million traveled abroad in 2005, only 13.4 percent of the total population of 127.3 million. Table 12.1 indicates that the number of Koreans visiting China in particular saw the most dramatic increase, reaching over four million in 2010, a number that has well surpassed those visiting Japan, thus marking China as the most frequently visited country of South Korean travelers (Moon 2009). Recently, the number of Chinese visiting South Korea has also increased significantly. As a result, the movement of people between China and South Korea has become an important research topic in migration and tourism studies in Korea.

With the increase in number, the types of Korean tourism to China have also been greatly diversified. On the basis of a long shared history, many religious and cultural expeditions have been organized by Koreans to visit the sites that possess specific narratives in relation to the history of Korean Confucianism, Buddhism, and even Catholicism (which had close ties with Chinese Catholicism in its early history). The places include famous temples, shrines, birth places, and places visited by great Korean monks, priests, and sages (Yang 2010). What can be classified as nature tourism, specifically aiming at grandiose natural scenery such as mountains and rivers, is also becoming very popular among Koreans, as are Chinese culture and history tours visiting old capitals and their surrounding areas, such as Beijing, Xi'an, and Nanjing, as well as Shanghai (Park 2011).

Table 12.1 • Destination Countries of Korean International Travelers

	1998	2001	2004	2007	2010
Japan	822,358	1,169,620	1,569,175	2,600,801	2,439,816
China	484,009	1,297,746	2,334,781	4,776,752	4,076,400
HongKong	122,577	234,051	305,351	76,231	891,024
Thailand	166,867	446,886	754,093	1,083,652	815,913
Philippines	62,616	203,682	377,217	653,310	740,622
U.S.A.	425,330	670,456	627,575	806,175	1,107,518
Australia	62,742	148,402	172,265	108,319	215,600
Others	553,944	1,230,691	1,868,446	2,419,737	2,201,471
Total	2,700,443	5,401,534	8,008,903	13,324,977	12,488,364

Source: Korea Tourism Organization (KTO)
http://korean.visitkorea.or.kr/kor/tt/sub_main.jsp

With the proliferation of economic and industrial ties between the two countries, business-related tourism is now a frequent experience for Korean male travelers, often combined with golf and sex tourism (Lee 2010).

The earlier post-normalization wave of Korean tourism to China, however, centered on what I call here national history tourism. Popular destinations of these Korean travelers were concentrated near the Chinese border with North Korea and in the three northeastern provinces of Liaoning, Jilin, and Heilongjiang. This is where most of the Koreans fleeing from Japanese colonial oppression and exploitation at the beginning of the twentieth century settled, and where a large number of Korean Chinese are still living in autonomous regions such as Yanbian and Changbai (Kim 2006; Kim and Ryu 2008; Yun 2008). In particular, Mount Paekdu (literally, Whitehead), located on the North Korean and Chinese border, has long been seen as sacred and central to the myths of Korean national origin (Ch'oe 1973[1927]). It began to attract pilgrimages from Korea even before the official opening in the early 1990s (Chông 1989; Park 2003). Along with Mount Paekdu, the remains of the two ancient kingdoms of Korea, Koguryô and Palhae, and the sites of anti-Japanese struggles of modern times are also in this general area (Song 1998; Ch'oi 1998; Kim 2000; Manabe 2000, 2001).

While the opportunities to travel to these hitherto forbidden historic lands were enthusiastically embraced by Koreans, the visits soon caused sensitivity from the Chinese perspective. While Korean tourists were initially welcomed as a source of potential economic gain to the region, and while the flood of

Korean tourists indeed contributed toward a new awareness of these sites and improvement of access to them, Korean nationalistic behavior (such as waving the South Korean national flag) at Mount Paekdu and other historic sites that now fall under Chinese sovereignty apparently made Chinese authorities wary of possible territorial encroachment from Korea, especially if the unification of the two Koreas were to occur. Suspicions also arose in relation to the growing intimacy between the Korean Chinese people and their motherland. Many Korean Chinese have relatives in South Korea and began to visit South Korea in large numbers to meet those relatives as well as to search for work. This consequently led to a series of new control and surveillance measures by the Chinese government, including the formulation of a state-led project that has come to be known as the Northeast Project.[2]

Consuming History and Place by Imagination

The focal point of Korean national history tourism to China, at least at the earlier stage, was Mount Paekdu, located on the Chinese border with North Korea. As many of the tourist brochures described it, to most Koreans it "is not simply a mountain but a place from which the Korean nation is originated" (www.tourvis. com, cited July 2008). Its symbolic status is indicated in the starting phrases of the Korean national anthem: "Until the waters of the East Sea dry up and the earth of Mount Paekdu is trodden away, God bless and long live our country …"[3] From the perspective of geomancy Mount Paekdu also figures as a sacred place from which all the mountains of the Korean Peninsula emanate. Given its symbolic and religious significance to Koreans, the denial of access to the place (as a consequence of the division of the country following the Japanese defeat in WWII) has been frustrating. Many South Korean visitors find it particularly saddening that they can only reach the place via Chinese territory (and with payment to China for the access). They feel that they ought to be able to climb the mountain through their own land in North Korea – an option that is not possible due to the division of the country and the antagonism that still exists between the two Koreas.

Given this background, many Korean politicians, businessmen, and scholars who were able to visit China before the onset of mass tourism felt that a visit to Mount Paekdu had to be included in their itinerary no matter what the primary purpose of their travel was. In fact, Korean tourism to China was quite elitist at the beginning. The trip was still very expensive and the visitors were subject to numerous regulations. In this regard, a visit to Mount Paekdu had an element of pilgrimage and many emotionally moving experiences were reported (e.g. Chông 1989; Yi 1991; Song 1993). According to Mr. C., a Korean Chinese interviewed in July 2008 in Seoul who had worked in the tourism business from 1993 until 1997 (when he went out of business due to the recession at the time of the Korean economic crisis), only those who had a certain amount of property were given visas at that time, and a four-day (three-night) trip to Beijing with a visit to Mount Paekdu cost approximately 2.5 million won per person (about US $2,500 at that time).

Despite the difficulties of access at the beginning stage and the unduly high costs, Mr. C. said that most Korean visitors over the age of fifty wanted to visit the mountain. Young people showed less interest, but those active in the Unification Movement were also frequent visitors to the mountain. Mount Paekdu had an important symbolic status for a unified Korea and members of civic groups working for unification (such as college students, intellectuals, and cultural and religious leaders) sometimes held a ritual on top of the mountain praying for a quick realization of Korean unification. Such rituals often involved worship of Tan'gun, the mythical founding ancestor of the Korean nation. Other religious sects also held rituals at the place, praying for unification of the country and prosperity of the people – although religious and other activities connoting the Korean nation and state have subsequently been strictly forbidden by Chinese authorities.[4]

The initial concentration of Korean national history tourism on Mount Paekdu was later extended to Koguryô remains found dispersed in Liaoning and Jilin Provinces, Huanren and Ji'an (Hwan'in and Chib'an in Korean reading) in particular. As places that had previously been the capitals of Koguryô,[5] they had numerous tombs with valuable murals, castle remains, monuments, and steles. To Koreans, visiting these places, whose history is embodied in the material remains, is satisfying in terms of nostalgia and national pride. They are places of a glorious Korean history about which they have learned so much in school textbooks but that have only existed in "dreams and fantasies" because they have not been allowed to set foot on the sites. That kind of reaction is seen in the following comments:

> To our people, Koguryô is a period that has a special meaning. It was a great state, full of spirit, possessing strong forces and occupying the widest territory in Korean history. It was a fiercely independent country that was able to confront several Chinese dynasties on an equal basis.

> In this regard, Koguryô has always existed as a dream to the Korean people who have so often suffered from foreign invasions in a tiny land. Whenever we wished to forget the weakness in ourselves or needed strength faced with national difficulties, the history of Koguryô came back to us as a source of pioneering spirit and gallantry.

> Yet, to us at the southern end of the Korean Peninsula, Koguryô had always been something like a mirage due to the temporal and spatial separation. This Koguryô that disappeared from us 1,400 years ago and had been felt so distant,

existing only in dreams and fantasies, has all of sudden come back to life and started moving [with the opening of China].

(Koguryô Research Foundation 2004: 6, translated by Okpyo Moon)

It is with such sentiments that place and history are consumed by Korean tourists visiting Koguryô sites in northeast China and, as in the case of Mount Paekdu, there have apparently been some displays of intense nationalistic feelings that are sometimes characterized as the "Korean version of colonialism." In the words of one Japanese scholar:

> The Korean version of colonialism manifested here [in Korean tourist behavior] is to dream about the revival of the "proud history of a conqueror" with virtual historical reality as a shield. To be re-conquered here are the "Northern Barbarians" [...] that is, the Manchurians and the Chinese Communists. [...] It is interesting to note that this Korean version of colonialism is inseparably connected with Petit Chinese Centralism (*shōchūkashisō*) that despises all nationalities other than the Han Chinese. It underlies a kind of expansionist nationalism that may be termed "Great Koreanism" (*daichōsenshugi*) which is also directed against a Japan (*wa*) that is situated at the bottom level of all Eastern Barbarians (*tōi*). It clearly shows a **Korean version of the colonialist gaze** combined with Great Koreanism.

(Manabe 2000: 88, translated and emphasis added by Okpyo Moon)

It is most interesting that this interpretation is offered by a Japanese scholar who has elsewhere attempted a rather arbitrary distinction between Japanese tourist behavior in Manchuria in northern China and Korean tourist behavior at Koguryô sites. She insists that, while both cases can be understood in the framework of a memory industry, Japanese Manchurian tourism, quite unlike that of Koreans, "shows only the character of nostalgia and study, and has no element of nationalism" (Manabe 2007: 4). Gao Yuan (2006), on the other hand, reports that there is a conspicuous concentration of Japanese tourists in Dalian in northeast China, the city developed by the Japanese as a base for colonial expansion into Manchuria as well as a military stronghold against the Russians at the beginning of the twentieth century. She reports, in particular, a case in which a Japanese businessman was actively involved in the reconstruction of a Russo-Japanese war memorial site in Lushun district of Dalian, where the ceasefire agreement was signed following the victory of Japan. The site had been destroyed by Russians after WWII and then left neglected until the Japanese arrived on the scene after the resumption of diplomatic ties between China and Japan in 1972. This site was reconstructed with a strong initiative from a Japanese businessman who possessed connections in Dalian's economic sector, and was designated by the

Chinese government as an important site for the patriotic education of Chinese. The signboard at the site reads:

> It was at this very place where two imperial powers brought upon the Chinese people serious disaster and injustice by attacking Lushun, fought each other there and made peace between them. The reason we preserve these remains is to inform our descendants of historical facts to make them stand up with fury [about what happened] and to help them work for world peace.
>
> (quoted from Gao and translated by Okpyo Moon)

The official message of the signboard notwithstanding, Gao Yuan notes that the place was mostly consumed by Japanese and not Chinese tourists. Criticisms were raised within China that the place was being shamelessly used as a spot for a "cheap sale of national disgrace" (*kokuji no yasuuri*) (Gao Yuan 2006: 53–56). Given the fact that the Russo-Japanese War in 1905, and the final victory of Japan that was concluded at this particular place in Lushun, provided critical momentum for the subsequent Japanese invasion of Manchuria, there is little doubt that it is the glorious and victorious past of Greater Japan that is remembered and consumed here by the "nostalgic" Japanese tourists.

Re-appropriation of History and Forfeiture of Memory

What the case of Lushun indicates is that, in the context of reconstructing, developing, marketing, and consuming a tourist site, histories can be read quite differently and that the interests and objectives of states, local authorities, businessmen, tourists, and tourism managers may also vary widely. With regard to the Koguryô sites, the Chinese government carried out a massive reconstruction project in the early 2000s. Like Lushun and other historic sites in the area, these Koguryô sites had been deserted and neglected until tourists began to appear on the scene in the early 1990s:

> Ten years ago, the place was pathetic, Ji'an of Jilin Province, China, the site of Guonei City of old Koguryô where the Stele of Great King Kwanggaet'o stands. At the Ji'an City museum, a curator used to come out to unlock the door if an application was submitted. The high-handed arrogance of the curator was no joke. The inscriptions were all so badly worn out that they were unreadable even at a short distance. But the visitors were brow-beaten not to go near the objects.
>
> It has completely changed recently. Anyone who pays the entrance fee can enter the premises of the pavilion that houses the [Kwanggaet'o] Stele. Instead, all the visitors are now subjected to the fixed remarks of the guide emphasizing

Koguryô as a mere regional kingdom of China [and not a Korean kingdom]. It is the Chinese official standpoint since the Northeast Project that Koguryô had never been an independent state but was merely one of the many local feudal states of China.

(Yi Tôk-il 2008, translated by Okpyo Moon)

It was more devastating at Shanguqingzi in Manchu autonomous region where early Koguryô tombs are concentrated. Even the shapes of the tombs were barely recognizable. Much of the area where the tombs are located had been turned into corn fields. Moreover, the entrance fees of Koguryô remains in Ji'an and Huanren Cities are set unreasonably high: 60 *yuan* for Wunu Mountain City, 60 *yuan* for Shanguqingzi, 30 *yuan* for the Tomb of the Great King Kwanggaet'o, 30 *yuan* for the Tomb of the Great General [King Changsu], 30 *yuan* for Wandu Mountain City and so forth. Altogether it is more than thirty thousand *won* in Korean currency (approximately US $30 at the time).

(*Tong-A Ilbo*, 24 August 2006, translated by Okpyo Moon)

It seems, then, that the flood of Korean tourists in the 1990s provided an initial impetus for the Chinese to re-discover and develop these neglected historical sites of Koguryô. Later, more extensive reconstruction projects were launched along with efforts to register the areas as UNESCO World Heritage sites.[6] Along with those efforts, a systematic re-mapping of history was also attempted through the Northeast Project, presenting Koguryô as part of the regional history of China rather than being solely or uniquely Korean. Some Chinese scholars even insisted that Koguryô and Palhae, the two ancient kingdoms that Koreans view with pride, were founded by Mohe (Malgal) peoples, purported ancestors of modern-day Manchus, who ruled China's Qing Dynasty (Ahn 2006; http://en.wikipedia.org/wiki/Goguryeo). Chinese characterization of Koguryô as a regional power center of China has spawned heated disputes with both North Korea and South Korea.

The progress of scholarly disputes aside, Korean tourists began to be subjected to more severe surveillance by the Chinese authorities who exercise sovereignty over those sites.

The city of Ji'an as a whole can be said to be a Koguryô museum. Wherever one goes, one comes across the remains of Koguryô such as ancient tombs, stele of Great King Kwanggaet'o, Guonei City, Wandu Mountain City, and so on. Chinese authorities have begun to reconstruct some of them. They moved some 300 farm houses in the neighborhood and made it into a tourist spot. One now has to pay thirty *yuan* to enter the premises [of the Kwanggaet'o Stele].

It's spiteful of them, though, to collect entrance fees every time by using other people's [i.e. Korean] culture. One has to pay fees again at Changgunch'ong [that is believed to be the tomb of Koguryô King Changsu but marked simply as *Jiangjunfen*, a tomb of a general, in Chinese]. As these are the places where most Korean tourists visit, the tourism-related income must be considerable. [But] if anyone tries to take a picture holding a Korean flag, s/he is immediately stopped. They also hate any kind of group placard.

(18 November 2008, *Ch'ungbuk Ilbo*, translated by Okpyo Moon)

The re-appropriation of Koguryô related sites by the Chinese, especially around the time of UNESCO World Heritage registration in 2004, has been far-reaching and systematic. Signboards were re-written. Tour guides working in the area, mostly Korean Chinese, received specific instructions. Manifestations of religious or nationalistic feeling relating to Korea became subject to disciplinary measures such as verbal warnings, fines, and threats of arrest. Even simple displays of respect such as bowing were strictly forbidden. Any signs implying Korean connections have been eroded systematically while Manchurian connections have been emphasized.

Similar measures of re-appropriation have been applied to Mount Paekdu. In 2005, for example, it was designated as one of the Chinese Ten Great Mountains even though it has long remained a relatively minor scenic attraction for majority (Han) Chinese. The central government recently took over from the Yanbian Korean Chinese autonomous region the management rights of the Paekdu mountain resort and its surrounding areas.[7] In order to improve access to the mountain, new routes have been constructed and, in the summer of 2008, a new Changbaishan airport was opened from which people can reach the mountain without going through Yanbian Korean Chinese autonomous region. The improved access has certainly contributed toward bringing more Chinese tourists. While more than 90 percent of those visiting the mountain were Koreans until the late 1990s, the composition has changed and now more than 80 percent are said to be Han Chinese (Professor J. at Yanbian University interviewed in July 2007). The Committee for Development and Management of Changbaishan, an organization newly set up after the central government's takeover, is also planning to build comprehensive resort facilities at the mountain, including numerous ski slopes, rafting courses, and climbing courses. One objective of these plans is no doubt to de-sacralize the place by turning it into a recreation area.

The remaking of Mount Paekdu and its surrounding area into a natural resort and recreation area void of any cultural and national meanings related to Korea can be quite offensive to Korean tourists. Many Koreans deplore the conditions under which the precious historical remains, perceived as being "their own," have been placed. They feel particularly resentful about the constraints placed upon them by the Chinese on how they may appreciate these heritage sites, and also about the fact that they have to pay the Chinese to visit "their own heritage." Even as paying tourists, they feel that they are not free, at least explicitly, to think, remember, dream, or fantasize the history embedded in these places. The way the sites are represented by the Chinese effectively dictates how to consume the sites and forfeits their connections to Korean historical memory.

Conclusion

Conflicts and tension surrounding the ownership of historic and cultural heritage are found not only between China and Korea as discussed in this chapter, but also in many other parts of the world where national borders have been drawn and re-drawn, often by external forces such as colonial powers, and where as a consequence historic and cultural remains are found dispersed across current borders. Many Southeast Asian countries such as Thailand, Cambodia, and Vietnam have such disputes, as so do Mediterranean countries like Greece and Macedonia. Given that the nationalization of heritage has been one of the key projects adopted by modern nation-states as a means of formulating and consolidating national identity, maintaining integration, and also of securing economic gain through tourism (Anderson 1983; Herzfeld 1991), there is little doubt that such questions of disputed heritage ownership will constitute one of the core topics in future studies of international tourism.

What is most suggestive in this regard is the fact that the disputes, and the discrepancies between imagination and experienced reality at the destinations, do not always stop the movement of people in the context of tourism. As can be seen in the case of Korean national history tourism in northeast China, the resentment and uneasiness Korean tourists experience at these destinations do not seem to have discouraged people from visiting. On the contrary, it seems that published travelogues and recounted stories of personal experiences (available also on the internet) may stimulate more people to visit in order to witness with their own eyes how their views of history are being distorted. Consequently, the continued growth of tourism could further encourage Korean Chinese locals to travel between China and Korea, increasing the tensions between Chinese authorities and Korean Chinese, between Chinese authorities and Korean tourists, and between Korean Chinese and Korean tourists. This kind of tourism thus presents us with a kind of encounter between guests and hosts in which antagonism, rather than peace or reconciliation, grows with increased contact. Such a finding suggests the importance of including tourism in the further interdisciplinary research that seeks to understand how circuits of human mobility are configured in particular places, for particular groups of people, and to what particular ends (Freedman 2011: 1009, re-quoted by Lindquist 2009: 7).

Notes

1. I would like to acknowledge that this chapter contains part of the results obtained in a joint research project supported by the Academy of Korean Studies in 2008 and some parts of the chapter overlap with a paper that was published by the same author in a Korean-language journal, *Pigyo Munhwa Yŏn'gu* (Cross-Cultural Studies) in 2010 (Moon 2010).

2. The full title of the project is "The research project of the history and current state of the northeast frontier." It was launched in 2002 and completed in 2007. The main objectives of the project were to eliminate potential disputes by providing new concepts and interpretations of the Chinese nation and its history (Yun 2003: 185-186). According to the project, the history of Koguryô and its remains are part of Chinese history, as is the case for any ethnic group that once occupied territory that falls with the current borders of China.

3. The lyrics of the Korean national anthem were written by Yun Ch'i-ho in 1896 and had originally been sung to the tune of the British folk melody, Auld Lang Syne. The Korean composer An Ik-t'ae wrote the current melody in 1936 at the time of the Berlin Olympic Games. It was not recognized as the official Korean national anthem until after Independence in 1945.

4. Another frequent set of visitors were those who had left family members in North Korea as they fled to the South following the division of the country. From the top of Mount Paekdu, they can look down on North Korea below and pray for the well-being of those relatives. For a time they can be seemingly re-united.

5. It was in present-day Huanren County in Liaoning Province where Koguryô first set up a capital in 37 BC. In 3 AD, the capital was moved to Guonei City in Ji'an, Jilin Province. In 427 AD, Koguryô moved its capital to P'yŏngyang in North Korea, but it is said that Ji'an with Guonei City and Wandu Mountain City remained supporting capitals of Koguryô until 668 AD (Koguryô Research Foundation 2004, 2005).

6. In 2004, UNESCO added to its World Heritage list the "Capital Cities and Tombs of the Ancient Koguryô Kingdom" in present-day China. These included Wunu Mountain City in Huanren, Guonei City, and Wandu Mountain City in Ji'an, including some forty scattered tombs and the Stele of King Kwangaet'o. The same year, UNESCO also added to its list the "Complex of Koguryô Tombs" in present-day North Korea.

7. The Chinese pronunciation of Mt. Paekdu is *Baitoushan*, but the mountain is referred to by a different name in China, *Changbaishan*.

References

Ahn, Yŏnsôn. 2006. *Korea China Textbook War: What's It All About?* History News Network, http://hnn.us/articles/21617.html.

Anderson, Benedict. 1983. *Imagined Communities: Reflections on the Origin and Spread of Nationalism.* London: Verso.

Ch'oe Nam-Sôn. 1973 (1927). *Paekdusan Kûnch'amgi* [Paying a respectful visit to Mt. Paekdu], *Yukdang Ch'oe Nam-Sôn Chônjip* [Collected Works of Yukdang Ch'oe Nam-Sôn]. 6: 11–152. Seoul: Hyônamsa.

Ch'oi Han-Sông. 1998. "Chungguk yônbyôn chiyôk ûi kwan'gwang chawon kwa han'guk tanch'e kwan'gwang e taehan koch'al" [An investigation of tourist resources in Yanbian region of China and Korean group tourism]. *Geography and Environment Education* 6(2): 111–126.

Chông Pyông Il. 1989. *Han'gug'in ûi Manju* [Manchuria for Koreans]. Seoul: Hoam Ch'ulpansa.

D'Amore, L.J. 1988. "Tourism – A vital force for peace." *Annals of Tourism Research* 15: 269–283.

Gao Yuan. 2001. "Kioku sangyō toshite no tsūrizumu: sengo ni okeru nihonjin no manshū kankō" [Tourism as memory industry: Postwar Japanese tourism to Manchuria]. *Gendaishisō* 29(4): 219–229. Tokyo: Seitosha.

———. 2006. "Kokuchi to kankō" [National disgrace and tourism], pp. 43–60 in *Nitchūkan nashonarizumu no dōjidaisi* [Contemporary history of Japanese, Chinese and Korean nationalism], ed. Dōjidaisi gakkai [Society for Contemporary History]. Tokyo: Nihon keizai hyōronsha.

Gichard-Anguis, Sylvie, and Okpyo Moon, eds. 2009. *Japanese Tourism and Travel Culture.* London: Routlege.

Herzfeld, Michael. 1991. *A Place in History: Social and Monumental Time in a Cretan Town*. Princeton: Princeton University Press.

Higgens-Desbiolles, Freya. 2003. "Reconciliation tourism: Tourism healing divided societies!" *Tourism Recreation Research* 31(1): 44–60.

Kim, Jae Min. 2000. "Report: A study of tourist demand and accommodation in the Mt. Paekdusan/Changbaishan area." *Tourism Economics* 6(1): 73–83.

Kim Kwang-ok. 2006. "Ch'ongron: Chongjok ûi hyôndaejôk palmyông kwa silch'ôn" [Introduction: Modern invention and practices of ethnicity], pp. 15–83 in *Chongjok kwa minjok: kû tanil kwa popyôn ûi shinhwa rûl nômôsô* [Ethnicity and nation: Beyond the myth of unity and universality], ed. Kim Kwang-ok. Taewoo Academic Series 577. Seoul: Acanet.

Kim, Pyông-ho and Ryu Ch'un-ok. 2008. "Chosônjok sahoe munje e taehan sago" [A consideration of the social issues of Korean Chinese], pp. 203–217 in *21segi chungguk esô ûi han'gukhak yôn'gu ûi saeroun chip'yông* [New horizons of Korean Studies in China in the 21st century], edited by T'ae P'yông-mu. Beijing: Minzu Publishing.

Koguryô Research Foundation [Koguryô yôn'gu chaedan], ed. 2004. "Tashi ponûn Koguryôsa" [History of Koguryô revisited]. Koguryô Research Foundation.

———, ed. 2005. "Koguryô munmyông kihaeng" [A journey into the civilization of Koguryô]. Koguryô Research Foundation.

Lee, Ch'angho. 2010. "Han'gug'in ûi Chungguk golf kwan'gwang gwa yônjangdoen pammunhwa" [Korean golf tourism and extended nightlife in China], in *Pigyo Munhwa Yôn'gu* [Cross-Cultural Studies] 16(1): 81–125.

Lindquist, Johan A. 2009. *The Anxieties of Mobility: Migration and Tourism in the Indonesian Borderlands*. Honolulu: University of Hawai'i Press.

Manabe Yūko. 2000. "Gendai kankoku no nashonarizumu to tsūrizumu" [Nationalism and tourism in modern Korea], pp. 79–90 in *Tabi no bunka kenkyūshō hōkoku* [Research Report of the Institute of Travel Culture].

———. 2001. "Kankokujin no esunisiti keisei to hakutōsan junrei" [Formation of Korean ethnicity and pilgrimage to Mount Paekdu]. *Gendai Kankoku Chōsen Kenkyū* [Modern Korean Studies] 1: 55–66. Tokyo: Society for Modern Korean Studies.

———. 2007 "Shanghai daikanminkoku rinjiseifu kyusi no sōshutsu to tsurizumu" [Creating the old site of Shanghai Korean provisional government and tourism], pp. 3–38 in *Chūsin to shūen kara mita nikkan shakai no shosō* [Japanese and Korean societies seen from the center and the periphery], eds. Abito Ito and Kyung-Koo Han. Tokyo: Keiogijuku daigaku shuppankai.

Moon, Okpyo. 2009. "Japanese tourists in Korea: Colonial and postcolonial encounters," pp. 147–171 in *Japanese Tourism and Travel Culture*, eds. Sylvie Gichard-Anguis and Okpyo Moon. London: Routledge.

———. 2010. "Kiôk gwa sangsang ûi hyônjang: chungguk ûl ch'atnûn han'gug'in minjok yôksa kwan'gwang" [Sites of memory and imagination: Korean national history tourism to China], in *Pigyo Munhwa Yôn'gu* [Cross-Cultural Studies] 16(1): 7–42.

Park, Christian J. 2005. "Politics of Geumgangsan tourism: Sovereignty in contestation." *Review of Korean Studies* 8(3): 113–136.

Park, Joonkyu. 2011 "National Identity and Tourism: South Korea's Consumption of China through Zhangjiajie Nature Tourism." *Tongbuk'a Kwan'gwang Yôn'gu* [Northeast Asia Tourism Studies] 7(4): 1–26.

Park, Yong-hi. 2003. "Han'gug'in ûi chungguk munhwa insik: yôhaenggi punsôk ûl chungsim ûro" [Korean understanding of Chinese culture: An analysis of travel writings]. *Munhwa Kwan'gwang Yôn'gu* [Culture Tourism Studies] 5(1): 151-167. Korean Society for Culture Tourism Studies.

Rojek, Chris and John Urry. 1997. *Touring Cultures: Transformations of Travel and Theory*. London: Routledge.

Smith, Valene L. 1989. "Introduction" in *Hosts and Guests: The Anthropology of Tourism* (2nd edition), ed. Valene Smith. Philadelphia: University of Pennsylvania Press.

Sofield, Trevor H.B. and Fung Mei Sarah Li. 1998. "Tourism development and cultural policies in China." *Annals of Tourism Research* 25(2): 362–392.

Song, Ki-ho. 1993. *Palhae rûl ch'ajasô* [Looking for Palhae]. Seoul: Son Ch'ulpansa.

Song, Ki-hôn. 1998. "Han'guk, chungguk kan ûi kwan'gwang kyoryu wa munhwa paljôn e kwanhan sajôk koch'al" [A historical study of tourist exchange and cultural development between China and Korea]. *Kwan'gwang chôngch'aek yôn'gu* [Tourism Policy Studies] 4(1): 225–242.

Tan, Chee-Beng, Sidney C.H. Cheung, and Yang Hui, eds. 2001. *Tourism, Anthropology and China*. Bangkok: White Lotus.

Wen, Zhang. 1997. "China's domestic tourism: Impetus, development and trends." *Tourism Management* 18(8): 565–571.

Yang, Han-Sun. 2010. "Pulgyo yujôkji sullye rûl t'onghaebon han'gug'in ûi chungguk munhwa kwan'gwang" [Buddhist heritage pilgrimage and Korean cultural tourism to China], in *Pigyo Munhwa Yôn'gu* [Cross-Cultural Studies] 16(1): 43–79.

Yi, Pyông-t'ae. 1991. *Pukkyông, Yônbyôn, kûrigo Paekdusan: Ch'ikwa ûisa Yi Pyôngt'ae ûi chungguk kihaeng* [Beijing, Yanbian and Mount Paekdu: Dentist Yi Pyôngt'ae's travelogue of China]. Seoul: Sahyôngak.

Yi Tôk-il. 2008. "Kwanggaet'o taewangbi rûl ch'ajasô" [Looking for the Stele of the Great King Kwanggaet'o], in *Ach'im Ullim*, Regular Electronic Mail Service of Korean Ministry of Culture, Tourism and Sports.

Yun Hwi-Tak. 2003. "Hyôndae chungguk ûi pyôngang minjok inshik kwa tongbuk kongjông" [Understanding the nation and its frontiers in modern China and the Northeast Project]. *Yôksabip'yông* [History Critique] Winter 2003: 184–205.

Yun, Pyông-sôk. 2008. "Pukkando han'in (chosôn'in) sahoe wa myôngdong hakkyo" [The society of the ethnic Koreans in Jiandao, northeast China and Myôngdong School], in Proceedings of International Conference Commemorating the 100th Anniversary of Myôngdong School, *The Life, Agony and Culture of Ethnic Koreans in Jiandao, Northeast China*. Foundation for the Studies of Northeast Asian History.

Part III:
Work, Ethnicity, and Nationality

CHAPTER 13

In the Shadows and at the Margins: Working in the Korean Clubs and Bars of Osaka's Minami Area

Haeng-ja Sachiko CHUNG[1]

In this chapter, I discuss the unique spatial and temporal constellations of an emerging Korean ethnic business community in Japan. From fall 2000 to summer 2001, I resided in an area called Shimanouchi, which was a mixed residential and commercial area on the eastern border of Minami (meaning "south" in Japanese). Minami is north of Namba Station, one of the largest stations in Osaka. It is one of the oldest and largest entertainment districts in Japan, dating back to the early seventeenth century, nearly four hundred years ago. Formerly a formal ward of the city, it became a part of Chuo-ku (Central Ward) of Osaka City after the re-organization of wards in 1989. Minami was surrounded by four major avenues (and train lines): Nagahori Dori Avenue (Nagahori Tsurumi-ryokuchi Line) on the north; Sennichi-mae Dori Avenue (Sennichimae Line) on the south; Yotsubashi Suji Avenue (Yotsubashi Line) on the west; and Sakai Suji Avenue (Sakai Suji Line) on the east.

The mid-eastern edge of Minami was called "Koreatown" by Korean migrants who worked in the area. The core of Minami's Koreatown lies in the east end of six blocks of Minami, which is about 150 meters (500 feet) from the east end to the west, and 300 meters (1,000 feet) from the south end to the north. The north end is Suhoumachi Dori Street, which is also called *Yoroppa Dori* (European Street). The south end is Soemon-cho, which is parallel to and close by the famous Dotonbori River. The east end is Sakai Suji Avenue and the west end is Tamayamachi Street.

When I conducted my research in 2000–2001, a few hundred Korean clubs and bars were estimated to operate in Minami. I distinguish the bars, often called "snacks" and "lounges," from the clubs. Distinctions have not always been clearly made in previous research, but it is important to note that clubs and bars are different in terms of number, status, and cost. The clubs were fewer in number and more expensive, yet generally more visible in Minami because of their class as well as licensed status. More than one thousand hostesses, entertainers, madams, and support staff worked at the thirty-three licensed Korean clubs in Minami to entertain primarily Japanese-born male customers by offering spaces and companions to drink and talk. Sex was not a part of service (cf., Chung 2011). Costs were high. The minimum charge for a single customer at Club Rose, for example, was approximately US $200, but a typical customer paid an extra hundred or two for drinks, snacks, and desserts. By contrast, the bars were far more numerous, with a couple of hundred operating from around 7 p.m. to midnight and/or from midnight into the early morning. These bars were generally smaller and more affordable than the clubs, with the minimum charge for a customer at approximately $100.

Other Korean ethnic businesses, such as restaurants, boutiques, flower shops, beauty salons, host clubs, and grocery stores, were also concentrated in and around the area. Yet, many of the Korean clubs and bars in Minami did not obviously look or sound Korean, and only a few ethnic markers existed in Koreatown: some Korean restaurants, Korean grocery stores, some Korean letters used for signs, and occasional Korean conversations. The Korean club at which I conducted research as a hostess, for example, had the European-sounding name "Club Rose," and the Korean bar at which I worked had the Japanese-sounding name "Tani."[2] Neither had any obvious ethnic markers to suggest from the outside that they were Korean establishments.[3]

Therefore, beyond the community members, this ethnic town was little known and received less academic attention (Chung 2002) than the older Korean ethnic community known as Ikaino around Tsuruhashi station in Osaka (e.g., Chapman 2008; Fukuoka 2000; Koh 1998; Lee and De Vos 1981; Lie 2008; Mitchell 1967; Morris-Suzuki 2007; Ryang 2000; Ryang and Lie 2008; Weiner 1989; Wender 2005). While both areas shared a Korean heritage, the interactions between them were rather more limited than I had originally expected, despite relative geographic proximity. Minami is only a couple of subway stops away from Tsuruhashi. The majority of Koreans in Minami were newcomers who began coming to Japan in the 1980s. The majority of Koreans in Ikaino were so-called "oldcomers" and their descendants. Their residence in Japan originated in the Japanese colonization of Korea (1910–1945). Ikaino thus has a longer ethnic history. The spatial distance between Minami and Ikaino of 3 km (2 miles) symbolically represents the temporal gap of migration periods between oldcomers and newcomers, which resulted in social, cultural, and linguistic gaps as well.[4]

I conducted research as a paid hostess at Korean Club Rose and Bar Tani in Koreatown. I specifically created the term "labor participant observation" to highlight the research advantage that lies in participating in a community as a worker (cf., Allison 1994; Chung 2008, 2011; Frank 2002; Kondo 1991; Tsuda 2003; Zheng 2009). I also conducted interviews of migrant Koreans, resident Koreans, Korean Japanese, and ethnic Japanese as well as library research to supplement my participant observation. My research was long-term, multi-sited, and multi-method. Before I began conducting research on Korean migrant hostesses, I was aware that the spatial arrangements of Korean businesses in Minami represented a geographical pattern of ethnic businesses common in other parts of the world: specifically the concentration of various kinds of ethnic businesses in a single area. Furthermore, soon after I began working as a paid hostess at Club Rose from 8 p.m. to midnight during the business week, I learned that approximately a quarter of the Korean migrant club workers had second jobs in Minami. This second job was called the "second shift." Bar Tani was one of the Korean second-shift bars that operated from midnight to as late as 7 a.m. I also conducted research there after I finished my work at Club Rose.

These Korean clubs and bars were exclusive in that they only served members and their guests. While approximately 900 Korean clubs and bars were estimated to operate in the Osaka area in the mid-1990s (KBS-TV 1995 in Sawazaki and Sung 1997), a total of 608 clubs and bars, including Japanese and Korean, were formally registered in the Central Ward of Osaka alone at the end of 1999, according to the Osaka City Statistical Data (2000). Minami was a multi-purpose entertainment district and was known as a drinking district (*nomiya-gai* in Japanese) as well. The Korean clubs and bars were built next to and around Japanese clubs and bars. The majority of Korean clubs and bars opened from early evening to midnight (the first shift) and were licensed. They obtained business permits from the police, committed to a multiple-year lease, paid large non-refundable rental fees, provided deposits upfront, and renovated the spaces. These more visible first-shift operations thus required more careful planning and substantial capital. The other type of Korean bars, which opened after midnight, were called "the second shift" (*ibu* in Korean) and were not formally registered. Therefore, they lacked "visibility" not only in formal statistics and quantitative research but also among ethnic Japanese.

In Minami, Korean clubs and bars alone accounted for at least two hundred establishments in 2001 (see Table 13.1). Yet, Korean clubs and bars have received little anthropological investigation as a sector of ethnic businesses in Japan. For example, there are only brief mentions of Korean hostesses in the past scholarship on Koreans in Japan (e.g., Lee and De Vos 1981; Lie 2001). In addition, the high concentration of similar clubs and bars – both Korean and non-Korean – would seem to increase the competition over customers and undermine profits. Why, then, were Korean clubs and bars concentrated in the small area where many Japanese clubs and bars were already operating? How did they cope with the limited space and high-rent? This chapter will address these questions in the case study of Minami's Korean clubs and bars. In particular, I will analyze why so many similar businesses (clubs and bars) operate in only a fraction of Minami by applying "agglomeration theory."

In the "agglomeration theory," business entities attract more customers when they are clustered (Fujita and Thisse 2002: 18). The theory suggests that the benefits are greater than the losses incurred by potential competition. The so-called garment district in Seoul, the financial district in London, and the diamond district in New York are well-known examples that support the agglomeration theory (cf. Fujita and Thisse 2002: 8). Anthropologists have documented similar concentration of ethnic businesses in case studies of Chinatown and Koreatown in New York City (e.g., Guest 2003; Park 1997). The benefits are greater than the loss from the competition. In Minami, not only Korean but also Japanese and other ethnic clubs and bars together created an adult entertainment district that attracted customers. This shows that the agglomeration theory is relevant both within and beyond ethnic boundaries.

Furthermore, Korean clubs and bars played crucial roles for the newly emerging Korean ethnic business community. Many other Korean businesses, such as restaurants and video shops, operated within and around Koreatown (about 0.2 square miles, 125 acres, or 600 square yards). Amalia Lucia Cabezas (1998: xii) discusses businesses such as hotels, boutiques, and domestic work services that are generated to cater to migrant and transient sex-worker populations in Sosua, the Dominican Republic. I argue that the agglomeration theory also helps to explain the concentration of different kinds of businesses within an ethnic area.

Through my fieldwork, I discovered the subtle yet elaborate mechanisms that support the agglomeration of Korean clubs and bars both in the spatial concentration and overlap of businesses. Some of these clubs and bars had two separate operations in the same spaces at different times. The spatial overlap was manifested in the form of time-sharing of spaces, names, and equipment by dual-shift operations. The investigation of the dual-shift operations would provide a unique contribution to the agglomeration theory, which primarily focuses on spatial concentration, by adding a temporal dimension (e.g., two different operations of a similar type of business in the same space but at different times).

I argue that a particular contradiction that migrant hostesses face also contributed to the emergence of time-sharing dual operations; although they worked as professional companions called "hostesses," there was no hostess visa in Japan; in other words, many migrant hostesses did not have proper visas to work as hostesses (Chung 2011). Some entered Japan with tourist or student visas and stayed in Japan legally, but these visas did not permit them to work as hostesses. Other migrants obtained "entertainer visas," many of which were issued for migrant women who were to perform on stage at ethnic clubs and bars rather than work as hostesses. In other words, a significant portion of migrant Korean hostesses were engaged in extra-visa activities and were uncertain of how long they could continue to work as hostesses in Japan due to their precarious visa statuses. This sense that they would have only "limited time" made some of them to want to work as much as possible while they could stay in Japan. This urge led to a new business scheme by compressing the spatial arrangement in a temporal manner in the shadows and at the margins: operating dual businesses in one space at different hours. Before discussing this time-sharing, I would like to offer some brief socio-historical background of Korean hostesses in modern Japan.

Korean Hostesses in Japan

While the demand for hostesses remained strong, the number of Japanese women who were willing to become hostesses declined as their employment opportunities gradually expanded after WWII. Some clubs and bars suffered from labor shortages during the years of Japan's booming economy (Hinako 1986: 153; Abito, Matsui and Tanaka 1988: 29–30). Even though the club/bar business itself was prosperous, the lack of employees led many clubs to bankruptcy (*hitode busoku tôsan*) (Kuwahara 1991: 170). The severe shortage of hostesses resulted in the diversification of workers in terms of country of origin. Some bars and clubs began recruiting hostesses from abroad by using brokers and production agencies. For example, approximately 36,000 hostesses worked at 3,000 clubs and bars in Tokyo's Ginza area (Kuwahara 1991: 1). By the 1980s, more than one hundred of these clubs had hired migrant hostesses from Thailand, Brazil, Columbia, Mexico, Spain, Korea, and Taiwan (Kuwahara 1991: 160–162) – in spite of the initial resistance to hiring migrants (Usuki 1986: 178). More and more migrant workers came to be employed for such short-handed businesses from the 1980s.

The legacy of the Japanese colonial occupation of Korea and "comfort women" between 1910 and 1945, (e.g., Soh 2008), and the resulting "postcolonial predicament" (Morris-Suzuki 2007: 65-68) contributed to the concentration of resident Koreans in the somewhat stigmatized part of the entertainment business in Japan (Chung 2004, 2011). Newcomer migrant Koreans also filled the gap of supply and demand of hostesses in Japan.

Korean migrant hostesses were a rarity and novelty until the 1970s (O 1990: 47–48), but by the 1980s, they had become conspicuous (Usuki 1986: 177). By 1990, the prime time of Japan's bubble economy, the club business prospered and recruited even more Korean hostesses. The South Korean media also promoted migration to Japan by featuring "successful" migrant Koreans who obtained permanent Japanese residency or citizenship. Some hostesses eventually became club owners and madams. Others married Japanese or resident Koreans and stabilized their legal status by obtaining a spousal visa. These "success stories" inspired more South Koreans to come to Japan (cf. Usuki 1988: 91). The disparity in economic conditions between Japan and South Korea also encouraged a migrant flow.

Approximately 3,000 Korean clubs and bars were in operation in Japan by the mid-1990s. Among them, 1,200 were in Tokyo, and 900 were in Osaka where Minami is located (KBS-TV 1995 in Sawazaki and Song 1997). Despite this influx of migrants to the club and bar industries and the fact that hostessing became one of the most common occupations for migrant women, Japan's gender-biased immigration policy has not addressed this change or created hostess visas. This policy contradiction contributed to criticism from the United States that there was trafficking of these women (Chung 2004, 2012). Based on my research, however, Korean migrant hostesses were far more concerned about their precarious visa status than being "trafficked" by brokers. In fact, I never observed or heard about any trafficked Korean migrant hostesses during my research. Ironically, the Japanese immigration policy created and sustained migrant hostesses' vulnerability. This was one of the reasons that the second-shift system was created and a quarter of high-end Korean club workers were willing to work the second shift to earn extra incomes. This system of dual shifts in Korean clubs and bars further intensified the agglomeration of other Korean ethnic businesses into Koreatown because of increased business opportunities.

The Gravitation of Korean Ethnic Businesses to Korean Clubs and Bars

Based on my ethnographic data and analysis of the telephone directory and advertisements of the April 2001 issue of a Korean monthly community magazine, *Tongrami*, I compiled Table 13.1, which summarizes Korean businesses in the Minami area. This free magazine was written in Korean and distributed in Korean communities in Osaka. I have added a dozen other businesses and services, which were not included in *Tongrami* but I confirmed through my fieldwork. In some cases, the exact number of establishments was impossible to verify, and I just list "a couple," "a few," and "quite a few" based upon my interviews of workers, managers, and customers. The exact number of such businesses and services was hard to discern because many of them were not officially registered or came and went quickly due to their freelance operations, precarious licenses, and/or their workers' unstable visa statuses.

All these different businesses offered various services and amenities. Due to the limitations of space here, I will provide brief descriptions of some of the most numerous businesses. Aside from the clubs (ranked number three on the list) and bars (ranked number one on the list), the largest category of Korean businesses in Minami was restaurants, of which there were fifty-three. Korean club/bar workers and customers often ate their meals, scheduled their business meetings, and arranged paid-dates called *dohan* at these restaurants. At Club Rose, like many other clubs and bars, a customer could have a date with a hostess, entertainer, or madam before the club's business hours if he would pay an extra fee to the club. Then the club reimbursed a portion of the fee to the hostess, entertainer, or

Table 13.1 • The Korean Ethnic Service Sector in and around Minami

Kind of businesses	Number
First- and second-shift hostess bars	A few hundred
Restaurants	53
First-shift hostess clubs	33
Christian churches	14
Boutiques	13
Beauty salons	12
Rental video shops	12
Unregistered taxi drivers (*narashi*)	10
Grocery stores	5
Internet cafés	5
Host clubs	4
Jewelry stores	3
Real estate agencies	2
Dressmakers	2
Public baths with saunas	2
Psychics	2
Nightclubs	2
Legal aid offices	1
Shoe-repair shops	1
Rental comic book stores	1
Dry-cleaning shops	1
Consumer credit firms	1
Esthetic clinics (facial and body massage)	1
Freelance keyboard accompanists	Quite a few
Flower shops	A couple
Liquor stores	A couple
Massage parlors	A few
Escort clubs	Several
Female sex solicitor agents	Quite a few
Criminal organizations (*Kkanpae*)	A few
Underground casinos	A few
Visa brokers	A few
Japanese husbands who provide spousal visas	A few hundred
Domestic workers	Quite a few

madam. The term *dohan* literally means "to come together or to accompany." A customer paid all the expenses during the date.

Senior Director Hong of Club Rose once noted that the "Korean meals in Minami often taste better than ones in South Korea because hostesses and customers have discriminating palates (*shita ga koeteru*) and are willing to pay high prices." With their buying power, frequent uses, and willingness to pay higher prices, the customers and workers of the clubs and bars contributed to the restaurants' sales and to attract restaurant businesses in the area.

Hostesses and madams' buying power supported by their relatively higher income enabled them to pay hundreds of dollars or even thousands of dollars for their clothes, which they wore at work. Based on the kinds of clothes worn by hostesses and madams, it was clear that they were important clienteles for boutiques. At least thirteen boutiques were confirmed. A fresh and attractive appearance was a minimum job requirement for hostesses and madams. Therefore, they frequently purchased expensive costumes, suits, and shoes. To accommodate hostesses' working hours, these boutiques tended to stay open until very late at night. Some club and bar customers also purchased items at the boutiques as gifts for hostesses, madams, and entertainers.

Appearance management was not limited to clothes. Hairstyling was another crucial element. Twelve Korean beauty salons made up about ten percent of the beauty salons in Minami. Considering that the Korean population consisted of around one percent of Japan's population, this statistic of ten percent reflected the strong and steady demands of Korean customers in Minami. Almost all Korean clubs required their hostesses and madams to have their hair set professionally at salons every day before they came to work. Each visit to the beauty salon cost a hostess or madam US $25–30. These beauty salons also offered a service to dress a hostess in a kimono for a fee of about US $30. When I interviewed a hair salon owner, she confirmed the importance of hostesses and madams for her business and said, "The number of hostesses in Minami affects our business." Hostesses and madams were among the major clients of these beauty salons.

Another necessary service for many club/bar workers was the taxi. The taxi business profited greatly by catering to the needs of the customers and the workers at the clubs and bars. In Japanese, an unregistered taxi was called *shirotaku*, which literally means "white taxi." Curiously, Korean migrants called them *narashi*, which I believe to be a mispronunciation of the Japanese term *nagashi* that means "cruising." I confirmed that ten unregistered taxi drivers operated around Minami. This is a point of interest because a taxi driver offering a ride for a fee without governmental registration is illegal in Japan. Therefore, these migrant Korean drivers made their vehicles indistinguishable from ordinary private cars and did not look like taxis at all. Because they were not able to pick up customers on the street, the unregistered taxi drivers offered competitive fares and built their own clientele through ethnic networks and connections. These unregistered taxis were particularly convenient for club/bar workers when regular taxis became scarce after midnight.

Many hostesses and madams used taxis instead of public transportation for several reasons. First, using public transportation did not match the fashionable and out of the ordinary image they tried to present to customers. Second, most public transportation was no longer running by the time they finished work. Third, those hostesses who did not have proper visas wanted to avoid any encounters with immigration officers. If they walked the streets less often, they believed that they could reduce the risk of being interrogated by the officers. In addition, many of them made long-term contracts with the unregistered taxi drivers who offered cheaper rates, guaranteed a ride home, and provided access to local news and gossip within the Korean community. Finally, these drivers could offer some familiarity and comfort to them. When I was walking on the street with my hostess colleague Erika, she waved her hand and walked to a car stopped for traffic light. Following her, I got in the car and learned that it was one of the unlicensed Korean taxis. The drivers were usually migrant Korean men who used the vehicles, which were not distinguishable from the ordinary non-commercial cars. The frequent users recognized these unregistered taxis based on drivers' faces. Erika looked more relaxed and was more talkative than when we took regular registered Japanese taxis.

Sharing a ride with other club workers also occurred in both the registered and unregistered taxis. The sharing was sometimes an effect of the agglomeration of Korean clubs and bars in Koreatown as well as more common practices in South Korea than in Japan. A contracted unregistered taxi might thus pick up one hostess or more at each apartment, bring them to each club and bar in the early evening, pick them up again near the clubs and bars at the end of the night, and return them to their apartments.

These drivers paid a nominal fee of about US $50 to *yakuza*, the Japanese mafia who "supervised" the area, as monthly "rent" for parking spaces to pick up their contracted Korean customers. One club customer explained this system: "Conflicts over scarce convenient parking spaces among the unlicensed taxis occurred in the past, and *yakuza* intervened to keep 'peace' in the area. *Yakuza* assigned a space and time for each unlicensed taxi driver and patrolled the area to enforce the spatial and temporal assignment in exchange for nominal fees." This type of *yakuza* intervention has been observed in other contexts in Japan, and overrepresentation of resident Koreans among *yakuza* has also been noted (Hill 2003). In Minami's Koreatown, I speculate ethnic affinity between migrant Koreans and resident Koreans contributed to regulating the unregulated businesses of unlicensed taxi and *yakuza*.

Services catering to the club and bar workers were not limited to commercial or "criminal" domains. Religious establishments were also within the orbit of the clubs and bars' influence. Korean migrant hostesses and madams were known for their extensive physical contributions (e.g., cooking Korean food, cleaning, and doing dishes) and monetary donations to the churches in exchange for emotional comfort, ethnic social networks, and "redemption for their guilt to be in a 'sinful' occupation" according to Older Sister Kim, the hostess at Club Rose.[5] The fourteen Korean Christian churches served Korean migrants in the Minami area and its vicinity. A quarter of the hostesses and madams at Club Rose were earnest Christians who attended church at least weekly and contributed their physical labor and at least ten percent of their income.

These broad and intricate linkages among the clubs, bars, and other Korean "businesses" deserve more discussion than they can receive here, but I hope that even this partial discussion illustrates how important Korean clubs and bars were to the formation of the Korean business and religious communities in Minami. The remainder of this chapter focuses on how the thirty-three first-shift clubs played a central role in the existence of the smaller-scale bars.

Clubs and Bars

Korean clubs and bars played a central role in enticing various Korean ethnic establishments into Minami. The first-shift Korean clubs in particular functioned as a magnet in attracting second-shift bars by providing not only human resources (e.g., entrepreneurs, customers, workers) but also infrastructure (e.g., facilities and equipment). Senior Director Hong of Club Rose confidently argued that the concentration of the clubs and bars in the area benefitted all of the parties involved:

> When customers decide to come to Korean clubs, most of them have not decided which club they want to go to until they actually come to Minami. So, it is advantageous to stay close to other Korean clubs. Even if Club Rose is not their first choice, the customers often go to another club. Therefore, Club Rose could be the second club they visit if not the first

Senior Director Hong emphasized the merits of being close to other clubs; the advantages were greater than any losses suffered through competition. In the case of Minami, it was not only Korean clubs/bars, but also Japanese and other ethnic clubs/bars which were located close together. In fact, when I conducted research at Japanese clubs, I encountered numerous Japanese customers who went to Korean clubs afterwards. This suggests the value of intra-ethnic agglomeration as well as inter-ethnic agglomeration. Furthermore, the concentration of numerous kinds of Korean ethnic businesses suggests inter-business agglomeration as well.

Agglomeration of Korean clubs and bars was so intense in Minami that one space sometimes hosted two businesses. In Minami, a number of Korean clubs and bars had a dual-shift system. They shared the same space, name, and equipment but in different time periods by two different groups of people. For example, one middle-aged Korean madam rented space and ran the first shift at Bar Tani from 7 p.m. to midnight with a Korean female manager and several migrant Korean hostesses. Erika, a Korean hostess at Club Rose, sublet the space and equipment of Bar Tani and ran a second shift with different staff from midnight through the early morning, as late as 7 a.m. The first and second shift inevitably shared the same bar name, "Tani," because the name was printed on the neon signs outside the bar and building and on the matches and coasters used in the bar. Although the profits made during each shift belonged to the individual management responsible, both parties benefited by splitting the costs of utilities and rent. I argue that a single bar location having both first-shift and second-shift operations is a more intensified form of agglomeration than previously theorized (e.g., Fujita and Thisse 2002). Formal statistics often fail to recognize such secondary operations and thus underestimate the actual number of clubs/bars in the area.

These unique Korean second-shift operations were usually only known to a relatively small circle of customers or Korean migrant workers at the clubs and bars. Most second-shift bars were technically "illegal" since the law did not allow such late night operation. Therefore, no official statistics were available to establish the exact number of the second-shift bars. Associate Madam Yun at Club Rose, who ran her own second-shift bar, and Mao who worked there and at Club Rose as a hostess, estimated the number as follows: Somewhere between thirty and fifty people worked at each of the thirty-three first-shift Korean clubs around Koreatown in Minami. Approximately twenty to thirty percent of the club hostesses and madams, which meant a few hundred, ran or worked at second-shift bars. Some of these bars were run by one person, as in the case of Ayu, as explained below. Some of them employed a few Korean migrants as Bar Tani did. Therefore, they estimated a couple of hundred Korean second-shift bars operated in Minami.

Erika ran the second shift at Bar Tani with three other migrant Korean women: Kana, the number two hostess of Club Rose; "Older Sister," a woman in her late thirties; and Kumi, a hostess who worked for another Korean club during the first shift. Working arrangements varied: Kana came to Bar Tani whenever she had her own customers to entertain, which could be as frequently as several times a week. Older Sister, unlike the others, did not work during the first shift, and she came to work at Bar Tani almost every night. Initially, Kana and Kumi were business partners, but Kana subsequently become more of a contractor, and Kumi took a leave of absence due to her illness.

I obtained the opportunity of participant observation as a paid hostess as a replacement for Kumi. To my surprise, Erika assigned me a responsible role soon after she hired me. I was often the first person to go to Bar Tani for the second shift. While I was finishing my work at Club Rose, Erika often urged me to rush to Bar Tani, which was only a couple of blocks away. The physical proximity of Club Rose and Bar Tani enabled us to do dual shifts back to back. I walked to Bar Tani around midnight, where the madam and several hostesses of the first shift were still entertaining customers. The customers were singing karaoke, drinking alcohol beverages, and talking with hostesses. As I entered the kitchen, I greeted "Manager," a Korean woman in her twenties by saying "Good morning," which was the common greeting in the club/bar industries in Japan no matter what time it was. She also had multiple responsibilities as manager, cook, and dishwasher. Standing next to her, I began to prepare the dry snacks for the second shift. We worked collegially, so did other members. When the first shift was short-handed, we helped them and vice versa during the overlapped hours.

The working style and conditions at the second-shift Bar Tani were much more fluid and multi-tasking than the ones at the first-shift Club Rose. So too were the reasons for opening a second-shift bar. Erika explained why she began her second-shift bar:

> Some customers want to spend more time with us even after Club Rose closes. I used to go to other bars and restaurants with them, but I realized that it was more profitable to bring the customers to my own bar. So, I began the second shift by renting the space of Bar Tani with a couple of other hostesses.

Once again, physical proximity was a factor, making it easy to solicit customers from Club Rose to Bar Tani.

Other informal "contractors" also benefited from the agglomeration. If a madam, hostess, or manager, who was not formally associated with the second-shift Bar Tani, brought a customer and spent time with him, Erika usually re-imbursed half of what the customer paid. For example, if the customer paid US $100 to Bar Tani, Erika gave US $50 back to the madam, hostess, or manager of the other club. This transaction often occurred under the table, and many customers seemed to be unaware of it. The informal contractor thus looked as if she was spending her "private time" with the customer – at least from the customer's point of view. Even if some customers noticed such practices, they still seemed to be happy spending time with a high-end club hostess or madam at second-shift Bar Tani for less expense. As this example suggests, the agglomeration of the Korean clubs and bars offered a chance of entrepreneurship and freelance contract opportunities with limited initial investment, created more jobs, and provided flexible working styles by bringing spaces, workers, and customers into close physical proximity. This physical proximity allowed the migrant workers to have more than one job if they wished and created different "services," which stimulated their personal aspirations and the local economic activities.

Economically, more opportunities also arise from product differentiation, which plays a key role in agglomeration as it "relaxes price competition and consequently allows" businesses to attract more customers (Fujita and Thisse 2002: 18). Although the prime product at clubs and bars was inter-personal services and companionship, the service styles and costs at the first-shift Club Rose differed from those of the second-shift Bar Tani. At Bar Tani, both Erika and Kana created a more casual atmosphere and solicited customers and hostesses to sing and drink more than they did at their first-shift jobs at Club Rose.

From the customers' point of view, the second-shift bars offered the customer the option of spending more time with his favorite hostess, presumably at a lower cost than at the first-shift high-end Club Rose. Mr. Matsui, a Japanese-born Korean customer in his early forties, often went to another second-shift bar called Bar Seven after Club Rose closed. Bar Seven was also conveniently located within walking distance of Club Rose. When he wanted to spend more time with Chiyon, the number one hostess of Club Rose, he went to Bar Seven, which Chiyon ran. This physical (only a few blocks between Club Rose and Bar Seven) and temporal proximity (back-to-back from Club Rose to Bar Seven) benefited Chiyon, her customers, and a couple of dancers from Club Rose to whom Chiyon offered second-shift informal employment. Mr. Matsui was one of the customers they occasionally recruited at Club Rose and brought to Bar Seven.

Sharing workers and customers is one of the marketing and management strategies called "demand smoothing." Some Korean migrant workers in Minami tried to increase the service demand during slow periods and decrease the demand during busy periods by encouraging reservations, adapting different fee scales, and extending their working hours. The second-shift bars enabled them to use these strategies. Agglomeration gives another advantage to smooth demand (cf. O'Flaherty 2005: 17–20). Overall, the ethnic business agglomeration of Koreatown in Minami provided entrepreneurial opportunities for those who ran the clubs and bars, entertainment variations for the customers, and flexible employment opportunities for those who looked for other income sources. Dual shifts also enabled the workers to use their hairdos, dresses, and make-up for two jobs.

Running second-shift bars, however, was not easy, as Ayu's experience indicates. Ayu was a 26-year-old popular hostess working at Club Rose who used to run her own second-shift bar. She said:

> I was infatuated by the idea of running my own second-shift bar. Once this idea came into my mind, I could not get rid of it. So, I asked some of my clients, whom I met through my work at the [first-shift] clubs, to help me to open the second-shift bar. It was not too difficult to find the space, and it was not too expensive compared to opening the first-shift bars. I opened my own bar within a couple of months. But it did not take too long for me to realize it was not an easy business. Most of all, it became physically challenging and mentally tiring.

Many hostesses flirted with the idea of having their own bars or clubs at some point in their career. However, running her own bar entailed more than just being a hostess. Ayu had to pay rent, utilities, and salaries to her employees. She also had to take care of other logistics, such as ordering bottles of whiskey and beer, and buying snacks and fruits. In addition, she herself cleaned the utensils, the bathroom, and the kitchen before locking up and leaving the bar. Running a bar not only required her to entertain customers but also imposed many other responsibilities of which she had been unaware. Those "invisible" responsibilities were taken care of by other administrative and support staff at the first-shift Club Rose. Although running her own second-shift bar as "madam" was psychologically and socially satisfying at the beginning, Ayu could not sustain her physical and mental energy, and her second-shift bar only lasted for a few months. The proximity of the first-shift job and the second-shift job made dual shifts possible, but having two jobs required not only extra time but also enormous efforts. Therefore, those who managed two jobs at first and second shifts were limited to approximately a quarter of the overall Club Rose workers, even many felt pressed about the length of time they could work in Japan.

Conclusion

The agglomeration of Korean clubs and bars contributed greatly to the development and expansion of the migrant Korean community and its economic activities in Minami's Koreatown because of its prominent consumption patterns and buying power. As a result, ethnic amenities, such as ethnic food and personal services, became easily available to the Korean clubs/bars and their workers. The availability of these ethnic amenities in Minami further attracted other types of commercial and religious establishments. This chapter sheds light on less visible Korean second-shift bars as a prime example of an agglomeration of ethnic businesses that were attracted to the Korean first-shift clubs and bars.

Multiple factors of agglomeration of clubs and bars contributed to the proliferation of the second-shift bars. The time-sharing of space and equipment reduced the initial investment for the second shift. Since the first-shift clubs and bars retrieved a part of their costs by subletting the space, they too benefited. In addition, customers – primarily Japanese and Koreans – could use these secondary venues to spend more time with their favorite migrant Korean hostesses after the first-shift clubs and bars closed. The second-shift bars also tended to be more lenient of workers' visa status because these bars themselves were not licensed. Furthermore those who could not work at first-shift bars and clubs because of their less suitable attributes in terms of age, appearance, experience, and clientele, had the chance to earn an income, like "Big Sister,"– albeit for lower wages and late-night working hours. Finally, the second-shift bars offered additional work or entrepreneurship for top-notch hostesses of first-shift clubs who wanted to make extra money or to pursue their dream of running their own bars.

This mechanism of agglomeration became most salient at places like Bar Tani. Having a first-shift bar and second-shift bar occupy the same space at different times, Bar Tani represents an intriguing form of temporal and spatial agglomeration: one physical space housing two different bars during different shifts and generating two separate business entities. The dual-shift business model enables better utilization of scarce land space in Minami, generates more jobs and profit, and reinforces inter- and intra-ethnic ties. Unlike a factory night-shift imposed by management, this second shift emerged from the workers as entrepreneurs.

This time-sharing business scheme was a particularly effective strategy for migrants who felt they had only limited time to work in Japan due to their precarious visa status. The agglomeration of Korean clubs and bars in Minami thus provided economic opportunities for a wide range of migrant workers, in terms of age, visa status, and earning power. These business operations – in the shadows and at the margins – deserve more attention in the research on migration, ethnic businesses, entrepreneurship, flexible labor, and entertainment and hospitality industries.

Notes

1. I am grateful to Gary Herrigel for introducing me to the concept of agglomeration and to David Haines, Keiko Yamanaka, Shinji Yamashita, the participants at the workshop held at UC Berkeley in 2008, and anonymous reviewers for their insightful comments and questions.
2. All the names used in this chapter are pseudonyms.
3. All the translations from Japanese and Korean are mine.
4. All mileage and footage is approximate.
5. See Chapter 13, "Psychological Impacts of Colonialism and Emotional Labor" (Chung 2004) for a discussion of the in-depth relationship between Christian churches and Korean hostesses in Minami.

References

Abito, Ruben, Yayori Matsui, and Hiroshi Tanaka. 1988. "Zadankai / Gaikokujin Rôdô-sha no Genzai: Sono Jittai to Korekara no Taiô." Vol. 249 in *Gendai no Esupuri, Japayuki-san no Ima: Gaikokujin Rôdôsha o Meguru Mondai-ten*, eds. Hiroshi Tanaka and Ayako Miyoshi. Fukuoka. Genyudo.

Allison, Anne. 1994. *Nightwork: Sexuality, Pleasure, and Corporate Masculinity in a Tokyo Hostess Club*. Chicago: University of Chicago Press.

Cabezas, Amalia Lucia. 1998. "Discourses of prostitution: The case of Cuba," in *Global Sex Workers: Rights, Resistance, and Redefinition*, eds. Kamala Kempadoo and Jo Doezema. New York: Routledge.

Chapman, David. 2008. *Zainichi Korean Identity and Ethnicity.* London: Routledge.

Chung, Haeng-ja S. 2002. "Korean hostess clubs in Minami, Osaka: Preliminary findings on workers, activities, and income." *The Journal of Human Rights* 24(2): 41–58. Osaka: Research Center for Human Rights, Osaka City University.

———. 2004. *Performing Sex, Selling Heart: Korean Nightclub Hostesses in Japan.* Ph.D. dissertation. The Department of Anthropology, University of California, Los Angeles.

———. 2008. "Deconstructing the notions of 'Korean' 'nightclub' 'hostesses' in Japan and proposing 'labor participant observation'." Paper presented at the Contemporary Anthropology Workshop at the University of Tokyo, Komaba (in Japanese).

———. 2009. "Gender and ethnicity at work: Korean Nightclub Rose in Japan," in *Gender and Labor in Korea and Japan: Sexing Class,* eds. Elyssa Faison and Ruth Barraclough. London: RoutledgeCurzon.

———. 2011. "'Zainichi' Hosutesu to Kankokujin Hosutesu: 'Sanyo Kansatsu,' 'Kanjo Rodo,' and 'Viza Seisaku' wo Chusin ni. ("'Resident Korean" Hostesses and "Migrant Korean' Hostesses in Japan: 'Participant Observation,' 'Emotional Labor,' and 'Visa Policy'.)" *Senso to Sei* 30. Tokyo: Senso to Sei Henshu-shitsu (in Japanese).

———. 2012. "Amerika Kokumusho no 'Jinshin Baibai Hokokusho' ni Tsukareta Nihon no Biza Seisaku no mujun: 'Hosutesu Biza' ga Nai Nihon de Hataraku Iju Hosutesutachi." (Contradictions of the Japanese Visa Policy Pointed Out By the 'Trafficking In Persons Report' of the United States' Department of State)." Migrants Network 147 (February-March): 12–15 (in Japanese).

Frank, Katherine. 2002. *G-Strings and Sympathy: Strip Club Regulars and Male Desire.* Durham: Duke University Press.

Fujita, Masahisa, and Jacques-Francois Thisse. 2002. *Economies of Agglomeration: Cities, Industrial Location, and Regional Growth.* Cambridge: Cambridge University Press.

Fukuoka, Yasunori. 2000. *Lives of Young Koreans in Japan.* Melborne: Trans Pacific Press.

Guest, Kenneth. 2003. *God in Chinatown: Religion and Survival in New York's Evolving Immigrant Community.* New York: New York University Press.

Hill, Peter B. E. 2003. *The Japanese Mafia: Yakuza, Law, and the State.* Oxford: Oxford University Press.

Hinako, Satoru. 1986. "Japayuki-san no Keizai-gaku: Japayuki Bijinesu – Sono Rekishi, Haikei, Shisutemu." *Bessatsu Takarajima 54: Japayuki-san Monogakatari.*

Koh, Sun-Hui. 1998. *20 Seiki no Tainichi-Chaejudō-jin: Sono Seikatsu Katei to Ishiki.* Tokyo: Akashi Shoten.

Kondo, Dorine. 1991. *Crafting Selves: Power, Gender, and Discourses of Identity in a Japanese Workplace.* Chicago: University of Chicago Press.

Korean Broadcasting System Television (KBS-TV). 1995. *"Kofuku 50-ne Tokubetsu Kikaku Dokyumentari."*

Kuwahara, Ietoshi. 1991. *Naisho Naisho* Vol.3. Tokyo: Sanmák Shuppan.

Lee, Changsoo, and George De Vos, eds. 1981. *Koreans in Japan: Ethnic Conflict and Accommodation.* Berkeley: University of California Press.

Lie, John. 2001. *Multiethnic Japan.* Cambridge: Harvard University Press.

———. 2008. *Zainichi (Koreans in Japan): Diasporic Nationalism and Postcolonial Identity.* Berkeley: University of California Press.

Mitchell, Richard H. 1967. *The Korean Minority in Japan.* Berkeley: University of California Press.

Morris-Suzuki, Tessa. 2007. *Exodus to North Korea: Shadows from Japan's Cold War.* Lanham: Rowman & Littlefield.

O, Sonhwa. 1990. *Sukaato no Kaze (Chima Param): Nihon Eiju wo Mezasu Kankoku no Onna-tachi.* Tokyo: Sankosha.

O'Flaherty, Brendan. 2005. *City Economics.* Cambridge: Harvard University Press.

Park, Kyeyoung 1997. *The Korean American Dream: Immigrants and Small Business in New York City.* Ithaca: Cornell University Press.

Ryang, Sonia, ed. 2000. *Koreans in Japan: Critical Voices from the Margin.* London: Routledge.

Ryang, Sonia, and John Lie, eds. 2008. *Diaspora without Homeland: Being Korean in Japan.* Berkeley: University of California Press.

Sawazaki, Yasushi and Tong-gyu Sung. 1997. *"Fûzoku Sangyô ni Jûji suru Rainichi Kankokujin no AIDS/STD ni Kakawaru Sêkôdô to sono Haikê ni kansuru Kenkyû."* Heisei 9-nendo Kôsê Kagaku Kenkyûhi Hojokin Kenkyû Buntan Kenkyû Hôkokusho.

Soh, Sarah C. 2008. *The Comfort Women: Sexual Violence and Postcolonial Memory in Korea and Japan.* Chicago: University of Chicago Press.

Tsuda, Takeyuki. 2003. *Strangers in the Ethnic Homeland: Japanese Brazilian Return Migration in Transnational Perspective.* New York: Columbia University Press.

Usuki, Keiko. 1986. "Aru Kankokujin Hosutesu no 'Japan' Funsenki." *Bessatsu Takarajima* 54: *Japayuki-san Monogakatari.* pp.10–37. Tokyo : JICC Shuppankyoku.

———. 1988. "Japayuki Genshô o Miru," in *Gendai no Esupuri, Japayuki-san no Ima: Gaikokujin Rôdôsha o Meguru Mondai-ten* 249 : 85–99, eds. Hiroshi Tanaka and Ayako Miyoshi.

Weiner, Michael A. 1989. *The Origins of the Korean Community in Japan, 1910–1923.* Atlantic Highlands: Humanities Press International.

Wender, Melissa L. 2005. *Lamentation as History: Narratives by Koreans in Japan, 1965–2000.* Stanford: Stanford University Press.

Zheng, Tiantian. 2009. *Red Lights: The Lives of Sex Workers in Postsocialist China.* Minneapolis: University of Minnesota Press.

CHAPTER 14

African Traders in Chungking Mansions, Hong Kong

Gordon MATHEWS[1]

Over the past decade there has been a massive increase in African traders coming to south China (Pawson 2005; Zhou 2006; French and Polgreen 2007) and to Hong Kong, particularly to Chungking Mansions, where I have been doing research over the past four years. Chungking Mansions is a ramshackle seventeen-story building with around 170 wholesale goods dealers on its first two floors and 120 cheap guesthouses and restaurants on its upper floors; some 2,000 African traders may stay there on any given night, and sometimes shop and live there for weeks at a time. In this chapter, I examine the business and migrations of these traders, and consider how they pursue their fortunes in an attempt to understand their lives. I also consider the larger economic implications of their global trade.

The Reasons and Routes of Traders

These traders have been drawn to the area by the newly emergent industrial might of China, as filtered through Hong Kong, and also by the fact that goods in China, real and fake, can be bought so cheaply. To use the terms of world systems theory, China is the powerhouse of the semi-periphery. These traders from the extreme periphery, "off all kinds of maps" (Allen and Hamnett 1995: 2; see also Ferguson 2007: 25-49), go to China, or to China's entrepôt, Hong Kong, to buy manufactured goods, new, used, or copies of products from the core, that their fellow Africans can afford. They embody "informal globalization" or "low-end globalization" (Ribeiro 2006; Mathews 2007, 2011) – globalization that takes place through individuals dealing with one another largely on the basis of trust and working with a high degree of risk, often carrying their goods themselves across the globe. This form of business migration is neither new nor unprecedented: consider, for example, the "informal commercial importers" in Haiti as described by Ulysse (2007), as well as elsewhere in the Caribbean (Browne 2004: 56), and the street entrepreneurs in Ciudad del Este in Paraguay (Ribeiro

2006), as well as the Congolese traders in Paris described by MacGaffey and Bazenguissa-Ganga (2000). But what does seem new is the sheer scale of their activity. Even approximate figures on the scale of this trade are difficult to arrive at, due to the informal, semi-legal nature of this trade; but my rough estimate is that 20 percent of the mobile phones now in use in sub-Saharan Africa have passed through Chungking Mansions.[2]

These African entrepreneurs trade in mobile phones and clothing most typically, but also in goods ranging from electronics to building materials to used car parts to knock-off Jacuzzi baths. The trade is not only one-way: while most traders transport goods from China and Hong Kong to sell in their home countries, some work in the other direction, carrying precious stones from various African countries to Paris, Bangkok, and Hong Kong. The livelihoods of these traders are predicated on the availability of tourist visas and airplane tickets, and above all, on the mobile phone, making it easy to stay in constant touch with one's home-country buyers and markets.

I have met traders from virtually every country in sub-Saharan Africa, with the largest contingent from Tanzania, Kenya, Nigeria, and Ghana. Some traders, particularly those dealing in fabrics, building materials, and furniture, go into China for their orders. They may obtain a visa for China in their home countries, or, if they come from a country that Hong Kong allows – which includes most African countries although visa controls have been tightening in recent years[3] – simply fly to Hong Kong and obtain visa-free entry at the airport, and then quickly obtain a China visa at Chungking Mansions. I know one female African trader of garments who uses her time in Hong Kong to buy single items of clothing that she thinks will sell well in her home country. She then goes into China and commissions a factory to make up to 30,000 copies for her under her own label, which she sends back to East Africa. Other traders stay in Hong Kong, but go to different Hong Kong locales for used car parts or for wholesale clothing styled especially for Africans. Still others spend their entire business trips in Chungking Mansions, buying clothing or especially mobile phones within the building, and venturing out only to have a meal at McDonald's, or to drink beer with their fellow traders at the 7-Eleven around the corner, which functions as a stand-up bar.

The great majority of traders do not try to stay in Hong Kong beyond their visa's expiration date; their profits depend upon their ability to rapidly go back and forth with their goods between Hong Kong and their home countries, as well as upon their staying on the legal side of immigration laws. But a small percentage of Africans coming to Hong Kong from various countries (Nigeria is perhaps most common) either declare themselves as asylum seekers to the UNHCR or the Hong Kong government, or simply overstay their visas. Immigration police regularly come to Chungking Mansions and check the passports of possible overstayers; but because Chungking Mansions is such a labyrinth, they generally only catch a small number of people, with the rest drifting off into the stairways and the crowds. Some asylum seekers or overstayers operate business networks with buyers in their home countries, networks that may be hampered by the fact that they cannot leave Hong Kong. Others work illegally in Chungking Mansions – HK $3,000 per month is a standard wage (US $1 = HK $7.8) – while still other asylum seekers live off the very limited assistance provided by the Hong Kong government. Many of these people hope to become legitimate traders in the future, but aside from their legal difficulties they cannot easily get the capital to begin.

Hong Kong Versus China as Places to Trade

One critical question that African traders must consider is whether to buy goods in Hong Kong or China. Prices are somewhat higher in Chungking Mansions than in mainland China, but security is greater and products are seen as being more reliable. For this reason, mobile phone and electronics buyers in particular often prefer Chungking Mansions over mainland China as a place in which to do business. As one young West African trader told me:

> The second time I came to Hong Kong, I bought 200 mobile phones in China, but 100 were no good.... I went back to China and told them – they told me they'd give me back my money in six months; eventually they only paid me for fifty of the phones. After that, I never buy mobiles in China; I'd prefer to buy them in Chungking Mansions.

Other, bigger and more established traders have evolved systems that enable them to feel more secure in their Chinese business. A Kenyan trader dealing in office equipment told me that when the goods are being packed in the container, he takes photographs of every step, and the young female owner of the Chinese company he works with makes a CD, giving one copy to him and keeping a copy, so that both sides have an exact visual record of what was packed. Another trader, a Tanzanian, found out recently that the Chinese factory he buys from was giving him a "foreigner's price," charging him more than they would an ethnic Chinese. He then hired a Singaporean – a Mandarin speaker and ethnic Chinese – and gave him a commission for handling the business on "Chinese terms." As this example implies, linguistic ability is important. The several African fixers I know in Guangzhou, the large Chinese city an hour north of Hong Kong, hook up their fellow Africans with Chinese factories and often make very large profits indeed, judging from the sumptuousness of the Guangzhou apartments that some of them possess; they are mostly fluent Putonghua (Mandarin) speakers. Others, non-Chinese speakers, get by using interpreters or computer translation devices.

Still others stay in Hong Kong and particularly in Chungking Mansions, where English is the lingua franca.

In Chungking Mansions too, African traders are cheated from time to time if they are not wary. Let me focus particularly on the phone market, since mobile phones are the most widely sold wholesale commodity in Chungking Mansions. There are an array of different kinds of phones in Chungking Mansions: new branded China models, 14-day phones (European models that have been warehoused after being returned by their original buyers), refab phones (14-day phones refurbished in China), used phones, China-made knock-offs, such as "Nokla" and "Sory-Ericson," and copies, bearing the same logo as the original, of European, Japanese, or Korean models, of varying degrees of quality. With such a diversity of goods, it is easy to cheat an ignorant buyer. Pakistani phone-sellers regale me with stories of how they got an African trader to buy 500 or 1,000 14-day phones as if they were new. But this is unusual, in that most African traders have a good idea of the nature of the game. As a Nigerian trader told me, "Both buyer and seller know what's real and what's fake, even though they can never say that." As a Pakistani phone dealer told me, "For wholesaler buyers from Africa, probably no more than five percent get cheated. They know the business! But when outside traders come and don't know, they must pay."

Because African banks are not generally trusted in the Hong Kong and Chinese milieu, traders tend to deal in cash: I have seen traders pull out US $50,000 in cash from their wallets or bags, and sometimes leave this money trustingly on a counter of a Chungking Mansions phone stall. Although these phone stalls may be quite duplicitous in other ways, I have almost never heard of a trader being directly robbed of his money in Chungking Mansions.[4] In China, however, this may happen. As one West African trader cautioned me, "In mainland China, a lot of traders have been mugged, threatened with long knives, once they sense you've got money…. " But at the same time, the chance for making really large amounts of money is greater in China than in Hong Kong. As a Nigerian trader told me, "China is there for large scale, for the big fish, not the small fish. The small fish will stay in Hong Kong – they need Hong Kong." At present, there are many more Africans in Guangzhou, the capital of Guangdong Province in China, an hour north of Hong Kong, than there are in Hong Kong, seeking to make their fortunes, but at considerable risk. I have seen traders from the Congo and Nigeria in Guangzhou spending hundreds of U.S. dollars in an evening's entertainment, so affluent have they become, but I also know of many more African traders being left utterly penniless, going home with no more than the shirt on their back.

Bringing Goods Home

Some traders carry goods in their luggage, up to 40 kilos, and pay the extra costs of airfreight as needed. These traders are bringing back mobile phones or electronics, particularly delicate, or else clothing, particularly light, especially when vacuum-packed. Others rent or share containers: expensive but necessary for goods such as tiles or car parts. For most traders, getting the goods transported is not the primary problem they face; instead, it is customs in their home country. A West African trader told me, "If I pay customs, I lose everything. If you buy one hundred mobile phones, you must give up fifty. It's better to give the customs person mobile phones as a present. You have to cheat: it's the only possible way…" (See Chalfin 2004 for a discussion of Ghanaian customs). An East African trader said, "In my country, the problem is customs – it would be insane to leave the container open for a night, because you'll never see anything again. I try to arrange everything in one day, even if I have to pay the customs officers overtime." A Nigerian trader in, primarily, China-made computers, said to me:

> For computers, officially I pay five percent duties. But I can't take just one thing in the consignment. And those other things will not be declared. What you declare, you pay to the government. But what customs sees that you don't declare, that's where the corruption comes in. It might be stuff for my friends – they might see my shirt, my suit, and say, "I'd like three of those!" If you declared this, it would be declared as contraband – you couldn't get it in the country – so you've got to put it in your consignment, conceal it there. Some customs guys will take $50, others $200, others $1,000; some need a suit, others shoes, to get the job done. They'll say, "I really like that wristwatch" – you know what they want. Yes, customs is that hardest part of my business – the worst part is getting my goods through the system.

Once these traders arrive back home, there are a variety of ways in which they bring their goods to market. I know a clothing dealer from Zambia who packs his clothes in a truck and drives off to villages, selling them off the back of the truck. I also know of Nigerian phone dealers who simply sell their entire consignment to the central phone market in Lagos. Many other traders have stores in urban areas, for example in Nairobi or Dar-es-Salaam or Kampala, and others belong to larger companies.

The rule is that the more individual and the smaller volume of trade, the greater the risk, both because customs can more easily exploit those who lack connections, and because the vicissitudes of an unpredictable global market at home and abroad can so easily destroy those traders who lack the backing of companies or patrons. Let me give two examples of such risk. One trader was blindsided by a fire on 20 December 2007, perhaps set by real-estate speculators, in which the largest clothing market in Lagos burned to the ground. Because his buyers were based in this market, he suddenly found that he had no customers for the clothing he had bought in Hong Kong. I met several African traders in June 2008 who were desperately trying to return to their businesses in south China, but could not, due to the Chinese government's sudden tightening of visa policies in the run-up to the Olympics. A West African told me, "I will lose everything if I cannot get back to Guangzhou by next week." He could not, and returned to Africa empty-handed.

Who These Traders Are

There are a wide range of traders at Chungking Mansions, but all are well off compared to their countrymen and women, in that they can afford to hop on a plane to come to another part of the world. These traders have been able to obtain the capital to fly to Hong Kong and make an initial investment in goods for resale in their home societies. Only the upper crust in Africa has the thousands of U.S. dollars necessary to finance such a step. I asked one trader from Cameroon what he would do if he had problems with customs in his country, and he said, "Oh I'd just call my father. He'd take care of everything...." I have met traders who tell me, for example, that their uncle was Idi Amin's Agricultural Minister, or the Ghanaian Commissioner of Prisons; some of these traders are no doubt embellishing their connections but it is possible that many are not.

Some of the traders I have spoken with are highly experienced. Many of my interviews have been conducted with men in their thirties, forties and fifties who have been in the trading business for decades, although they all only came to Hong Kong and China in recent years. Many of these traders have made a hundred or more trips between Hong Kong and their home countries; and many shake their heads in wonder at younger traders. Christian Lo (2006: 52) has shown that for young Ghanaian traders, coming to Hong Kong has served as a rite of passage, a way of gaining status at home. This is true, but there is also the matter of economics – there is a huge price to pay for failure, as Lo outlines in his discussion of failed Ghanaian traders who stay in Hong Kong to work illegally (2006: 53–54, 59–60). A Tanzanian trader in his thirties discussed young traders at length:

> They get money from family inheritance, family donations – US $15,000, $20,000 – and they come to Hong Kong with all the family hopes.... They are likely to fail because they don't understand the market, and go home only with a few hundred dollars.... Some of them come to me and ask me for advice. I tell them, "Don't go to China! Just buy in Chungking Mansions and go straight back home!".... When I go to the 7-Eleven outside Chungking Mansions, there

are ten or so traders from different countries that I've known for a while – we've become friends; we meet at the airport, or in Dubai. These are the professionals. They may be running with capital of a quarter-million U.S. dollars. The others I never see again. They don't know what a copy is – that if you buy an Armani suit in China, it's not original! Hong Kong customs officers won't allow that. Some African traders really don't know this....

The young traders I have spoken with confirm this view. A Kenyan trader in his early twenties insisted to me that he would have no problem getting his 600 copy Boss suits over the border between China and Hong Kong because "Hong Kong is now part of China. China is the parent and Hong Kong is the child. The child will never hurt the parent. So Hong Kong must let all copies through customs – otherwise, it will hurt the Chinese economy." I suggested to him that he had been lucky so far in getting through Hong Kong customs without having his goods confiscated, but he did not believe me. (He may be partially correct in his analysis – only a very small percentage of fake goods are confiscated at the border – but this has less to do with Hong Kong's fealty to China than with its own neoliberalism, as I later discuss, as well as the fact that the Hong Kong-China border crossing at Lo Wu is the busiest in the world.)

What do these traders make of their global travels? Some maintain that they are completely uninfluenced by the new worlds they see: "I'm here only to do business. I don't want to learn about other societies. I only want to make money." Others are filled with disdain towards Chinese. Many Africans have experienced how Hong Kong Chinese will not sit next to them on buses, and see this as racism rather than fear of the unknown (as my own Hong Kong students sometimes tell me, "I've never spoken to an African before....") – although by most accounts, this is diminishing, as people in Hong Kong and southern China become more accustomed to Africans. A few traders become more or less immersed in their new cultural surroundings. One Congolese trader described himself as "a Chinese with black skin"; when I saw him interact in Mandarin, backslapping his laughing Chinese friends in Guangzhou, he did seem wholly at ease in his new society, despite the ever-present visa difficulties he experiences on the mainland. A Ghanaian trader told me that his Chinese supplier, a factory owner in China with whom he stays when he goes to Guangzhou, "is like a father to me.... He teaches me Chinese culture." This close relation is highly unusual among the traders I know, but it does happen. I also witnessed two East African traders, one based in China and the other in Hong Kong, getting into a heated drunken argument over the two societies, one shouting that "Hong Kong has more human rights than China. Hong Kong people look down upon Chinese!" and the other proclaiming that "Everything in Hong Kong is from China! If it weren't for China, Hong Kong wouldn't exist!" This is the kind of argument that Hongkongers and Chinese might have, but in this case it was two Africans, each vociferously defending his temporarily adopted home.

I often asked these traders, "Would you rather live in your home country or in Hong Kong?" Most proclaimed their love for their home country, but also indicated that their travels had changed them – several indicated that they could not really "go home again," since they had seen the world outside. They could physically return to Kenya, or Tanzania, or Nigeria, or Ghana, but it could never be the same place as it was before they left – they had changed because of their travels. Perhaps, as we will now discuss, the goods they bring back to their home countries also shape those who buy them.

The Significance of Traders

These traders exist for a simple reason: most African countries manufacture little or nothing. As a trader in clothing told me, "To make goods in Nigeria costs more than importing them. In Nigeria, the energy is unreliable – you have to buy diesel; you have to run the generator, the costs are so high – why waste your time and money? It's easier to go overseas; in China they can make your order in weeks." This situation led some of the traders I interviewed to bemoan the state of Africa today. In another Nigerian trader's words, "Why can't my country make anything for its own people?.... Why is my country so poor even though it has so many natural resources?.... What's wrong with Africa?" he asked, with considerable anguish. His answer was the legacy of colonialism, although he acknowledged that that ended fifty years ago: "Why are our leaders so bad today? Why is there so much corruption?" He could not answer these questions.

I often asked these traders whether they feel their role is positive or negative for their customers and their countries. Are they simply buying shoddy goods with which to cheat their customers (who, I am told, sometimes do not understand the difference between "real" and "fake")? Some traders acknowledge exploitation: "I get good mobile phones for my family and friends in the city, but cheap fakes for villagers. They don't know any better," one West African trader told me. However, most fake goods are functional for at least a while – definitely clothing, and most mobile phones and electronic goods as well – and high-quality fakes are practically as good as the original at a fraction of the price. The prices charged to their fellow countryman for these goods reflect the costs incurred by these traders' global routes as well as their desire for profits, but the sheer number of traders means that competition keeps their prices down. Accordingly, most traders I spoke with maintained that the role they played was a fundamentally positive one. An intellectual Congolese trader said that traders like him are "expanding the imaginations" of the poor, by showing them what high-quality goods are like – giving them the chance to see good things will mean that they no longer take for granted that everything around them must be broken and shabby, he claimed. As a reflective Kenyan trader told me, "Nobody in my country can buy an original brand of suit, or an original phone by a famous company. It's too expensive! But these copies can show them good things. They are good!.... They bring the world to Africa!" It is indeed these traders and the goods they carry that bring, through China and Hong Kong, the world to Africa, for better or for worse.[5]

What is the role of China and Hong Kong in this process? The role of China is clear – it is the source of a cornucopia of goods, often flawed or fake but serviceable, at attractive prices that make China the industrial powerhouse of the world. But Hong Kong also has a key role to play. Hong Kong has, by some accounts, the freest economy in the world (*Economist* 2005: 31), and it is easy for most of these traders to pass through Hong Kong. Most can get tourist visas at the airport, as we have seen; most can buy copy goods in China and travel unhindered to Hong Kong; almost all can buy copy goods in Hong Kong unmolested; and all can depart Hong Kong with their goods unexamined. All in all, Hong Kong is a neoliberal paradise, in which traders, if they do not carry drugs or practice overt thievery, are left to go about their business freely. If developing African countries cannot stop trade deemed illicit because of corruption and ineffective state control, developed Hong Kong will not stop this trade because of its assumption that business triumphs over all else. This is far less likely to happen in the United States or Japan or other developed societies; but this happens in Hong Kong, and this, in the largest sense, is how Hong Kong exists as an entrepôt between China and the world. Many Africans are also in south China, as we have discussed, but because of visa restrictions in China, as well as fuller airport connections in Hong Kong, Chungking Mansions remains a center of African trade in the Chinese world. This is one of Hong Kong's unique distinctions in the realm of Asian migration.

These traders may have a limited future; already Chinese middlemen and companies are moving into many African countries, and will perhaps increasingly replace these traders. In the far future, to the extent that Africa is able to re-enter the world map, this kind of migration may no longer be necessary. For now, though, these traders are bringing back the goods of China, bringing globalization to places that otherwise would be largely shut off from the world. In this they resemble that traveler of yore, Marco Polo.

Notes

1. The research for this chapter was funded by a Competitive Earmarked Research Grant (CERG), Research Grants Council, Hong Kong, Project ID 2110148; my research assistant Jose Antonio Rojas Uzcategui has provided very useful data for the chapter on Nigerian traders. Much of this chapter has appeared in my recent book on Chungking Mansions (Mathews 2011).

2. Phone stalls sell an average of 20,000 phones a month, I am told, at least before the economic downturn which began in late 2008; the large majority of buyers are African. There are one hundred phone stalls in Chungking Mansions, and thus some 24 million phone sales a year in Chungking Mansions. There were 126 million mobile phone subscriptions in sub-Saharan Africa in 2007, with many individuals having multiple subscriptions (Richard Ling, personal communication). This makes the assumption of 20 percent seem broadly plausible. Phone traders tell me that, if anything, this percentage is too low.

3. As of 2008, Hong Kong immigration requires advance visas from 17 African countries, including Cameroon, Ghana, and Nigeria; 36 countries are allowed visa-free entry, valid for anywhere from 14 to 90 days (Immigration Department 2008). Hong Kong remains substantially more liberal in its visa policies towards African countries than China (Heron 2008).

4. I have heard of African traders being robbed in other ways. One cautionary tale regularly making the rounds in Chungking Mansions is of the African trader accosted by one of the mainland Chinese sex workers cruising Nathan Road near Chungking Mansions' entrance. He takes her to his room and takes a shower; she, seeing US $60,000 hidden in his underwear, takes the money and races to the train station located near the entrance to Chungking Mansions, with trains leaving every five minutes to the mainland Chinese border. He comes out and sees her and his money gone, and races in hot pursuit, but never sees her again.

5. I spoke with a former Nokia employee, who said that, although Nokia would never say so on record, in fact the company was not troubled by the widespread sale of copies of its phones in Africa. She suggested that the copy phones were seen as intermediaries to the real thing: "An African in his twenties might buy the copy and see how good Nokia is. In his thirties, when he has more money, then he may buy the real thing." Indeed, copied Nokia phones do not compete with original Nokia phones in the African marketplace, but rather with Chinese brands of phones in the same price range.

References

Allen, John and Chris Hamnett, eds. 1995. *A Shrinking World? Global Unevenness and Inequality.* Oxford: Oxford University Press.

Browne, Katherine E. 2004. *Creole Economics: Caribbean Cunning Under the French Flag.* Austin: University of Texas Press.

Chalfin, Brenda. 2004. "Border scans: Sovereignty, surveillance, and the customs service in Ghana." *Identities: Global Studies in Culture and Power* 11: 397–416.

Economist, The. 2005. *Pocket World in Figures: 2006 Edition.* London: Profile Books.

Ferguson, James. 2007. "Globalizing Africa? Observations from an inconvenient continent," pp. 25–49 in *Global Shadows: Africa in the Neoliberal World Order.* Durham: Duke University Press.

French, Howard W. and Lydia Polgreen. 2007. "Entrepreneurs from China flourish in Africa." *New York Times*, 18 August. http://www.nytimes.com/2007/08/18/world/africa/18malawi.html.

Heron, Liz. 2008. "Africans latest to be hit by visa restrictions." *South China Morning Post.* May 11.

Immigration Department, Government of the Hong Kong Special Administrative Region. 2008. http://www.immd.gov.hk/ehtml/hkvisas_4.htm.

Lo, Christian. 2006. "Making it at the Chung-king Mansions: Stories from the bottom end of globalization." Master's thesis, Dept. of Social Anthropology, Norwegian University of Science and Technology, Trondheim, Norway.

MacGaffey, Janet, and Remy Bazenguissa-Ganga. 2000. *Congo-Paris: Transnational Traders on the Margins of the Law.* Bloomington, IN: Indiana University Press.

Mathews, Gordon. 2007. "Chungking Mansions: A center of 'low-end globalization.'" *Ethnology* XLVI(2): 169–183.

———. 2011. *Ghetto at the Center of the World: Chungking Mansions, Hong Kong.* Chicago: University of Chicago Press.

Pawson, Lara. 2005. "Africa's thriving trade with China." BBC News. 9 March. http://news.bbc.co.uk/1/hi/world/africa/4332273.stm.

Ribeiro, Gustavo Lins. 2006. "Economic globalization from below." *Etnográfica*, Vol. X(2): 233–249.

Ulysse, Gina A. 2007. *Downtown Ladies: Informal Commercial Importers, a Haitian Anthropologist, and Self-Making in Jamaica.* Chicago: University of Chicago Press.

Zhou, Raymond. 2006. "Out of Guangzhou, Africa trade booms." NewsGD.com http://www.newsgd.com/news/guangdong1/200605230049.htm/.

CHAPTER 15

Negotiating "Home" and "Away": Singaporean Professional Migrants in China

Brenda S.A. YEOH and Katie WILLIS

In recent years, studies of transnational labor migration have broadened their focus from the movement of low-skilled workers across international boundaries to include the increasing numbers of professionals and managers engaged in work-related migration in association with the intensification of economic globalization processes. Emphasis on the hyper-mobility of these elite transnational subjects has tended to depict them as mobile individual careerists circulating in an intensely fluid world of intra- and inter-firm transfers and career mobility. While definitions are somewhat elusive, these "knowledge nomads," circulating "talent workers," "transnational capitalist class," or "transnational elites" are often constructed relationally to the "knowledge economy." Tulgan (2001: 37), for example, asserts that firms today are heavily dependent on "human talent," "judgment," and "the human brain," in order to successfully navigate "the new economy" characterized by a high-speed business environment that requires organizations to be able to deploy resources in a flexible and timely manner. Thrift (2000: 676; emphasis added) writes that knowledge has become an "*asset class* that a business must foster, warehouse, manage and constantly work upon in order to produce a constant stream of innovation." In this way, highly skilled economic migrants play a weighty role as almost non-substitutable drivers of the new creativity-obsessed business model.

The notion of "talent" is vitally connected to international mobility, essentially because talented individuals are scarce and in great demand globally. Such individuals are highly mobile, often circulating from global city to global city (Findlay et al. 1996); at the same time, mobility across international borders in itself enhances their symbolic value and social-cultural capital (Yeoh and Lai 2008). For example, Beaverstock (2005: 256), in his study on highly skilled British inter-company transferees in Manhattan, suggests that international mobility has allowed these "transnational elites" to accumulate highly regarded "intellectual and social capital ... through [their] business interaction in the New York business community" and elsewhere. The ease with which such mobile individuals operate in different contexts and their perceived openness to engaging with "the other," has created an image of transnational elites as either cosmopolitans who are "basically indifferent to where they lived" or "cosmopolites" who are "habitants of a vast universe" (Tuan 1996, cited in Robbins 1998: 3).

The freedom of supposedly frictionless movement has, however, been increasingly queried by researchers highlighting the "body politics" within which all migrants, including highly skilled ones, are embedded (Silvey 2006). They are not free-floating individuals, but rather bearers of culture, ethnicity, class and gender (Kofman and Raghuram 2005, 2006; Yeoh and Willis 2005a; Ley 2010; Lan 2011). Additionally, while mobility may certainly be facilitated by economic privilege and the demands for "talent" and the injection of foreign capital to drive economic growth (Ong 1999), state policies, business practices and networks, as well as broader cultural norms and expectations, can restrict movement, or channel it in particular directions (Yeoh and Huang 2011). As Ley (2010: 253) states, "The framing of 'cosmopolitan capitalists' seems to have overlooked the inconveniences of geographical difference."

This critique also extends to debates around engagement with co-present others. Rather than being distanced from other migrant or non-migrant populations, or possessing the cultural capital to move easily between groups, highly skilled migrants are implicated in particular forms of "contact" or "collision" (Willis 2010) with others in the global city. Previously, we have drawn on Mary Louise Pratt's concept of "contact zones" (Pratt 1992) to consider the cultural politics involved in the construction of these zones comparing British and Singaporean migrants to China (Yeoh and Willis 2005b). In Pratt's work, the focus was on encounters between previously geographically separate populations, brought together due to the European colonial project. Her emphasis on the role of these encounters in identity construction highlights the relational nature of identity through both co-presence in particular material spaces, but also interactions between individuals and groups.

Drawing on a case study of Singaporean professional, managerial, and entrepreneurial elites in China (both mainland China and the Hong Kong SAR),[1] this chapter builds on earlier work on contact zones to consider the ways in which the migration experiences of the highly skilled are embedded in the multiple social, economic, and political practices of being simultaneously "home" and "away." These experiences play out at different scales – for example, the household and the nation – and are refracted through asymmetries of power along crosscutting gender, class, race, and nationality lines. We argue that the contact zones that highly skilled migrants carve out are marked by different kinds of simultaneous engagement with "home" and "away" and deserve more careful differentiation than the current literature has demonstrated. In other words, the literature usually assumes that the highly skilled are more able to transcend global-local bina-ries given superior resources and many more degrees of freedom to shape their encounters with both host- and home-countries than lower-skilled counterparts. At the same time, the current scholarship still has little to say about how the global and the local are dissolved or folded into each other. In this chapter, we focus on two sets of negotiations between "home" and "away": (a) within the sphere of everyday life in local-transnational space in China; and (b) through the lens of identity negotiations around nationality, race, and gender. Before doing so, a brief review of the context for increasing Singaporean economic migration to China is in order.

The increasing numbers of highly skilled Singaporeans venturing as economic migrants to China and other parts of the Asian region in the 1990s and onward stemmed from the Singapore government's "regionalization drive" to expand Sin-gapore's economic space beyond its shores to reach out to new markets, inventing for the city-state a "hinterland" comprising "2.8 billion people, with hundreds of millions in the middle income group" within a seven-hour flight radius of Singapore (Goh 2001). Singapore companies and Singaporeans themselves were exhorted to embrace a culture of "risk-taking" and "innovation" and venture forth into the hinterland. In particular, securing a niche in China and riding on the back of its phenomenal growth were seen to be key concerns, leading to the establishment of a number of government flagship projects in China, as well as the encouragement of Singapore businesses and "enterprising Singaporeans" to "strike out in business" (Goh 2001). From the development of Suzhou Industrial Park – a cooperative project between China and Singapore some fifteen years ago – the number of Singaporean ventures in China has continued to grow and recent examples include the joint eco-city project in Tianjin as well as the Raf-fles City project in Ningbo, Zhejiang (*Channel NewsAsia* 2009; Chong 2009a, 2009b). Singaporeans have thus joined the ranks of the transnational business and professional elite from the developed world in attempting to engage the greater Asian region and transform it into Singapore's hinterland. While there are no exact figures detailing the number of Singaporeans in China, news articles in 2006 estimated that around 10,000 Singaporeans were spread throughout the country and that the numbers were expected to grow (Quek 2006). A year later, the same press reported that 6,527 Singaporeans were registered with the Singa-pore Consulate as living in Shanghai, but that unofficial estimates were that the total number of Singaporeans in Shanghai alone was around 10,000 (Leong and Lee 2007). The Singaporean community in China is said to be a varied group, comprising CEOs sent to start up their company's China operations, entrepre-neurs, restaurateurs, chefs, architects, executives, educators, fresh graduates, and even student-interns (Leong and Lee 2007).

This chapter is based on interviews between 1997 and 1999 with 150 Sin-gaporeans (73 men and 77 women) who were living or had lived in mainland

China or the Hong Kong SAR. We interviewed Singaporeans who were working or had worked in China, as well as spouses (all women) who had accompanied their husbands to China. While ethnic Chinese make up the vast majority of Singapore's population (approximately 75 percent), all of our interviewees were Chinese Singaporeans. Research was conducted in Beijing, Shanghai, Suzhou, Wuxi, Guangzhou and Hong Kong as these were key sites for Singaporean investment, as well as for foreign direct investment more generally and the concomitant hiring of foreign professionals. Participants were recruited through personal contacts and Singapore Clubs, as well as through snowball sampling. For more information about the methodology see Yeoh and Willis (2005a).

Making Sense of Everyday Life in the Contact Zone

In navigating contact zones in everyday life and in putting the emphasis on the unequal relations which shape these contact zones, we had considered the usefulness of the terms "culturalist" and "colonialist" as metaphors to describe the power geometries implied in the way in which transnational elites encounter China (Yeoh and Willis 2005b).[2] We will take each of these metaphors in turn.

Culturalists?

Among Singaporean transnational elites in China, the language of the contact zone was largely framed by the ideology of masculinist entrepreneurship propelled by the state (Yeoh and Willis 2004). While most Singaporean migrants interviewed defined their relationship with China primarily in terms of career, business, and economic motivations, there were also some who framed their migration in terms of a secondary discourse centered on heritage and a "return to roots." The notion of encountering China as a cultural, return-to-roots experience was appealing for the Singaporean Chinese, one which colored their motivation to accept a China posting, rather than a posting to another Asian location, or even to North America or Europe. For many interviewees, the chance to live and work in China was framed as an ideal opportunity to discover a real sense of "Chineseness" and Chinese culture, one which had been diminished over the generations in Singapore. Some talked of China as an ancestral homeland or motherland, while others focused on named "ancestral villages" to ground their feelings of return to a specific location where they expected to feel a sense of connection and belonging. This mobilizing of ideas of "cultural return" resonates with state discourses about the value of ethnic similarities in business practices as part of the regionalization strategy.[3]

Colonialists?

The "return-to-roots" discourse and enthusiasm for "encountering China" were, however, far more muted in negotiating everyday life in the contact zone. Despite claims of connectivity in terms of culture and language, Singaporeans in China generally maintain separate social lives beyond the workplace. Especially among those working for multi-national corporations, embassies, or government-linked institutions, residences are concentrated in particular areas, either because of Chinese regulations regarding housing for foreigners (in mainland China), or because of residential preferences (in Hong Kong). Among "expat wives" in particular, contact with the local Chinese was particularly limited as their social worlds hardly extended beyond the expatriate condominium in which they lived and the international schools which their children attended. Forays into the city itself were conducted in the comfort and isolation of their husbands' chauffeur-driven company cars, while "social conversations" were transacted over transnational space, through phone calls and emails to family and friends back "home." Over time, most of those not engaged in paid employment developed social ties with other non-local women, either through more formal forms of networks such as the Singapore Club, or more informally through their children's schools or contacts with friends from "home" also living in the same city. Day-to-day pragmatic adjustments to life in China tended to focus on differences between Singapore and China in terms of China's lack vis-à-vis Singaporean standards, from the "shocking" incivilities in public places (in contrast to the highly managed public order and street discipline in Singapore), to the "low quality" of local Chinese maids (unacceptable to Singaporean households which are used to relying on live-in, 24/7 foreign domestic workers to sustain the middle-class way of life). As Turner (2007) puts it, globalization and global mobilities paradoxically produce "new systems of closure" as seen in the (re)emergence of the "enclave society," not dissimilar in nature to colonial enclaves.

Strategic and Sticky Identities in the Contact Zone

While the literature on identity formation among long-term immigrants-turned-settlers is equipped with a postmodern lexicon of concepts such as fragmentation, hybridization, syncretism, creolization, deterritorialization, or diasporization of social identities (see also Anthias 2002, who argues for an abandonment of the term "identity" for narratives of "translocational positionality"), the transient nature of social experience among transnational elites in the contact zone seems to engender identity politics of a different sort.

Negotiating national-racial identity?

It was common for most Singaporeans in China to retreat into the safety net of a fixed, known, and clearly bounded identity rather than embrace a deterritorialized or ambivalent allegiance. Encounters with the more disordered, uncertain environment of "the other" tended to lead to an elevation of national self and pride in national systems and the Singaporean way of doing things rather than a greater flexibility of mind and strategies of cultural hybridity. For example, Singaporean transnational elites declared that they felt "more Singaporean" in China than ever before and were careful in distinguishing themselves as "Chinese Singaporeans" and not "China Chinese." This reflected their desire to distance themselves from what they perceived as the leached culture of China, particularly with regard to celebrations such as Chinese New Year and the month-long Hungry Ghost festival, as well as the degenerate morality of China. While distancing themselves from China they were also shifting the "true" site of Chinese tradition and culture offshore, and proclaimed themselves fortunate that their forefathers "took the trouble" to leave China for the *nanyang* ("south seas") (Yeoh and Willis 1999). While there were some exceptions, and the vehemence with which interviewees expressed their opinions varied greatly, the vast majority of the Singaporeans interviewed articulated such views. In short, the identity politics of being "home" and "away" as negotiated in the contact zone retained a strategic "stickiness" (borrowing Hanson and Pratt's [1995] term which they used in a different context) in the face of transience and mobility (Yeoh and Willis 2005c).

Negotiating gender identity?

Traversing transnational space as part of Singapore's go-regional drive seemed to be a hegemonically masculinized enterprise in which men and women remained complicit in the reproduction of patriarchy beyond national shores. Transnational entrepreneurialism extended and crystallized male roles as exemplary fighters, breadwinners, adventurers, husbands, fathers, and lovers, against a background where women somehow remained sequestered in a supportive, domestic sphere. Regional experience not only prepared men for career advancement but provided an important testing ground to hone characteristics such as courage and risk-taking behavior.

In contrast, most Singaporean married women participated in the regionalizing effort not as economic agents but as preservers of the family and moral guardians of the nation (Yeoh and Willis 1999). While most women stated that they had been involved to some degree in the decision to move to China, for the majority, the decision to come to China was based on supporting their husband in what was an excellent career opportunity and/or one which would be beneficial for the family as a whole, particularly in economic terms. Away from the familiar environment of Singapore and its support structures, the majority of married Singaporean women interviewed withdrew from the paid labor force on moving to China. This allowed them to provide their husbands and children with the care and support required to maintain the reproduction of the regionalizing family.

The move to being a full-time housewife was not necessarily an unwelcome one for the women themselves, for many were quick to point out the advantages such as having more time with the children, or giving themselves a break from the rigors of pursuing a career in Singapore; however, the individual circumstances of these women writ large implied that, as a whole, regionalization did little to destabilize the home-nation's gender norms but instead further hardened the lines that divided men's and women's identities, and strengthened the ties that bind women to the home. In short, married Singaporean women – many of them well-educated and formerly engaged in paid, high-status employment in the home-nation – were valorized not for their economic skills but for their skills in reconstituting and holding together the household on foreign terrain.[4]

They were not so much "deskilled" as "re-domesticated." In part, their revalorization for the domestic front when the family "goes transnational" was accentuated because at "home" in Singapore the hard edge of domestic work had been passed on to migrant women (mainly from the Philippines, Indonesia, and Sri Lanka) who entered Singapore as live-in domestic workers. The crisis of the domestic sphere in rapidly globalizing cities such as Singapore – resolved within the borders of the nation-state by drawing on the underpaid reproductive labor of women from countries further down the development ladder – resurfaces in transnational space. Resolving the crisis away from the home-nation requires the re-domestication of elite Singaporean women to replace their maids' labor with their own, for the quintessential Singaporean product – "the foreign maid" – is not transnationally portable (only one of our interviewees had been able to bring her Filipina maid with her to China; the rest relied on Chinese women, often rural migrants). In transnationalizing the gender division of family labor, the regionalization thrust has, to a large extent, further deepened the difference between men and women's roles; while men spearhead the drive as economic pioneers, entrepreneurs, and professional and managerial elites, most Singaporean women participate in the regionalizing effort in supportive roles, often as appendages to men (Yeoh and Willis 2005a).

Conclusion

What the era of transnational migration and hypermobilities has demonstrated is that "identities based on such macro-societal paradigms as nation, ethnicity, and race may become ambivalent, partial, multiple, hybrid, and contradictory, but *they may also be reinvented as primordial certainties*" (Aguilar 1996: 6; emphases added). Indeed, Ley (2004: 159-160) cautions that transnational elites are not necessarily associated with "the expansive possibilities of new hybrid experience" or immediately identifiable as "cosmopolitans [who] think globally, aim to exceed their own local specificities, welcome unfamiliar cultural encounters and express the wish to move toward a true humanity of equality and respect, free of racial, national and other prejudices." To move beyond our suspicion that elite mobilities are not necessarily accompanied by an advancement of cosmopolitan sensibilities, we have argued for a need to focus attention on the cultural politics of the contact zone in transnational space. By showing how actually occurring everyday encounters in the contact zone are framed and how identities of race, nationality, and gender are negotiated vis-à-vis "the other-in-place," we reject the fiction of frictionless mobility among transnational elites and confirm Ley's (2004: 162) argument that "cosmopolitanism itself is always situated, always imbued with partiality and vulnerability."

Notes

1. This chapter draws together some of the key arguments presented in our earlier publications (in the *Asian and Pacific Migration Journal*, *Geoforum*, and the *Journal of Ethnic and Migration Studies*) arising from our project on Singaporean and British skilled migration to China. We would like to acknowledge project funding from the Lee Foundation (Singapore), an HSBC Holdings Small Grant from the Royal Geographical Society (with the Institute of British Geographers) and the United Kingdom's Economic and Social Research Council (no. L214 25 2007).

2. We were alerted to these terms as a way of framing British experiences in China by 'Nicholas,' a British engineer whom we interviewed in Beijing. He also identified an 'imperialist' attitude or form of engagement (see Yeoh and Willis 2005b).

3. Former Senior Minister Lee Kuan Yew (quoted in do Rosario 1993: 17), for example, stressed the need to exploit "network capitalism" to its fullest as a means of capturing business opportunities in China, arguing that there is "no need [for ethnic Chinese] to be apologetic about wanting to maximize benefits through each other's contacts and access to opportunities" since the "Anglo-Saxons do it, the Jews do it, so do the Hindus and the Muslims."

4. Single women were not necessarily immune from the effects of gendered ideologies of the family and the nation. While many single Singaporean women worked alongside their single and married male counterparts as economic migrants in China, social expectations concerning marriage and marriageability meant that these women did not consider their forays in transnational space to be long-term. Instead, returning to the home-nation was considered prudent if they were concerned with not jeopardizing their marriage prospects (see Willis and Yeoh 2003).

References

Aguilar, Filomeno. 1996. "Filipinos as transnational migrants: Guest editor's preface." *Philippine Sociological Review* 44: 4–11.

Anthias, Floya. 2002. "Where do I belong? Narrating collective identity and transnational positionality." *Ethnicities* 2(4): 491–514.

Beaverstock, Jonathan V. 2005. "Transnational elites in the city: British highly-skilled inter-company transferees in New York City's financial district." *Journal of Ethnic and Migration Studies* 31(2): 245–268.

Channel NewsAsia. 2009. "Sino-Singapore Tianjin Eco-city panel reviews project's progress." *Channel NewsAsia*, 3 June.

Chong, Glenda. 2009a. "S'pore firms showing great interest in Ningbo city in Zhejiang." *Channel NewsAsia*, 6 June.

———. 2009b. "Singapore, China celebrate 15th anniversary of Suzhou Indust'l Park." *Channel NewsAsia*, 26 May.

do Rosario, Louise. 1993. "Network capitalism: personal connections help Overseas Chinese investors." *Far Eastern Economic Review* 156: 17 (2 December).

Findlay, Allan M., Lin N. Li, John J. Jowett, and Ronald Skeldon. 1996. "Skilled international migration and the global city: a study of expatriates in Hong Kong." *Transactions of the Institute of British Geographers* 21: 49–61.

Goh Chok Tong, 2001. Prime Minister Goh Chok Tong's National Day Rally 2001 Speech at the University Cultural Centre, National University of Singapore on Sunday, 19 August 2001 at 8.00 pm. Singapore Government Press Release, Media Division, Ministry of Information and the Arts.

Hanson, Susan, and Geraldine Pratt. 1995. *Gender, Work, and Space*. London: Routledge.

Kofman, Eleanore, and Parvati Raghuram. 2006. "Women and global labour migrations: incorporating skilled workers." *Antipode* 38(2): 282–303.

———, eds. 2005. "Gender and Skilled Migrants: Into and Beyond the Workplace." Special issue of *Geoforum* 36(2): 149–154.

Lan Pei-Chia. 2011. "White privilege, language capital and cultural ghettoisation: Western high-skilled migrants in Taiwan." *Journal of Ethnic and Migration Studies* 37(10): 1669–1693.

Leong, Sanda, and Sze Yong Lee. 2007. "Shanghai Shine." *The Straits Times*, 22 September.

Ley, David. 2004. "Transnational spaces and everyday lives." *Transactions of the Institute of British Geographers* NS, 29: 151–164.

———. 2010. *Millionaire Migrants: Trans-Pacific Life Lines*. Oxford: Wiley-Blackwell.

Ong, Aihwa. 1999. *Flexible Citizenship: The Cultural Logics of Transnationality*. Durham, NC: Duke University Press.

Pratt, Mary Louise. 1992. *Imperial Eyes: Travel Writing and Transculturation*. London: Routledge.

Quek, Tracy. 2006. "Bringing MOE syllabus to S'pore kids in China." *The Straits Times*, 23 June.

Robbins, Bruce. 1998. "Introduction Part I: Actually existing cosmopolitanism," pp. 1–19 in *Cosmopolitics: Thinking and Feeling Beyond the Nation*, eds. Pheng Cheah and Bruce Robbins. Minneapolis: University of Minnesota Press.

Silvey, Rachel. 2006. "Geographies of gender and migration: Spatializing social difference." *International Migration Review* 40(1): 64–81.

Thrift, Nigel. 2000. "Performing cultures in the new economy." *Annals of the Association of American Geographers* 90(4): 674–692.

Tulgan, Bruce. 2001. *Winning the Talent Wars*. New York: Norton.

Turner, Bryan. 2007. "The enclave society: towards a sociology of immobility." *European Journal of Social Theory* 10(2): 287–303.

Willis, Katie, 2010. "Social collisions," pp. 139–153 in *The Sage Handbook of Social Geographies*, eds. Susan Smith, Sallie Marston, Rachel Pain and John Paul Jones III. London: Sage.

Willis, Katie and Brenda Yeoh. 2003. "Gender, marriage and migration: The case of Singaporeans in China," pp. 101–119 in *Marriage and Migration in the Age of Globalisation: Asian Women as Wives and Workers*, eds. Nicola Piper and Mina Roces. Lanham, Maryland: Rowman and Littlefield.

Yeoh, Brenda S.A. and Shirlena Huang. 2011. "Introduction: Fluidity and friction in talent migration." *Journal of Ethnic and Migration Studies* 37(5): 681–690.

Yeoh, Brenda S.A. and Ah Eng Lai. 2008. "'Talent' migration in and out of Asia: Challenges for policies and places." *Asian Population Studies* 4(3): 235–245.

Yeoh, Brenda S.A. and Katie Willis. 1999. "'Heart' and 'wing', nation and diaspora: Gendered discourses in Singapore's regionalisation process." *Gender, Place and Culture* 6(4): 355–372.

———. 2004. "Constructing masculinities in transnational space: Singapore men on the 'regional beat'," pp.147–163 in *Transnational Spaces*, eds. Peter Jackson, Philip Crang and Clarie Dwyer. London: Routledge.

———. 2005a. "Singaporeans in China: Transnational women elites and the negotiation of gendered identities." *Geoforum* 36: 211–222.

——— 2005b. "Singaporean and British transmigrants in China and the cultural politics of 'contact zones'." *Journal of Ethnic and Migration Studies* 31(2): 269–285.

———. 2005c. "'Singapore unlimited'?: Transnational elites and negotiations of social identity in the regionalization process." *Asian and Pacific Migration Journal* 14(1–2): 71–95.

CHAPTER 16

"Guarded Globalization": The Politics of Skill Recognition on Migrant Health Care Workers

Mika TOYOTA[1]

This chapter seeks to unearth some of the hidden political and cultural logics of globalization that emerge in the case of the transnational migration of health care workers (nurses and qualified long-term care workers for the elderly) to Japan and Singapore. While care work is increasingly commodified in the global gendered labor market (Brown and Connell 2004; Browne and Braun 2008; Gamble 2002; Kingma 2006, 2008; Zimmerman, Litt and Bose 2006), what constitutes "skill" in care work is strictly regulated by state policies (Bach 2003; Hardill and MacDonald 2000; Iredale 2001, 2005; Raghuram and Kofman 2002) and, in particular, by a number of gate-keeping mechanisms that define what kind of care work counts and what does not (Choy 2003; Dahle 2005; Folbre 2006; Hagey et al. 2001). Care for the elderly is part of public welfare provision, the regulation of which is a key function of the modern nation-state.

While regulations relating to the immigration of health care workers, especially nurses and nursing aides, were liberalized in East Asia (e.g. Japan and Singapore) during the 1990s and intra-regional flows of migrant health care workers intensified, state policies in both sending and receiving countries continue to play an important role in redefining the meaning of "care work" through the operation of a number of gate-keeping mechanisms, including setting qualifications procedures. Passing the national certificate is a precondition for becoming a qualified nurse or care worker. As a result, care work, which used to be the "shadow work" of female family members, is now recognized as "paid work" and has been formalized by the state through providing training and assessing qualifications (Dyer et al. 2008). The state is thus increasingly involved in defining care work and its necessary qualifications, and the way in which it is built into the state's welfare system (Buchan and Calman 2004; Diallo 2004).

As Kofman and Raghuram have noted, providing welfare to the frail elderly is seen at least in part as a state responsibility, with the state usually playing a crucial role in regulating care industries (Kofman and Raghuram 2005: 151). The migration pathways of health care workers are thus filled with various obligatory screening processes. Recruitment agents, employers, professional bodies, and other state regulatory bodies may facilitate as well as undermine the process. Thus "any theorisation of skilled migration in welfare sectors would need to take into account the role of the state in the education and training of specific labour forces, the nature of labour shortages, the strength and effectiveness of protectionist bodies, such as professional organisations, their influence on immigration, and the recognition of migrant qualifications by states and within macroregions" (Raghuram and Kofman 2002: 2087).

National governments have a strong incentive to keep care work under their strict control. This control operates through a set of internal barriers and external borders. One is technical, and the other is socio-institutional, with the second functioning to reinforce the former. The result is a kind of "guarded globalization." On the one hand, transnational mobility of health care workers has been accelerated significantly with the assumption that the skills acquired in the origin country can be transferred to health care provision in the destination country; on the other hand, the procedure is closely monitored and shaped by national governments. What we are observing here are the processes of "de-skilling" and "re-skilling" of care work, which are seemingly contradictory yet taking place simultaneously. The state's accreditation standardizes and professionalizes the skills of care work, which are supposedly transferable across state borders. Yet qualifications obtained outside of the country are often excluded because the accredited skills are "country-specific." With this kind of de-skilling, the host country simply does not recognize the skill accreditation of the country of origin, hence the migrant health care workers with higher levels of skill often have to take jobs that are well below their level. The only way for the migrant workers to resolve this discrepancy is by a re-skilling process in which the professional bodies of host countries encourage foreign workers to take up training courses and thereby meet the official skill qualifications of the host country.

By illustrating these processes of de-skilling and re-skilling among foreign health care workers in Japan and Singapore, this chapter investigates the gatekeeping mechanisms for skill accreditation facilitated by meso-level actors as part of state policies, such as professional regulatory bodies, health care institutions, and recruitment agencies, in regulating and technically differentiating "care work" qualifications. The broader theoretical question I aim to ask is: Why does the state regard care work skill recognition as such a prerogative of sovereignty? I argue that skill recognition and technical differentiation have become a mode of exercise of national sovereignty at a time of increased transnational mobility of health care workers in the region.

The analysis of this chapter is based on fieldwork and interviews of officials at relevant ministries and organizations, which were conducted in Japan and Singapore from 2006 to 2008. The interview data were collected at the Ministry of Foreign Affairs, the Ministry of Justice, the Ministry of Health, Labor and Welfare, the Immigration Bureau of Japan, the Ministry of Economics, Trade and Industry, Nippon Keidanren (Japanese Business Federation), the Japanese Nursing Association in Japan in January 2007, the Ministry of Health, the Ministry of Community Development, Youth and Sports, the Ministry of Manpower, and the Singapore Nursing Board in Singapore in May 2007. Field visits and interviews were also conducted at hospitals and nursing homes which employ foreign care workers. In Singapore a semi-structured questionnaire was also used with foreign nurses from China, the Philippines, India and Myanmar (n=400). This was followed by in-depth interviews with foreign nurses working in Singapore either in hospitals or nursing homes (n= 35).

Gate-Keeping Mechanisms in Japan: The EPA Schemes

The Council on Economic and Fiscal Policy, headed by ex-Prime Minister Koizumi (2001-2006), approved the "Strategy in the Globalizing Economy" and acknowledged a policy agenda related to reforming Japanese migration policy. The discussion on reforming migration policy was shaped by worries as to whether the competitiveness of the Japanese economy would be weakened as a result of a shrinking labor force. According to a U.N. estimate, Japan needs an average annual net intake of about 381,000 in order to maintain its present population size (U.N. 2005). This has led to a growing acceptance of foreigners, especially of nurses and care workers as well as of technical people, in particular those with some facility in the Japanese language and with relevant vocational qualifications. In parallel with this new policy agenda, Economic Partnership Agreements (EPAs) were signed with the Philippines (September 2006) and Indonesia (August 2007). These agreements form part of a broader framework aimed at promoting economic integration. The EPA, however, relates not only to the flow of goods and services but also includes a chapter on specific commitments dealing with the movement of persons. It stipulates that Japan will receive 1,000 candidates (400 nurses and 600 certified care workers) from Indonesia and the Philippines in the first two years.

Currently Japan accepts mid/low-skilled foreign workers only as "foreign trainees" on a one-year contract. Almost 80 percent of the foreign trainees change their "trainee" status after one year of training. If they pass the official skill test, they become Technical Intern Trainees (TITs), which allows them to take on employment for up to three years in total (including the first year as trainees). Nurses and care workers are not limited to this standard; classified as "mid-skilled," they are excluded from the category of medical professionals under Japan's immigration law (interview data at Nippon Keidanren [Japanese Business

Federation], January 2007). Non-Japanese students obtaining nursing degrees in Japan are permitted to work as trainees for no more than seven years after qualifying (interview data at Japanese Nursing Association, January 2007).

They may be as well qualified as their Japanese equivalents but their foreign origins preclude them from working as registered nurses beyond this period. Furthermore because they cannot work after that seven-year period, they cannot remain in the country because they no longer have a job. So, ironically, despite training in the Japanese nursing education system and qualifying as nurses by passing the state certificate, they have to leave the country.[2]

Placing a limit on the period of stay of foreign nurses is explained officially as intended to prevent a "brain drain" from developing countries. The same reason is given for limiting the total intake of nurses and care givers under the EPA. The Ministry of Health, Labor and Welfare (MHLW) avers that the EPA scheme was implemented not for the purpose of offsetting the shortage of domestic care workers but to reinforce the economic partnership between the countries through human resource exchanges. As a result, those nurses and care workers from Indonesia and the Philippines coming to Japan under the EPA are categorized under a "special designated activity" (特定活動) which separates them from other "skilled" workers. Certainly the migration of health care workers from poor to richer countries has come under scrutiny not only from academics but also from international organizations such as the World Health Organization (WHO), the International Labour Office (ILO), and the International Organisation for Migration (IOM). There are growing concerns that large-scale migration of nurses and care workers may have a devastating impact on health care provision in the source countries. This is acknowledged, for example, in the recently released WHO code of practice on the international recruitment of health personnel (1 September 2008), which draws attention to the uneven gains and losses between the providers (the global south) and the receivers (the global north).

This larger concern, however, does not justify the injustice done to individual workers. Those enlisted into the Japanese training programs under the EPA system undertake a heavy burden. In August 2008, the first batch of 104 nurses and 104 practical care givers[3] (male 77, female 131 in total) from Indonesia arrived in Japan and were put on a six-month intensive Japanese language training course. After that they were to be dispatched all over Japan to take on practical vocational training in hospitals and elderly care institutions. A tight time-schedule was set up. To become certified nurses, they had to attain adequate language proficiency to take and pass their vocational certificates within three years for nurses and four years for certified care workers. If they were successful, their residential status would be extended for only another three years, but if they failed the language test or failed to obtain their certificate within the time prescribed they would be deported. Furthermore, they were given only one chance to take the exam.

For Indonesians starting with no knowledge, to master Japanese (speaking, writing, and reading knowledge of 3,500 words, including 700 Chinese characters) within six months and be ready to take the national certificate examination within the limited time – and while holding down a full-time job – was no easy undertaking. If we consider that in 2007 only 50.4 percent of native Japanese trying for the "certified care worker" qualification managed to pass, the magnitude of this task for foreigners is underlined. From the perspective of the nurses' career development, it must be seen as high risk, with the probability that they will end up wasting much time and money. This may partially explain why less than half of the first group of Indonesian applicants managed to qualify. This formal re-skilling procedure is a mammoth undertaking for foreign workers.

Anxiety about a "brain drain" does not fully account for the regulations and requirements regarding de-skilling and re-skilling. A more likely explanation is that the "brain drain" is a convenient argument used to disguise and paper over conflicting attitudes between different sections of Japanese officialdom; this has little to do with concern about poorer countries and their health needs or about individual health care workers. On one side in Japanese officialdom are the Ministry of Foreign Affairs, METI, and the Nippon Keidanren, all of which have been proactive in reforming and liberalizing labor migration policy. They have promoted the immigration of nurses and care workers and insisted that the basic framework of the JPEPA (Japan-Philippines EPA) should pave the way for future negotiations with other Southeast Asian neighbors (such as Thailand and Vietnam). On the other side are MHLW, the Japan Nursing Association, and the Labour Union League, all of which are against accepting less skilled foreign workers. They stress that the first priority is to cultivate the domestic labor market by mobilizing the currently inactive elderly and female labor force – including many dormant nurses and certified care workers – rather than importing foreigners.[4] The Ministry of Justice takes yet a different position, maintaining that only highly skilled labor should be accepted, without indicating any solution to the reality of the growing mismatches in the low to mid-skilled labor market in Japan.

While processes of economic liberalization lead to greater flows of transnational migrant care workers, the state's qualifications requirements set limits on this migration. Although the EPA scheme upholds the policy of equal payment for Japanese and foreign workers, it will only be applied after the foreign trainees successfully pass the national examination. As a result, it justifies maintaining wage differentials between foreign trainees and Japanese workers in the guise of recognizing difference in skill levels. The imposition of governmental certification requirements, together with immigration regulations, leads to justifying stratification between different states' qualifications, thereby creating hierarchy. A concomitant of this is the effective de-skilling of transnational health care workers. In this case, what matters is not only the nationality attached to the worker personally, but also the nationalism of the skill accreditation process. The state and meso-level actors (e.g. professional bodies) play a crucial role not only in set-ting the labor market regulations and in mediating immigration requirements, but also in shaping the genealogy and sociopolitical constructedness of the defi-nition of skills and qualifications ascribed to care work, which framework allows discrimination on nationality grounds through the medium of qualifications.

For their part, nursing home employers stress that the quality of care work does not always depend on the qualifications of the workers but on their charac-ter and ability to establish a rapport with patients and to work in a team. Simi-larly, some employers say that what matters most for care work is the attitude rather than the level of language ability, and that they could modify their patient data recording systems to cope with the lesser writing abilities of their foreign workers. Some employers with experience in hiring foreign workers (such as Fili-pina women married to Japanese) were initially worried about the negative image associated with foreign workers and the possibly negative reaction of the elderly, but then observed positive effects on the elderly clients as well as on peer work-ers.[5] In short, these employers perceive a gap between the formal skills required and the actual on-the-job needs.

Under the EPA scheme, the state does not provide any systematic job training program for foreign health care workers. The expenses of the initial six-month Japanese language program are shared by the Ministry of Foreign Affairs and METI. But once the care workers are dispatched to the designated institutions as trainees, the cost of language training and vocational training (which is estimated at around 600,000 yen [US $6,414] per person per year) is to be borne by the host institutions. Accepting foreign workers requires appointing Japanese men-tors, which might put a strain on the workload of other workers. There is indeed a high risk that even after providing the full language and vocational training, the foreign worker may not be able to pass the national certificate and may have to leave the country. Employers may not be against the idea of hiring foreign work-ers but most employers cannot afford to take on this burden.[6] It is therefore not surprising that fewer hospitals and nursing homes were ready to provide posts for foreign care workers under the EPA scheme than expected. While the two-year quota of nurses and certified care workers from Indonesia was 1,000 in total, only 208 posts were provided for the 2008 batch and initially only 104 posts were secured for the 2009 batch. Even after the extension of the deadline and consid-erable persuasive efforts by an intermediary agent set up by the government, only 477 posts had been secured for the 2009 batch as of 28 April 2009.

The EPA scheme does not seem to be meeting any of its goals. It places techni-cal qualification barriers which are unnecessarily high in terms of what it takes to do the job, while socio-institutionally neither resolving the problem of la-bor shortages within the Japanese care industry nor addressing the brain drain concerns of sending countries. What it does instead is "institutionalize" skill recognition and technical differentiation. These nation-specific qualification requirements are a powerful institutional mechanism that not only enhances the Japanese state's regulating power over care workers but also reinforces the notion of a global hierarchy of care workers.

Gate-Keeping Mechanisms in Singapore: Regulating the "Churn" of Foreign Workers

In the case of Singapore, national sovereignty is exercised by regulating the "churn" of migration – a continuous cycle of workers going out and coming into the country. There are four occupational categories of health care workers in Singapore: (1) Registered Nurses (RN); (2) Enrolled Nurses (EN); (3) Nursing Aides (NA); and (4) Health Care Attendants (HCA). If they are accepted to work at a higher level – either as Registered Nurse (RN) or Enrolled Nurse (EN) – health care workers receive a salary of over SGD 1,800 (US $1,234). In addition, they hold an employment pass (called an S-pass) and are allowed to apply for the Singapore P. R. (Permanent Residence) if desired. However, foreign trained nurses from the Philippines, China, India, or Myanmar have to work as Nursing Aides (NA) until they pass the nursing certificate authorized by the Singapore Nursing Board. They will then hold a work permit with a two-year contract, with a possible extension up to six years. As work permit holders, they are not allowed to marry a Singapore citizen or a Singapore P. R. Furthermore, it is mandatory to take a pregnancy test every six months. If they are found to be pregnant they are deported immediately. Those in the last category, Health Care Attendants, also hold work permits and the same regulations apply to them. For locals, no nursing training is needed at all to work as a Heath Care Attendant (HCA), but anyone from Myanmar has to have a university degree (Toyota 2009).

Most of the foreign health care workers pay SGD 1,500-2,700 (US $1,028-1,850) to a recruitment agent in order to obtain a post in Singapore.[7] Over their first six months of probation,[8] the workers have to pay off this debt through a top-slice deduction from their monthly salary. Neither nursing qualifications nor previous work experience in their home countries are necessarily reflected in their salary scale. Only the number of years of working experience in Singapore is taken into consideration. Thus it is not uncommon for the monthly salary of an HCA without nursing qualification but with longer working experience in Singapore to be higher than that of an NA with nursing qualification and experience but only newly arrived in Singapore. This can be rather demoralizing, especially for experienced foreign health care workers with nursing degrees who have to work as Nursing Aides (NA) without being able to properly deploy their professional knowledge and expertise in their new posts. As for Singaporeans, no nursing degree is required to become a Nursing Aide. Furthermore, salary scales are clearly differentiated between foreign heath care workers and Singaporeans (see Table 16.1).

Table 16.1 • Salary Scale of Foreign Health Care Workers in Singapore (1 USD =1.47 SGD)

	Non-Singapore citizen (working experience in Singapore)	Singapore citizen
Registered Nurse (RN)	SGD 1,400–2,700 (9 years) (US $950–1,834)	SGD 1,500–4,000 (US $1,019–2,718)
Enrolled Nurse (EN)	SGD 800–1,200 (3 years) (US $543–815)	SGD 1,150–2,900 (US $781–1,970)
Nursing Aide (NA)	SGD 400 (US $272) (1 year) SGD 450 (US $306) (2 year) SGD 600 (US $408) (5 years)	SGD 850–1,535 (US $578–1,043)
Health Care Attendant (HCA)	SGD 380 (US $258) (1 year) SGD 600 (US $408) (8 years)	SGD 750–1,175 (US $510–798)

Structurally it is very difficult for foreign health care workers to change their work place even if they are deeply dissatisfied with their working conditions. If the worker leaves the job before the contract ends, the employer has to pay a security bond amount of SGD 5,000 to the state. Thus the employer systematically regulates workers. The security bond is embedded in their salary, under the name of "loyalty allowance." According to the contract:

> You are eligible for a loyalty allowance upon successful completion of the contracted period. The amount will be pro-rated if the work permit expires earlier than the contractual period. Should you resign or if your employment is terminated by the Company for cause before the expiry of the contractual period, you should not be entitled to any loyalty allowance. The loyalty allowance is paid on the last payroll of the contractual period.

Furthermore, workers from Myanmar have to go through a guarantor system, which means that their guarantors will be punished and required to pay a fine if they break their contract. They usually borrow money from a family member or other relatives to pay the recruitment agent fee and they are expected to pay back these debts as well as some additional remittance. Therefore, no matter how bad the working conditions are, they try to bear it through the initial two-year contact with the hope that they can find a better job in the next round of the contract.

At nursing homes, there is a re-skilling procedure for the workers. For their part, the nursing home employers are keen for their own workers to obtain the ITE (Institute of Technical Education) Skill Certificate in Health Care, partly to improve their skills but, more importantly, to reduce the monthly levy that the employers have to pay to the state: employers have to pay a monthly levy of SGD 240 per person to hire foreign workers but after being trained and obtaining the certificate, the cost of the levy is reduced to SGD 50–60 per person. Furthermore, with more "trained" workers the assistance provided to the institution by the state increases. With this ITE Skill Certificate, the foreign worker's contract can be extended up to eighteen years. Some nursing homes impose years of bonds on the workers in exchange for the provision of an ITE Skill Certificate.

For those who have nursing degrees and working experience, this ITE certificate course is not necessarily a positive option. The ITE Skill Certificate entails 120 hours of lectures over six months,[9] but is far too basic for those who are already trained and have three or four years' experience as registered nurses in their home country. What they want is an opportunity to take the Singapore Nursing Board (SNB) exam and work as a professional nurse at the hospital. However, they cannot just go and take the exam by themselves. They have to have a recommendation from the employer. This is not a simple process. The workers have to face difficult negotiations with their employer because any employer who would like to retain the workers will not easily allow them to take the Singapore Nursing Board exam. Instead they encourage them to obtain the ITE certificate. Taking the ITE certificate can often mean being bonded to the same employer for years to come. Anyone hoping to start working as a nurse as soon as possible is thus not keen to take the ITE certificate, but if that intention is revealed to the employer, there is a risk of not getting a recommendation letter from the employer to take the SNB exam.

By the end of the first two-year contract, if workers have not received a recommendation from their employers for the SNB exam, they have to turn to a private agent. The agent fee for a recommendation is SGD 3,000, the equivalent of five to six months of salary. It is a large sum but they have no choice if they want to ensure that they get a nursing job in the second two-year contract. Foreign nurses come to Singapore with the intention of gaining new knowledge and experience and of advancing their professional skills. This leads them to decide to devote most of their savings to this purpose. During the first two-year contract, they can hardly make money as they are paying off their recruitment agent fee of SGD 1,500–2,700 during the first six months out of SGD 4,800 (SGD 400 x 12 months) and then paying the recommendation fee of SGD 3,000 out of SGD 5,400 (SGD 450 x 12 months). In this way, the agent fee is structurally embedded in their personal wage system. This structure not only leads to the proliferation of labor recruitment industries in Singapore but also helps to sustain a churn of migration, a continuous cycle of workers entering and leaving, managed and regulated by the state.

Conclusion

Globalization creates opportunities for health care workers to work outside of their countries, and the standardization and professionalization of nursing skills constitute an important mechanism to facilitate this process. Although technically skills should be transferable freely, in reality heath care workers cannot perform to the full level of their skills without the recognition and approval of the receiving state. Skill recognition is by no means purely a technical procedure or a neutral filter; it is rather a social process and a new arena where the state can exercise its sovereign power. State policies about skill recognition are not necessarily designed to exploit foreign health care labor, but the process of acquiring official state recognition effectively puts migrant care workers in disadvantaged positions in the labor market.

By using the notion "guarded globalization," I wish to call attention to the fact that globalization is a process full of tensions, setbacks (often intentional), and contradictions. The globalization of the heath care profession and transnational mobility of health care workers have become a necessity in Asia (and beyond) to address various demographic and social challenges, but the processes are carefully guarded, and even contained, by the established authorities. Globalization in this case should be understood as a complex process of negotiations between different social forces and we, as critical social scientists, should pay close attention to the human consequences of such negotiations.

Notes

1. This research (2007-2010) was supported by a grant (JSPS/JRP/06/FASS1) from the National University of Singapore and Japan Society for the Promotion of Science. The field research in Singapore was conducted with Prof. Brenda Yeoh and Associate Professor Shirlena Huang at the National University of Singapore and the fieldwork in Japan was led by Prof. Ruri ITO at the Hitotsubashi University.
2. Although the length of stay has recently been extended from three years to seven years for this specific mid-skilled category, the exclusion from legal residential status remained.
3. There are 49 care giver training institutions in Indonesia, producing 5,350 graduates per year. However, qualifications and definitions of "care givers" vary depending on the country in which they are working. For example, the qualification of "practical care giver" needed to work in Japan requires a General Diploma 3 (senior high school + 3 years) + 6 months training + 6 months intensive language training,

whereas the requirement for a "care giver" to work in Hong Kong or Taiwan is only a senior high school education + 3–6 months training. In Singapore, "care givers" are categorized as unskilled labor and the boundary between domestic maids and care givers is vague as both hold a Work Permit Pass.

4. It was reported by the Japanese Nursing Association (in 2007) that there were 550,000 certified but inactive nurses and almost half of the certified care workers were not currently working as care workers in Japan.

5. Interviews with employers of foreign health care workers were conducted in Japan in January and December 2007.

6. Yokohama city provides an interpreter and assistance with the labor cost and Tokyo prefecture provides assistance to support the Japanese language expenses of 1,000,000 yen per year per worker. But these cases are exceptions. The support given to the foreign trainees varies from place to place.

7. The survey among foreign health care workers in Singapore (n=400) was conducted in 2006–2007 as a part of the following project: "Transnational care workers, state policies and gender dynamics in ageing societies: a comparative study of Singapore and Japan." In-depth interviews were conducted in 2007–2008.

8. During the probationary period, the employer can return the worker to the recruitment agents.

9. Of those 120 hours, 60 hours are for Basic Health Care, 40 hours for Home and In-patient Care and 20 hours for Home Care.

References

Bach, Stephen. 2003. "International migration of health workers: Labour and social issues." Working Paper WP. 2009, Sectoral Activities Programme, Geneva: ILO.

Brown, Richard, and John Connell. 2004. "The migration of doctors and nurses from South Pacific island nations." *Social Science and Medicine* 58: 2193–2210.

Browne, Colette V., and Kathryn L. Braun. 2008. "Globalization, women's migration, and the long-term-care workforce." *The Gerontologist* 48(1): 16–24.

Buchan, James, and Lynn Calman. 2004. *The Global Shortage of Registered Nurses: An Overview of Issues and Actions.* Geneva: International Council of Nurses.

Choy, Catherine C. 2003. *Empire of Care: Nursing and Migration in Filipino American History.* Durham and London: Duke University Press.

Dahle, Rannveig. 2005. "Men, bodies and nursing," pp. 127–138, in *Gender, Bodies and Work*, eds. David Morgan, Berit Brandth, and Elin Kvande. Aldershot: Ashgate.

Diallo, Khassoum. 2004. "Data on the migration of health-care workers: Sources, uses, and challenges." *Bulletin of the World Health Organization* 82: 601–607.

Dyer, S., L. McDowell, and A. Batnitzky. 2008. "Emotional labour/body work: The caring labours of migrants in the UK's National Health Service." *Geoforum* 39: 2030–2038.

Folbre, Nancy. 2006. "Demanding quality: Worker/consumer coalitions and 'high road' strategies in the care sector." *Politics & Society* 34(5): 101–131.

Gamble, Debi. 2002. "Filipino nurse recruitment as a staffing strategy." *Journal of Nursing Administration* 32(4): 175–177.

Hagey, Rebecca, Ushi Choudhry, Sepali Guruge, Jane Turrittin, Enid Collins, and Ruth Lee. 2001. "Immigrant nurses' experience of racism." *Journal of Nursing Scholarship* 33(4): 389–394.

Hardill, Irene, and Sandra MacDonald. 2000. "Skilled international migration: The experience of nurses in the UK." *Regional Studies* 34(7): 681–692.

Iredale, Robyn. 2001. "The migration of professionals: Theories and typologies." *International Migration* 39(5): 7–26.

———. 2005. "Gender, immigration policies and accreditation: Valuing the skills of professional women migrants." *Geoforum* 36: 155–166.

Kingma, Mireille. 2006. *Nurses on the Move: Migration and the Global Health Care Economy.* Ithaca, NY: Cornell University Press.

———. 2008. "Nurse migration and the global health care economy." *Policy, Politics, & Nursing Practice* 9(4): 328–333.

Kofman, Eleonore, and Parvati Raghuram. 2005. "Gender and skilled migrants: Into and beyond the workplace." *Geoforum* 36: 149–154.

Raghuram, Parvati, and Eleonore Kofman. 2002. "The state, skilled labour markets and immigration: The case of doctors in England." *Environment and Planning A* 34: 2071–2089.

Toyota, Mika. 2009. "I am a nurse! Professional identity, state regulation and career pathways of Burmese care workers in Singapore," paper presented at the International Workshop on Transnational Migrant Identity in Asia: Intersecting Cultural, Social and Economic Dimensions, 17–18 December 2009, Singapore.

U.N. 2005. http://www.un.org/esa/population/publications/ReplMigED/Japan.pdf.

Zimmerman, Mary K., Jacquelyn S. Litt, and Christine E. Bose. 2006. *Global Dimensions of Gender and Carework.* Palo Alto, CA: Stanford University Press.

❧ Conclusion

Keiko YAMANAKA, David W. HAINES, J.S. EADES,
Nelson GRABURN, WANG Jianxin, and
Bernard P. WONG

In their conclusion to *The Age of Migration*, Castles and Miller (2009: 299) note the increasing ubiquity and significance of international migration throughout the world today. East Asia is no exception. As this volume amply demonstrates, owing to the region's rapid economic development, in the past three decades cross-border migration in the region has grown immensely in its volume, frequency, and complexity. As a result, the region's contemporary migration patterns are fluid and flexible in forms, categories, goals, directions, and durations. An examination of East Asian migration – its causes, processes and consequences – therefore requires multi-level, multi-faceted, and multi-sited research with close attention to specific historical roots and structural contexts in which human mobility patterns have been shaped and transformed over time and across space.

As Haines, Yamashita, and Eades suggest in the introduction to this volume, East Asian migration has arisen as a prominent field of international migration study and one critical to enhancing its overall coherence in many ways. For example, the frequent adoption of temporary guest worker systems by Asian labor-importing countries reveals the highly rigid immigration controls that limit immigrant rights and freedom in destination countries (e.g., Yamanaka and Piper 2005). Many of these East Asian countries suffer from sharply declining fertility and thus a rapidly aging population and labor force. Yet their governments often see low-skill foreign workers as necessary only to adjust to changing labor demands due to economic cycles. Consequently, while high-skill workers are much desired, low-skill workers are subject to rigid rules regarding their admission, employment, and residence. For most unskilled workers in East Asia, settlement with family in the country of destination, not to mention the acquisition of citizenship, is almost impossible (Seol and Skrentny 2009). Furthermore, in East Asia there are no regional conventions to harmonize the rights of migrant workers and their families, such as exist in Europe.

Over the years, the increasingly middle-class East Asian societies have given rise to highly gendered and racialized patterns of international labor migration (Piper

2008). Their expanding service economies and aging populations require a rotation of large numbers of reproductive labor workers from selected countries willing to send their nationals, mostly women, abroad (Rodriguez 2010). The intense economic competition among East Asian industrial countries means there continues to be a demand for temporary, inexpensive laborers – men and women – in the manufacturing and construction industries. Such gendered and racialized patterns of migration are also common in China where the household registration (*hukou*) system still operates to limit the geographic mobility of rural populations to large coastal cities with rapid economic growth. Lacking citizenship (or other rights to residence and public services) and labeled as backward people, rural migrants in urban areas constitute an enormous reservoir of circular temporary workers who are needed but not wanted (Pun 2005; Yan 2008; Han 2010).

Yet international migration is also known for its "relative autonomy" from public policy (Castles and Miller 2009: 299). The fluid and flexible patterns of East Asian migration confirm this pattern. Given the region's huge and growing gaps in economic development, a high proportion of the population in the periphery eagerly seek better opportunities in the core. In so doing, migrants mobilize any resources available for them to cross the border, find a job, and maintain it at their destination. The close historical and cultural ties between different groups across the contiguous land or sea borders of East and Southeast Asia provide fertile grounds for extensive social networks to develop among individuals sharing the same ethnicity, dialect, or origin. At the same time the region has witnessed the rapid growth of a migration industry providing migrants with a variety of services to cross the border and secure employment overseas. International migration has thus become not only a way of earning a livelihood for millions of migrants, but also a national project by which states secure foreign labor reserves (Rodriguez 2010).

In the following sections, we highlight some crucial themes and issues that appear in the many varied chapters of this volume. The discussion reflects an amalgamation and updating of views that we originally developed individually as discussants at the conferences in which early versions of the chapters in this volume were presented.

Aging, Skill, and Lifestyle

In East Asia's industrialized countries, the rapidly aging population resulting from extremely low fertility requires governments to develop comprehensive public welfare systems. However, the diminishing working-age population also depletes the pool of local workers, especially women, willing to take labor-intensive, low-paid jobs in such areas as domestic service, health care, and entertainment. State welfare policy in these countries is therefore tied to an immigration policy that targets low-skilled foreign women from less developed countries. These countries, however, differ significantly in their policies concerning deployment of female immigrant workers. As a result, two conspicuous patterns have emerged (Huang, Yeoh, and Rahman 2005).

In Singapore, Malaysia, Taiwan, and Hong Kong, governments have accepted large numbers of foreign women to work in private households as live-in domestic workers and elderly care workers. These governments have done so, because "foreign maids" free educated local women from their household responsibilities, thus encouraging them to participate in the labor force. Such privatization and commodification of reproductive labor has also enabled the governments to save enormous social welfare costs that would otherwise have to be invested in the expansion of public programs for the care of children and the elderly.

In sharp contrast, in Japan (and until recently, Korea), the government has not legalized the employment of transnational domestic workers in private households. This is largely attributable to the fact that very few Japanese families demand foreign maids in their homes. In post-WWII Japan, caring for family and household has been women's (wives') work. Even today, women are kept to their traditional domestic gender roles not only by social convention but also by governmental policies that provide tax deductions for homebound women. At work, wage discrimination against women is still common, effectively discouraging them from continuing employment or developing a career.

Recently, however, the reality of Japan's rapidly aging population has drastically changed the centuries-long tradition of family care for the elderly. In 2000, the state installed a national elderly care system replete with public insurance, service programs, training, and certification systems. This has quickly transformed elderly care from a home-based, unskilled, unpaid service into a market-based, skilled, paid service. As a result, the elderly care industry has expanded rapidly, drawing large numbers of Japanese (mostly female) workers wishing for a new career. However, they have soon found these jobs unattractive because of their labor-intensive nature, low wages, and low prestige. Consequently, the elderly care industry is suffering from high turnover rates, while facing a shrinking pool of job applicants.

These factors provide the context for Toyota's comparative study (Chapter 16) on foreign care givers in Japan and Singapore. In her analysis of state policies in these two middle-class countries, she demonstrates the convergence and divergence of approaches taken to solve labor shortages in elderly health care. Despite its urgent labor needs, Japan remains closed to large-scale immigration even at skilled levels. The country's economic partnership agreements with a few developing Asian countries oblige the government to accept a certain number of immigrant trainees into the health care industry. Nonetheless, as Toyota shows, the state has constructed excessively high barriers for foreign nurses to be retrained and pass the board exams in Japan. As a result, very few Asian trainees become certified health care workers in the country.

In sharp contrast, Singapore is well known for its liberal immigration policies for both skilled and unskilled workers. Toyota's case study provides a prototype of a Singapore model that rewards immigrant workers with differential benefits based not only their skills but also on their nationality and gender. The state regards them as indispensable to the city-state's economic vitality and has developed elaborate immigration schemes for both skill levels: the unskilled to work on a short-term rotation, and the skilled to stay on a permanent basis.

What explains the stark difference in immigration policies employed by Japan and Singapore? A clue lies in the different public policies concerning an aging population and female labor participation. Japan has adopted a national elderly care system by centralizing resources to serve its elderly population with the deployment of Japanese women in the health care industry. In contrast, Singapore has opted for a global capitalist approach to its shrinking labor force. By privatizing the reproductive labor offered by immigrant women, Singapore encourages its women to contribute to national economic growth, while minimizing state spending for public child and elderly care.

The increasingly feminized and racialized labor migration from Southeast Asia has been a solution for a small number of aging, middle-class societies in East Asia, most prominently Singapore, Taiwan and Hong Kong. In other middle-class societies, such as Japan and South Korea, increased income and improved pension programs permit some of the relatively wealthy elderly to move overseas for retirement, frequently to Southeast Asia. As Yamashita points out in his chapter (Chapter 11), for Japanese travelers most of Southeast Asia is "cheap, near, warm," a formula that accounts for much of the post-WWII North-South tourism the world over. This, in turn, reflects the "rich visitor to poorer destination" formula for mass recreational tourism.

There are, however, a variety of other forms, goals, and durations of traveling which go beyond this rich-poor dichotomy. The chapters by Yamashita (Chapter 11) and Moon (Chapter 12) are perfect examples of contemporary research on international migration among middle-class members of wealthy East Asian societies. Each involves people in their temporary communities in national and international settings, in no way isolated from the global system (Appadurai 1991). Each focuses on people in motion, or multi-habitation, or perhaps people "in between" (Clifford 1997). Each author has also had to move to follow these people, conducting multi-sited ethnography (Marcus 1995) – as is also true of the authors of many other chapters of this book.

The temporary and permanent flows of Japanese retirees to Southeast Asia discussed by Yamashita are an example of the increasingly common phenomenon of retirement to the "cheap, near, warm," that can also be found in Europe's colonization of the Mediterranean coasts and Americans' retirement to Mexico,

Central America, and Panama. All these are examples of the relatively recent topic of "lifestyle migration" (Benson and O'Reilly 2009). Yamashita's detailed ethnography of Japanese retirees controverts any remaining belief in Japanese homogeneity by showing the wide range of cultural and economic motivations and life styles, ranging from permanent married resettlement to bi-local marriage, to see-sawing back and forth travel, to escaping from Japan as cultural refugees. Significantly many of these retirees settle in places which they already know through prior overseas employment or recreational tourism. Commonly the target communities are in Malaysia, Indonesia, or the Philippines and are seen as an answer to the nostalgic search of the Japanese for a non-modern *furusato*, an ideal "old village community" with familiar rice paddies that appeals to their *kokoro*, "heart-mind."

In contrast to elderly Japanese travelers in Southeast Asia, the relationship between the South Korean citizens visiting the Chinese borderlands adjacent to North Korea generates feelings governed by past political relationships of a rather different kind. Moon shows us that these Koreans see the area they visit in terms of deep historical connections. The feeling of cultural ownership infuses international tourism in relation to Japan as well (Graburn 2008a, 2008b; Moon 1997). South Korean tourism to northeast China, like the on-and-off-again tourism to Mount Kumgangsan in North Korea since 1998, takes place because of history, not in spite of history. The region is "claimed" by Koreans as the land of *Koguryô*, a national place of origin and political flourishing. Because the land is also "claimed" by China, this is a good example of *Dissonant Heritage* (Tunbridge and Ashworth 1996). Clearly, many modern forms of tourism constitute serious cultural and historical interactions with profound meaning for the participants (Graburn 1977, 2004), even though the visits may be quite short in length. In East Asia – and perhaps in the world more generally – places of ethnic and national origins engender as much reverence as the abodes of the gods.

Cross-Border Marriages

Asia's economic and demographic divide has resulted in trends, as detailed above, that include such divergent elements as lifestyle migration and low-wage, often "feminized," flows, which reflect East Asia's great labor demands and Southeast Asia's relatively abundant labor supply. The remarkable increase in cross-border marriages originates from that same economic divide but entails intricate and complex interactions between economic inequality and more individualistic motivations. Cross-border marriages have thus emerged as a major focus of research and policy during the past few decades.

In terms of numbers, policy immediacy, public attention, and academic research, marriages between foreign women from less developed countries and men living in more developed countries (such as Korea and Japan) have tended to receive the most attention: they do indeed constitute the major portion of these marriages (Yamanaka 2006). As would be expected, these marriages involve difficult adjustments for the brides, and sometimes situations so abusive that women are forced to leave the marriage, if they can. Yet these marriages also provide some options for women that they do not otherwise have. As is described with particular clarity in Constable's edited volume *Cross-Border Marriages* (2005), an international marriage may provide a way up (or at least a way out) for women, possibly the only option for doing so that they will ever have in their lifetime. Using to good effect Lavely's (1991) notion of spatial hypergamy, several of the authors in that volume point out that even if a marriage requires downward mobility in status, it provides upward mobility toward a society that has more opportunities for the wives and certainly for their children.

The three chapters in this book by Grillot, Kudo, and Thai extend the understanding of the range of international marriages and also the very long historical view that is needed to understand the origins and futures, causes and effects of these marriages. Grillot's discussion (Chapter 8) is perhaps the most in tune with the bulk of international marriages in that these involve Vietnamese women in China, looking for improved marriage prospects. But the situation is far more complex than a simple stratagem for economic advancement in a border area where people are constantly in movement. Grillot begins her chapter with an assessment of the complex mutual perceptions through which Chinese men and Vietnamese women seek in each other an ideal spouse. They must make their calculations in a situation that is volatile and one in which the individual people are not particularly well-known and thus are especially subject to mutual stereotypes, both negative and positive. Grillot's material highlights the complexities in assessing cross-border marriage as it is understood by its participants, as they seek each other out, as they find each other, and as they construct often fitful, yet sometimes durable, alliances.

Kudo's work (Chapter 10) on Pakistani husbands and Japanese wives in Japan may seem to be entirely different. The wives must deal with men from a rather different culture and with a religion that is both different in its beliefs and in its degree of hold on people's lives. Their conversion to Islam itself requires their careful analysis as they sort out what is truly Islamic in their Pakistani husbands' accounts and practice of it. The specific issues raised by Kudo concern the fact that in their marriage both the husbands and the wives remain potentially mobile. The immigrant husbands move from low-wage jobs to insecure self-employed jobs. As they move occupationally, the families move residentially within Japan, and often to Pakistan. Suddenly these marriages look less like Pakistani men marrying in to Japanese society than women marrying in to Pakistani families which have their strongest physical and moral grounding in Pakistan. The nature of the wives' futures is never fully resolved and the result is something that looks very much like a transnational lifestyle. However, as with Grillot, the complex of mutual perceptions, expectations, and hopes that husbands and wives hold suggest that the meaning and practice of "transnational" may be more complex than is usually assumed, and less certain in its outcomes.

Thai (Chapter 9), in turn, deals with the initial forays into Vietnam of Vietnamese American men from the United States looking for wives. His study is particularly helpful in examining the full range of factors that facilitate the mutual inspections of the men and the women and that will make their alliances appealing but also difficult. As in Grillot's case, Vietnamese women are looking for "modern" husbands and certainly the men are looking to find "old-fashioned" wives who will validate their masculinity. But perhaps the issue on which Thai is clearest is class. These are marriages based on a fairly sharp status distinction between men and women. Here is exactly the spatial hypergamy that Lavely (1991) has noted. The Vietnamese women are marrying down in terms of education and occupation but marrying up in terms of opportunities simply because they are moving to the United States. There may be disappointment when these women find out where they fit in American society, but their expectation that America is indeed a rich country and may provide some of that wealth to them (and perhaps more to their children) is quite well founded.

All three chapters on international marriage migration are especially rich on the complex interactions between men and women at all stages of their lives together, and the way in which marriages across borders of nation, ethnicity, language, and class are yet further complicated by a web of uneasy mutual perceptions. Perhaps the one point that deserves reiteration, since it runs directly to the heart of this book's consideration of migration, is how very long the story of a cross-border marriage is. The marriage itself is only the beginning of an uncertain future of marital accommodation, life in a new place, and creation of a family with children growing up in a new "multicultural" household. The prolonged process by which a cross-border marriage shapes itself is a good reminder of the long story of migration that includes all the unpredictabilities and transformations that reverberate over space and through time.

Networks and Social Capital

If the two sections discussed above have generally dealt with international migrant flows which are officially sanctioned by the authority of the destination countries, be it for labor, lifestyle, or marriage, there are also very large internal, as well as international, flows that are more irregular in nature. Although often regarded as unlawful, these flows are tacitly incorporated into governmental policy in order to alleviate labor shortages in occupations and industries shunned by local workers. In mainland China, this process is seen in rural to urban migration that results in an indeterminate legal and social status for migrant workers in the cities. All these migrants, whether internal or international, must expend great effort to circumvent their irregular status and a frequently hostile reception. They do so by mobilizing a wide range of resources.

In China, most of the internal migration is to big coastal cities, and one major component of it involves ethnic minorities who become much like internal "foreigners" in the cities. They belong to the Chinese state, but less clearly to the Chinese nation, which is why they must be incorporated as officially designated ethnic minorities rather than simply as generic Chinese. Many of them come from populations that spread across borders, whether Tai to the south, Mongolian to the north, or Korean to the east. In looking at these minority migrants, Zhang (Chapter 3) relies on a pair of research projects that used various methods, but with a strong focus on surveys – and the surveys receive most of the attention in his chapter. Here is a reprise of the Redfieldian tracking of movement from the countryside into the city and thus a reminder of Redfield's work with the late Fei Hsiao-tung (Xiaotong) in China, at a time when sociology and anthropology were more intertwined in the study of migration and of cities. Zhang's invocation of Fei's notion of networks – that each person is at the center of spreading ripples that in their intersection with other spreading ripples are the social network – is thus quite appropriate.

That general methodological point aside, the implications of the survey findings are intriguing. The simple notion of the importance of social networks to migrant adaptation in cities yields immediately to variation and complexity. In his comparison of reliance on social networks for initial and current jobs no general pattern is found at all. Instead, the situations of different minorities vary. Behind these survey data lie the complicated political, social, economic, and cultural histories of China's many minorities. The radically different findings for even the same minorities in different cities is a reminder that the consideration of migrants in cities must also be a study of how variable cities in a single country can be in terms of the resources and obstacles they present to migrants.

Another flow of migration in China today that requires scholarly attention is that from outside the country. Compared to the internal flows, international migration to mainland China is still more limited, although growing rapidly (see Yeo, Chapter 5). For that reason, the case of Hong Kong is particularly interesting. Mathews (Chapter 14) provides a case study focusing on African traders based in Chungking Mansions, a localized migrant community and hub of global migration. By following the African transnationals to their "contact zones" (Yeoh and Willis, Chapter 15) and interviewing and observing their migratory processes, Mathews provides vivid and concrete ethnographic accounts of these African entrepreneurs as agents of low-end globalization. Few would imagine that Africans would find a way to participate in the "semi-periphery" of the global economy in these dilapidated ramshackle buildings. But because Hong Kong is a neoliberal paradise with free visa-entry and little interference in business, these ambitious African men can seek their fortune by buying cheap goods and copies of brand-name products that are made in the nearby factories of southern main-land China. Mathews' insightful account provides a helpful vantage point from which to understand transnational migrants in this particularly global city.

Turning to Japan, where the government's reluctance to develop comprehensive immigration policy has resulted in a variety of *de facto* immigrant workers in the country (Yamanaka 2010), the image of Japan as an ethnically "homogenous society" is flatly belied by the evidence; since the colonial period the import of labor into Japan from the Korean Peninsula and other colonies (Weiner 1994; Yamawaki 2003) has made homogeneity a myth, albeit one that has been powerfully resurrected in the post-WWII period (Oguma 2002). Furthermore, from the late 1980s on, newly arrived immigrant groups have come to occupy a range of niches in the Japanese labor market, differentiated by gender, education, and skills. These migrants hold a variety of immigration statuses, from legal long-term residents to illegal overstayers who enter the country on tourist or student visas. They possess varied types of social capital, ranging from skills in demand in the automotive or construction industries to social networks both within and beyond the boundaries of their groups of fellow ethnics, co-religionists, or fellow nationals. Some are able to make their own way in Japanese society relatively in-dependently, while others are forced to rely heavily on the efforts of local city hall officials or members of non-profit and non-governmental organizations (NPOs and NGOs) such as churches, charities, and informal groups of volunteers. The niches in the labor market that they occupy also mean that many of these groups have distinctive patterns of distribution throughout Japan.

The two studies by Chung (Chapter 13) and Yamanaka (Chapter 6) provide examples of the different types of social capital available to different immigrants with different visas and statuses in Japan. Chung's Korean bar hostesses in Osaka, most of whom are visa-overstayers, are comfortably sheltered by the well-estab-lished Korean enclave economy, and therefore enjoy relatively high autonomy despite their undocumented status. In contrast, Yamanaka's Japanese Brazilian workers and families in Hamamatsu (a city with a high concentration of for-eigners) tend to rely heavily on local citizens' groups to help them in their labor disputes and their education and health care needs. This is because they are new immigrants with little social capital, despite their ancestral roots in Japan that opened up special immigration status for them.

Chung's ethnographic account of Korean bar hostesses highlights the social and economic dynamism of immigrant workers despite Japan's strict immigra-tion policies. The sojourning bar hostesses with whom Chung interacted work in Koreatown, within Osaka's well-known entertainment district of Minami. There they find a safe haven with cultural comfort and security. Chung's focus is on the development of diverse ethnic businesses in this small ethnic enclave that support the needs of the hostesses themselves, including second-shift bars operating illegally after the regular bars are closed, restaurants and rental video shops serving bar hostesses and their customers, boutiques and beauty parlors who meet the hostesses' daily needs, and unregistered taxi drivers taking hostesses back and forth to their homes, especially after public transportation has stopped for the day. There are even fourteen Christian churches scattered throughout Koreatown to which bar hostesses give generous donations. Chung's account, based on her "labor participant observation" as a bar hostess, conveys vividly the ambivalent air which permeates this ethnic niche, emanating from the economic vitality but personal insecurity of Korean bar hostesses wishing to maximize the fruits of their illegal sojourning. Due to the hidden nature of the sites and the frequently late hours of the activities, the Japanese public (and even the police) may be unaware of this thriving underground economy. Chung's contribution to migration studies is not only in uncovering such an economy, but also in bringing to the fore the resistance and resilience of these immigrant women in outwitting state authority.

In contrast to Korean visa-overstayers in Osaka, the migrant workers described by Yamanaka in the Tokai region of central Japan work mainly in automotive parts and related industries. These include *Nikkeijin* (people of Japanese descent) from Latin America, mostly from Brazil but also some from Peru, whose long-term residence was legitimated by the government in 1990, and whose numbers increased steadily thereafter. There also other migrants employed as "industrial trainees" (in effect low-paid workers) and undocumented migrants, often working for smaller companies that suffer from chronic labor shortages. This large-scale immigration into the region has caused problems for the local authorities, not least that of providing education and services for a population that speaks mainly Portuguese and Spanish. Like immigrants elsewhere, these foreign workers have also attracted negative press attention for their assumed association with crime, even though there is very little evidence to back up that accusation (Herbert 1996). Despite the initial assumption that *Nikkeijin* would quickly adapt to life in Japan because of their familiarity with Japanese culture, their presence has led to allegations of discrimination, cultural friction, and a range of social problems. The result has been a transition from being a "positive" minority in Brazil to being a "negative" one in Japan (Tsuda 2003). The undocumented migrants, in turn, suffer from exploitation at the hands of employers and a lack of adequate health coverage.

As Yamanaka shows, a variety of local groups have sprung up in recent years to help with these problems, aided by changes in the laws governing NPOs (Shipper 2008). Even so, these groups face an uphill struggle through their lack of resources and official support. Of the three she describes, the first, a support group, suffered from a lack of manpower and money, while the second, an organization offering health services, was largely dependent on the efforts of a single doctor, until he himself became ill. The third group, a pressure group organized by a

Catholic priest and a social worker, also failed to persuade the local authorities to provide better health facilities for migrants, even though it may have raised local awareness of the problem.

In brief, the success of migrants in Japan seems largely to be determined by the social capital that they possess or can acquire. Migrants from other cultures lacking enough social capital are forced to rely much more on the good will and resources offered by local NPOs, volunteers, health professionals, the churches, and (mainly in the case of legal residents) local government. However, the chapter by Yamanaka shows that the Japanese state does react, even if only slowly, to the changing social structure of its population. Immigration law, policies in regard to foreign residents, labor law, and laws relating to civil society can and do change. Given the economic and demographic parameters of contemporary Japan, labor and migration policies are likely to remain high on the list of national priorities for some time to come, perhaps even provoking the government to think more carefully about migrant welfare as an essential part of the Japanese economic system.

Such emphases on the situation of migrants at their destination, however, tend to elide the extreme complexity of the routes by which migrants arrive. On this point, the chapters by Lainez (Chapter 1) and Xiang (Chapter 2) are crucial in illustrating how tortuous those routes can be. Lainez provides a careful consideration of trafficking in colonial Vietnam, particularly of women. Here it is not the networks of the people that are crucial, but the elaborate networks of the traffickers. Indeed, the more widely and strongly woven are the trafficking networks, the more hopelessly alone and defenseless are those who are trafficked. Xiang provides a more contemporary profile of the machinery of migration out of China, largely for temporary labor. Here too it is the networks of those who manage migration – not the migrants – that are most impressive, woven across national lines, but also up and down public and private bureaucratic chains in both the sending and receiving countries. Both chapters have important methodological implications: for Lainez it is the importance of finding the historical bases for what are often labeled as contemporary problems; for Xiang it is the importance of a combined tracking of both the experience and management of migration. Together, the two chapters provide a sharp reminder that any assessment of migration must attend to the complexity of the control of the migration process in and across public, governmental, and national lines.

Community and City

The discussions so far also show the increasing significance of cities throughout East Asia, be it Beijing, Hong Kong, or Osaka, where migrants' social ties develop and their social capital extends across regional and national boundaries. Today more than half of the world's population lives in cities, making cities both objects of analysis and sites within which analysis occurs. In this sense, where is better than East Asia to consider the interaction of migration and urbanization? But cities – common, unexceptional, and ordinary though they may now have become – are hardly uniform as entities or as contexts for human life.

Yeoh and Lam (Chapter 4) provide the example of Singapore, whose history is clearly one of multiple layers of migration. Located at the center of Southeast Asia, Singapore was cosmopolitan at heart and characterized by "a liberal open-door policy of immigration" during the colonial period. More recent data, presented in careful tabulations, show increasing numbers of foreigners, both official and unofficial. The particularly sharp increases in unofficial migrants are a useful reminder of how much of contemporary migration is controlled by making sure it is outside the bounds of normal civil protection. Singapore thus provides a vivid example of how understanding migrant lives in cities requires a comprehension of the way in which cities manage migrants – that the topics of migrants in cities and cities of migrants are fully intertwined.

Crucial to the Singapore experience is an acceptance – even a valorization – of diversity. Yet there is also considerable ambivalence about the nature of diversity. There is, on the one hand, official diversity that hinges on the use of racial categories; people, by birth, belong to one of a carefully defined set of categories that provide their official identity and, through that identity, their legal rights. One is thus Singaporean in general, but also Singaporean by virtue of belonging to a particular racial group within Singapore. This is equality through race – a rather benign use of racial categories compared to their more frequent use as rigid forms of social inequality. That issue of control through racial categories nevertheless persists, whether it leads to institutional equality or inequality among different races.

On the other hand, Yeoh and Lam note the ambivalence that emerges around hyphenated identities in Singapore. Cosmopolitanism would seem to dictate that new kinds of diversity should be accepted, and indeed Singapore accepts new variants of diversity whether through immigration or though marriage among Singapore's "races" or between Singaporeans and foreigners. Yet Yeoh and Lam also indicate how ambivalent and ambiguous the official response to such new identities is. Thus while these new migrants and marriages are "beginning to move understandings of racial categorization beyond the fixity 'of the formal racial scheme,' the hope remains that the 'hyphens' are transient phenomena that will dissolve with subsequent generations." Nevertheless, their ultimate stance is a positive one, as they are hopeful that "the intrinsic strengths of an already-plural society" will bear fruit in the "constant (re)making of this city of diversities."

In another example of a diverse city with numerous migrant communities, both internal and international, Yeo (Chapter 5) unveils a transnational landscape of the formation and development of a new community in Beijing inhabited by many migrants from South Korea. Yeo reviews the general situation of South

Korean migrants in urban China, focusing on their rapidly increasing population within the political, economic, geographic, and cultural context. According to Yeo, the formation of the specific South Korean community, Beijing's Wangjing Koreatown, hinges upon a dynamic power relationship among the foreign immigrants, the local administration, and the local Chinese community, including Chinese citizens of Korean descent who have acted as cultural interpreters for the new Korean arrivals. The making of this Koreatown in Beijing only became possible, then, as a result of transnational interactions among different ethnicities and nationalities.

This new global city, Beijing, is now home to many foreign nationals, often women and men with professional qualifications from more developed countries, including the North American and European countries, Japan, and Singapore. In their study of big cities in China, Yeoh and Willis (Chapter 15) found the highly mobile Singaporeans living in and making a "home away from home" in their ancestral homeland. As in the case of Chinese scientists and engineers in Silicon Valley, California, their case study confirms the fact that global human movements can originate from anywhere – from the core, periphery, and even semi-periphery – and are not unilinear in their direction. It is best to call this movement a "temporary circulatory migration movement" (Wong 2008). The actors who participate in this movement can be small-scale traders, highly educated professionals, as well as the capitalists, and multinational corporations.

Globalization has affected men and women differently. Yeoh and Willis note that Singaporean ex-patriot wives have to do the domestic work that was formerly performed by Filipina maids and others. They also point out that transnational existence has hardened the line between men's and women's identities and perpetuated a traditional patriarchy. The expatriate wives have lost their comfort and the social position they achieved in Singapore, while their Singapore husbands advance their careers and corporate positions by being in China. It is ironic that although they may have Chinese heritage, Singaporeans are different from local Chinese in that they are foreigners with little intention of assimilating themselves into the local Chinese culture. Instead, the Singapore wives segregate themselves in their high-end residential enclaves that are rather reminiscent of earlier colonial enclaves. Their use of the "ethnic card" in Beijing therefore is a good counter-example of the global culture that creates homogeneity by eliminating cultural heterogeneity, thus replacing particularism with universalism. On the contrary, as Yeoh and Willis show, globalization does not erase cultural differences and local identities.

Luong (Chapter 7) raises this issue of the lack of cultural erasure in a different context, that of internal migrants in Vietnam. They too go to cities, and most to "the City" (the former Saigon). But their original identities are not erased. Indeed, their migration is continually assessed and reassessed in terms of their original ties to community and, above all, to family. Luong traces a research process that elicited accounts of migration both by the migrants and by the members of their family "at home" in the sending communities. Here we find not change but durability, not the attenuation of ties but their continuity, not different perspectives on migration but a (generally) shared view by those who leave and those who stay. Migration is, then, not an event that changes networks (or generates new ones), but rather an event understood through continuing networks. It is helpful, here, to have a reminder that migration may be more a part of individual and collective identity, rather than a force that changes identity.

All these examinations of how migration experiences play out in different communities and cities, at both personal and family levels, for both internal and transnational migrants, inevitably raise broader questions. What are the connections between "home" and "away" for women and men of different ethnic and national groups who labor and live in increasingly global cities? How is everyday life linked with multiple homes, multiple cultures and communities, and changing household relations? What are the social and moral networks within which the meanings and decisions of migration are configured? The answers are not simple ones. Migration liberates yet often oppresses; it gives hope to migrants yet often crushes their dreams; it is based on migrant decisions yet is controlled by complex networks of public and private interests, of strangers and friends, of "others" and kin. This book has not fully resolved what the East Asian experience can contribute as a lesson and model for such broader questions in the study of human migration and mobility, but we hope it provides a step along the way, and a reminder of how broad and deep is the human experience of migration and mobility.

References

Appadurai, Arjun. 1991. "Global ethnoscapes: Notes and queries for a transnational anthropology," pp. 191–210 in *Recapturing Anthropology. Working in the Present,* ed. Richard G. Fox. Santa Fe: School of American Research Press.

Benson, Michaela, and Karen O'Reilly, eds. 2009. *Lifestyle Migration: Expectations, Aspirations and Experiences.* Farnham: Ashgate.

Castles, Stephen, and Mark J. Miller. 2009. *The Age of Migration* (4th Edition). New York: Guilford.

Clifford, James. 1997. *Routes: Travel and Translation in the Late Twentieth Century.* Cambridge: Harvard University Press.

Constable, Nicole, ed. 2005. *Cross-Border Marriages: Gender and Mobility in Transnational Asia.* Philadelphia: University of Pennsylvania Press.

Graburn, Nelson. 1977. "Tourism: The sacred journey," pp. 17–32 in *Hosts and Guests: The Anthropology of Tourism,* ed. Valene Smith. Philadelphia: University of Pennsylvania Press.

———. 2004. "Religious tourism and the Kyoto temple tax strike," pp. 125–139 in *Centres in Motion: Anthropological Perspectives on Pilgrimage and Tourism*, eds. E. Badone and S. Roseman. Urbana: University of Illinois Press.

———. 2008a. "When is domestic tourism international: Multiculturalism and tourism in Japan," pp. 218–240 in *Multiculturalism in the New Japan*, eds. Nelson Graburn, John Ertl, and R. Kenji Tierney. Oxford and New York: Berghahn Press.

———. 2008b. "The past and the other in the present: *Kokunai kokusaika kanko* – domestic international tourism," pp. 21–36 in *Japanese Tourism and Travel Culture*, eds. Sylvie Guichard-Anguis and Okpyo Moon. London: Routledge.

Han, Dong. 2010. "Policing and racialization of rural migrant workers in Chinese cities." *Ethnic and Racial Studies* 33(4): 593–610.

Herbert, Wolfgang. 1996. *Foreign Workers and Law Enforcement in Japan*. London: Tavistock.

Huang, Shirlena, Brenda S.A. Yeoh and Noor Abdul Rahman, eds. 2005. *Asian Women as Transnational Domestic Workers*. London: Marshall Cavendish Academic.

Lavely, William. 1991. "Marriage and mobility under rural collectivism," pp. 286-312 in *Marriage and Inequality in China*, eds. Patricia Ebrey and Rubie Watson. Berkeley: University of California Press.

Marcus, George E. 1995. "Ethnography in/of the world system: The emergence of multi-sited ethnography." *Annual Review of Anthropology* 24: 95–117.

Moon, Okpyo. 1997. "Tourism and cultural development: Japanese and Korean contexts," pp. 178–193 in *Tourism and Cultural Development in East Asia and Oceania*, eds. Shinji Yamashita, Kadir Din, and J.S. Eades. Bangi, Malaysia: University of Malaysia Press.

Oguma, Eiji. 2002. *A Genealogy of "Japanese" Self-Images*. Melbourne: Trans Pacific Press.

Piper, Nicola. 2008. "Feminisation of Migration and the Social Dimensions of Development: the Asian Case." *Third World Quarterly* 29(7): 1287–1303.

Pun Ngai. 2005. *Made in China: Women Factory Workers in a Global Workplace*. Durham: Duke University Press.

Rodriguez, Robyn. 2010. *Migrants for Export: How the Philippine State Brokers Labor to the World*. Minneapolis: University of Minnesota Press.

Seol, Dong-Hoon, and John Skrentny. 2009. "Why is there so little migrant settlement in East Asia?" *International Migration Review* 43(3): 578–620.

Shipper, Apichai W. 2008. *Fighting for Foreigners: Immigration and Its Impact on Japanese Democracy*. Ithaca: Cornell University.

Tsuda, Takeyuki. 2003. *Strangers in the Ethnic Homeland*. New York: Columbia University Press.

Tunbridge, John. E., and Gregory. J. Ashworth. 1996. *Dissonant Heritage: The Management of the Past as a Resource in Conflict*. Chichester and New York: J. Wiley.

Weiner, Michael. 1994. *Race and Migration in Imperial Japan*. London: Routledge.

Wong, Bernard P. 2008. *The Chinese in Silicon Valley: Globalization, Social Networks, and Ethnic Identity*. Lanham, MD: Rowman & Littlefield Publishers.

Yamanaka, Keiko. 2006. "Increasing international marriages in East Asia (Japan, South Korea, Taiwan): Migration, marriage and citizenship." Paper presented at the meeting of the Society for East Asian Anthropology, Hong Kong. Panel: *Marriage out of Place*, organized by David W. Haines.

————. 2010. "Civil society and social movements for immigrant rights in Japan and South Korea: Convergence and divergence in unskilled immigration policy." *Korea Observer* 41(4): 615–647.

Yamanaka, Keiko, and Nicola Piper. 2005. *Feminized Migration in East and Southeast Asia: Policies, Actions and Empowerment.* Occasional Paper 11. United Nations Research Institute for Social Development.

Yamawaki, Keizo. 2003. "Foreign workers in Japan: A historical perspective," pp. 38–51 in *Japan and Global Migration,* eds. Mike Douglass and Glenda Roberts. Honolulu: University of Hawai'i Press.

Yan, Hairong. 2008. *New Masters, New Servants: Migration, Development, and Women Workers in China.* Durham, NC: Duke University Press.

❧ About the Contributors

HAENG-JA CHUNG earned her Ph.D. from UCLA in 2004 and was subsequently a postdoctoral fellow at Harvard University and at Colorado College. She joined the department of anthropology at Hamilton College in 2006, where she received the John R. Hatch Class of 1925 Excellence in Teaching Award in 2008. She has conducted research for her book project on Korean nightclub hostesses in Japan with fellowship support from the Social Science Research Council and the Japan Society for the Promotion of Science, while being affiliated with the University of Tokyo from 2008–2010. Her new group project on the internet and changing landscapes of social movements is funded by the Toyota Foundation.

J.S. (JERRY) EADES is professor emeritus, Ritsumeikan Asia Pacific University, Beppu, Japan, and holds honorary research positions at the University of Kent and the School of Oriental and African Studies, London. He began his career in West Africa and the United Kingdom, and worked in Japan from 1991 to 2012. His recent publications include studies of migration, higher education, urbanization, tourism, and the environment in the Asia Pacific region.

NELSON GRABURN, educated at the universities of Cambridge, McGill, and Chicago, has taught at Berkeley since 1964. He has been a visiting professor or researcher at Minpaku (Osaka), and universities in Aix-en-Provence, Fukuoka, Porto Alegre (Brazil), London, and Beijing. Since 1959 he has researched social change, commercial arts, ethnic identity, tourism, and museums among the Canadian Inuit and, since 1974, tourism in, to, and from China and Korea, and domestic tourism and multiculturalism in Japan. His recent books include *Multiculturalism in the New Japan* (Berghahn 2008), edited with John Ertl and R. Kenji Tierney, and *Tourism and Glocalization: Perspectives in East Asian Studies* (National Museum of Ethnology 2010), edited with Han Min.

CAROLINE GRILLOT is a sinologist and social anthropologist (INALCO, Nanterre University). Born in France, she has lived in China for over a decade. She has been studying various communities living on the margins of Chinese society and is particularly interested in those whose values and social position challenge its imagined uniformity. She has just published a book on cross-border marriages at the Sino-Vietnamese border (IRASEC/Connaissances et Savoirs,

2010) and has completed her Ph.D. dissertation on this same topic at Macquarie University in Australia, in cotutelle with Vrije Universiteit Amsterdam. Her article "Between Bitterness and Sweetness" appeared in the *Journal of Vietnamese Studies* in 2012.

DAVID W. HAINES is professor of anthropology at George Mason University, following a dual career in academia and government. He is the author of *Cultural Anthropology: Adaptations, Structures, Meanings* (2005), *The Limits of Kinship: Vietnamese Households, 1954-1975* (2006), and *Safe Haven? A History of Refugees in America* (2010), as well as editor of several volumes on refugees and immigrants in the United States. He has twice been a Fulbright scholar (Western Europe and South Korea), and is a former president of the Society for Urban, National, and Transnational/Global Anthropology (SUNTA).

MASAKO KUDO is associate professor of anthropology at the Faculty for the Study of Contemporary Society, Kyoto Women's University. She has conducted long-term research among Japanese women married to Pakistani labor migrants in Japan. Her research interests include gender, family, migration, and transnationalism. Recent publications in English include "Becoming the Other in One's Own Homeland?" (*Japanese Review of Cultural Anthropology*, 2008) and "Negotiation of Difference in Multicultural Japan" (*Senri Ethnological Reports* 77, 2008).

NICOLAS LAINEZ was born in 1975 in Barcelona, Spain. After graduating from film school, he worked as a photojournalist in Southeast Asia. In 2004, he resumed academic studies and graduated with master's degrees in development studies from the Sorbonne University and social anthropology from the Ecole des Hautes Etudes en Sciences Sociales, where he is currently enrolled in a Ph.D. program. His research focuses on cross-border mobility, slavery, indebtedness, and women's issues. Since 2007, he has been affiliated with the Ho Chi Minh City University of Social Sciences and Humanities, and the Asia Research Institute (National University of Singapore). He has published "Commodification of Sexuality and Mother-Daughter Power Dynamics in the Mekong Delta," *Journal of Vietnamese Studies* 7(1) (2012).

THEODORA LAM is a Ph.D. candidate in the department of geography at the National University of Singapore, and a research associate in the Asian MetaCentre for Population and Sustainable Development Analysis. Her research interests include transnationalism, migration, gender studies, and children's geographies. She has co-edited two special journal issues: "Asian Transnational Families in Transition" in *International Migration* (2008, with Shirlena Huang and Brenda Yeoh), and "Asian Transnational Families" in *Global Networks* (2005, with Brenda

Yeoh and Shirlena Huang), and is also the co-author of articles in *International Development Planning Review* (2006) and *Asia Pacific Viewpoint* (2004).

HY V. LUONG is professor of anthropology at the University of Toronto. He has been conducting comparative research in both northern and southern Vietnam since 1987 and has published extensively on political economy, discourse, social organization, and migration in modern Vietnam. His recent books include *Tradition, Revolution, and Market Economy in a North Vietnamese Village, 1925-2006* (2010), and the edited volumes *Postwar Vietnam: Dynamics of a Transforming Society* (2003), *Migration, Urbanization, and Poverty in a Vietnamese Metropolis* (2009), and *The Dynamics of Social Capital and Civic Engagement in Asia* (2012, co-edited with Amrita Daniere).

GORDON MATHEWS teaches anthropology at the Chinese University of Hong Kong. He has written *What Makes Life Worth Living? How Japanese and Americans Make Sense of Their Worlds* (1996) and *Global Culture/Individual Identity: Searching for Home in the Cultural Supermarket* (2000). Most recently he has co-written *Hong Kong, China: Learning to Belong to a Nation* (2008) and co-edited *Pursuits of Happiness: Well-Being in Anthropological Perspective* (2009). He has been conducting research in Chungking Mansions since 2005, and has recently published *Ghetto at the Center of the World: Chungking Mansions, Hong Kong* (2011).

OKPYO MOON is professor of anthropology at the Academy of Korean Studies and has been a visiting professor at Harvard University (2000-2001) and at the National Museum of Ethnology, Osaka, Japan (2006-2007). She has carried out extensive research both in Japan and Korea focusing on family and gender, urban and rural community making, ethnic minorities, tourism, and heritage policies. Her recent publications include *Ethnic Relations of Overseas Koreans* (editor, 2006) and *Japanese Tourism and Travel Culture* (co-editor with Sylvie Gichard-Anguis, 2009).

HUNG CAM THAI (Ph.D., University of California, Berkeley) is associate professor of sociology and Asian American Studies at Pomona College and the Claremont University Consortium. He is also concurrently serving as Director of the Pacific Basin Institute and Chair of Department of Sociology. His monograph, *For Better or For Worse: Vietnamese International Marriages in the New Global Economy*, was published by Rutgers University Press in 2008. He has a forthcoming book with Stanford University Press, *Insufficient Funds: Money in Low Wage Transnational Families*.

MIKA TOYOTA is associate professor at Rikkyo University in Japan. She obtained her Ph.D. at the University of Hull, United Kingdom in 2000. Her current work examines the migration of transnational health care workers and the impact of retirement industry development in Southeast Asia. She has extensive field research experience in both Japan and Southeast Asia, and has published more than thirty refereed journal articles and book chapters in English and Japanese.

WANG JIANXIN is professor of anthropology at Sun Yat-sen University. He finished his undergraduate studies in law at Xinjiang University, China, and received his M.A. in cultural anthropology from Saitama University and his Ph.D. from the University of Tokyo. He studies Turkic-speaking Muslims and their Islamic culture in Central Asian countries and in Xinjiang, China. In recent years, he has also undertaken research on ethnic minority groups in Qinghai, Yunnan, and Guizhou provinces in China.

KATIE WILLIS is professor of human geography and director of the Politics, Development and Sustainability Group at Royal Holloway, University of London. Her main research interests are gender, migration, and health, with a particular focus on East Asia and Latin America. Her publications include *Theories and Practices of Development* (2011) and *Geographies of Developing Areas: The Global South in a Changing World* (2009, with Glyn Williams and Paula Meth).

BERNARD P. WONG is professor of anthropology at San Francisco State University, and has conducted fieldwork on the Chinese in Japan, Peru, the Philippines, and the United States. His research interests include the family, ethnic identity, cultural citizenship, globalization, and ethnic entrepreneurship. He is the author of several books, most recently *Family, Kin and Community* (2001) and *Chinese in Silicon Valley* (2006), as well as numerous journal articles. He is currently working on a book on the Chinese diaspora in the Pacific Rim countries.

XIANG BIAO is a University Lecturer in Social Anthropology at the University of Oxford. He is the author of *Making Order from Transnational Migration* (Princeton University Press, forthcoming), *Global "Body Shopping"* (Princeton University Press, 2007; winner of 2008 Anthony Leeds Prize), *Transcending Boundaries* (Chinese edition by Sanlian Press, 2000; English edition by Brill Academic Publishers, 2005) and numerous articles, in both English and Chinese, in academic journals and the public media.

KEIKO YAMANAKA is currently a lecturer in the departments of Ethnic Studies and International and Area Studies at UC Berkeley. She has conducted research on international labor migration, Asian American studies, ethnic and racial relations, gender studies, and Japanese studies. A native of Japan, her research has also carried her to other areas of Asia, such as China and Korea, to research issues concerning migrant workers and intercultural contact.

SHINJI YAMASHITA is professor of cultural anthropology at the University of Tokyo, and former president of the Japanese Society of Cultural Anthropology – the world's second largest national anthropology association. His major published work has been on tourism, including *Bali and Beyond* (2003), and the development of Japanese and Asian anthropology, including *The Making of Anthropology in East and Southeast Asia* (co-edited with Joseph Bosco and J.S. Eades, 2004). He is a frequent organizer and participant in efforts to develop a more fully global anthropology.

KWANG-KYOON YEO, researcher at Hanyang University in Korea, is completing his doctoral dissertation at Columbia University on the development of "Koreatown" in Beijing and its impact on local politics. His current research extends from this dissertation into comparative aspects of Korean communities in China, Japan, and the United States in contexts of transnational migration, social stratification, and globalization in East Asia.

BRENDA S.A. YEOH is professor in the department of geography, dean of the Faculty of Arts and Social Sciences, and research leader of the Asian Migration Cluster at the Asia Research Institute, National University of Singapore. Her research interests include gender, transnational migration, and the politics of space in colonial and postcolonial cities. Recent books with a migration theme include *Approaching Transnationalisms* (with Michael W. Charney and Tong Chee Kiong, 2003), *State/Nation/Transnation* (with Katie Willis, 2004), *Migration and Health in Asia* (with Santosh Jatrana and Mika Toyota, 2005), *Asian Women as Transnational Domestic Workers* (with Shirlena Huang and Noor Abdul Rahman, 2005), and *Migration and Diversity in Asian Contexts* (with Lai Ah Eng and Francis Collins, 2012).

ZHANG JIJIAO is professor in the Institute of Ethnology and Anthropology, Chinese Academy of Social Sciences. He has been especially active in the International Union of the Anthropological and Ethnological Sciences (IUAES), serving as founder and chair of the Commission on Enterprise Anthropology, and Co-chair of the Commission on Urban Anthropology in the China Union of the Anthropological and Ethnological Sciences (CUAES). His research fields include urban anthropology, urban migrant adaptation, and enterprise anthropology. His publications appear in English and Japanese as well as Chinese.

Index